# Ultimate Java Functional Projects

*Build, Architect, and Deploy Enterprise Java Applications with Spring Boot, Microservices, and Kubernetes*

**Bhargav Bachina**



www.orangeava.com

**First Published:** November 2025

**Published By:** Orange Education Pvt Ltd, AVA®

**Address:** 9, Daryaganj, Delhi, 110002, India

275 New North Road Islington Suite 1314 London,
N1 7AA, United Kingdom

**ISBN (PBK):** 978-93-49888-29-6

**ISBN (E-BOOK):** 978-93-49888-12-8

**Scan the QR code to explore our entire catalogue**

www.orangeava.com

## Dedicated To

*My beloved Parents and Wife:*

*Veeranjaneyulu Bachina,*
*Nagalaxmi Bachina,*
*Srividya Pullela*

*My Strength and Support System*

# About the Author

**Bhargav Bachina** is an eminent figure in the IT industry, celebrating a 13-year career distinguished by innovative leadership and advanced software architecture. With deep expertise spanning front-end, back-end development, and cloud computing, Bhargav's versatility shines through his mastery of Java, JavaScript, Python, and Node.js. His role as a visionary software architect is highlighted by his ability to craft comprehensive end-to-end solutions, with a commitment to excellence that has propelled numerous projects to success and established him as a pivotal thought leader.

Currently serving as the CTO of an educational startup, Bhargav is poised to launch a groundbreaking project that promises to add another achievement to his already impressive career. His role extends beyond company leadership, serving as a fractional CTO where his guidance is invaluable to emerging startups seeking his expertise, particularly those he mentors through LinkedIn.

Bhargav is also a prolific writer with a significant online presence. Over the past five years, he has authored over 700 articles on Medium, reaching a global audience of 8 million and gaining a substantial following of 22,000 readers. His insightful contributions continue to make waves on LinkedIn and provide valuable resources on GitHub, where he manages 431 repositories that frequently garner attention from the tech community.

Recently, Bhargav was honored with the 2024 Global Recognition Award for his substantial contributions to the technology and education sectors. Recognized for his strategic leadership and technical prowess in developing cutting-edge solutions for web and mobile platforms, Bhargav Bachina continues to be a beacon of industry excellence and a source of inspiration for IT professionals worldwide.

Outside of his professional life, Bhargav has a passion for watching movies, writing books, strength training, investing in real estate, and building tech things. These hobbies not only provide him with relaxation and enjoyment but also fuel his creativity and innovative thinking in his professional endeavors.

# About the Technical Reviewer

**Kablu Mandal** is a seasoned techno-functional professional with about 13 years of experience in software development, specializing in Core Java, Java EE, Spring Boot, Microservices, SOA, EJB and PKI-based CA solutions. He has a proven track record in delivering scalable, multi-tier enterprise applications across diverse domains, including e-Governance, identify Solutions, Digital Signatures, ManTech and e-learning Systems.

Currently, serving as Senior Manager at Protean eGov Technologies Ltd. (formerly NSDL e-Gov Ltd.), Kablu has led the design and implementation of mission-critical projects such as eSign, eDastakhat, Offline eSign, GST Suvidha Provider (GSP-ASP), Beckn Protocol APP, eWaybill systems, and National Academic Depository (NAD). His expertise spans across cryptography, PKI infrastructure, HSM integration, cloud-native deployment (Docker, Kubernetes), distributed systems, and enterprise-grade security protocols.

A Gold Medallist (University Topper) from Bharati VidyaPeeth University, Pune, with a Master of Science in Information Technology, Kablu brings strong technical acumen along with project management skills rooted in Agile and Scrum methodologies. He is adept at requirement analysis and architecture design, leading teams to deliver secure and efficient digital transformation solutions.

Recognized for his problem-solving ability, leadership, and mentoring skills, Kablu thrives in handling both technological and business challenges, while ensuring innovation, compliance, and scalability in every project he delivers.

# Acknowledgments

Embarking on the journey of writing ***Ultimate Java Functional Projects*** has been a deeply enriching experience that reflects not only my personal passion for Java and software architecture but also the collective support, collaboration, and inspiration from my family, peers, and the global developer community.

I extend my heartfelt gratitude to my family–my mother, **Nagalaxmi Bachina**, and my father, **Veeranjaneyulu Bachina**–for their unwavering encouragement throughout every stage of my academic and professional path. To my wife, **Srividya Pullela**, whose constant support and patience have been a pillar of strength, and my brother, **Sandeep Bachina**, whose belief in my pursuits has always been a source of motivation–I offer my sincerest thanks. Special appreciation goes to my children, who continue to be the spark behind my creativity and drive.

This book also stands on the foundation built by great mentors. I'm especially thankful to **Khanna Kakarla** for guiding me early in my software engineering journey, and to **Dhanunjaya Sir**, whose mentorship during my college days left a lasting impact on my career. Their insights and encouragement continue to influence my approach to engineering and education.

Professionally, I bring over 13 years of experience across frontend, backend, and cloud technologies. My academic journey at the **University of Missouri-Kansas City**, combined with hands-on exposure to technologies like Java, Spring Boot, Docker, Kubernetes, and cloud platforms such as AWS, GCP, and Azure, has enabled me to contribute to real-world projects and mentor teams globally.

As the **Startup CTO at Bachina Labs**, I have focused on solving engineering problems with scalable and modern solutions. This book reflects those lessons learned–both in theory and in practice.

I also want to thank the **Java community**, the maintainers of **Spring Boot**, and the broader ecosystem for making tools and knowledge freely accessible. Their commitment to open source and continuous innovation inspired many of the hands-on examples presented here.

This book is not just about syntax or frameworks–it's about building **production-grade**, scalable, and cloud-ready Java applications. It is intended for **Java developers**, **software engineers**, **DevOps professionals**, and **curious learners** eager to level up their skills from Java fundamentals to full-blown microservices deployed in cloud environments.

Thank you to the editorial and publishing teams whose support has brought this project to life. And finally, thank you, the reader, for choosing this book as your guide. I hope it empowers you with the confidence and practical tools needed to excel in your software development journey using Java.

# Preface

In today's fast-evolving software development landscape, mastering Java and its ecosystem is a gateway to building powerful, scalable, and production-ready applications. ***Ultimate Java Functional Projects*** is your practical companion through this journey–from foundational Java programming all the way to advanced cloud-native architectures. Whether you're just beginning or looking to deepen your expertise, this book is designed to guide you step by step with clarity, purpose, and real-world application.

Unlike generic tutorials, this book is not just a technical manual–it is a **learning experience-built chapter by chapter**, each unlocking new levels of understanding and hands-on ability. From core object-oriented principles to database-driven applications, from building microservices to exploring API gateways and resilient service patterns, this book helps you **build complete, enterprise-grade Java solutions** using the latest tools and practices.

**Part 1: Java Fundamentals**

**Chapter 1: Foundations of Java**: In this chapter, we embark on a concise journey through Java's history and foundational principles, merging theoretical insights with practical programming skills. We begin by charting Java's evolution and its principles of security, readability, and compatibility. The chapter then guides readers through setting up the Java development environment and unpacks Java's syntax and structure to lay the groundwork for effective coding. We further explore basic programming constructs, such as variables, data types, operations, control flow mechanisms, arrays, and strings, culminating in an understanding of methods and parameter passing. This approach sets a solid foundation, preparing readers for more advanced Java programming concepts while emphasizing code reusability and modularity.

**Chapter 2: Object-Oriented Programming in Java**: This chapter offers a concise yet comprehensive exploration into the principles of Object-Oriented Programming (OOP) in Java, focusing on foundational elements like classes and objects, and extending into lifecycle management through constructors. It delves into inheritance and polymorphism, essential for reusability and flexibility in code, alongside abstraction and encapsulation, which safeguard against unauthorized access and enhance maintainability. The narrative progresses to cover advanced OOP concepts, fostering a deeper understanding of Java's capabilities, and rounds off with a segment on best practices, guiding readers towards writing efficient, robust, and maintainable Java applications. This chapter serves as an essential guide for anyone looking to master OOP principles in Java.

**Chapter 3: Advanced Java Features**: This chapter delves into advanced Java features, enhancing your programming toolkit for more sophisticated applications. It starts with Generics, introducing type safety and flexibility, and moves to Lambda Expressions and Functional Interfaces, marking Java's foray into functional programming. The chapter covers the comprehensive Java Collections Framework for efficient data management, followed by the Stream API for modern, functional-style data processing. Concurrency and Multithreading sections address building responsive applications, while Reflection and Annotations discuss introspection and metadata-driven programming. Advanced I/O techniques are explored for high-performance file and network operations. Exception Handling is revisited in-depth, ensuring robust error management strategies. Finally, Java Database Connectivity (JDBC) is thoroughly explained, enabling direct interaction between Java applications and databases. This chapter equips you with the necessary skills to tackle complex programming challenges in Java.

**Part 2: Building Weather App with Spring Boot**

**Chapter 4: Understanding Spring Boot Basics**: This chapter introduces Java Spring Boot, a powerful framework for building Java applications quickly and with minimal configuration. It starts with an introduction to Spring Boot, highlighting its purpose and advantages, followed by an overview of its architecture, emphasizing its convention-over-configuration approach. The chapter further explores how Spring Boot simplifies application development through intelligent dependencies and auto-configuration. It introduces Spring Boot Starters, which provide ready-to-use sets of dependencies for various types of applications. Readers will also learn about customizing applications using Spring Boot's application properties. Finally, the chapter culminates in building a simple "Hello World" application, illustrating the ease and efficiency of developing with Spring Boot, making it an invaluable resource for modern Java developers.

**Chapter 5: Database Integration and Weather App Development**: This pivotal chapter takes developers through the end-to-end process of integrating a MySQL database into a Java project using the Java Persistence API (JPA) and then leveraging this integration to build a sophisticated weather application. Initially, the chapter covers the essential steps for setting up and configuring a MySQL database to facilitate efficient data management. It transitions into configuring the Java project for optimal JPA integration, illustrating seamless database connection and the creation of JPA entities to reflect database structures within Java code accurately. Following database setup, the chapter delves into executing data access operations through JPA, enhancing the application's dynamic data handling capabilities. Shifting gears, the narrative progresses to the construction of a weather application, emphasizing practical application of learned database skills within a real-world project. This section addresses implementing the Spring MVC architecture and integrating weather APIs for live data. Additionally, we explore building the application's frontend using Thymeleaf, coupled with robust exception handling and validation techniques. The development process is further enriched with unit testing using JUnit and end-to-end testing with Rest-Assured, ensuring a thoroughly validated application. Both segments are tied together with discussions on using Liquibase for database version control and Maven for building the project, presenting a holistic view of modern Java application development from database setup to application deployment.

**Part 3: Advancing Further with Java Project Development**

**Chapter 6: Building a Chat Application with Java**: This chapter guides you through building a chat application using Java, detailing each step from setup to execution. Starting with setting up the project environment using the Java SDK and an IDE, it lays the foundation for application development. The section on designing the chat application covers the architectural considerations and user interface design. Implementing the WebSocket protocol is discussed next, enabling real-time, bidirectional communication between clients and the server. The server-side implementation is then explored, focusing on handling client connections and message broadcasting. Security and user management are addressed, ensuring that user data is protected and access is controlled. Frontend development is covered, detailing how to create an interactive and user-friendly interface. Finally, the chapter concludes with instructions for running the application, allowing you to test and deploy your chat solution effectively. This comprehensive guide provides all the necessary details to create a fully functional chat application with Java. The integration of OpenAI introduces a revolutionary dimension to the chat application, transforming it with chatbots that can understand and generate human-like text, making conversations more engaging and interactive

**Chapter 7: Implementing Symmetric Encryption in Java**: This chapter delves into implementing symmetric encryption in Java, starting with an introduction that sets the stage for the importance and applications of encryption in securing data. It progresses to explain the fundamentals of symmetric encryption, where the same key is used for both encryption and decryption. The section on setting up the Java environment prepares readers for practical implementation, ensuring they have the necessary tools and libraries. The core of the chapter, implementing symmetric encryption in Java, guides readers through the process of encrypting and decrypting data, complemented by insights into working with initialization vectors for enhanced security. It emphasizes best practices and security considerations to avoid common pitfalls and ensure data remains secure. The chapter concludes with practical examples and exercises, providing hands-on experience to reinforce the concepts learned and apply them effectively in real-world scenarios.

**Part 4: Building Microservices**

**Chapter 8: From Microservices Foundations to Your First Application**: This comprehensive chapter serves as an all-encompassing guide to understanding and implementing microservices with Spring Boot, tailored for developers stepping into the microservices world. Initially, it lays the groundwork by introducing the concept of microservices architecture, contrasting it with traditional monolithic frameworks and discussing the advantages and challenges of adopting a microservices approach. Key components such as service discovery, configuration management, and gateway routing are explained to equip readers with the knowledge needed to design a microservices infrastructure. Transitioning from theory to practice, the chapter proceeds to guide developers through setting up their development environment, encompassing the installation of necessary tools such as Java, Spring Boot, Docker, and Postman, along with setting up IntelliJ Community Edition and a MySQL database. Practical advice on utilizing Spring Initializr for bootstrapping projects provides a smooth segue into the hands-on development phase. The narrative culminates with a detailed walkthrough for creating a first Spring Boot microservice. Starting from a simple RESTful service, it covers defining endpoints, understanding and applying Spring Boot annotations and dependencies, configuring application properties, and the build and run process. The chapter concludes with practical steps for testing the newly developed microservice, ensuring readers can confidently build, deploy, and validate their own microservices from scratch.

**Chapter 9: Service Discovery and Registration**: This chapter explores the concept of service discovery and registration, essential components in microservices architecture for managing and locating services dynamically. It begins with an introduction to service discovery patterns, explaining how they facilitate communication and efficiency among distributed services. The chapter then guides readers through setting up a Eureka Server, which acts as a central registry for services. Following the setup, it covers configuring microservices to function as Eureka clients, enabling them to register with and discover other services. The concept of self-registration is dissected to understand how services autonomously register and maintain their presence. Finally, the chapter concludes with testing procedures to ensure that service discovery and registration are functioning correctly within the microservices ecosystem. This section aims to provide a comprehensive understanding and practical experience in implementing service discovery and registration using Eureka.

**Chapter 10: Microservices Communication**: This chapter delves into the vital aspect of communication within microservices architectures, distinguishing between synchronous and asynchronous methods. It begins with an overview, comparing synchronous communication, typical for immediate responses, against asynchronous approaches, which allow for decoupled and scalable interactions. The chapter progresses to practical implementations, showcasing how to construct RESTful clients using Spring's RestTemplate and the newer, non-blocking WebClient. It introduces Feign Client for simplifying REST calls through a declarative approach. The narrative then shifts towards asynchronous mechanisms, explaining the role of message brokers and the principles of event-driven architecture, essential for distributed systems. The chapter concludes with hands-on examples of implementing asynchronous communication using popular message brokers like RabbitMQ or Kafka, illustrating how they enable efficient message handling and service decoupling in microservices environments.

**Chapter 11: API Gateway and Edge Services**: This chapter focuses on API Gateways and Edge Services, key components in managing microservices architectures. It begins by explaining the crucial role of API Gateways in providing a single entry point for all client requests, facilitating request routing, load balancing, and authentication. The chapter then guides readers through configuring Spring Cloud Gateway, demonstrating how to set up, route, and filter requests effectively to various microservices. It covers implementing advanced patterns such as rate limiting and circuit breakers to ensure the API gateway efficiently manages traffic and maintains service availability. Finally, the chapter delves into securing microservices, discussing the integration of JWT and OAuth2 for robust authentication and authorization at the gateway level, ensuring secure access to microservices.

**Chapter 12: Configuring Centralized Configuration**: This chapter addresses the vital aspect of centralized configuration in microservices architecture, starting with an introduction to its principles and advantages. It guides through setting up the Spring Cloud Config Server, which serves as the central hub for managing configuration properties across multiple services. The narrative then explains how to configure individual microservices as config clients, allowing them to fetch their settings from the central server. It explores mechanisms for refreshing configuration properties at runtime without restarting services, enhancing operational efficiency. Lastly, the chapter covers best practices for securing sensitive configuration information, ensuring that your microservices environment is both dynamic and secure.

**Chapter 13: Microservices Resilience and Fault Tolerance**: This chapter delves into resilience and fault tolerance within microservices, crucial for maintaining robust and reliable systems. It starts with an understanding of what resilience means in the context of distributed systems and why it is essential. The chapter then guides through implementing the Circuit Breaker pattern using Resilience4j, a fault tolerance library designed for Java8 and functional programming, enhancing system stability. Additionally, it covers configuring advanced resilience strategies such as Bulkhead, RateLimiter, and Retry mechanisms, further fortifying services against failures.

The concept and implementation of fallback methods are discussed, providing strategies to ensure graceful degradation of functionality. Finally, the chapter emphasizes the importance of monitoring and logging for maintaining system health, utilizing Spring Boot Actuator for insights into microservices performance and issues.

**Chapter 14: Effective Data Handling and Testing Strategies in Microservices**: This chapter merges critical aspects of data management and testing within a microservices architecture, providing a holistic view on maintaining integrity, consistency, and performance while ensuring reliability and quality through systematic testing. It starts by addressing the data management challenges in microservices, introducing the Database per Service pattern to ensure loose coupling and scalability. We explore transaction management strategies, the concept of eventual consistency, and the Saga pattern to maintain data consistency across distributed services. Additionally, the integration of JPA and Hibernate highlights practical approaches to persistent data handling while adhering to microservices principles. Transitioning from data management to testing, the chapter lays out a structured approach to microservices testing. It covers the spectrum from unit and integration tests, ensuring component reliability and interaction, to contract testing with Spring Cloud Contract, enhancing service consistency. The narrative then guides through end-to-end testing methodologies for comprehensive system validation. Lastly, we delve into mocking external services and databases, essential for isolating services during testing. This combined focus equips developers with the strategies and tools necessary for robust data management and effective testing in a microservices environment.

**Part 5: Java Cloud Options**

**Chapter 15: Cloud Options with Java**: This chapter offers a thorough introduction to cloud computing for Java developers, outlining the diverse cloud options available and their specific offerings. It begins with a foundational overview of cloud computing principles and the advantages they bring to Java development. The chapter then navigates through the various cloud platforms, including AWS, GCP, Azure detailing the services and tools each provides for Java applications. It emphasizes the unique features and strengths of each platform, aiding in selecting the most suitable environment for specific Java projects. Additionally, the chapter covers best practices for Java development in the cloud, focusing on efficiency, scalability, and security, ensuring readers are well-equipped to leverage the cloud effectively for their Java applications.

This book is more than just a technical reference–it is a comprehensive learning companion designed to guide you through the vast landscape of modern Java development. Each chapter is thoughtfully structured to build on the knowledge gained in the previous one, creating a logical and progressive journey from foundational Java concepts to advanced programming patterns and real-world applications. Whether you are a beginner eager to master core Java or an experienced developer exploring Spring Boot, microservices, and cloud deployment, this book equips you with the practical skills and architectural insights required to succeed. Let's embark on this enriching journey into Java development together empowering you to build robust, scalable, and secure applications for the future. Happy coding!

# Get a Free eBook

We hope you are enjoying your recently purchased book! Your feedback is incredibly valuable to us, and to all other readers looking for great books.

If you found this book helpful or enjoyable, we would truly appreciate it, if you could take a moment to leave a short review with a 5 star rating on Amazon. It helps us grow, and lets other readers discover our books.

As a thank you, we would love to send you a free digital copy of this book, and a **30%** discount code on your next cart value on our official websites:

**www.orangeava.com**

**www.orangeava.in** (For Indian Subcontinent)

☑ **Here's how:**

**Leave a review for the book on Amazon.**

Take a screenshot of your review, and send an email to **info@orangeava.com** (it can be just the confirmation screen).

Once, we receive your screenshot, we will send you the digital file, within 24 hours.

Thank you so much for your support – it means a lot to us!

# Downloading the code bundles and colored images

Please follow the links or scan the QR codes to download the ***Code Bundles and Images*** of the book:

**https://github.com/ava-orange-education/Ultimate-Java-Functional-Projects**

The code bundles and images of the book are also hosted on ***https://rebrand.ly/8f3727***

In case there's an update to the code, it will be updated on the existing GitHub repository.

# Errata

We take immense pride in our work at **Orange Education Pvt Ltd,** and follow best practices to ensure the accuracy of our content to provide an indulging reading experience to our subscribers. Our readers are our mirrors, and we use their inputs to reflect and improve upon human errors, if any, that may have occurred during the publishing processes involved. To let us maintain the quality and help us reach out to any readers who might be having difficulties due to any unforeseen errors, please write to us at :

**errata@orangeava.com**

Your support, suggestions, and feedback are highly appreciated.

## DID YOU KNOW

Did you know that Orange Education Pvt Ltd offers eBook versions of every book published, with PDF and ePub files available? You can upgrade to the eBook version at **www.orangeava.com** and as a print book customer, you are entitled to a discount on the eBook copy. Get in touch with us at: **info@orangeava.com** for more details.

At **www.orangeava.com**, you can also read a collection of free technical articles, sign up for a range of free newsletters, and receive exclusive discounts and offers on Print Books and eBooks.

## PIRACY

If you come across any illegal copies of our works in any form on the internet, we would be grateful if you would provide us with the location address or website name. Please contact us at **info@orangeava.com** with a link to the material.

## ARE YOU INTERESTED IN AUTHORING WITH US?

If there is a topic that you have expertise in, and you are interested in either writing or contributing to a book, please write to us at **business@orangeava.com**. We are on a journey to help developers and tech professionals to gain insights on the present technological advancements and innovations happening across the globe and build a community that believes Knowledge is best acquired by sharing and learning with others. Please reach out to us to learn what our audience demands and how you can be part of this educational reform. We also welcome ideas from tech experts and help them build learning and development content for their domains.

## REVIEWS

Please leave a review. Once you have read and used this book, why not leave a review on the site that you purchased it from? Potential readers can then see and use your unbiased opinion to make purchase decisions. We at Orange Education would love to know what you think about our products, and our authors can learn from your feedback. Thank you!

For more information about Orange Education, please visit **www.orangeava.com**.

# Table of Contents

# PART 1
# Java Fundamentals

(CHAPTERS 1–3)

# Chapter 1
# Foundations of Java

## Introduction

Java has been a foundational language in the world of software development since its inception in the mid-1990s. Known for its versatility and platform independence, Java has played a critical role in everything from web applications to enterprise-level systems. In this chapter, we will explore the **History of Java** to understand its evolution and the factors that have contributed to its long-standing popularity. We will then delve into the **Java Philosophy and Principles** that guide its design and emphasize the importance of simplicity, portability, and security. You will also learn how to **Set Up the Java Environment**, ensuring that you are equipped with the right tools to write, compile, and run Java code. Following this, we will cover the **Syntax and Structure** of Java, providing you with a clear understanding of the language's fundamental components.

As you progress through the chapter, you will gain hands-on experience by taking your **First Steps in Java Programming**, where you will write your first Java programs and become familiar with **Basic Java Syntax and Operations**. We will explore **Expressions and Control Flow Statements**, key elements for making logical decisions within your code. The chapter also introduces you to **Arrays, Strings, and Data Handling**, crucial for managing and manipulating data, along with **Basic Input and Output in Java**, which allows for interaction with users and external systems. Finally, we wrap up with an **Introduction to Methods and Parameter Passing**, enabling you to create modular, reusable code that enhances the maintainability of your applications. By the end of this chapter, you will have established a solid foundation in Java, which is ready to build upon as you dive into more advanced topics.

## Structure

The chapter covers the following topics:

- History of Java
- Java Philosophy and Principles
- Setting Up the Java Environment
- Understanding Java Syntax and Structure
- Arrays, Strings, and Data Handling
- Basic Input and Output in Java

## History of Java

The history of Java is a remarkable journey spanning over three decades and began in the early 1990s. Slowly, it evolved into one of the most widely used programming languages worldwide. Java's creation was driven by the need for a versatile, secure, and platform-independent language suitable for the growing world of networked computing. From its inception, Java has continuously adapted to new technological demands, becoming a key player in enterprise software development, mobile applications, cloud computing, and more. This section takes you through Java's evolution, from its early days to its latest version, Java 21.

## The Origins of Java: The Green Team and the Oak Project

Java's story begins in 1991 with a small team of engineers at Sun Microsystems, which was also known as the "*Green Team.*" It was led by James Gosling, Mike Sheridan, and Patrick Naughton, who aimed to develop a programming language for embedded consumer electronic devices like interactive televisions and remote controls. The project was initially called "*Oak*," after the oak tree that stood outside Gosling's office.

The primary goal of the Oak project was to create a language that was robust, portable, and architecture-neutral. Such a language was crucial for devices with limited resources and varying hardware architectures. The team wanted to develop a language with the "*Write Once, Run Anywhere*" capability. This need for platform independence laid the foundation for Java's most significant feature: its ability to run on any device with a Java Virtual Machine (JVM).

## The Shift to Java and the Rise of the Internet

As the Oak project progressed, the team realized that the interactive television market was not ready for the technology. However, the rise of the Internet in the mid-1990s presented a new opportunity. The team at Sun Microsystems recognized that the language they had developed could be perfect for the web, which was rapidly gaining popularity.

In 1995, the language was renamed "*Java*" after a type of coffee, and Sun Microsystems publicly announced its release as a core component of its new platform for the Internet. The initial release included the Java Development Kit (JDK) 1.0, which came with the Java runtime environment, a compiler, and the APIs necessary to build Java applications.

## Java 1.0 and the Applet Revolution

Java 1.0 was officially launched in 1996, and one of its groundbreaking features was the applet. Applets were small Java programs that could be embedded into web pages and executed within a browser. This capability was revolutionary because it allowed developers to create interactive and dynamic content for the web at a time when most websites were static and text-based.

Applets showcased Java's potential and drew significant attention from developers, but they also highlighted the importance of security. Java was designed with a strong focus on security from the beginning, and the applet sandbox model ensured that untrusted code could not perform unauthorized operations on a user's machine.

# The Expansion of Java: Java 2 Platform and the Enterprise Edition

The late 1990s and early 2000s marked the expansion of Java beyond applets and into enterprise computing. In 1998, Sun Microsystems released Java 2, which rebranded the language's versions into three editions:

- **Java Standard Edition (J2SE)** for desktop and server environments
- **Java Enterprise Edition (J2EE)** for enterprise-level applications
- **Java Micro Edition (J2ME)** for embedded systems and mobile devices

Java 2 brought significant enhancements, including the Swing GUI toolkit, the Collections Framework, and the introduction of JavaBeans, servlets, and JavaServer Pages (JSP) for building dynamic web applications. Java's "*Enterprise Edition*" became especially popular in building large-scale, distributed systems in enterprises, thereby cementing Java's reputation as a leading language for backend development.

# Java Community Process (JCP) and OpenJDK

To foster a more open development environment and community involvement, Sun Microsystems introduced the **Java Community Process (JCP)** in 1998. The JCP allowed developers, organizations, and other stakeholders to contribute to the evolution of the Java platform through Java Specification Requests (JSRs).

In 2006, Sun Microsystems made a groundbreaking move by releasing Java as an open-source project under the GNU General Public License (GPL). This initiative, known as **OpenJDK**, opened up the development of Java to a broader community and reinforced its position as a community-driven language.

## Java SE 5, 6, and the Emergence of Modern Java

With Java SE 5 (released in 2004) and Java SE 6 (released in 2006), Java began to modernize its syntax and libraries to accommodate the growing demands of developers. Java SE 5 introduced features like generics, metadata annotations, enumerated types, and the enhanced for loop. These additions greatly improved Java's type safety and reduced boilerplate code.

Java SE 6 focused on performance improvements, better integration with native operating systems, and enhanced support for scripting languages through the inclusion of the **`javax.script`** API. It also included updates to the Java Virtual Machine (JVM) for better memory management and garbage collection.

## Java 7, 8, and the Rise of Functional Programming

Java SE 7, released in 2011, brought several significant improvements, including the try-with-resources statement, the **`switch`** statement with strings, and the fork/join framework for parallel programming. However, it was Java SE 8, which was released in 2014, that marked a major turning point in Java's evolution.

Java SE 8 introduced lambda expressions, the Stream API, and functional interfaces, bringing functional programming paradigms to Java. These features greatly simplified complex data manipulation and processing tasks, making it more expressive and concise. Java 8 also introduced the **`java.time`** package, a modern date and time API that replaced the cumbersome **`java.util.Date`** and **`Calendar`** classes.

# Oracle's Stewardship and the New Release Cadence

In 2010, Oracle Corporation acquired Sun Microsystems, taking over the stewardship of Java. Under Oracle's guidance, Java continued to evolve with a new, faster release cadence. Starting with Java 9 in 2017, Oracle committed to releasing new versions every six months, ensuring that the language could adapt more rapidly to the changing needs of developers.

Java 9 introduced the Java Platform Module System (JPMS), also known as Project Jigsaw, which modularized the JDK and made Java applications more scalable and maintainable. Subsequent releases like Java 10, 11 (the next Long-Term Support release) and later versions have continued to bring incremental improvements, performance optimizations, and new language features, such as the var keyword for local variable type inference.

## Java 10 to 16: Rapid Evolution

From Java 10 (2018) to Java 16 (2021), Java saw rapid innovation with new language features and performance improvements:

- **Java 10** introduced the `var` keyword for local variable type inference.
- **Java 11** (the next Long-Term Support release) added new APIs, removed outdated features, and enhanced performance.
- **Java 12 to 16** brought features like switch expressions, text blocks, records, pattern matching, and sealed classes, which simplified coding and made Java more concise and expressive.

## Java 17: The New LTS and Stability

Java 17, released in September 2021, became the next Long-Term Support (LTS) release after Java 11. It included features like enhanced pattern matching, sealed classes, and the removal of deprecated features such as the Applet API. Java 17 provided a stable platform for developers looking for long-term support, reflecting Oracle's commitment to a predictable release cycle.

## Java 18 to 21: Continued Innovation

Java 18 through Java 21 continued the trend of adding powerful features and improvements to the language:

- **Java 18** (March 2022): Introduced features like the Simple Web Server and UTF-8 by default, improving the language's accessibility and usability
- **Java 19** (September 2022): Brought in incubating features such as virtual threads and structured concurrency as part of Project Loom, which was designed to improve concurrency handling
- **Java 20** (March 2023): Continued to refine virtual threads and structured concurrency while introducing additional preview features like pattern matching for records.
- **Java 21** (September 2023): Became the next LTS release, stabilizing features like virtual threads and pattern matching for records and adding value-based classes with Project Valhalla. Java 21 also introduced sequenced collections and continued enhancing memory as well as performance management.

## Java Today and the Future

Today, Java is one of the most popular programming languages in the world, widely used in enterprise applications, Android development, cloud computing, and big data technologies. With its strong backward compatibility, vibrant ecosystem, and active community, Java continues to evolve and meet the needs of modern software development.

Looking to the future, Java is expected to keep innovating with features like Project Loom (lightweight concurrency), Project Valhalla (value types), and Project Panama (foreign function and memory API). These projects aim to make Java more performant and adaptable, ensuring that it stays relevant in the long run.

Thus, the history of Java is a proof of its adaptability, robustness, and community-driven evolution. From its humble beginnings as a language for consumer electronics to its dominance in enterprise software and beyond, Java has proven itself as a versatile and enduring language. As we look forward, Java's ongoing development promises to keep it at the forefront of programming, providing developers with powerful tools to tackle future challenges.

# Java Philosophy and Principles

The success and longevity of Java as a programming language can be attributed to its technical features, guiding philosophy, and core principles. From its inception, Java was designed to be simple, robust, and platform-independent, making it highly suitable for a wide range of applications, from embedded systems to large-scale enterprise solutions. This section thus delves into the philosophy that has shaped Java and the fundamental principles that continue to guide its evolution.

Java was created in the early 1990s by James Gosling and his team at Sun Microsystems. The primary goal was to develop a language that could run on multiple platforms, handle networked environments, and be robust enough to avoid common programming errors. The philosophy behind Java emerged from the shortcomings of its predecessors, such as C and C++, and the desire to create a language that could overcome these limitations while embracing the strengths of modern programming paradigms.

## Simple and Familiar

Java was designed to be easy to learn and use. It draws heavily from C and C++ but omits complex and error-prone features such as pointers, operator overloading, and multiple inheritance. This approach reduces the cognitive load on developers and eliminates a class of common programming errors.

- **Familiar Syntax**: Java's syntax is similar to C and C++, which makes it familiar to developers coming from these backgrounds. This familiarity reduces the learning curve and enables rapid adoption.
- **Readability**: Java emphasizes readability and simplicity, with a clear and structured approach to programming. This results in more maintainable code that is easier for teams to work with over time.
- **Elimination of Complex Features**: By removing low-level features like pointers, Java avoids the complexities of direct memory manipulation, thereby reducing errors and improving security.

## Object-Oriented

Java is inherently object-oriented, which means that it is designed around the concept of objects and classes. This paradigm promotes modular, reusable, and maintainable code, which is crucial for building complex applications.

- **Encapsulation**: Java encourages encapsulation, where data and behavior are bundled together within classes. This hides the internal implementation details and exposes only the necessary functionalities.
- **Inheritance**: Java supports inheritance, allowing classes to inherit properties and methods from other classes. This promotes code reuse and a hierarchical class structure.
- **Polymorphism**: Java allows polymorphism, where a single interface can represent different underlying forms (data types). This is vital for designing flexible and scalable applications.
- **Abstraction**: Java emphasizes abstraction, enabling developers to focus on essential qualities while hiding unnecessary details, making complex systems more manageable.

## Robust and Secure

Java was designed with a strong emphasis on reliability, robustness, and security. These principles are fundamental to Java's philosophy and have played a significant role in its widespread adoption in security-sensitive domains like finance, healthcare, and telecommunications.

- **Memory Management**: Java's automatic garbage collection eliminates the need for developers to manually manage memory allocation and deallocation, reducing memory leaks and pointer errors.

- **Exception Handling**: Java's robust exception handling framework ensures that errors are caught and handled gracefully, preventing system crashes and maintaining stability.
- **Security Features**: Java has a comprehensive security model that includes a built-in sandbox environment for running untrusted code, bytecode verification, and secure class loading. This makes Java a preferred choice for applications requiring strong security guarantees.

# Platform Independence

"*Write Once, Run Anywhere*" (WORA) is perhaps the most well-known principle of Java. It achieves platform independence through its use of the Java Virtual Machine (JVM), which allows Java programs to run on any device or operating system that has a compatible JVM.

- **Bytecode Compilation:** Java code is compiled into platform-independent bytecode, which is executed by the JVM. This abstraction layer allows Java applications to run seamlessly on different platforms without any modification.
- **JVM Abstraction:** The JVM serves as an intermediary between the Java program and the underlying operating system, handling all platform-specific operations and ensuring consistent behavior across environments.
- **Standard Libraries:** Java's extensive standard libraries provide a uniform interface for commonly used functions like file I/O, networking, and database connectivity, further promoting platform independence.

# High Performance

While Java is an interpreted language, which can introduce some overhead, the developers behind Java have continuously improved its performance over the years. Techniques such as Just-In-Time (JIT) compilation, HotSpot optimization, and native libraries have significantly enhanced Java's execution speed.

- **Just-In-Time Compilation**: The JVM uses JIT compilation to convert bytecode into native machine code at runtime. This results in faster execution times, as the code runs directly on the hardware rather than being interpreted.
- **Optimized Libraries**: Java's standard libraries are optimized for performance, enabling developers to build high-performance applications without worrying about low-level optimization.
- **Adaptive Optimization**: The HotSpot JVM includes advanced features like adaptive optimization, which continuously analyzes program behavior and optimizes code paths dynamically, further improving performance.

# Multithreading and Concurrency

Java was designed from the ground up to support multithreading, allowing multiple threads of execution to run concurrently within a single program. This is particularly useful for developing responsive and scalable applications.

- **Built-In Support for Threads**: Java provides built-in support for threads at the language level, with a rich set of APIs for managing thread creation, synchronization, and communication.
- **Synchronization**: Java offers synchronized blocks and methods to manage access to shared resources, preventing race conditions and ensuring data integrity.

- **Concurrency Utilities**: With the addition of the `java.util.concurrent` package, Java provides high-level abstractions for concurrent programming, such as thread pools, executors, and atomic variables, simplifying complex multithreading scenarios.

## Distributed Computing

Java was designed with networked and distributed computing in mind. This focus has made Java a natural fit for building networked applications, from web services to cloud-native applications.

- **Networking Libraries**: Java provides an extensive set of libraries for networking, including support for TCP/IP, UDP, HTTP, and higher-level protocols like RMI (Remote Method Invocation).
- **Remote Method Invocation (RMI)**: RMI allows Java programs to invoke methods on remote objects, enabling seamless communication between distributed components.
- **Enterprise Integration**: Java's Enterprise Edition (Java EE, now Jakarta EE) provides a robust framework for building distributed, transactional, and secure applications, including support for EJBs, servlets, JSP, JAX-RS, and more.

## Evolution and Backward Compatibility

Java's evolution has always been driven by a balance between innovation and backward compatibility. New features are added carefully to avoid breaking existing applications, ensuring a smooth transition for developers upgrading to newer versions.

- **Backward Compatibility**: Java has a strong track record of maintaining backward compatibility, meaning that applications built on older versions can still run on newer versions with little or no modification.
- **Modular Evolution**: Starting with Java 9, the introduction of the Java Platform Module System (JPMS) allowed for modular development, making Java more scalable and adaptable while retaining compatibility.
- **Community-Driven Process**: Through the Java Community Process (JCP), Java has evolved in a way that reflects the needs and feedback of its extensive developer community, ensuring that changes are practical and valuable.

Java's philosophy and principles like simplicity, object-orientation, robustness, security, platform independence, high performance, multithreading, distributed computing, and backward compatibility, have shaped it into one of the most enduring and widely adopted programming languages. These guiding principles have ensured that Java remains a relevant and powerful language for modern software development, and is capable of adapting to the evolving landscape of technology.

Java's continued adherence to these principles ensures that it remains a top choice for developers and organizations looking for a reliable, scalable, and secure programming language. As Java evolves, it continues to embody these core values, driving innovation while maintaining the stability and reliability that developers have come to expect from it.

# Setting Up the Java Environment

Setting up the Java environment is an essential step to start developing Java applications. A proper setup includes installing the Java Development Kit (JDK), configuring environment variables, and choosing an Integrated Development Environment (IDE) or text editor for writing and compiling the Java code. This section will cover all the necessary steps for setting up the Java environment across different platforms, including Windows, macOS, and Linux.

# Installing the Java Development Kit (JDK)

The Java Development Kit (JDK) is a software development environment used for developing Java applications. It includes the Java Runtime Environment (JRE), an interpreter/loader (Java), a compiler (javac), an archiver (jar), a documentation generator (Javadoc), and other tools necessary for Java development.

# Choosing the Right JDK Version

Selecting the right Java Development Kit (JDK) version is a crucial first step when beginning any Java project, as it impacts compatibility, performance, support timelines, and access to modern language features.

- **JDK Versions**: Oracle provides several JDK versions, such as JDK 8, 11, 17, and 21. JDK 8 and JDK 11 that are widely used in production environments and are considered Long-Term Support (LTS) versions. JDK 17 and JDK 21 are the most recent LTS releases and consist of the latest features and improvements.
- **OpenJDK vs. Oracle JDK**: OpenJDK is the open-source implementation of the Java Platform, Standard Edition, and is available for free under the GNU General Public License (GPL). Oracle JDK includes commercial features and comes with a different license. For most developers, OpenJDK is sufficient.

**Installing the JDK on Different Operating Systems**

Installing the Java Development Kit (JDK) correctly is the first step to enabling Java development on your system. While the core installation process is similar across platforms, each operating system has its own best practices, tools, and environment configurations.

**Windows:**

1. Download the JDK installer from the Oracle website or the OpenJDK website.
2. Run the installer and follow the on-screen instructions.
3. Once installed, add the `bin` directory of the JDK to the **PATH** environment variable.

**macOS:**

1. Download the `.dmg` installer from the Oracle or OpenJDK website.
2. Open the downloaded file and follow the installation instructions.
3. Alternatively, you can use a package manager like `Homebrew` to install OpenJDK with the command: `brew install openjdk`.
4. Set the `JAVA_HOME` environment variable using: `export JAVA_HOME=$(/usr/libexec/java_home)`.

**Linux:**

1. You can use the package manager to install OpenJDK. For Debian-based distributions (like Ubuntu), run: `sudo apt install openjdk-17-jdk`.
2. For Red Hat-based distributions (like CentOS), run: `sudo yum install java-17-openjdk`.
3. You can also download the tar.gz file from the Oracle or OpenJDK website and manually install it.

# Configuring Environment Variables

After installing the JDK, you need to configure environment variables to ensure that the Java compiler and runtime are accessible from the command line.

**Setting Up Environment Variables on Different Operating Systems**

**Windows:**

1. Right-click on "**This PC**" or "**Computer**" and select "**Properties**."
2. Click on "**Advanced system settings**" and then "**Environment Variables**."
3. Add a new system variable named **JAVA_HOME** and set its value to the path of your JDK installation (for example **C:\Program Files\Java\jdk-17**).
4. Edit the **Path** variable and add **%JAVA_HOME%\bin.**

**macOS:**

1. Open the Terminal.
2. Edit the **.bash_profile** or **.zshrc** file, depending on your shell, using nano **~/.bash_profile or nano ~/.zshrc.**

   ```
   export JAVA_HOME=$(/usr/libexec/java_home)
   export PATH=$JAVA_HOME/bin:$PATH
   ```
3. Save and reload the profile using **source ~/.bash_profile** or **source ~/.zshrc.**

**Linux:**

1. Open the terminal and edit the **.bashrc** or **.bash_profile** file using a text editor like **nano.**
2. Add the following lines

   ```
   export JAVA_HOME=/usr/lib/jvm/java-17-openjdk-amd64
   export PATH=$JAVA_HOME/bin:$PATH
   ```
3. Save and run **source ~/.bashrc** or **source ~/.bash_profile** to apply the changes.

# Verifying the Java Installation

After installing the JDK and configuring environment variables, it is crucial to verify that the setup is correct.

1. Open a terminal or command prompt.
2. Run the following command to check the installed Java version:

   ```
   java –version
   ```

# Choosing an Integrated Development Environment (IDE)

An Integrated Development Environment (IDE) significantly enhances productivity by providing features like syntax highlighting, code completion, debugging, and project management. Here are some popular IDEs for Java development:

- **IntelliJ IDEA**: IntelliJ IDEA, developed by JetBrains, is one of the most popular IDEs for Java development. It offers both a Community Edition (free) and an Ultimate Edition (commercial). IntelliJ IDEA provides powerful features such as intelligent code completion, refactoring, debugging, and integration with build tools and version control systems.

- **Eclipse IDE**: Eclipse is a free and open-source IDE widely used for Java development. It provides a robust set of tools and plugins, including Maven and Gradle integration, a powerful debugger, and a wide range of extensions for different languages and frameworks.
- **NetBeans**: NetBeans is an open-source IDE sponsored by Apache and is another popular choice for Java developers. It provides excellent support for Java SE, Java EE, and JavaFX development, along with features like code templates, refactoring, and built-in support for version control.
- **VS Code with Java Extensions**: Visual Studio Code (VS Code), with Java extensions like "`Java Extension Pack`," offers a lightweight and customizable development environment for Java. It is especially popular among developers who prefer a minimalistic and highly customizable setup.

# Setting Up Build Tools

Build tools are essential for managing project dependencies, compiling codes, and packaging applications. Two of the most popular build tools for Java are Maven and Gradle.

- **Apache Maven**: Maven is a widely used build automation tool for Java projects. It uses an XML file (**pom.xml**) to manage project dependencies, build configurations, and plugins. You can install Maven by downloading it from the official website (https://maven.apache.org/) and configuring the **PATH** environment variable.
- **Gradle**: Gradle is another popular build tool that uses a Groovy-based DSL or Kotlin-based DSL for its build scripts. It is known for its flexibility and performance, especially with large projects. You can install Gradle by downloading it from the official website (https://gradle.org/) and adding it to the PATH environment variable.

# Setting Up Java Projects in an IDE

After installing the JDK, configuring environment variables, and selecting an IDE, the next step is to set up your first Java project.

1. **Creating a New Java Project**:
    a. Open your chosen IDE (such as IntelliJ IDEA, Eclipse and NetBeans).
    b. Create a new project and select "`Java`" as the project type.
    c. Configure the project SDK to point to your installed JDK.
    d. Add a new class with a `main` method to start coding.
2. **Configuring Build Tools**: If you are using Maven or Gradle, the IDE will typically prompt you to add a `pom.xml` (Maven) or `build.gradle` (Gradle) file to manage dependencies and build configurations.

# Managing Multiple Java Versions with Java Version Managers

In development environments, it is common to work with multiple Java versions, especially when maintaining legacy applications or developing new ones that require the latest features. Java Version Managers are tools that help developers seamlessly switch between different Java versions on their machine without having to manually change environment variables each time. These tools simplify the process of managing multiple JDKs and make the development workflow more efficient.

### SDKMAN! - The Software Development Kit Manager

**SDKMAN!** (Software Development Kit Manager) is a popular tool for managing multiple versions of Java (and other SDKs) on Unix-based systems, including Linux and macOS. It allows developers to easily install, switch, and configure different versions of Java with simple command-line commands.

**Key Features of SDKMAN!**

- **Install Multiple Java Versions**: Install any JDK version, from OpenJDK to Oracle JDK, AdoptOpenJDK, Amazon Corretto, and more.
- **Easily Switch between Versions**: Change the default Java version for your environment with a single command.
- **Remove Unused Versions**: Remove specific Java versions that are no longer needed to free up space.
- **Support for Other SDKs**: In addition to Java, SDKMAN! supports managing other SDKs like Scala, Groovy, Kotlin, and more.

**Installing SDKMAN!**

```
// Open your terminal and run the following command
curl -s "https://get.sdkman.io" | bash
// After installation, initialize SDKMAN! by running
source "$HOME/.sdkman/bin/sdkman-init.sh"
// To ensure SDKMAN! is installed correctly, run
sdk version
```

**Using SDKMAN! to Manage Java Versions**

```
// To view all the available Java versions for installation, run
sdk list java
// To install a specific version of Java, use the following command
sdk install java 17.0.2-open
// To switch between installed Java versions, use the command
sdk use java 11.0.12-zulu
// To set a default Java version for all terminal sessions, run
sdk default java 11.0.12-zulu
// If you need to uninstall a specific Java version, run
sdk uninstall java 16.0.1-open
```

**Other Java Version Managers**

In addition to SDKMAN!, there are other tools available for managing Java versions:

- **jEnv**: A tool specifically for managing Java environments on Unix-based systems. It provides a similar experience to SDKMAN! but focuses solely on Java. jEnv does not install JDKs itself; it works with already installed versions and provides a way to switch between them.
- **Jabba**: Another cross-platform Java version manager that can be used on Windows, macOS, and Linux. Jabba is a lightweight tool that focuses on downloading and managing different versions of Java.

Managing multiple Java versions is a common requirement in modern development environments, and tools like SDKMAN! provide a simple and efficient way to handle this task. By using such tools, developers can quickly switch between different Java versions, ensuring compatibility across various projects and streamlining their workflow.

# Understanding Java Syntax and Structure

Understanding the syntax and structure of Java is fundamental for any developer who wants to write effective and maintainable code. Java's syntax is designed to be simple and familiar, borrowing heavily from C and C++ while eliminating many of their complexities and pitfalls. This chapter provides a comprehensive overview of Java's syntax and structure, covering essential elements such as data types, operators, control flow statements, classes, and methods. By the end of this chapter, you will have a solid foundation in Java programming, enabling you to write clear and efficient code.

# Basic Structure of a Java Program

Every Java program is made up of one or more classes, and each class contains methods that define the behavior of the program. The most basic Java program consists of a class definition with a main method, which serves as the entry point of the application.

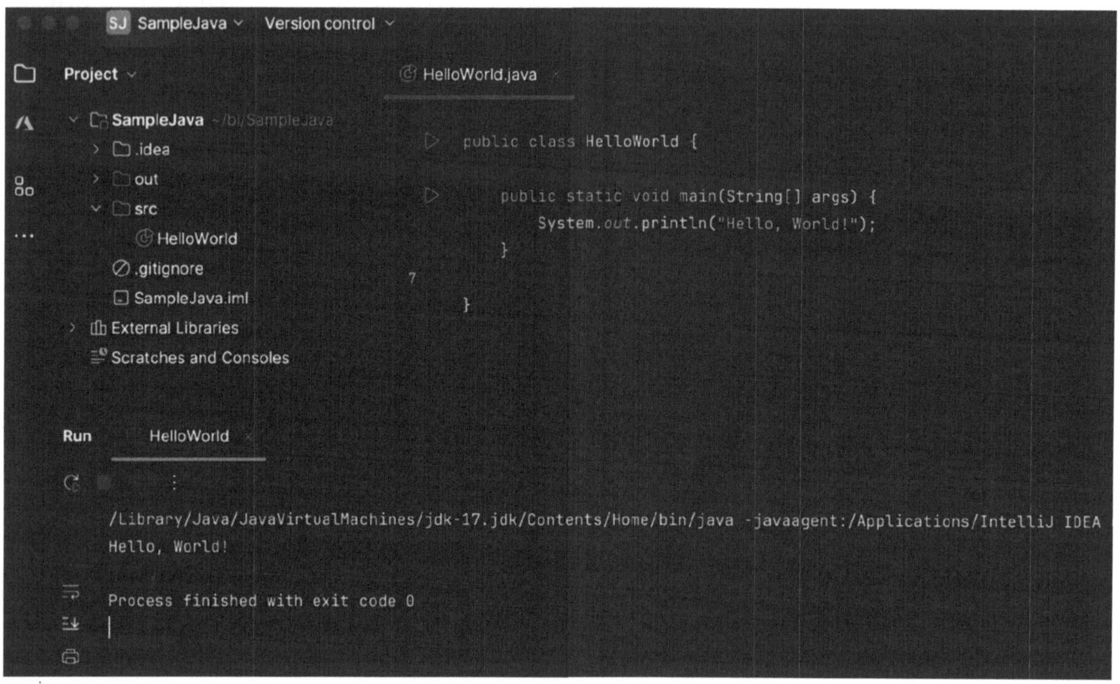


***Figure 1.1:*** *Running the Hello World*

**Key Components:**

- **Class Definition**: Every Java program must have at least one class definition. The class is defined using the `class` keyword followed by the class name (`HelloWorld`, in this case).
- **Main Method**: The `main` method is the entry point of any Java application. It is always defined with the signature `public static void main(String[] args)`. The `String[] args` parameter is used to pass command-line arguments to the program.
- **Statements**: Java statements are executed in the order they appear within a method. The `System.out.println("Hello, World!");` statement is used to print text to the console.

# Java Syntax Elements

Java's syntax is composed of various elements that are crucial for building programs. Let us look at the most fundamental elements:

- **Identifiers:** Identifiers are names used to identify variables, methods, classes, packages, and other entities. They must begin with a letter, a dollar sign (**$**), or an underscore (_), followed by letters, digits, dollar signs, or underscores. Java is case-sensitive, so **`Variable`** and **`variable`** are considered as different identifiers.

- **Keywords:** Java has a set of reserved words known as keywords. These keywords have predefined meanings in the language and cannot be used as identifiers. Some examples of Java keywords are **`class`**, **`public`**, **`static`**, **`void`**, **`int`**, **`if`**, **`else`**, **`for`**, **`while`**, **`return`**, and so on.
- **Comments:** Comments are used to document code and are ignored by the compiler. Java supports three types of comments:

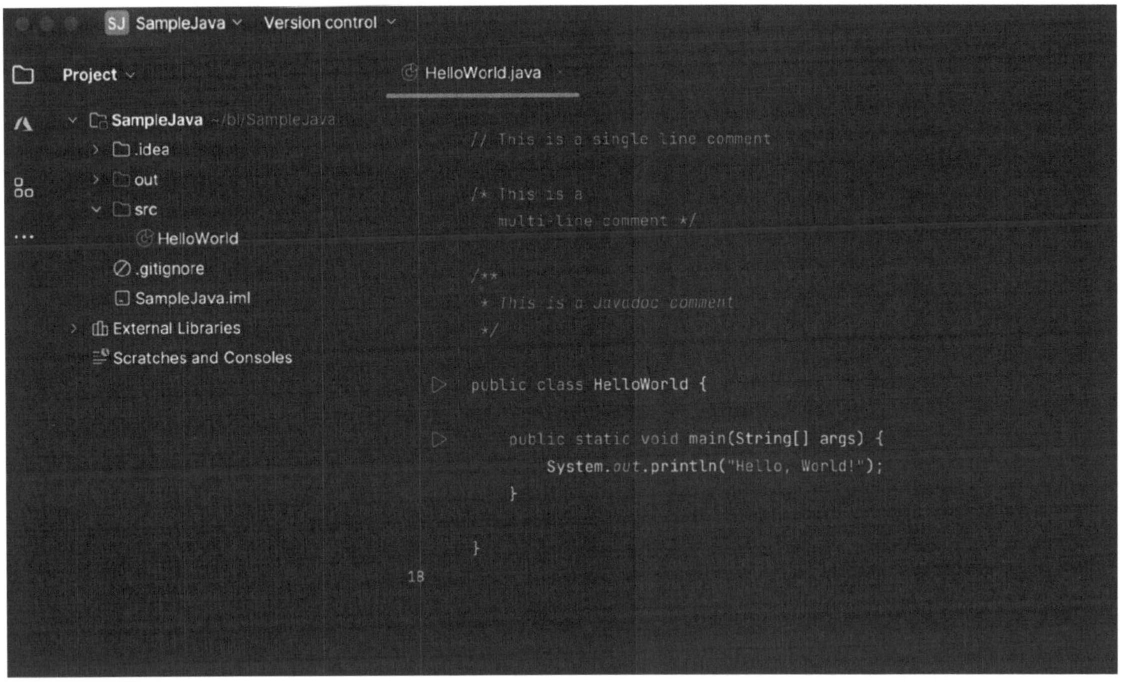


**Figure 1.2:** *Different Types of Comments*

# Java Data Types

Java is a strongly typed language, meaning every variable must have a declared data type. Data types specify the size and type of values that variables can hold.

## Primitive Data Types

Java has eight primitive data types that represent basic types of data:

- **`byte`**: 8-bit integer (for example, **`byte b = 100;`**)
- **`short`**: 16-bit integer (for example, **`short s = 1000;`**)
- **`int`**: 32-bit integer (for example, **`int i = 10000;`**)
- **`long`**: 64-bit integer (for example, **`long l = 100000L;`**)
- **`float`**: 32-bit floating-point number (for example, **`float f = 10.5f;`**)
- **`double`**: 64-bit floating-point number (for example, **`double d = 10.5;`**)
- **`char`**: 16-bit Unicode character (for example, **`char c = 'A';`**)
- **`boolean`**: Represents true or false values (for example, **`boolean flag = true;`**)

# Reference Data Types

Reference data types are used to refer to objects. They include class types, interface types, array types, and more. Unlike primitive types, reference types do not hold the data value itself but a reference (memory address) to the object in memory.

```
String name = "Java"; // 'name' is a reference variable pointing to a String
object
```

# Operators in Java

Operators in Java are special symbols used to perform operations on variables and values. Java provides a rich set of operators to manipulate variables.

**Types of Operators**

- **Arithmetic Operators: +, -, *, /, %**
- **Relational Operators: ==, !=, >, <, >=, <=**
- **Logical Operators: &&, ||, !**
- **Assignment Operators: =, +=, -=, *=, /=, %=**
- **Increment and Decrement Operators: ++, -**
- **Ternary Operator: ? :**

```
int a = 10, b = 5;
int sum = a + b;  // Addition
boolean result = (a > b);  // Greater than
boolean logicalResult = (a > b) && (a != b);  // Logical AND
a += 5;  // Equivalent to 'a = a + 5;'
a++;  // Increment by 1
int min = (a < b) ? a : b;  // Ternary operation
```

# Control Flow Statements

Control flow statements are used to determine the flow of execution in a Java program based on conditions or loops.

**Conditional Statements**

- **`if` Statement**: Executes a block of code if a specified condition is true

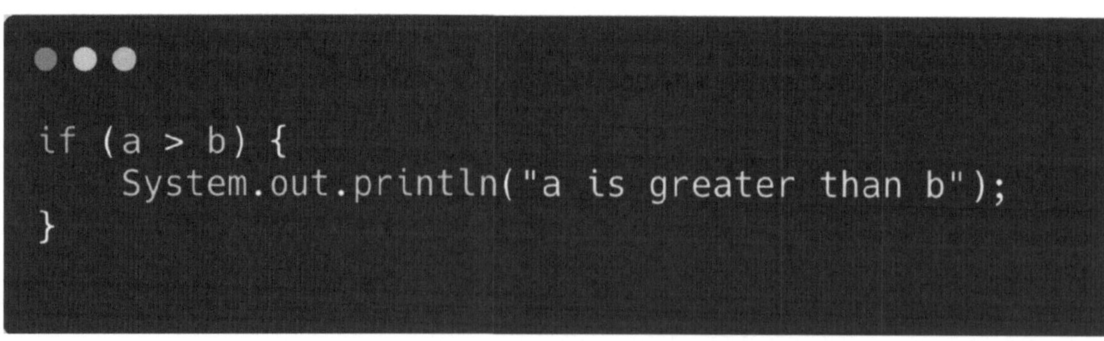


**Figure 1.3**: *Simple If Statement*

- **`if-else` Statement**: Provides an alternative block of code if the condition is false

```
if (a > b) {
    System.out.println("a is greater than b");
} else {
    System.out.println("a is not greater than
b");
}
```

**Figure 1.4:** *If else Statement*

- **`switch` Statement**: Allows the execution of a block of code among multiple options

```
int day = 2;
switch (day) {
    case 1:
        System.out.println("Monday");
        break;
    case 2:
        System.out.println("Tuesday");
        break;
    default:
        System.out.println("Other Day");
}
```

**Figure 1.5:** *Switch Statement*

**Looping Statements**

- **`for` Loop**: Repeats a block of code a fixed number of times

```
for (int i = 0; i < 5; i++) {
    System.out.println(i);
}
```

**Figure 1.6:** *for loop*

- **`while` Loop**: Repeats a block of code as long as a condition is true

```
int i = 0;
while (i < 5) {
    System.out.println(i);
    i++;
}
```

***Figure 1.7:*** *While Loop*

- **`do-while` Loop**: Executes a block of code at least once, then repeats as long as a condition is true

```
int i = 0;
do {
    System.out.println(i);
    i++;
} while (i < 5);
```

***Figure 1.8:* Do** *While Loop*

# Java Classes and Objects

Java is an object-oriented language, and understanding classes and objects is essential for Java programming.

- **`Class`**: A class is a blueprint for creating objects. It defines the properties (fields) and behaviors (methods) that objects of the class will have.

```
public class Car {
    String color;
    int year;

    void displayInfo() {
        System.out.println("Color: " + color + ", Year: " + year);
    }
}
```

***Figure 1.9:*** *Java Class*

- **`Object`**: An object is an instance of a class. It is created using the **`new`** keyword.

```
Car myCar = new Car();   // Creating an object of the Car class
myCar.color = "Red";     // Accessing fields
myCar.year = 2020;
myCar.displayInfo();     // Calling methods
```

**Figure 1.10:** *Creating an Object*

Understanding Java's syntax and structure is fundamental to becoming proficient in Java programming. By mastering the basic components, such as classes, methods, and packages, you can lay the groundwork for creating well-structured and organized Java applications. Knowledge of **data types** and **how they function in Java** allows you to handle data effectively, ensuring that your programs are both memory-efficient and robust. Grasping the **nuances of operators**–from arithmetic to logical operators–enables you to perform a wide range of operations, manipulate data, and control program flow.

Learning how to use **control flow statements** like **`if`**, **`switch`**, **`for`**, **`while`**, and **`do-while`** empowers you to make decisions and repeat tasks, which is essential for developing dynamic and interactive applications. **Understanding expressions** and the concept of **operator precedence** helps in writing concise and effective codes, reducing errors caused by improper evaluation of complex expressions.

By building a strong foundation in these fundamental concepts, you prepare yourself to tackle more advanced Java topics with confidence. This knowledge will not only help you write better code but also enable you to understand and leverage Java's powerful libraries and frameworks, ultimately allowing you to build sophisticated, high-performance applications that meet real-world needs. As you continue to learn and practice, the principles and syntax covered in this chapter will serve as the building blocks upon which all your future Java development is based.

# Arrays, Strings, and Data Handling

Efficient data handling is a critical skill for any Java developer. Java provides powerful built-in support for managing data using arrays and strings, which are fundamental components for storing, manipulating, and processing data. Arrays provide a way to store multiple elements of the same type, while strings offer a convenient and efficient way to handle text data. This chapter covers the fundamentals of arrays and strings in Java, along with various techniques and classes for effective data handling. By the end of this chapter, you will have a deep understanding of how to use these structures to build robust and efficient applications.

# Working with Arrays

An array is a data structure that allows you to store multiple values of the same type in a single variable. Arrays are one of the most basic and commonly used data structures in Java.

## Defining and Initializing Arrays

Arrays are fundamental data structures in Java that allow you to store multiple values of the same type in a single variable. Before working with them effectively, it is essential to understand how arrays are defined, initialized, and accessed.

- **Single-Dimensional Arrays**: These are the simplest type of arrays, which store a list of elements.

```
int[] numbers = new int[5]; // Declaration with size
int[] initializedNumbers = {1, 2, 3, 4, 5}; // Declaration with initialization

// You can access elements using an index, which starts at 0

System.out.println(numbers[0]); // Output: 1
```

**Figure 1.11:** *Defining and Accessing Arrays*

- **Multi-Dimensional Arrays**: These are arrays of arrays, commonly used for matrices.

```
int[][] matrix = new int[3][3]; // 2D array
int[][] predefinedMatrix = { {1, 2, 3}, {4, 5, 6}, {7, 8, 9} }; // Initialization

// Access elements using row and column indices
System.out.println(matrix[0][1]); // Output: 2
```

**Figure 1.12:** *Accessing Elements*

# Common Array Operations

This example illustrates how to work with arrays in Java. To modify an array element, use its index, like setting `numbers[2] = 10` to change the third element to 10. You can iterate over arrays using a standard for loop to access elements by index or an enhanced `for-each` loop to directly work with each element. The array's length can be determined using the `.length` attribute, which returns the total number of elements and allows you to manage and control iterations effectively. These are fundamental techniques for handling arrays in Java programming.

```
// Accessing and Modifying Elements: Access elements by their index and modify them directly.
numbers[2] = 10; // Set the third element to 10

// Iterating Over Arrays: Use for, for-each, or while loops to iterate over array elements.
for (int i = 0; i < numbers.length; i++) {
    System.out.println(numbers[i]);
}

// Using enhanced for loop
for (int number : numbers) {
    System.out.println(number);
}

// Array Length: Use the .length attribute to determine the size of the array.
System.out.println(numbers.length); // Output: 5
```

**Figure 1.13:** *Common Array Operations*

## Common Array Algorithms

This Java code demonstrates key array operations: searching, sorting, and merging. For searching, it uses a linear search to locate a target element within an array and prints its index. For sorting, the code utilizes the **Arrays.sort()** method to sort an array in ascending order. Finally, it shows you how to merge two arrays into one by using **System.arraycopy()** to copy elements from each source array into a new, larger array. These basic operations are essential for effectively handling arrays in Java programming.

```
// Searching: Finding an element in an array using linear search or binary search
int target = 3;
for (int i = 0; i < numbers.length; i++) {
    if (numbers[i] == target) {
        System.out.println("Element found at index: " + i);
        break;
    }
}

// Sorting: Sorting an array using built-in methods like Arrays.sort()
import java.util.Arrays;
Arrays.sort(numbers); // Sorts the array in ascending order

// Merging: Combining two arrays into one larger array
int[] array1 = {1, 2, 3};
int[] array2 = {4, 5, 6};
int[] mergedArray = new int[array1.length + array2.length];

System.arraycopy(array1, 0, mergedArray, 0, array1.length);
System.arraycopy(array2, 0, mergedArray, array1.length, array2.length);
```

***Figure 1.14:*** *Common Array Algorithms*

## Array Utility Methods

Java provides the **java.util.Arrays** class, which contains various utility methods for arrays:

- **Arrays.toString(array)**: Converts the array to a string representation
- **Arrays.equals(array1, array2)**: Compares two arrays for equality
- **Arrays.fill(array, value)**: Fills the array with a specified value

# Working with Strings

Strings are one of the most commonly used data types in Java. Java provides a rich set of classes and methods for handling strings, such as **String**, **StringBuilder**, and **StringBuffer**.

**Introduction to the String Class:**

- **Immutable Strings**: In Java, strings are immutable, meaning once created, their values cannot be changed. Any modification results in a new string object.
- **String Pool**: Java maintains a pool of strings for memory optimization. Strings created using literals are stored in the string pool, whereas those created with **new** are stored in the heap.

```java
String str1 = "Hello";
String str2 = str1.concat(" World"); // str1 remains "Hello", str2 is "Hello World"

String s1 = "Java"; // Stored in string pool
String s2 = new String("Java"); // Stored in heap
```

**Figure 1.15:** *String Class*

# Common String Methods

This code snippet demonstrates essential Java string operations. It covers basic methods like **`length()`** to get a string's length, **`charAt()`** to access a character at a specific index, and **`substring()`** for extracting parts of a string. It also shows comparison methods like **`equalsIgnoreCase()`** for case-insensitive comparisons. For string manipulation, it uses methods like **`trim()`** to remove whitespace, **`toLowerCase()`** and **`toUpperCase()`** for case conversion, and **`replace()`** for replacing characters. These methods are crucial for handling and manipulating strings efficiently in Java.

```java
// Basic Methods: length(), charAt(index), substring(beginIndex, endIndex), indexOf(), lastIndexOf()
String text = "Java Programming";
System.out.println(text.length()); // Output: 16
System.out.println(text.charAt(5)); // Output: P

// Comparison Methods: equals(), equalsIgnoreCase(), compareTo()
String s1 = "java";
String s2 = "Java";
System.out.println(s1.equalsIgnoreCase(s2)); // Output: true


// String Manipulation: toLowerCase(), toUpperCase(), trim(), replace(oldChar, newChar)
String s = " Hello ";
System.out.println(s.trim()); // Output: "Hello"
```

**Figure 1.16:** *Common String Methods*

# `StringBuilder` and `StringBuffer`

When working with mutable sequences of characters in Java, such as building or modifying strings dynamically, **`StringBuilder`** and **`StringBuffer`** provide efficient and flexible alternatives to the immutable **`String`** class. Understanding their differences and ideal use cases is essential for writing performant and thread-safe code.

- **Mutable Strings**: **`StringBuilder`** and **`StringBuffer`** provide mutable alternatives to the **`String`** class.
    - **`StringBuilder`** is non-synchronized and offers better performance.
    - **`StringBuffer`** is synchronized, making it thread-safe but slower.

```java
StringBuilder sb = new StringBuilder("Hello");
sb.append(" World");
System.out.println(sb); // Output: "Hello World"

StringBuffer sb = new StringBuffer("Hello");
sb.append(" World");
System.out.println(sb); // Output: "Hello World"
```

**Figure 1.17:** *StringBuilder and StringBuffer*

# Data Handling with Collections

Java's Collections Framework provides a set of classes and interfaces for handling data efficiently. It includes **List, Set, Map,** and **Queue** interfaces, each with multiple implementations for different use cases.

## Lists: Ordered Collections

When working with groups of elements in Java where order matters and duplicates are allowed, lists offer a flexible and widely used collection type. As ordered collections, lists maintain the sequence of insertion and provide indexed access to elements, making them ideal for scenarios that require dynamic, sequential data handling.

- **`ArrayList` and `LinkedList`**: Examples of **`List`** implementations
- **Common Operations**: Adding, removing, searching, sorting, and iterating elements

```java
List<String> names = new ArrayList<>();
names.add("John");
names.add("Jane");
System.out.println(names); // Output: [John, Jane]
```

**Figure 1.18:** *Defining List*

## Sets: Unordered Collections without Duplicates

When your application requires a collection that automatically eliminates duplicates, and does not enforce element ordering, sets are the ideal choice. In Java, sets are designed to store unique elements efficiently, making them perfect for membership testing, de-duplication, and mathematical set operations like union and intersection.

- **`HashSet` and `TreeSet`**: Examples of **`Set`** implementations
- **Unique Properties**: No duplicate elements, and different sets provide ordering guarantees

```
Set<Integer> numbers = new HashSet<>();
numbers.add(1);
numbers.add(2);
numbers.add(1); // Duplicates are not allowed
```

***Figure 1.19:*** *Defining Sets*

## Maps: Key-Value Pairs

When data needs to be stored and retrieved using a unique identifier, maps provide a powerful and efficient solution. In Java, maps represent collections of key-value pairs, where each key maps to a specific value, enabling quick lookups, updates, and deletions based on the key.

- **`HashMap` and `TreeMap`**: Examples of **`Map`** implementations
- **Use Cases**: Suitable for situations requiring fast lookup, insertion, and deletion operations

```
Map<String, Integer> map = new HashMap<>();
map.put("Alice", 25);
map.put("Bob", 30);
System.out.println(map.get("Alice")); // Output: 25
```

***Figure 1.20:*** *Defining Maps*

# Working with Data Streams

Java provides extensive support for handling input and output (I/O) operations, such as reading from or writing to files.

**Reading and Writing Files**

- **Using `FileReader` and `FileWriter`**: For character-based I/O operations
- **Using `BufferedReader` and `BufferedWriter`**: For more efficient I/O operations

```
// FileWriter
FileWriter writer = new FileWriter("output.txt");
writer.write("Hello, World!");
writer.close();

// BufferedReader
BufferedReader reader = new BufferedReader(new
FileReader("input.txt"));
String line = reader.readLine();
```

***Figure 1.21:*** *FileWriter and BufferedReader*

## Working with Byte Streams

When dealing with raw binary data, such as reading from or writing to image files, audio files, or network sockets, byte streams provide a low-level, efficient mechanism for input and output operations in Java.

- **Using `FileInputStream` and `FileOutputStream`:** For reading and writing binary data

```
FileInputStream fis = new FileInputStream("data.dat");
int data = fis.read( );
```

**Figure 1.22:** *FileInputStream*

Mastering arrays, strings, and data handling is crucial for any Java developer. These foundational concepts are essential for writing efficient and robust programs that process and manipulate data. By understanding how to use arrays for structured data storage, strings for text processing, collections for flexible data manipulation, and streams for I/O operations, you will be equipped to handle any data-centric challenge in Java development. With this knowledge, you can build scalable, high-performance applications that effectively manage and process complex data sets.

# Basic Input and Output in Java

Input and output (I/O) operations are fundamental to any programming language, enabling programs to interact with users, files, and external systems. In Java, the java.io and **`java.nio`** packages provide comprehensive support for handling both basic and advanced I/O operations. This section will cover the basic concepts of Java I/O, including console input/output, file handling, and working with data streams. By the end of this chapter, you will have a strong foundation in Java's I/O mechanisms, allowing you to write applications that effectively interact with users and handle data efficiently.

# Console Input and Output

Console input and output are the most basic forms of I/O operations in Java. The **`System.out`** and **`System.in`** streams are used to interact with the console for output and input, respectively.

## Console Output with `System.out`

In Java, displaying messages to the console is a fundamental operation for debugging, logging, and user interaction. **`System.out`** provides a simple and effective way to output text and monitor program behavior during development.

- **Using `print()` and `println()`:** The **`System.out`** object provides methods to print data to the console. The **`print()`** method outputs text without a newline, while **`println()`** adds a newline at the end of the output.
- **Formatted Output with `printf()`:** The **`printf()`** method provides formatted output similar to the **`printf()`** function in C.

```
System.out.print("Hello, "); // Output: Hello,
System.out.println("World!"); // Output: World! (with a newline)


System.out.printf("Hello, %s! You are %d years old.%n", "Alice", 30);
// Output: Hello, Alice! You are 30 years old.
```

***Figure 1.23:*** *Console Output*

## Console Input with `Scanner`

Reading user input from the console is a fundamental part of interactive Java applications, and the Scanner class offers a flexible and straightforward way to capture and process this input efficiently.

- **Using the `Scanner` Class**: The **`Scanner`** class, available in the **`java.util`** package, provides an easy way to read different types of input from the console.
- **Reading Different Types of Input**: The **`Scanner`** class provides various methods to read different data types:
    - **`nextInt()`**: Reads an integer
    - **`nextDouble()`**: Reads a double
    - **`nextLine()`**: Reads a line of text
    - **`next()`** and **`nextBoolean()`**: Reads a single word and a boolean, respectively

```
import java.util.Scanner;

public class ConsoleInputExample {
    public static void main(String[] args) {
        Scanner scanner = new Scanner(System.in);
        System.out.print("Enter your name: ");
        String name = scanner.nextLine();
        System.out.println("Hello, " + name + "!");
        scanner.close(); // Always close the scanner to prevent resource leaks
    }
}
```

***Figure 1.24:*** *Console Input with Scanner*

# File Input and Output

Java provides robust support for file handling through the **`java.io`** package. You can perform various file operations such as reading, writing, creating, deleting, and appending.

# Reading from Files

- **Using `FileReader` and `BufferedReader`**: `FileReader` reads characters from a file, while `BufferedReader` provides efficient reading of text, buffering characters for faster performance.

```
import java.io.BufferedReader;
import java.io.FileReader;
import java.io.IOException;

public class FileReadingExample {
    public static void main(String[] args) {
        try (BufferedReader reader = new BufferedReader(new FileReader("input.txt"))) {
            String line;
            while ((line = reader.readLine()) != null) {
                System.out.println(line);
            }
        } catch (IOException e) {
            e.printStackTrace();
        }
    }
}
```

**Figure 1.25:** *File Reading Example*

- **Using `FileInputStream` for Binary Data**: `FileInputStream` is used to read raw binary data from a file.

```
import java.io.FileInputStream;
import java.io.IOException;

public class BinaryFileReadingExample {
    public static void main(String[] args) {
        try (FileInputStream fis = new FileInputStream("data.dat")) {
            int data;
            while ((data = fis.read()) != -1) {
                System.out.print((char) data); // Casting to char for readable output
            }
        } catch (IOException e) {
            e.printStackTrace();
        }
    }
}
```

**Figure 1.26:** *Binary File Reading Example*

# Writing to Files

Persisting data by writing it to files is a common requirement in many Java applications, and Java provides simple yet powerful classes like `FileWriter` and `BufferedWriter` to handle this efficiently.

- **Using `FileWriter` and `BufferedWriter`**: `FileWriter` writes characters to a file, while `BufferedWriter` provides efficient writing by buffering characters.

```
import java.io.BufferedWriter;
import java.io.FileWriter;
import java.io.IOException;

public class FileWritingExample {
    public static void main(String[] args) {
        try (BufferedWriter writer = new BufferedWriter(new FileWriter("output.txt"))) {
            writer.write("Hello, World!");
            writer.newLine(); // Adds a new line
            writer.write("Writing to a file in Java.");
        } catch (IOException e) {
            e.printStackTrace();
        }
    }
}
```

**Figure 1.27:** *File Writing Example*

- **Using `FileOutputStream` for Binary Data**: **`FileOutputStream`** is used to write binary data to a file.

```
import java.io.FileOutputStream;
import java.io.IOException;

public class BinaryFileWritingExample {
    public static void main(String[] args) {
        try (FileOutputStream fos = new FileOutputStream("binary.dat")) {
            fos.write("Hello, Binary World!".getBytes());
        } catch (IOException e) {
            e.printStackTrace();
        }
    }
}
```

**Figure 1.28:** *Binary File Writing Example*

# Working with Streams

Java I/O is based on streams, which represent an input or output source. Streams can be categorized into two types: byte streams (for handling binary data) and character streams (for handling character data).

## Byte Streams

- **`InputStream` and `OutputStream`**: The **`InputStream`** and **`OutputStream`** classes are the base classes for all byte streams. They are used for reading and writing the binary data.
    - **`FileInputStream` and `FileOutputStream`**: Read and write binary data from and to files
    - **`BufferedInputStream` and `BufferedOutputStream`**: Provide buffering for input and output streams, improving performance
- **Reading and Writing Using Byte Streams**

```
import java.io.FileInputStream;
import java.io.FileOutputStream;
import java.io.IOException;

public class ByteStreamExample {
    public static void main(String[] args) {
        try (FileInputStream fis = new FileInputStream("input.dat");
             FileOutputStream fos = new FileOutputStream("output.dat")) {
            int byteData;
            while ((byteData = fis.read()) != -1) {
                fos.write(byteData); // Writing each byte read from input file to output file
            }
        } catch (IOException e) {
            e.printStackTrace();
        }
    }
}
```

**Figure 1.29:** *Byte Stream Example*

# Character Streams

- **Reader and Writer**: The Reader and Writer classes are the base classes for all character streams. They are used for reading and writing the text data.
    - **`FileReader` and `FileWriter`**: Read and write character data from and to files
    - **`BufferedReader` and `BufferedWriter`**: Provide efficient character-based input and output with buffering

# File Management Operations

Java provides various classes and methods to manage files and directories. The File class in the **java.io** package offers methods to create files, delete them, rename them, and check their properties.

### Creating and Deleting Files

- **Creating Files**: Using the **`createNewFile()`** method of the **`File`** class

```
import java.io.File;
import java.io.IOException;

public class FileCreationExample {
    public static void main(String[] args) {
        File file = new File("newfile.txt");
        try {
            if (file.createNewFile()) {
                System.out.println("File created: " + file.getName());
            } else {
                System.out.println("File already exists.");
            }
        } catch (IOException e) {
            e.printStackTrace();
        }
    }
}
```

**Figure 1.30:** *File Creation Example*

- **Deleting Files**: Using the **`delete()`** method of the **`File`** class

```
File file = new File("newfile.txt");
if (file.delete()) {
    System.out.println("File deleted: " + file.getName());
} else {
    System.out.println("Failed to delete the file.");
}
```

***Figure 1.31:*** *Deleting Files*

**Working with Directories**

- **Creating Directories**: Using the **`mkdir()`** and **`mkdirs()`** methods
- **Listing Files and Directories**: Using the **`list()`** and **`listFiles()`** methods

```
// Creating a Directory
File dir = new File("newdir");
if (dir.mkdir()) {
    System.out.println("Directory created: " + dir.getName());
}

// Listing Directories
File directory = new File("existingdir");
String[] fileList = directory.list();
for (String fileName : fileList) {
    System.out.println(fileName);
}
```

***Figure 1.32:*** *Creating and Listing Directories*

# Serialization and Deserialization

Serialization is the process of converting an object into a byte stream, while deserialization is the process of converting a byte stream back into an object. Java provides **`ObjectInputStream`** and **`ObjectOutputStream`** classes for these operations.

# Serializing an Object

In Java, object serialization enables you to convert an object into a byte stream, making it possible to store or transmit the object while preserving its state.

- **Implementing Serializable Interface**: The class of the object to be serialized must implement the **Serializable** interface.

```java
import java.io.Serializable;

public class Person implements Serializable {
    private static final long serialVersionUID = 1L;
    private String name;
    private int age;

    public Person(String name, int age) {
        this.name = name;
        this.age = age;
    }
}

// Writing an Object to a file

import java.io.FileOutputStream;
import java.io.ObjectOutputStream;
import java.io.IOException;

public class SerializationExample {
    public static void main(String[] args) {
        Person person = new Person("Alice", 30);
        try (FileOutputStream fos = new
FileOutputStream("person.ser");
             ObjectOutputStream oos = new
ObjectOutputStream(fos)) {
            oos.writeObject(person);
        } catch (IOException e) {
            e.printStackTrace();
        }
    }
}
```

***Figure 1.33:*** *Serialization Example*

## Deserializing an Object

Deserialization is the process of reconstructing an object from its serialized form (a byte stream). In Java, this is typically done using **`ObjectInputStream`**, which reads data from a file (or any input stream) and restores the original object.

```
import java.io.FileInputStream;
import java.io.ObjectInputStream;
import java.io.IOException;

public class DeserializationExample {
    public static void main(String[] args) {
        try (FileInputStream fis = new FileInputStream("person.ser");
             ObjectInputStream ois = new ObjectInputStream(fis)) {
            Person person = (Person) ois.readObject();
            System.out.println("Deserialized Person: " + person.getName() + ", " + person.getAge());
        } catch (IOException | ClassNotFoundException e) {
            e.printStackTrace();
        }
    }
}
```

***Figure 1.34:*** *Deserialization Example*

Java provides a comprehensive set of tools for handling basic input and output operations, from simple console I/O to complex file handling and data serialization. By mastering these techniques, you will be able to create robust applications that interact seamlessly with users and external systems. Understanding how to work with streams, manage files, and perform serialization/deserialization is crucial for building scalable, efficient, and data-driven Java applications.

# Conclusion

This chapter provided a comprehensive introduction to Java, covering its evolution, core principles, and fundamental programming concepts. We began with the **History of Java**, tracing its growth from a language for consumer electronics to a dominant force in software development. Understanding **Java's Philosophy and Principles** revealed the key design goals–simplicity, portability, security, and robustness–that have made it a preferred choice for developers worldwide.

We then moved to **Setting Up the Java Environment**, while guiding you through installing the JDK and configuring an IDE to set up a productive development environment. The section on **Understanding Java Syntax and Structure** laid the groundwork for writing well-structured code, focusing on classes, methods, data types, and control flow statements. The chapter also explored **Arrays, Strings, and Data Handling**, demonstrating how to manage and manipulate data effectively in Java, followed by **Basic Input and Output in Java**, which covered essential techniques for interacting with users and handling files.

With these fundamentals in place, the next chapter will dive into **Object-Oriented Programming (OOP)** in Java. You will learn about the key OOP concepts like **classes, objects, inheritance, polymorphism, encapsulation, and abstraction**, which are vital for building robust, scalable, and maintainable Java applications.

# CHAPTER 2
# Object-Oriented Programming in Java

## Introduction

Object-Oriented Programming (OOP) is at the heart of Java, shaping the way developers design and structure their code. This chapter introduces you to the core concepts of OOP, which are essential for building robust and scalable Java applications.

We begin with **Understanding Classes and Objects**, the fundamental building blocks of OOP that enable you to model real-world entities within your code. Next, we explore **Constructors and Object Lifecycle**, detailing how objects are created, initialized, and managed throughout their existence. Then, we will discuss the principles of **Inheritance** and **Polymorphism** to demonstrate how Java allows for code reuse and flexibility by enabling classes to inherit properties and behaviors from other classes and by allowing objects to take on multiple forms.

The chapter continues with **Abstraction** and **Encapsulation**, two key concepts that help in managing complexity and protecting data within your applications. Abstraction simplifies complex systems by hiding unnecessary details, while encapsulation ensures that an object's internal state is safeguarded from unintended interference. We will also cover **Advanced OOP Concepts** to strengthen your understanding of OOP in Java, which is followed by a section on **Best Practices to** guide you about how to write clean, maintainable, and efficient code.

By the end of this chapter, you will have a strong grasp of OOP in Java, enabling you to create more organized and effective software solutions.

## Structure

In this chapter, the following topics will be covered:

- Understanding Classes and Objects
- Constructors and Object Lifecycle
- Introduction to Methods and Parameter Passing
- Inheritance
- Polymorphism
- Abstraction
- Encapsulation
- Advanced OOP Concepts

## Understanding Classes and Objects

Classes and objects are the fundamental concepts of Object-Oriented Programming (OOP) in Java. A **class** serves as a blueprint for creating objects, defining their properties (attributes) and behaviors (methods). An **object**, on the other hand, is an instance of a class that embodies these properties and behaviors. Understanding how to design and work with classes and objects is crucial for writing clean, efficient, and scalable Java code. This chapter delves into the concepts of classes and objects, their components, how to create and use them, and the best practices for designing classes in Java.

# Understanding Class

A **class** in Java is a blueprint or template that defines the structure and behavior of objects. It encapsulates data (fields) and functions (methods) that operate on that data. Classes provide a way to define new types, and organize code in a logical and reusable manner.

## Structure of a Class

A basic class definition in Java includes:

- **Fields (Attributes)**: Variables that represent the state or properties of the class
- **Methods (Functions)**: Blocks of code that define the behavior of the class and operate on its fields

Here is a simple example of a class definition in Java:

```java
public class Car {
    // Fields (Attributes)
    private String color;
    private String model;
    private int year;

    // Constructor
    public Car(String color, String model, int year) {
        this.color = color;
        this.model = model;
        this.year = year;
    }

    // Methods (Functions)
    public void startEngine() {
        System.out.println("The engine is starting.");
    }

    public void stopEngine() {
        System.out.println("The engine is stopping.");
    }

    public String getColor() {
        return color;
    }
}
```

**Figure 2.1:** *Structure of a Class*

## Components of a Class

- **Fields**: Fields are variables declared inside a class but outside any method. They represent the state or properties of the class.
- **Methods**: Methods define the behavior of the class. They perform operations and can modify the state of the object.

## Understanding an Object

An **`object`** is an instance of a class. It represents a real-world entity and contains both state (fields) and behavior (methods). When a class is defined, no memory is allocated until an object of that class is created.

## Creating an Object

An object is created using the new keyword, followed by the class constructor:

**Instantiating a Class:**

```
Car myCar = new Car("Red", "Toyota", 2021);
```

- **`Car`** is the class name.
- **`myCar`** is the reference variable.
- **`new Car(...)`** is the constructor call that creates the object.

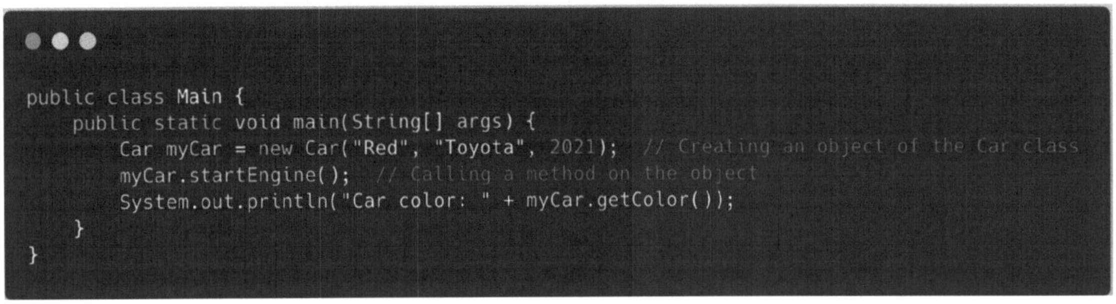


***Figure 2.2:*** *Creating an Object*

## Accessing Object Members

- Objects can access their fields and methods using the dot `.` operator:

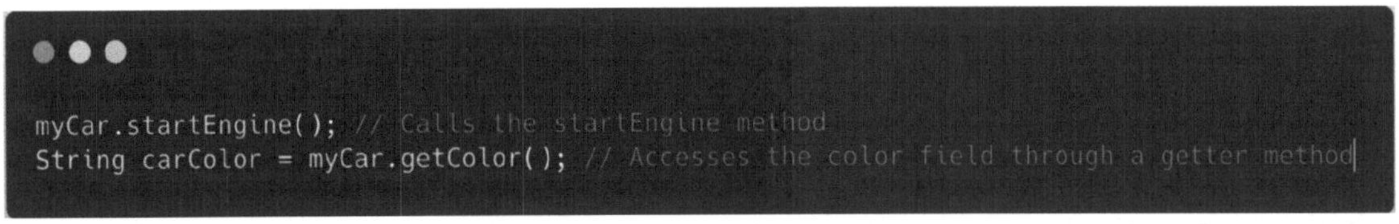


***Figure 2.3:*** *Accessing Object Members*

## Constructors in Java

A **constructor** is a special method that initializes an object when it is created. It has the same name as the class and does not have a return type. Constructors can be overloaded to create objects in different ways.

## Types of Constructors

- **Default Constructor**: Provided by Java if no constructor is defined. It initializes objects with default values.
- **Parameterized Constructor**: Takes parameters to initialize the fields of the class.

```java
// Default constructor
public class Car {
    public Car() {
        // Default constructor
    }
}

// Parameterized Constructor
public Car(String color, String model, int year) {
    this.color = color;
    this.model = model;
    this.year = year;
}
```

***Figure 2.4:*** *Types of Constructors*

## Methods in Classes

Methods define the behaviors of an object and provide a way to perform operations. They can take parameters, perform operations, and return results.

## Defining Methods

A method in Java consists of:

- **Access Modifier**: Determines the visibility (for example, `public`, `private`)
- **Return Type**: Specifies the type of value returned by the method (void if no return)
- **Method Name**: A descriptive name following naming conventions
- **Parameters**: Optional inputs enclosed in parentheses
- **Method Body**: Code enclosed in curly braces `{}`

## Calling Methods

Methods are called on an object using the dot `.` operator:

```
// method
public int add(int a, int b) {
    return a + b;  // Returns the sum of two integers
}

// calling methods
Car myCar = new Car("Red", "Toyota", 2021);
myCar.startEngine();  // Calls the startEngine method
```

***Figure 2.5:*** *Calling Methods*

# Access Modifiers and Encapsulation

Java provides four access modifiers that determine the visibility of classes, methods, and fields:

- **`public`**: Accessible from any other class
- **`private`**: Accessible only within the declared class
- **`protected`**: Accessible within the same package or subclasses
- **`default`** (no modifier): Accessible within the same package

Encapsulation is a core principle of OOP that involves bundling the data (fields) and methods that operate on the data into a single unit (class) and restricting access to the internals of that class.

```
public class BankAccount {
    private double balance;  // Private field

    public double getBalance() {  // Public getter method
        return balance;
    }

    public void deposit(double amount) {  // Public setter method
        if (amount > 0) {
            balance += amount;
        }
    }
}
```

***Figure 2.6:*** *Encapsulation*

# Static Members and Methods

In Java, the static keyword is used to define class-level fields and methods that are shared among all instances of a class. Static members belong to the class, not to any specific object.

- **Static Fields:** Static fields are shared among all instances of a class.
- **Static Methods:** Static methods are associated with the class rather than any object.

```
// static fields
public class Car {
    private static int numberOfCars = 0;  // Static field

    public Car() {
        numberOfCars++;  // Increment for each new object created
    }

    public static int getNumberOfCars() {  // Static method
        return numberOfCars;
    }
}


// static methods
public class MathUtils {
    public static int add(int a, int b) {
        return a + b;
    }
}

// Call without creating an object
int sum = MathUtils.add(5, 3);
```

***Figure 2.7:*** *Static Members and Methods*

## Object-Oriented Principles: Classes and Objects

Classes and objects embody the four principles of object-oriented programming:

- **Encapsulation**: Bundling data and methods together and restricting direct access to some of an object's components
- **Inheritance**: Creating new classes based on the existing ones, promoting code reuse
- **Polymorphism**: Allowing methods to do different things based on the object it is acting upon
- **Abstraction**: Hiding complex implementation details and showing only the necessary features

Understanding classes and objects is fundamental to Java programming and is the foundation for mastering object-oriented programming. By defining classes with well-structured fields and methods, leveraging constructors, encapsulating data with access modifiers, and utilizing static members, you can create robust, reusable, and maintainable Java applications. With this knowledge, you can explore more advanced topics in Java, such as inheritance, polymorphism, abstraction, and design patterns, which build on these core concepts and allow developers to create powerful and flexible software design.

# Constructors and Object Lifecycle

Constructors and the object lifecycle are fundamental concepts in Java that every developer must understand to create robust and maintainable applications. A **constructor** is a special method used to initialize objects when they are created. It plays a crucial role in setting up the initial state of an object. Understanding how constructors work, their types, and how they fit into the lifecycle of an object is essential for effective Java programming. This chapter delves into constructors, their types, their role in the object lifecycle, and best practices for designing constructors in Java.

# Understanding a Constructor

A **constructor in Java** is a block of code that is called when an instance of an object is created. Unlike regular methods, constructors do not have a return type, not even void, and they must have the same name as the class in which they reside.

## Characteristics of Constructors

- **No Return Type**: Constructors do not have a return type.
- **Same Name as Class**: A constructor's name must match the name of the class.
- **Automatically Called**: A constructor is automatically called when an object is instantiated using the new keyword.
- **Can Be Overloaded**: Multiple constructors can be defined with different parameter lists (constructor overloading).

## Purpose of Constructors

- **Initialize Objects**: Constructors are primarily used to set initial values for the object's fields.
- **Setup Resources**: They can be used to set up initial configurations, allocate resources, or perform any setup required when an object is created.

# Types of Constructors

Java provides several types of constructors that serve different purposes. Understanding these types helps in effectively initializing objects:

## Default Constructor

A **default constructor** is automatically provided by the Java compiler if no constructors are defined in a class. It initializes object fields to their default values (for example, 0 for integers, null for objects). If any constructor is explicitly defined, the default constructor is no longer provided by the compiler.

```
public class Car {
    private String model;
    private int year;

    // Default constructor automatically provided by Java
    public Car() {
        // Fields initialized to default values: model = null, year = 0
    }
}
```

**Figure 2.8:** *Default Constructor*

## No-Argument Constructor

A **no-argument constructor** is a constructor that does not take any parameters. It is often used to initialize fields with default or predetermined values.

```java
public class Car {
    private String model;
    private int year;

    // No-argument constructor
    public Car() {
        this.model = "Unknown";
        this.year = 2020;
    }
}
```

***Figure 2.9:*** *No-Argument Constructor*

## Parameterized Constructor

A **parameterized constructor** takes arguments that are used to initialize fields with specific values when an object is created. This allows for greater flexibility and control over object creation.

```java
public class Car {
    private String model;
    private int year;

    // Parameterized constructor
    public Car(String model, int year) {
        this.model = model;
        this.year = year;
    }
}

// usage
Car car1 = new Car("Toyota", 2022);  // model = "Toyota", year = 2022
```

***Figure 2.10:*** *Parameterized Constructor*

## Copy Constructor

A **copy constructor** creates a new object as a copy of an existing object. It is often used to duplicate objects while ensuring that mutable fields are properly handled.

```
public class Car {
    private String model;
    private int year;

    // Parameterized constructor
    public Car(String model, int year) {
        this.model = model;
        this.year = year;
    }

    // Copy constructor
    public Car(Car otherCar) {
        this.model = otherCar.model;
        this.year = otherCar.year;
    }
}

// usage
Car car1 = new Car("Honda", 2021);
Car car2 = new Car(car1);  // Copies the properties of car1 into car2
```

**Figure 2.11:** *Copy Constructor*

## Constructor Overloading

**Constructor overloading** allows a class to have more than one constructor with different parameter lists. This provides flexibility in object creation and enables different ways to initialize an object.

```
public class Car {
    private String model;
    private int year;

    // No-argument constructor
    public Car() {
        this("Unknown", 2020);  // Calls the parameterized constructor
    }

    // Parameterized constructor
    public Car(String model) {
        this(model, 2020);
    }

    // Overloaded constructor with two parameters
    public Car(String model, int year) {
        this.model = model;
        this.year = year;
    }
}

// usage
Car car1 = new Car();  // Uses no-argument constructor
Car car2 = new Car("Ford");  // Uses single-parameter constructor
Car car3 = new Car("BMW", 2023);  // Uses two-parameter constructor
```

**Figure 2.12:** *Constructor Overloading*

# The Object Lifecycle

The **object lifecycle** refers to the phases an object goes through during its existence in a Java application–from creation to destruction. Understanding this lifecycle helps developers manage resources, ensure proper initialization, and prevent memory leaks.

## Object Creation

Before an object in Java can be used, it must go through a well-defined lifecycle involving instantiation, initialization, and memory allocation. This process ensures that the object is fully prepared with all its required fields and behaviors. Here is a breakdown of the steps involved:

- **Instantiation**: When an object is created using the new keyword, memory is allocated for the object on the heap.
- **Constructor Call**: The appropriate constructor is called to initialize the object's fields.
- **Initialization Block**: Any instance initialization block (a block defined within a class but outside of a method) is executed.

```
Car car = new Car("Audi", 2021);  // Object creation and initialization
```

## Object Usage

Once an object is instantiated and properly initialized, it becomes an active participant in the Java program. At this stage, the object can be interacted through method calls and field access, and continues to exist in memory as long as it is reachable.

- Once created, an object can be used to call methods, access fields, and perform operations.
- Objects remain in memory as long as they are reachable from a live thread or are referenced by other objects.

## Object Destruction and Garbage Collection

- **Garbage Collection**: Java handles memory management through a process called garbage collection. When an object is no longer reachable, it becomes eligible for garbage collection, which means that the memory it occupies can be reclaimed.
- **Finalization (Deprecated in Java 9)**: The **`finalize()`** method was previously used to perform cleanup before an object is destroyed, but it has been deprecated due to unpredictability and performance issues.

## Best Practices for Object Destruction:

- Use try-with-resources for closing resources (for example: files, sockets).
- Avoid reliance on **`finalize()` (Deprecated in Java 9)** for cleanup; instead, use explicit cleanup methods.

# Best Practices for Using Constructors

To ensure clean and maintainable codes, consider the following best practices when designing constructors:

- **Minimize the Number of Parameters**: Too many parameters can make constructors hard to use and maintain. Consider using builders or factory methods.
- **Use `this()` for Constructor Chaining**: Avoid code duplication by using **`this()`** to call another constructor from within a constructor.

- **Avoid Business Logic in Constructors**: Constructors should focus on initializing fields. Complex logic should be placed in methods.
- **Ensure Proper Exception Handling**: If a constructor throws an exception, it can prevent an object from being fully constructed. Handle exceptions appropriately and document potential errors.
- **Use Immutable Objects When Possible**: For simpler and safer designs, prefer immutable objects where fields are final, and no setters are provided.
- **Consider Factory Methods or Builder Patterns**: For complex objects, use factory methods or the Builder pattern to improve readability and maintainability.

Constructors are essential for initializing objects in Java, and understanding their role in the object lifecycle is key to designing robust and reliable applications. By mastering different types of constructors, constructor overloading, and best practices, developers can create flexible, maintainable, and efficient Java programs. Proper management of object creation and destruction ensures that applications run smoothly, avoid memory leaks, and remain performant. With a solid grasp of these concepts, you will be equipped to handle more advanced object-oriented design principles in Java.

# Introduction to Methods and Parameter Passing

Methods are fundamental building blocks in Java programming, allowing developers to encapsulate code into reusable blocks that perform specific tasks. They enhance modularity, code organization, and reusability, making code easier to understand, maintain, and test. **Parameter passing** is how data is sent to methods to perform operations. This section covers the basics of defining and using methods, different types of methods, and the concepts of parameter passing in Java.

## Understanding Methods in Java

A **method** is a block of code within a class that performs a specific task. It typically has a name, a return type, and may accept parameters. Methods are used to define the behaviors of objects, perform operations, and return results.

## Anatomy of a Method

The general structure of a method in Java consists of:

- **Access Modifier**: Controls the visibility of the method (like `public`, `private`, and `protected`)
- **Return Type**: Specifies the type of value the method returns. If the method does not return a value, it is specified as void
- **Method Name**: A unique name following Java naming conventions (`camelCase`)
- **Parameter List**: A comma-separated list of input parameters enclosed in parentheses ()
- **Method Body**: A block of code enclosed in curly braces `{}` that defines what the method does

```
public int add(int a, int b) {
    return a + b;  // Adds two integers and returns the result
}
```

a. **Access Modifier: `public`** means this method can be accessed from other classes

b. **Return Type: `int`** specifies that this method returns an integer

c. **Method Name: `add`** is the name of the method

d. **Parameters: `int a`, `int b`** are the parameters

e. **Method Body:** The code block `{ return a + b; }` contains the logic to perform

## Defining and Calling Methods

Methods are defined inside a class and can be called using an object of that class. Here is an example of defining and calling a method:

```
public class Calculator {
    // Method to add two numbers
    public int add(int num1, int num2) {
        return num1 + num2;
    }

    public static void main(String[] args) {
        Calculator calc = new Calculator(); // Create an object of Calculator
        int result = calc.add(5, 3);  // Call the add method
        System.out.println("Sum: " + result);  // Output: Sum: 8
    }
}
```

***Figure 2.13:** Defining and Calling a Method*

## Types of Methods

Java supports various types of methods based on their behavior, visibility, and return types. These are mentioned as follows:

## Instance Methods

**Instance methods** are associated with an instance of a class (an object). They can access instance variables and other instance methods. Instance methods are defined without the **`static`** keyword.

```
public class Car {
    private String model;

    // Instance method
    public void setModel(String model) {
        this.model = model;
    }
}
```

***Figure 2.14:** Instance Method*

## Static Methods

**Static methods** belong to the class rather than any particular object instance. They are defined using the **`static`** keyword and can be called without creating an instance of the class.

```
public class MathUtils {
    // Static method
    public static int multiply(int a, int b) {
        return a * b;
    }
}

// Called without creating an object
int result = MathUtils.multiply(4, 5);
```

**Figure 2.15:** *Static Methods*

# Method Overloading

**Method overloading** allows a class to have more than one method with the same name but different parameter lists. It is a form of compile-time polymorphism.

```
public class Printer {
    public void print(String text) {
        System.out.println(text);
    }

    // Overloaded method with different parameter type
    public void print(int number) {
        System.out.println(number);
    }
}

// usage
Printer printer = new Printer();
printer.print("Hello");  // Calls the method with String parameter
printer.print(123);      // Calls the method with int parameter
```

**Figure 2.16:** *Method Overloading*

# Parameter Passing in Java

Java supports **parameter passing** to methods to provide input values. Java uses **`Pass by Value`**, meaning a copy of the actual parameter's value is passed to the method. This applies to both primitive data types and objects.

# Passing Primitive Data Types

When a **primitive data type** (for example: **`int`**, **`char`**, or **`double`**) is passed to a method, the method gets a copy of the value. Changes to the parameter inside the method do not affect the original argument.

```java
public class Example {
    public static void modifyValue(int num) {
        num = 10;  // This change is local to this method
    }

    public static void main(String[] args) {
        int value = 5;
        modifyValue(value);
        System.out.println("Value after method call: " + value);  //Output: 5
    }
}
```

**Figure 2.17:** *Passing Primitive Data Types*

# Passing Object References

When **object references** are passed to a method, a copy of the reference is passed, not the actual object. However, the method can modify the object's internal state because the reference points to the same memory location.

```java
public class Car {
    String model;

    public static void changeModel(Car car) {
        car.model = "Tesla";  // Modifies the original object
    }

    public static void main(String[] args) {
        Car myCar = new Car();
        myCar.model = "Toyota";
        changeModel(myCar);
        System.out.println("Car model after change: " + myCar.model);  // Output: Tesla
    }
}
```

**Figure 2.18:** *Passing Object References*

# Passing Arrays

Arrays in Java are passed by reference, meaning changes made to the array elements inside the method will affect the original array.

```java
public class ArrayExample {
    public static void modifyArray(int[] arr) {
        arr[0] = 99;  // Modifies the original array
    }

    public static void main(String[] args) {
        int[] numbers = {1, 2, 3};
        modifyArray(numbers);
        System.out.println("First element after modification: " + numbers[0]);  // Output: 99
    }
}
```

**Figure 2.19:** *Passing Arrays*

## Returning Values from Methods

A method can return a value using the return keyword. The return type must match the type specified in the method definition.

- **Returning a Primitive Type**
- **Returning an Object:** Methods can also return objects as shown in the following figure:

```
// returning primitive type
public int add(int a, int b) {
    return a + b;  // Returns the sum of two numbers
}

// returning object
public class CarFactory {
    public Car createCar() {
        return new Car("Toyota", 2021);  // Returns a new Car object
    }
}
```

***Figure 2.20:** Returning Values*

## Varargs (Variable-Length Arguments)

Java supports **varargs** (variable-length arguments), which allows methods to accept zero or more arguments of the same type. **Varargs** are useful when you do not know the number of arguments in advance.

```
public class Calculator {
    public int sum(int... numbers) {  // Varargs parameter
        int sum = 0;
        for (int num : numbers) {
            sum += num;
        }
        return sum;
    }
}

// usage
Calculator calc = new Calculator();
int result = calc.sum(1, 2, 3, 4, 5);  // Accepts multiple arguments
```

***Figure 2.21:** Varargs*

## Best Practices for Methods and Parameter Passing

- **Use Descriptive Method Names**: Method names should clearly describe the action performed, for example: **`calculateTotal()`**.

- **Keep Methods Small and Focused**: A method should perform a single task to enhance readability and maintainability.
- **Minimize the Number of Parameters**: Too many parameters can make methods difficult to understand. Consider using objects to group-related parameters.
- **Ensure Proper Error Handling**: Validate parameters and handle errors gracefully to make methods more robust.
- **Use `Varargs` Judiciously**: While **`varargs`** are flexible, they should not be overused, as they can lead to ambiguity and reduce type safety.
- **Avoid Side Effects**: Methods should avoid altering global states or modifying parameters unintentionally.

Understanding methods and parameters passing is crucial for writing modular and reusable Java code. Methods encapsulate behavior, allowing for clean and organized code, while parameter passing enables methods to operate on different data inputs. By mastering method overloading, returning values, and the nuances of parameter passing in Java, you can write more flexible and maintainable code, paving the way for advanced programming techniques and design patterns in Java development.

# Inheritance

**Inheritance** is one of the fundamental principles of OOP that allows one class to inherit fields and methods from another class. It promotes code reuse and establishes a relationship between classes, enabling developers to build hierarchical class structures. Inheritance is a powerful feature in Java that facilitates the creation of more modular, maintainable, and scalable code. This chapter will provide a comprehensive understanding of inheritance in Java, its types, how it is implemented, and best practices for using inheritance effectively.

# Understanding Inheritance

Inheritance allows a new class (subclass or child class) to inherit the properties and behaviors (fields and methods) of an existing class (superclass or parent class). This enables the subclass to reuse, extend, and modify the functionalities defined in the superclass.

## Basic Terminology

Before diving into inheritance in Java, it's important to understand some foundational terminology that defines the relationship between classes in an object-oriented hierarchy.

- **Superclass (Parent Class)**: The class whose properties and methods are inherited by another class; also known as the base or parent class.
- **Subclass (Child Class)**: The class that inherits from another class; also known as the derived or child class.

## Benefits of Inheritance

- **Code Reusability**: Reduces redundancy by reusing code already written in the superclass
- **Modularity**: Enhances code organization by creating a hierarchical relationship between classes
- **Maintainability**: Easier to maintain and extend code by modifying the superclass, which automatically affects all subclasses

- **Extensibility**: Subclasses can add new fields and methods or override the existing ones to provide specific behavior

# Implementing Inheritance in Java

Inheritance in Java is implemented using the extends keyword. A subclass inherits all non-private members (fields and methods) from the superclass.

# Basic Inheritance Example

- **Superclass**: **`Vehicle`**
- **Subclass**: **`Car`**
- **Inheritance Relationship**: Car inherits from Vehicle, gaining access to the **`brand`** field and **`start()`** method.

```
// Superclass
public class Vehicle {
    protected String brand = "Vehicle Brand";  // Protected access modifier allows subclass access

    public void start() {
        System.out.println("Vehicle is starting...");
    }
}

// Subclass
public class Car extends Vehicle {  // Car inherits from Vehicle
    private String model;

    public Car(String model) {
        this.model = model;
    }

    public void displayInfo() {
        System.out.println("Brand: " + brand);  // Accessing inherited field
        System.out.println("Model: " + model);
    }
}

public class Main {
    public static void main(String[] args) {
        Car myCar = new Car("Toyota");
        myCar.start();  // Inherited method from Vehicle
        myCar.displayInfo();
    }
}
```

***Figure 2.22:*** *Basic Inheritance Example*

# Access Modifiers and Inheritance

- **`private`**: Members declared as private in the superclass are not accessible to the subclass.
- **`protected`**: Members declared as protected are accessible to the subclass.
- **`public`**: Members declared as public are accessible to the subclass.
- **`default` (no modifier)**: Members with no modifier are accessible within the same package.

# Types of Inheritance in Java

Java supports different types of inheritance:

## Single Inheritance

Single inheritance occurs when a class inherits from one superclass.

```
public class Animal {
    public void eat() {
        System.out.println("Animal is eating...");
    }
}

public class Dog extends Animal {  // Single inheritance: Dog inherits from Animal
    public void bark() {
        System.out.println("Dog is barking...");
    }
}
```

**Figure 2.23:** *Single Inheritance*

## Multilevel Inheritance

Multilevel inheritance occurs when a class inherits from another class, which in turn inherits from another class.

```
public class Animal {
    public void eat() {
        System.out.println("Animal is eating...");
    }
}

public class Dog extends Animal {  // Dog inherits from Animal
    public void bark() {
        System.out.println("Dog is barking...");
    }
}

public class Labrador extends Dog {  // Labrador inherits from Dog, which inherits from Animal
    public void fetch() {
        System.out.println("Labrador is fetching...");
    }
}
```

**Figure 2.24:** *Multilevel Inheritance*

## Hierarchical Inheritance

Hierarchical inheritance occurs when multiple classes inherit from the same superclass.

```java
public class Animal {
    public void eat() {
        System.out.println("Animal is eating...");
    }
}

public class Dog extends Animal {  // Dog inherits from Animal
    public void bark() {
        System.out.println("Dog is barking...");
    }
}

public class Cat extends Animal {  // Cat also inherits from Animal
    public void meow() {
        System.out.println("Cat is meowing...");
    }
}
```

**Figure 2.25:** *Hierarchical Inheritance*

## Why Java Does Not Support Multiple Inheritance

Java does not support multiple inheritance (a class inheriting from more than one class) to avoid the **Diamond Problem**, which occurs when a class inherits from two classes having the same method, thus causing ambiguity. Instead, Java provides **interfaces** to achieve multiple inheritance of behavior, which will be discussed later.

# Method Overriding in Inheritance

**Method overriding** allows a subclass to provide a specific implementation for a method already defined in its superclass. It is a form of runtime polymorphism.

## Overriding a Method

To override a method, the subclass method must have the same name, return type, and parameter list as the superclass method.

```java
public class Animal {
    public void makeSound() {
        System.out.println("Animal makes a sound...");
    }
}

public class Dog extends Animal {
    @Override  // Annotation to indicate method overriding
    public void makeSound() {
        System.out.println("Dog barks...");
    }
}

// usage
Animal myDog = new Dog();
myDog.makeSound();  // Output: Dog barks...
```

**Figure 2.26:** *Overriding a Method*

## Using the super Keyword

The **super** keyword is used to refer to the superclass. It is commonly used to access **superclass** methods and constructors.

```
public class Animal {
    public void makeSound() {
        System.out.println("Animal makes a sound...");
    }
}

public class Dog extends Animal {
    @Override
    public void makeSound() {
        super.makeSound();  // Calls the superclass method
        System.out.println("Dog barks...");
    }
}
```

**Figure 2.27:** *Super Keyword*

## The Object Class

In Java, every class implicitly inherits from the **Object** class, which is the root of the class hierarchy. The **Object** class provides several useful methods that can be overridden:

- **toString()**: Returns a string representation of the object
- **equals(Object obj)**: Compares two objects for equality
- **hashCode()**: Returns a hash code value for the object

```
public class Car {
    private String model;
    private int year;

    public Car(String model, int year) {
        this.model = model;
        this.year = year;
    }

    @Override
    public String toString() {
        return "Car Model: " + model + ", Year: " + year;
    }
}
```

**Figure 2.28:** Object Class

## Best Practices for Using Inheritance

While inheritance can be a powerful feature in object-oriented programming, it must be used thoughtfully to avoid design pitfalls and ensure maintainable code. The following best practices help developers use inheritance effectively and responsibly in Java applications.

- **Favor Composition over Inheritance**: Use inheritance to model **`is-a`** relationships. If the relationship is not clear, consider using composition (having fields that reference other classes) instead.
- **Use @Override Annotation**: Always use the @Override annotation when overriding methods to avoid errors and improve code readability.
- **Avoid Deep Inheritance Hierarchies**: Deep hierarchies can be difficult to manage and understand. Keep the inheritance chain shallow to maintain simplicity.
- **Ensure Proper Use of Super**: Use super to call superclass methods when necessary, especially when extending methods in subclasses.
- **Keep `Superclasses` Closed for Modification**: **`Superclasses`** should be designed carefully to prevent changes that could break subclasses. Consider using the **Open/Closed Principle**–open for extension, but closed for modification.

Inheritance is a powerful feature in Java that enables code reuse, modularity, and scalability. By understanding how to implement inheritance, override methods, and use the super keyword, developers can build robust and maintainable Java applications. However, it is essential to use inheritance judiciously, while keeping design principles and best practices in mind in order to avoid pitfalls like tight coupling and the diamond problem. With a solid understanding of inheritance, you can effectively leverage OOP to design flexible and reusable code structures.

# Polymorphism

**Polymorphism** is one of the four fundamental principles of object-oriented programming (OOP) in Java, alongside inheritance, encapsulation, and abstraction. Polymorphism allows one interface to be used for a general class of actions, making it possible to write more flexible and reusable code. It enables a single method, operator, or object to take on many forms, allowing developers to build dynamic applications that can handle multiple data types and behaviors. This chapter explores the concept of polymorphism, its types, how it is implemented in Java, and best practices for using polymorphism effectively in Java applications.

# Understanding Polymorphism

Polymorphism in Java allows objects of different classes to be treated as objects of a common superclass. It provides a way to perform a single action in different forms, enhancing flexibility and maintainability in code.

## Key Concepts of Polymorphism

- **Polymorphism**: The ability of an object to take on many forms and allow methods to perform different tasks based on the object that is invoking it.
- **Compile-Time Polymorphism**: Also known as **method overloading**, where multiple methods have the same name but different parameters.
- **Run-Time Polymorphism**: Also known as **method overriding**, where a subclass provides a specific implementation of a method that is already defined in its superclass.

# Types of Polymorphism

Polymorphism in Java can be broadly classified into two types:

## Compile-Time Polymorphism (Method Overloading)

**Compile-time polymorphism**, or **method overloading** occurs when multiple methods with the same name are defined in the same class, but with different parameter lists (different type, number, or both). The method to be executed is determined at compile time.

- **Advantages**: Method overloading improves code readability and allows methods to perform similar operations with different types of inputs.

```
public class MathOperations {
    // Method to add two integers
    public int add(int a, int b) {
        return a + b;
    }

    // Overloaded method to add three integers
    public int add(int a, int b, int c) {
        return a + b + c;
    }

    // Overloaded method to add two double values
    public double add(double a, double b) {
        return a + b;
    }
}

// usage
public class Main {
    public static void main(String[] args) {
        MathOperations math = new MathOperations();
        System.out.println("Sum of two integers: " + math.add(2, 3)); // Calls the method with two
integer parameters
        System.out.println("Sum of three integers: " + math.add(2, 3, 4)); // Calls the method with
three integer parameters
        System.out.println("Sum of two doubles: " + math.add(2.5, 3.5)); // Calls the method with two
double parameters
    }
}
```

**Figure 2.29:** *Compile Time Polymorphism*

## Run-Time Polymorphism (Method Overriding)

**Run-time polymorphism**, or **method overriding**, occurs when a subclass provides a specific implementation of a method that is already defined in its superclass. The method to be executed is determined at runtime based on the object's type.

- **Advantages**: Method overriding allows for dynamic method dispatch, where the method to be invoked is determined at runtime. This makes the code more flexible and easier to extend.

```
public class Animal {
    // Superclass method
    public void makeSound() {
        System.out.println("Animal makes a sound");
    }
}

public class Dog extends Animal {
    // Overridden method
    @Override
    public void makeSound() {
        System.out.println("Dog barks");
    }
}

public class Cat extends Animal {
    // Overridden method
    @Override
    public void makeSound() {
        System.out.println("Cat meows");
    }
}


// usage
public class Main {
    public static void main(String[] args) {
        Animal myAnimal = new Dog();  // Polymorphic reference
        myAnimal.makeSound();  // Output: Dog barks

        myAnimal = new Cat();  // Reassign to a different subtype
        myAnimal.makeSound();  // Output: Cat meows
    }
}
```

***Figure 2.30**: Runtime Polymorphism*

## Using Interfaces for Polymorphism

Interfaces in Java provide a way to achieve polymorphism. By defining a set of abstract methods in an interface, classes that implement the interface can provide their own specific implementations. This allows objects to be treated uniformly based on the interface type.

- **Benefits of Using Interfaces**: Interfaces provide a way to decouple code, making it easier to maintain and extend. They also allow for multiple inheritance of type, enabling a class to implement multiple interfaces.

```
// Interface
public interface Shape {
    void draw();
}

// Implementing class 1
public class Circle implements Shape {
    @Override
    public void draw() {
        System.out.println("Drawing a Circle");
    }
}

// Implementing class 2
public class Rectangle implements Shape {
    @Override
    public void draw() {
        System.out.println("Drawing a Rectangle");
    }
}

// usage
public class Main {
    public static void main(String[] args) {
        Shape myShape = new Circle();  // Polymorphic reference to Circle
        myShape.draw();  // Output: Drawing a Circle

        myShape = new Rectangle();  // Polymorphic reference to Rectangle
        myShape.draw();  // Output: Drawing a Rectangle
    }
}
```

***Figure 2.31:*** *Interfaces*

## The `instanceof` Operator

The **`instanceof`** operator in Java is used to test whether an object is an instance of a specific class or implements a specific interface. This is often used in polymorphic code to determine the actual type of an object before performing certain operations.

```
public class Main {
    public static void main(String[] args) {
        Animal myAnimal = new Dog();

        if (myAnimal instanceof Dog) {
            System.out.println("This is a Dog.");
        } else if (myAnimal instanceof Cat) {
            System.out.println("This is a Cat.");
        } else {
            System.out.println("This is an Animal.");
        }
    }
}
```

***Figure 2.32:*** *instanceof Operator*

## Covariant Return Types

**Covariant return types** allow a method in a subclass to override a method in its superclass and return a more specific type. This enhances polymorphism by providing more flexibility in method overriding.

```
class Animal {
    public Animal getAnimal() {
        return new Animal();
    }
}

class Dog extends Animal {
    @Override
    public Dog getAnimal() {  // Covariant return type: returns a Dog instead
of Animal
        return new Dog();
    }
}
```

**Figure 2.33:** *Covariant Return Types*

## Polymorphism with Abstract Classes

**Abstract classes** provide a way to define a common interface for all subclasses while allowing each subclass to provide its specific implementation. Abstract classes are a powerful tool for achieving polymorphism.

```
public abstract class Vehicle {
    public abstract void start();  // Abstract method
}

public class Car extends Vehicle {
    @Override
    public void start() {
        System.out.println("Car is starting...");
    }
}

public class Bike extends Vehicle {
    @Override
    public void start() {
        System.out.println("Bike is starting...");
    }
}

// usage
public class Main {
    public static void main(String[] args) {
        Vehicle myVehicle = new Car();  // Polymorphic reference
        myVehicle.start();  // Output: Car is starting...

        myVehicle = new Bike();  // Polymorphic reference
        myVehicle.start();  // Output: Bike is starting...
    }
}
```

**Figure 2.34:** *Polymorphism with Abstract Class*

## Best Practices for Using Polymorphism

- **Use Interfaces to Define Common Behavior**: Define common behaviors using interfaces, allowing classes to implement their own specific methods.
- **Favor Composition over Inheritance**: Use inheritance to model "`is-a`" relationships, but prefer composition to avoid tight coupling.
- **Use the `@Override` Annotation**: Always use the **`@Override`** annotation when overriding methods to avoid errors and enhance readability.
- **Avoid Overloading Methods Unnecessarily**: Use method overloading judiciously to maintain readability and avoid confusion.
- **Use Polymorphism to Decouple Code**: Polymorphism helps decouple code by reducing dependencies on specific implementations, making it easier to extend and maintain.

Polymorphism is a powerful concept in Java that allows for flexible and dynamic code, making applications easier to extend and maintain. By understanding and effectively implementing compile-time and run-time polymorphism, leveraging interfaces and abstract classes, and following best practices, developers can build robust and scalable Java applications. Polymorphism enables objects to take on many forms, providing the foundation for flexible and reusable code that can adapt to future changes and requirements.

# Abstraction

**Abstraction** is a key concept in object-oriented programming that focuses on hiding the complex implementation details and showing only the essential features of an object. In Java, abstraction allows developers to define a blueprint for a class while leaving the details of its implementation to subclasses or other classes. This chapter delves into the concept of abstraction, how it is implemented in Java using abstract classes and interfaces, and best practices for leveraging abstraction to build flexible and maintainable Java applications.

# Understanding Abstraction

Abstraction is the process of simplifying complex systems by modeling classes appropriate to the problem and working at the most relevant level of inheritance for a specific aspect of the problem. It helps in reducing programming complexity by hiding irrelevant details from the user.

## Key Concepts of Abstraction

- **Abstraction**: Focusing on the essential characteristics of an object while ignoring its internal details.
- **Abstract Class**: A class that cannot be instantiated and is intended to be subclassed. It can contain both abstract methods (without implementation) and concrete methods (with implementation).
- **Interface**: A reference type in Java that is used to specify a contract that classes must follow. Interfaces only contain abstract methods (until Java 8) and constants.

# Implementing Abstraction in Java

Java provides two primary ways to achieve abstraction: **abstract classes** and **interfaces**.

# Abstract Classes

An **abstract class** is a class that cannot be instantiated on its own and must be subclassed. It can contain both abstract methods (methods without a body) and concrete methods (methods with a body).

## Defining an Abstract Class

An abstract class is defined using the `abstract` keyword. It can have fields, constructors, and methods like a regular class, but it can also have abstract methods that must be implemented by subclasses.

- **Concrete Method**: `displayBrand()` provides an implementation
- **Abstract Method**: `start()` does not provide an implementation and must be implemented by subclasses

```
// Abstract class
public abstract class Vehicle {
    private String brand;

    // Constructor
    public Vehicle(String brand) {
        this.brand = brand;
    }

    // Concrete method
    public void displayBrand() {
        System.out.println("Brand: " + brand);
    }

    // Abstract method
    public abstract void start();
}
```

**Figure 2.35:** *Definition of Abstract Class*

## Extending an Abstract Class

A subclass must extend the `abstract` class and provide implementations for all abstract methods.

- **Usage of super**: The subclass constructor calls the superclass constructor using `super()`.
- **Overriding Abstract Methods**: The `Car` class overrides the `start()` method.

```
// Subclass that extends an abstract class
public class Car extends Vehicle {
    public Car(String brand) {
        super(brand);  // Calls the constructor of the superclass
    }

    @Override
    public void start() {  // Implements the abstract method
        System.out.println("Car is starting...");
    }
}

public class Main {
    public static void main(String[] args) {
        Vehicle myCar = new Car("Toyota");
        myCar.displayBrand();  // Output: Brand: Toyota
        myCar.start();  // Output: Car is starting...
    }
}
```

***Figure 2.36:*** *Extending an Abstract Class*

# Interfaces

An **interface** in Java is a reference type that can contain only abstract methods (methods without a body) and constants (until Java 8). Interfaces provide a way to achieve **100% abstraction** because they do not contain any concrete methods (until Java 8).

# Defining an Interface

An interface is defined using the interface keyword. Methods in an interface are public and abstract by default.

```
// Interface definition
public interface Drivable {
    // Abstract method
    void drive();
}
```

# Implementing an Interface

A class implements an interface using the implements keyword. It must provide concrete implementations for all abstract methods defined in the interface.

- **Polymorphism with Interfaces**: The **`myBike`** object is treated as a Drivable type, showcasing polymorphism.

```java
// Class implementing the interface
public class Bike implements Drivable {
    @Override
    public void drive() {
        System.out.println("Bike is driving...");
    }
}

public class Main {
    public static void main(String[] args) {
        Drivable myBike = new Bike();
        myBike.drive();  // Output: Bike is driving...
    }
}
```

**Figure 2.37:** *Implementation of Interface*

# Multiple Interface Inheritance

Java allows a class to implement multiple interfaces, thereby supporting multiple inheritance of type.

```java
public interface Electric {
    void chargeBattery();
}

public class ElectricCar implements Drivable, Electric {
    @Override
    public void drive() {
        System.out.println("Electric car is driving...");
    }

    @Override
    public void chargeBattery() {
        System.out.println("Charging the battery...");
    }
}

public class Main {
    public static void main(String[] args) {
        ElectricCar myElectricCar = new ElectricCar();
        myElectricCar.drive();  // Output: Electric car is driving...
        myElectricCar.chargeBattery();  // Output: Charging the battery...
    }
}
```

**Figure 2.38:** *Multiple Interface Inheritance*

# Abstract Classes vs. Interfaces

Java provides both abstract classes and interfaces to achieve abstraction, and each has its own use cases. The following table mentions the differences between them:

**Differences between Abstract Classes and Interfaces**

| Feature | Abstract Class | Interface |
|---|---|---|
| **Methods** | Can have both abstract and concrete methods | Can have only abstract methods (until Java 8) |
| **Multiple Inheritance** | Does not support multiple inheritance | Supports multiple inheritance |
| **Fields** | Can have instance variables | Can only have public, static, final fields |
| **Constructors** | Can have constructors | Cannot have constructors |
| **Access Modifiers** | Can have any access modifier for methods and fields | Methods are public by default |
| **Use Case** | Use when there is a common base class | Use when classes share a common set of behaviors |

***Table 2.1:*** *Abstract Classes vs Interfaces*

# When to Use Abstract Classes vs. Interfaces

Choosing between abstract classes and interfaces is a fundamental design decision in object-oriented programming. Understanding the distinctions between them helps ensure that your code remains flexible, reusable, and aligned with best design principles.

- Use an `Abstract` class when:
  - There is a need for shared code among several closely related classes.
  - You want to provide a common base class that can contain fields and concrete methods.
- Use an Interface when:
  - There is a need to specify behavior without imposing a class hierarchy.
  - Multiple classes from different inheritance chains need to implement the same behavior.

# Best Practices for Using Abstraction

- **Use Abstraction to Simplify Complex Systems**: Hide unnecessary details from the user and expose only what is essential.
- **Leverage Interfaces for Loose Coupling**: Use interfaces to define contracts and decouple code, making it easier to extend and maintain.
- **Prefer Composition Over Inheritance**: Use interfaces to achieve composition and avoid deep inheritance hierarchies.
- **Keep Abstract Classes Simple**: Abstract classes should focus on shared functionality and provide a clear contract for subclasses.
- **Use Abstraction Judiciously**: Avoid over-abstraction, as it can lead to unnecessary complexity.

Abstraction is a powerful OOP concept that helps developers create flexible and maintainable Java applications by focusing on essential details and hiding the complexity of implementation. By using abstract classes and interfaces effectively, you can design systems that are easier to understand, modify, and extend. Understanding the differences between abstract classes and interfaces, and following best practices for abstraction, will enable you to write clean, modular, and scalable code that adheres to the principles of object-oriented design.

# Encapsulation

**Encapsulation** is a fundamental concept of OOP in Java that binds together data (fields) and the methods that operate on the data, restricting direct access to some of the object's components. It protects the internal state of an object and ensures that the object is used as intended. Encapsulation is often achieved by using access modifiers to restrict access to fields and methods and providing public getter and setter methods to access and update these fields. The following section explores the concept of encapsulation, how to implement it in Java, and best practices to effectively use encapsulation in your Java applications.

## Understanding Encapsulation

Encapsulation keeps the internal details of an object hidden from the outside world while exposing only necessary functionality through well-defined interfaces. This allows the internal implementation to change without affecting other parts of the program that use the object and provides a clear separation between an object's abstract interface and its concrete implementation.

## Key Concepts of Encapsulation

- **Data Hiding**: Protects the internal state of an object from unwanted modification and misuse
- **Controlled Access**: Provides controlled access to the fields of an object through methods (getters and setters)
- **Modularity and Maintainability**: Enhances modularity by keeping the internal workings of a class hidden from the outside world. This makes it easier to refactor and maintain code

## Implementing Encapsulation in Java

Encapsulation in Java is primarily achieved using **access modifiers** to control access to the fields and methods of a class. The main access modifiers in Java are private, protected, public, and the default (package-private).

## Using Access Modifiers

- **`private`**: The member is accessible only within the class it is declared in.
- **`protected`**: The member is accessible within its own package and by subclasses.
- **`public`**: The member is accessible from any other class.
- **`Default (package-private)`**: The member is accessible only within its own package.

**Example of Encapsulation Using private Fields**

In the following example, the **`BankAccount`** class uses private access modifiers to encapsulate the balance field and provides public methods to access and modify this field.

- **Data Hiding**: The balance field is private and cannot be accessed directly from outside the **`BankAccount`** class.
- **Controlled Access**: The **`getBalance()`**, **`deposit()`**, and **`withdraw()`** methods provide controlled access to the balance field.

```
public class BankAccount {
    private double balance;  // private field to restrict direct access

    // Constructor to initialize balance
    public BankAccount(double initialBalance) {
        if (initialBalance > 0) {
            this.balance = initialBalance;
        } else {
            this.balance = 0;
        }
    }

    // Getter method to access balance
    public double getBalance() {
        return balance;
    }

    // Setter method to update balance
    public void deposit(double amount) {
        if (amount > 0) {
            balance += amount;
        }
    }

    // Method to withdraw money from the account
    public boolean withdraw(double amount) {
        if (amount > 0 && balance >= amount) {
            balance -= amount;
            return true;
        } else {
            return false;
        }
    }
}

// usage
public class Main {
    public static void main(String[] args) {
        BankAccount account = new BankAccount(1000);
        account.deposit(500);  // Deposit amount
        System.out.println("Current balance: $" + account.getBalance());  //
Access balance through getter
        account.withdraw(300);  // Withdraw amount
        System.out.println("Balance after withdrawal: $" +
account.getBalance());
    }
}
```

**Figure 2.39:** *Encapsulation Example*

## Read-Only and Write-Only Classes

Encapsulation also allows the creation of **read-only** or **write-only** classes:

- **Read-Only Class**: Only getter methods are provided; the field cannot be modified after object creation.
- **Write-Only Class**: Only setter methods are provided; the field value can be set but not read.
- **Read-Only Nature**: Once the name is set through the constructor, it cannot be modified since there is no setter method.

## Benefits of Encapsulation

Encapsulation provides several benefits that enhance the robustness and maintainability of code:

- **Improved Security**: Sensitive data is hidden from outside access, reducing the risk of unintended changes and misuse.
- **Simplified Maintenance**: The internal implementation can be changed without affecting other parts of the code that depend on the class.
- **Enhanced Code Reusability**: Encapsulated code can be reused without revealing or altering its internal logic.
- **Loose Coupling**: By restricting direct access to fields, encapsulation helps in achieving loose coupling between classes, making code more modular and easier to manage.

## Encapsulation and Object-Oriented Design Principles

Encapsulation plays a vital role in object-oriented design principles such as **Single Responsibility Principle** (SRP) and **Information Hiding**.

- **Single Responsibility Principle (SRP)**: A class should have only one reason to change. Encapsulation helps in adhering to this principle by restricting the exposure of fields and maintaining focused and cohesive methods.
- **Information Hiding**: Encapsulation ensures that a class's internal representation is hidden from outside. This protects the integrity of the data and ensures that only valid states are allowed.

## Best Practices for Using Encapsulation

- **Use private Fields with public Getters and Setters**: Use private access for fields and provide public getters and setters for controlled access.
- **Validate Input in Setter Methods**: Ensure that setters validate input to maintain a valid state.
- **Avoid Exposing Internal Fields Directly**: Avoid using public fields as they expose internal implementation and reduce flexibility.
- **Use Encapsulation to Implement `Read-Only` and `Write-Only` Classes**: Depending on the requirements, create read-only or write-only classes to enforce access control.
- **Favor Composition Over Inheritance**: Use encapsulation to create modular components that can be reused and composed, rather than tightly coupling classes with inheritance.

Encapsulation is a powerful concept in Java that helps in hiding the internal state of objects and providing a controlled interface for accessing and modifying that state. By using access modifiers effectively and adhering to best practices, you can create robust, maintainable, and secure Java applications. Encapsulation enhances modularity, simplifies maintenance, and improves code readability, all of which are critical for developing scalable and flexible object-oriented systems.

# Advanced OOP Concepts

Advanced object-oriented programming (OOP) concepts build on the foundational principles of OOP–encapsulation, inheritance, polymorphism, and abstraction–to provide more sophisticated and powerful tools for designing robust and scalable applications. These advanced concepts, such as **composition**, **association**, **aggregation**, **composition**, **dependency injection**, and **design patterns**, offer greater flexibility and control in software development. This section explores these advanced OOP concepts in Java, their implementation, and best practices for leveraging them to create well-structured and maintainable code.

# Composition over Inheritance

**Composition** is a design principle that favors creating complex types by combining objects of other types, rather than inheriting from a base class. It promotes greater flexibility and avoids the pitfalls of deep inheritance hierarchies.

## Understanding Composition

Composition involves creating classes that are composed of one or more objects of other classes. This "`has-a`" relationship is different from inheritance's "`is-a`" relationship.

```
public class Engine {
    public void start() {
        System.out.println("Engine starting...");
    }
}

public class Car {
    private Engine engine;  // Composition: Car has an Engine

    public Car() {
        this.engine = new Engine();  // Engine is created when Car is created
    }

    public void drive() {
        engine.start();  // Delegation
        System.out.println("Car is driving...");
    }
}
```

***Figure* 2.40:** *Composition over Inheritance*

**Advantages of Composition:**

- Promotes code reuse without the drawbacks of inheritance
- Easier to change the behavior by changing the composed objects
- Reduces coupling between classes

# Association, Aggregation, and Composition

Association, aggregation, and composition are types of relationships between classes that determine how they interact and depend on each other.

- **Association** is a relationship where one object is connected to another and represents the "**uses-a**" relationship.

  **Example**: A Teacher and a Student have an association, as a teacher "**uses**" students in a classroom.

```java
public class Teacher {
    private String name;

    public Teacher(String name) {
        this.name = name;
    }

    public void teach() {
        System.out.println(name + " is teaching.");
    }
}
```

**Figure 2.41:** *Association*

- **Aggregation** is a special form of association where one class can have a collection of other classes. It represents a "**whole-part**" relationship but with independent lifecycles.

  **Example**: A Department and Teacher have an aggregation relationship because a department can exist without its teachers.

```java
public class Department {
    private List<Teacher> teachers; // Aggregation: Department has Teachers

    public Department() {
        teachers = new ArrayList<>();
    }

    public void addTeacher(Teacher teacher) {
        teachers.add(teacher);
    }
}
```

**Figure 2.42:** *Aggregation*

- **Composition** is a stronger form of aggregation where the contained object cannot exist without the container object. It is a "**whole-part**" relationship with dependent lifecycles.

  **Example**: A **House** and a **Room** have a composition relationship because a room cannot exist without a house.

```
public class Room {
    private String name;

    public Room(String name) {
        this.name = name;
    }
}

public class House {
    private List<Room> rooms;  // Composition: House contains Rooms

    public House() {
        rooms = new ArrayList<>();
        rooms.add(new Room("Living Room"));
        rooms.add(new Room("Bedroom"));
    }
}
```

***Figure 2.43:*** *Composition*

# Dependency Injection

**Dependency Injection (DI)** is a design pattern used to implement **Inversion of Control (IoC)**, allowing objects to receive their dependencies from an external source rather than creating them internally. This enhances modularity and testability.

**What is Dependency Injection?**

- **Dependency**: An object that another object needs to function.
- **Injection**: The process of providing dependencies from an external source, typically through constructors, setters, or interfaces.

```
public class Engine {
    public void start() {
        System.out.println("Engine starting...");
    }
}

public class Car {
    private Engine engine;

    // Constructor Injection
    public Car(Engine engine) {
        this.engine = engine;
    }

    public void drive() {
        engine.start();
        System.out.println("Car is driving...");
    }
}

// usage
public class Main {
    public static void main(String[] args) {
        Engine engine = new Engine();
        Car car = new Car(engine);  // Injecting dependency
        car.drive();
    }
}
```

***Figure 2.44:*** *Dependency Injection*

**Benefits of DI:**

- Improves code flexibility and reusability
- Makes code easier to test by allowing the use of mock objects
- Reduces coupling between classes

# Design Patterns in Java

**Design patterns** are proven solutions to common problems that arise during software development. They allow developers to create more flexible, reusable, and maintainable code.

## Common Design Patterns

**Singleton Pattern**: Ensures a class has only one instance and provides a global point of access.

```
public class Singleton {
    private static Singleton instance;

    private Singleton() {}  // Private constructor

    public static Singleton getInstance() {
        if (instance == null) {
            instance = new Singleton();
        }
        return instance;
    }
}
```

***Figure 2.45:*** *Singleton Pattern*

**Factory Pattern**: Provides a way to create objects without specifying the exact class of the object being created.

```
public interface Animal {
    void makeSound();
}

public class Dog implements Animal {
    @Override
    public void makeSound() {
        System.out.println("Bark");
    }
}

public class AnimalFactory {
    public static Animal createAnimal(String type) {
        if (type.equals("Dog")) {
            return new Dog();
        }
        return null;
    }
}
```

***Figure 2.46:*** *Factory Pattern*

**Observer Pattern**: Defines a one-to-many dependency between objects so that when one object changes state, all its dependents are notified and updated automatically.

```
public interface Observer {
    void update(String message);
}

public class ConcreteObserver implements Observer {
    @Override
    public void update(String message) {
        System.out.println("Received update: " + message);
    }
}
```

***Figure 2.47:*** *Observer Pattern*

# Best Practices for Advanced OOP Concepts

- **Prefer Interfaces over Abstract Classes**: Use interfaces to define contracts and abstract classes to provide shared code and structure.
- **Encapsulate What Varies**: Use composition and dependency injection to manage changing requirements and implementations.
- **Apply Design Patterns Where Appropriate**: Use design patterns to solve common problems in software design, but avoid over-engineering.
- **Keep Class Responsibilities Single**: Follow the Single Responsibility Principle (SRP) to keep classes focused on one task.
- **Promote Loose Coupling**: Use dependency injection and interfaces to reduce dependencies between classes and improve testability.

# Conclusion

This chapter covered the foundational principles of object-oriented programming (OOP) in Java, providing a deep dive into essential concepts such as understanding classes and objects, constructors and object lifecycle, methods and parameter passing, inheritance, polymorphism, abstraction, encapsulation, and advanced OOP concepts. By mastering these concepts, developers can design robust and reusable code structures that are easy to understand, extend, and maintain. These OOP principles form the backbone of Java programming, enabling the creation of scalable and modular applications that promote code reuse, flexibility, and adherence to best practices.

Classes and objects provide the blueprint for modeling real-world entities, while constructors and the object lifecycle define how these objects are initialized, used, and ultimately destroyed. Methods and parameter passing enhance code modularity and enable the reuse of logic through encapsulated behaviors. Inheritance and polymorphism introduce dynamic behavior and allow developers to reuse and extend existing code, thereby supporting flexible application design. Abstraction hides complexity by exposing only relevant features, while encapsulation ensures data integrity by restricting direct access to internal object states through controlled interfaces.

Advanced OOP concepts such as interfaces, abstract classes, and design patterns empower developers to architect sophisticated software systems. These tools help in the creation of highly cohesive and loosely coupled components, enhancing the maintainability and scalability of applications. With a solid grasp of OOP fundamentals, we are now ready to explore more advanced topics that deepen Java programming skills. In the next chapter, we will focus on generics to provide type safety and eliminate casting issues, lambda expressions and functional interfaces to introduce functional programming paradigms, the Java Collections Framework to efficiently manage data structures, and the Stream API for processing data in a concise and functional style.

# CHAPTER 3
# Advanced Java Features

## Introduction

As you move ahead in your Java programming journey, mastering the language's more sophisticated features becomes crucial for developing high-performance and scalable applications. This chapter delves into the powerful tools and techniques that allow you to write more efficient, flexible, and maintainable Java code.

We will begin with **Generics**, a feature that enables you to write type-safe code while maintaining flexibility. After that, we will explore **Lambda Expressions and Functional Interfaces**, which introduces a more functional style of programming in Java and makes your code more concise and expressive. Then, we will cover **Java Collections Framework**, which provides you with a comprehensive understanding of how to store, manipulate, and retrieve data efficiently.

Next, we will delve into the **Stream API**, a powerful tool for processing data in a functional manner, and **Concurrency and Multithreading**, which are essential for developing applications that can perform multiple tasks simultaneously. You will also learn about **Reflection and Annotations**, which offer deeper insights into Java's runtime behavior and enable the creation of more dynamic and flexible code.

The chapter continues with **Advanced I/O** techniques, expanding your ability to handle input and output operations beyond the basics. **Exception Handling** is also discussed in depth, equipping you with the knowledge to manage errors and exceptions effectively in your programs. Finally, we cover **Java Database Connectivity (JDBC)**, enabling you to integrate your Java applications with databases, a critical skill for developing data-driven applications.

By the end of this chapter, you will have a comprehensive understanding of Java's advanced features, which will allow you to confidently tackle complex programming challenges.

## Structure

This chapter will address the following topics:

- Generics
- Lambda Expressions and Functional Interfaces
- Java Collections Framework
- Stream API
- Concurrency and Multithreading
- Reflection and Annotations
- Advanced I/O
- Exception Handling
- Java Database Connectivity (JDBC)

# Generics

**Generics** is one of the most powerful features introduced in Java 5 that enables types (classes and interfaces) to be parameters when defining classes, interfaces, and methods. Using generics provides compile-time type safety and allows developers to catch and fix errors during the compilation process rather than at runtime. Generics can create reusable, type-safe code and eliminate the need for typecasting, making Java programs more robust and easier to maintain. This chapter explores the concept of generics in Java, their syntax and usage, and best practices to write cleaner and more reliable code using them.

# Understanding Generics

Generics enable types (classes, interfaces, methods) to be parameterized. Instead of working with Object types, generics provide a way to work with specific types while maintaining flexibility. This means that you can write a generic class or method that works with any data type, increasing code reusability.

## Benefits of Using Generics

- **Type Safety**: Generics provide stronger type checks at compile time, reducing the risk of `ClassCastException` at runtime.
- **Code Reusability**: A single generic class or method can be used with different types without needing multiple versions.
- **Elimination of Casts**: Generics eliminate the need for explicit type casting, making code cleaner and easier to read.
- **Improved Performance**: Generics avoid boxing and unboxing when dealing with collections, leading to better performance.

# Generic Classes

A **generic class** can operate on objects of various types while providing compile-time type safety. Generic classes are declared with a type parameter inside angle brackets **<>** after the class name.

## Defining a Generic Class

The following example demonstrates how to define a simple generic class:

- **Type Parameter <T>**: The T in the **Box<T>** class is a type parameter that will be replaced with an actual type when an instance of Box is created.

```
public class Box<T> {  // 'T' is a type parameter
    private T content;

    public void setContent(T content) {
        this.content = content;
    }

    public T getContent() {
        return content;
    }
}
```

***Figure 3.1:*** *Type Parameter*

## Using a Generic Class

**Type Safety**: When creating an instance of Box, the type parameter is specified, which ensures that only that type can be used in the Box instance.

```
public class Main {
    public static void main(String[] args) {
        Box<String> stringBox = new Box<>();  // Replace 'T' with 'String'
        stringBox.setContent("Hello, Generics!");
        System.out.println("String content: " + stringBox.getContent());

        Box<Integer> integerBox = new Box<>();  // Replace 'T' with 'Integer'
        integerBox.setContent(123);
        System.out.println("Integer content: " + integerBox.getContent());
    }
}
```

***Figure 3.2:*** *Generic Class*

# Generic Methods

**Generic methods** introduce their own type parameters. They can be static or instance, and the type parameter is declared before the return type.

## Defining a Generic Method

The following example demonstrates a generic method that accepts any type of array, and prints its elements:

- **Type Parameter `<T>`**: Declared before the return type void

```java
public class GenericMethodExample {
    // Generic method to print an array
    public static <T> void printArray(T[] array) {
        for (T element : array) {
            System.out.print(element + " ");
        }
        System.out.println();
    }
}
```

***Figure 3.3:*** *Generic Method*

## Using a Generic Method

**Type Inference**: Java can infer the type parameters automatically based on the method arguments, so explicit type specification is not necessary.

# Bounded Type Parameters

**Bounded type parameters** restrict the types that can be used as arguments for a type parameter. The most common bounded type parameter is `T` extends `SomeClass`, which restricts the parameter from being a subtype of `SomeClass`.

## Upper Bounded Wildcards

An **upper-bounded wildcard** allows the generic to accept any subtype of a specified type.

```java
public class BoxUtil {
    // Upper bounded wildcard method
    public static void printNumbers(Box<? extends Number> box) {
        System.out.println("Number: " + box.getContent());
    }
}

// Usage
public class Main {
    public static void main(String[] args) {
        Box<Integer> intBox = new Box<>();
        intBox.setContent(100);

        BoxUtil.printNumbers(intBox); // Works because Integer extends Number
    }
}
```

***Figure 3.4:*** *Upper Bounded Wildcard*

## Lower Bounded Wildcards

A **lower-bounded wildcard** allows the generic to accept any supertype of a specified type.

```
public class BoxUtil {
    // Lower bounded wildcard method
    public static void addNumbers(Box<? super Integer> box) {
        box.setContent(123);
    }
}
```

**Figure 3.5:** *Lower Bounded Wildcard*

# Generic Interfaces

A **generic interface** defines methods that can be used with different data types, enhancing code flexibility and reuse.

**Defining a Generic Interface**

```
public interface Pair<K, V> {  // Generic interface with two type parameters
    K getKey();
    V getValue();
}

public class OrderedPair<K, V> implements Pair<K, V> {
    private K key;
    private V value;

    public OrderedPair(K key, V value) {
        this.key = key;
        this.value = value;
    }

    @Override
    public K getKey() { return key; }

    @Override
    public V getValue() { return value; }
}

// usage
public class Main {
    public static void main(String[] args) {
        Pair<String, Integer> pair = new OrderedPair<>("One", 1);
        System.out.println("Key: " + pair.getKey() + ", Value: " +
pair.getValue());
    }
}
```

**Figure 3.6:** *Generic Interface*

# Generics and Type Erasure

Java implements generics using **type erasure**, which means that generic types are converted to Object at runtime, and type checks are applied only at compile time. This ensures compatibility with legacy code but also introduces some limitations.

## Type Erasure and Limitations

- **No Runtime Type Information**: At runtime, all generic information is erased, so `List<Integer>` and `List<String>` are both treated as List.
- **Cannot Create Generic Arrays**: Due to type erasure, creating an array of a generic type is not allowed.

  ```
  List<String>[] stringLists = new List<String>[10];  // Compile-time error
  ```

# Best Practices for Using Generics

- **Use Meaningful Type Parameter Names**: Use descriptive names like `T` for type, `K` for key, `V` for value, and so on
- **Prefer Generics Over Object References**: To ensure type safety and avoid `ClassCastException`
- **Avoid Raw Types**: Always specify a type parameter when using generics
- **Use Wildcards When You Do Not Need Full Flexibility**: Wildcards (`?`, `?` extends `T`, `?` super `T`) provide more flexibility in method parameters
- **Understand the Limitations of Type Erasure**: Be aware that generics are only for compile-time safety and that type information is erased at runtime itself

Generics in Java are a powerful way to write flexible, reusable, and type-safe code. By understanding how to define and use generic classes, methods, interfaces, and the concept of bounded type parameters, you can significantly improve the robustness and readability of your code. However, it is important to be mindful of the limitations due to type erasure and follow best practices to make the most out of generics. Moving forward, *Chapter 4, Understanding Spring Boot Basics* will explore other advanced Java features such as **Lambda Expressions**, **Functional Interfaces**, and the **Stream API**, which when combined with generics provide even more powerful tools for modern Java development.

# Lambda Expressions and Functional Interfaces

**Lambda expressions** and **functional interfaces** were introduced in Java 8, revolutionizing the way we write code by bringing functional programming capabilities to the language. Lambda expressions enable you to treat functionality as a method argument or to write concise and readable code that can be passed around as a parameter. **Functional interfaces** serve as the foundation for lambda expressions, providing a target type for them.

## Understanding Lambda Expressions

A **lambda expression** is a compact way of writing anonymous functions (methods without a name) that can be treated as instances of functional interfaces. They provide a clear and concise way to represent one-method interfaces using an expression.

## Benefits of Lambda Expressions

- **Concise Code**: Reduces the need for boilerplate code, such as anonymous inner classes
- **Improved Readability**: Code is easier to read and understand
- **Enables Functional Programming**: Allows users to write clean and functional-style code in Java
- **Enables Stream API**: Works seamlessly with the Stream API to enable declarative data processing

## Syntax of Lambda Expressions

The syntax of a lambda expression consists of three parts:

- **Parameter List**: Enclosed in parentheses `()`
- **Arrow Token**: The "`arrow`" token `->` separates the parameter list from the body
- **Body**: The code block (or expression) that defines the functionality

```
(parameters) -> expression

(parameters) -> { statements }
```

# Using Lambda Expressions

Lambda expressions are typically used to provide the implementation of functional interfaces, especially when working with collections, streams, and event handling.

## Examples of Lambda Expressions

**Example 1: Using a Lambda Expression to Implement a Functional Interface**

```
// Functional interface
@FunctionalInterface
interface MathOperation {
    int operate(int a, int b);
}

public class Main {
    public static void main(String[] args) {
        // Lambda expression to provide implementation for operate()
        MathOperation addition = (a, b) -> a + b;
        System.out.println("Addition: " + addition.operate(5, 3));  // Output: Addition: 8

        MathOperation multiplication = (a, b) -> a * b;
        System.out.println("Multiplication: " + multiplication.operate(5, 3));  // Output:
Multiplication: 15
    }
}
```

***Figure 3.7**: Lambda Expression*

**Explanation**: The lambda expression `(a, b) -> a + b` provides a concise implementation for the `operate()` method of `MathOperation`.

**Example 2: Lambda Expression with Collections**

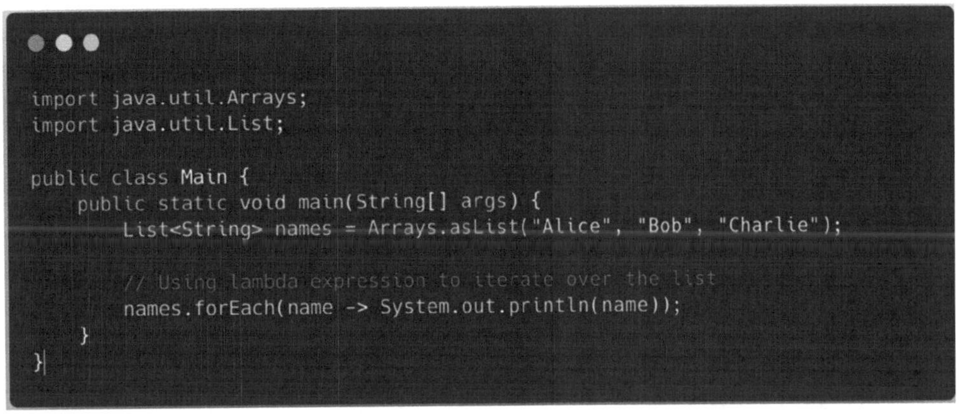


***Figure 3.8:*** *Lambda Expression with Collections*

**Explanation**: The lambda expression **`name -> System.out.println(name)`** is passed to the **`forEach`** method to print each element of the list.

## Types of Lambda Expressions

**No Parameter Lambda Expression**: `() -> System.out.println("Hello, World!")`

**Single Parameter Lambda Expression**: `(a) -> a * 2`

**Multiple Parameter Lambda Expression**: `(a, b) -> a + b`

**Lambda Expression with Multiple Statements**:

```
(int a, int b) -> {
    int result = a + b;
    System.out.println("Result: " + result);
    return result;
}
```

# Functional Interfaces

A **functional interface** contains only one abstract method. They are the foundation for lambda expressions, which provide implementations for these interfaces. Functional interfaces can have multiple default or static methods, but must have only one abstract method.

# Defining a Functional Interface

A functional interface is defined using the **`@FunctionalInterface`** annotation, which is not mandatory but is good practice to ensure the interface meets the criteria.

```
@FunctionalInterface
interface Calculator {
    int calculate(int a, int b);
}
```

# Common Functional Interfaces in `java.util.function`

Java provides several built-in functional interfaces in the **`java.util.function`** package:

- **`Predicate<T>`**: Represents a function that takes a single argument and returns a boolean.

  `Predicate<String> isLongerThanFive = s -> s.length() > 5;`

- **`Function<T, R>`**: Represents a function that takes one argument and produces a result.

```
Function<Integer, String> intToString = i -> "Number: " + i;
```

- **`Consumer<T>`**: Represents an operation that takes a single input argument and returns no result.

```
Consumer<String> printString = s -> System.out.println(s);
```

- **`Supplier<T>`**: Represents a function that supplies a result without taking any arguments.

```
Supplier<Double> randomValue = () -> Math.random();
```

- **`BinaryOperator<T>`**: Represents an operation upon two operands of the same type, producing a result of the same type.

```
BinaryOperator<Integer> add = (a, b) -> a + b;
```

# Method References

Method references are a shorthand notation of a lambda expression that calls an existing method. They provide a clean and readable way to refer to methods without executing them.

## Types of Method References

- **Reference to a Static Method**: **`ClassName::staticMethodName`**

```
Function<String, Integer> parseInt = Integer::parseInt;
```

- **Reference to an Instance Method of a Particular Object**: **`instance::instanceMethodName`**

```
Consumer<String> print = System.out::println;
```

- **Reference to an Instance Method of an Arbitrary Object of a Particular Type**: **`ClassName::instanceMethodName`**

```
Predicate<String> isEmpty = String::isEmpty;
```

- **Reference to a Constructor**: **`ClassName::new`**

```
Supplier<List<String>> listSupplier = ArrayList::new;
```

# Using Lambdas with the Stream API

Lambda expressions are heavily used with the Stream API to perform operations on collections in a functional style.

**Example: Using Lambdas with Streams**

```
import java.util.Arrays;
import java.util.List;
import java.util.stream.Collectors;

public class Main {
    public static void main(String[] args) {
        List<String> names = Arrays.asList("Alice", "Bob", "Charlie", "David");

        // Using lambda expressions with streams to filter and collect names
        List<String> filteredNames = names.stream()
                                          .filter(name -> name.length() > 3)
                                          .map(String::toUpperCase)
                                          .collect(Collectors.toList());

        System.out.println(filteredNames); // Output: [ALICE, CHARLIE, DAVID]
    }
}
```

***Figure 3.9:*** *Lambda with Streams*

# Best Practices for Using Lambda Expressions and Functional Interfaces

- **Prefer Method References When Possible**: Method references are more concise and readable.
- **Keep Lambda Expressions Short and Simple**: Avoid complex logic within lambda expressions; use methods instead.
- **Use Built-In Functional Interfaces**: Leverage Java's built-in functional interfaces from `java.util.function` before creating custom ones.
- **Use `@FunctionalInterface` Annotation**: This annotation ensures that the interface cannot have more than one abstract method.
- **Avoid Overusing Lambdas**: Lambdas should be used to simplify code, not to make it more complex or harder to debug.

Lambda expressions and functional interfaces bring powerful functional programming capabilities to Java, enabling developers to write more concise, expressive, and readable code. By leveraging these features, you can write cleaner and more maintainable Java programs, especially when working with collections and the Stream API. Understanding how to use lambda expressions, functional interfaces, and method references effectively is essential for modern Java development. In *Chapter 4*, we will explore the **Java Collections Framework** and how it works with generics and lambda expressions to manage groups of objects efficiently.

# Java Collections Framework

The **Java Collections Framework (JCF)** is a powerful and essential part of the Java Standard Library that provides a set of classes and interfaces for storing, manipulating, and managing groups of objects. Collections are one of the most commonly used data structures in Java programming and the framework provides a unified architecture for representing and manipulating collections, allowing developers to write high-performance, reusable, and easily maintainable code.

# Overview of the Java Collections Framework

The Java Collections Framework consists of several interfaces and classes that provide different types of data structures and utilities for manipulating data. It was introduced in Java 2 (JDK 1.2) and has since evolved to include powerful tools such as **Generics**, **Lambda Expressions**, and **Streams,** which work with collections in a more functional style.

## Key Benefits of the Collections Framework

- **Unified Architecture**: Provides a consistent API for all collections, including lists, sets, and maps
- **Type Safety with Generics**: Collections support generics, enabling compile-time type checking and reducing runtime errors
- **Rich Set of Algorithms**: Offers a set of standard algorithms like sorting, searching, and shuffling that can be used on different collections
- **Thread Safety and Concurrency**: Provides thread-safe collections and utilities to handle concurrent access in multithreaded environments
- **Performance Optimization**: Collections are optimized for performance, allowing developers to choose the right data structure for the task at hand

# Core Interfaces of the Collections Framework

The Java Collections Framework is built on several core interfaces, each defining a different type of collection.

## Collection<E> Interface

The **Collection<E>** interface is the root interface of the Java Collections Framework. It provides the common methods that all collections must implement, such as **add()**, **remove()**, **size()**, and **clear()**.

**Key Methods:**

- boolean add(E element)
- boolean remove(Object o)
- int size()
- void clear()
- boolean isEmpty()
- boolean contains(Object o)

```
import java.util.ArrayList;
import java.util.List;

public class Main {
    public static void main(String[] args) {
        List<String> fruits = new ArrayList<>();
        fruits.add("Apple");
        fruits.add("Banana");
        fruits.add("Orange");

        System.out.println(fruits.get(1));  // Output: Banana
    }
}
```

***Figure 3.10:*** *List Interface*

## Set<E> Interface

The **Set<E>** interface represents an unordered collection that does not allow duplicate elements. It is useful when you want to maintain a unique set of elements.

- **Common Implementations: HashSet, LinkedHashSet, TreeSet**
- **Key Methods:**
    - boolean **add(E element)**
    - boolean **remove(Object o)**
    - boolean **contains(Object o)**
    - **int size()**

```
import java.util.HashSet;
import java.util.Set;

public class Main {
    public static void main(String[] args) {
        Set<String> uniqueNames = new HashSet<>();
        uniqueNames.add("Alice");
        uniqueNames.add("Bob");
        uniqueNames.add("Alice");  // Duplicate, will not be added

        System.out.println(uniqueNames);  // Output: [Alice, Bob]
    }
}
```

***Figure 3.11:*** *Set Interface*

## Queue<E> Interface

The `Queue<E>` interface represents a **collection designed for holding elements prior to processing**. Queues typically order elements in a FIFO (First-In-First-Out) manner.

- **Common Implementations**: `LinkedList`, `PriorityQueue`
- **Key Methods**:
  - `boolean offer(E e)`
  - `E poll()`
  - `E peek()`

```
import java.util.LinkedList;
import java.util.Queue;

public class Main {
    public static void main(String[] args) {
        Queue<Integer> queue = new LinkedList<>();
        queue.offer(1);
        queue.offer(2);
        queue.offer(3);

        System.out.println(queue.poll());  // Output: 1
    }
}
```

***Figure 3.12:*** *Queue Interface*

## Map<K, V> Interface

The `Map<K, V>` interface represents a collection of key-value pairs. A Map cannot contain duplicate keys, and each key maps to at most one value.

- **Common Implementations:** `HashMap`, `LinkedHashMap`, `TreeMap`, and `Hashtable`
- **Key Methods:**
  - `V put(K key, V value)`
  - `V get(Object key)`
  - `V remove(Object key)`
  - `boolean containsKey(Object key)`
  - `Set<K> keySet()`

```
import java.util.HashMap;
import java.util.Map;

public class Main {
    public static void main(String[] args) {
        Map<String, Integer> ageMap = new HashMap<>();
        ageMap.put("Alice", 25);
        ageMap.put("Bob", 30);

        System.out.println(ageMap.get("Alice"));  // Output: 25
    }
}
```

***Figure 3.13:*** *Map Interface*

# Common Implementations of Core Interfaces

Java provides several standard implementations of the core collection interfaces, where each is optimized for different scenarios. These are mentioned as follows:

## `ArrayList<E>` vs. `LinkedList<E>`

- `ArrayList<E>`: Provides fast random access to elements `(O(1))`, but slow insertions and deletions (O(n)) as it requires shifting elements
- `LinkedList<E>`: Provides fast insertions and deletions `(O(1))`, but slow random access `(O(n))` as it requires traversing the list

## `HashSet<E>` vs. `TreeSet<E>`

- `HashSet<E>`: Provides constant-time performance `(O(1))` for basic operations (`add`, `remove`, `contains`), but does not guarantee any order
- `TreeSet<E>`: Implements `NavigableSet` and provides guaranteed `log(n)` time cost for the basic operations and maintains sorted order

## `HashMap<K, V>` vs. `TreeMap<K, V>`

- `HashMap<K, V>`: Provides constant-time performance (`O(1)`) for basic operations (`get` and `put`), but does not guarantee any order
- `TreeMap<K, V>`: Implements `NavigableMap` and provides `log(n)` time cost for the basic operations and maintains sorted order based on keys

# Using Generics with Collections

The Java Collections Framework heavily relies on **Generics** to provide type safety and eliminate the need for type casting.

- **Type Safety**: The **`List<String>`** ensures that only String objects can be added, providing compile-time type safety.

```
import java.util.ArrayList;
import java.util.List;

public class Main {
    public static void main(String[] args) {
        List<String> strings = new ArrayList<>(); // Type-safe, only allows Strings
        strings.add("Java");
        strings.add("Collections");

        for (String s : strings) {
            System.out.println(s.toUpperCase());
        }
    }
}
```

***Figure 3.14:*** *Type Safety*

# Concurrent Collections

Java provides the following concurrent collections that are thread-safe and optimized for multithreaded environments and are part of the **`java.util.concurrent`** package:

- **`ConcurrentHashMap<K, V>`**: A thread-safe version of HashMap that allows concurrent read and write operations.
- **`CopyOnWriteArrayList<E>`**: A thread-safe version of **`ArrayList`** that creates a new copy of the array whenever it is modified.
- **`BlockingQueue<E>`**: An interface that represents a thread-safe queue supporting operations and wait for the queue to become non-empty or non-full.

# Best Practices for Using Collections

- **Choose the Right Collection for the Task:** Use List for ordered collections, Set for unique elements, Map for key-value pairs, and Queue for FIFO processing
- **Prefer `ArrayList` over `LinkedList` for Most Use Cases:** **`ArrayList`** provides better performance for most read-heavy use cases
- **Use Generics to Ensure Type Safety:** Always specify the type parameter when using collections to avoid **`ClassCastException`**
- **Avoid Using Raw Types:** Raw types can lead to runtime errors and lack type safety
- **Use Concurrent Collections in Multithreaded Environments:** Avoid manual synchronization and use collections from **`java.util.concurrent`** for better performance

- **Prefer `Collections.unmodifiableList()` for Read-Only Lists:** Use unmodifiable views to prevent modification of collections when they are not required

The **Java Collections Framework** is a core component of Java's utility library as it provides a standardized architecture for managing and manipulating groups of objects. It offers a wide range of interfaces and classes, such as **List**, **Set**, **Queue**, and **Map**, where each has various implementations optimized for different use cases. Through collections, developers can write more flexible, efficient, and type-safe code that is easier to maintain and extend. Understanding the differences between collection types, such as **`ArrayList`** vs. **`LinkedList`**, **`HashSet`** vs. **`TreeSet`**, and **`HashMap`** vs. **`TreeMap`**, is essential for selecting the right data structure to optimize performance for specific operations. Additionally, leveraging **Generics** with collections ensures compile-time type safety, reducing runtime errors and improving code reliability. As Java applications often operate in multithreaded environments, knowing when to use **concurrent collections** like **`ConcurrentHashMap`** and **`CopyOnWriteArrayList`** is crucial for thread safety and performance. By following best practices for using collections, such as choosing the right collection type and avoiding raw types, developers can create robust, efficient, and scalable Java applications.

# Stream API

The **Stream API** was introduced in Java 8 as a powerful and flexible way to process collections of data in a functional style. The Stream API allows developers to perform complex data operations like filtering, mapping, reducing, and collecting in a concise and readable manner. Streams represent a sequence of elements that can be processed in parallel or sequentially, enabling highly efficient data processing pipelines.

# Understanding the Stream API

A **Stream** is a sequence of elements that supports various operations to perform computations on those elements. Unlike collections, streams do not store data but are used to convey data from a source (like a collection) through a pipeline of operations. Streams are designed to work with **lambda expressions** and **functional interfaces**, enabling a more declarative style of programming.

## Key Characteristics of Streams

- **Lazy Evaluation**: Streams are evaluated lazily, meaning that operations are performed only when necessary, which improves performance.
- **Functional Style**: Streams enable a declarative approach to data processing.
- **Pipeline of Operations**: Streams allow chaining of multiple operations (filter, map, reduce) to build a pipeline.
- **Non-Interference**: Streams do not modify the underlying data source.
- **Parallel Processing**: Streams support parallel execution, making it easier to leverage multi-core processors.

# Creating Streams

Streams can be created from various sources, such as collections, arrays, or I/O channels. The most common way to create a stream is to do so from a collection using the **`stream()`** method.

### Creating Streams from Collections

```
import java.util.Arrays;
import java.util.List;
import java.util.stream.Stream;

public class Main {
    public static void main(String[] args) {
        List<String> names = Arrays.asList("Alice", "Bob", "Charlie");

        // Creating a stream from a collection
        Stream<String> nameStream = names.stream();

        // Creating a parallel stream from a collection
        Stream<String> parallelStream = names.parallelStream();
    }
}
```

***Figure 3.15:*** *Streams with Collections*

### Creating Streams from Arrays

```
import java.util.stream.Stream;

public class Main {
    public static void main(String[] args) {
        String[] fruits = {"Apple", "Banana", "Orange"};

        // Creating a stream from an array
        Stream<String> fruitStream = Stream.of(fruits);
    }
}
```

***Figure 3.16:*** *Creating Streams from Arrays*

### Creating Streams Using `Stream.generate()` and `Stream.iterate()`

```
import java.util.stream.Stream;

public class Main {
    public static void main(String[] args) {
        // Creating an infinite stream using Stream.generate()
        Stream<Double> randomNumbers =
Stream.generate(Math::random).limit(5);

        // Creating an infinite stream using Stream.iterate()
        Stream<Integer> evenNumbers = Stream.iterate(0, n -> n + 2).limit(5);

        randomNumbers.forEach(System.out::println);
        evenNumbers.forEach(System.out::println);
    }
}
```

***Figure 3.17:*** *Using Generate and Iterate*

# Stream Operations

Streams support two types of operations: **intermediate** and **terminal**. Intermediate operations are lazy and return a new stream, while terminal operations produce a result or a side-effect and terminate the stream pipeline.

## Intermediate Operations

Intermediate operations transform a stream into another stream. They are lazy and only executed when a terminal operation is called.

- **`filter(Predicate<T>)`**: Returns a stream consisting of elements that match a given predicate

  ```
  List<String> names = Arrays.asList("Alice", "Bob", "Charlie");
  names.stream().filter(name -> name.startsWith("A")).forEach(System.out::println);
  // Output: Alice
  ```

- **`map(Function<T, R>)`**: Returns a stream consisting of the results of applying a given function to each element

  ```
  List<String> names = Arrays.asList("Alice", "Bob", "Charlie");
  names.stream().map(String::toUpperCase).forEach(System.out::println);
  // Output: ALICE, BOB, CHARLIE
  ```

- **`sorted()`**: Returns a stream with elements sorted according to natural order or a provided comparator

  ```
  List<String> names = Arrays.asList("Alice", "Bob", "Charlie");
  names.stream().sorted().forEach(System.out::println);
  // Output: Alice, Bob, Charlie
  ```

  **`distinct()`**: Returns a stream with distinct elements based on **`equals()`**.

  ```
  List<String> names = Arrays.asList("Alice", "Bob", "Alice");
  names.stream().distinct().forEach(System.out::println);
  // Output: Alice, Bob
  ```

# Terminal Operations

Terminal operations produce a result or side-effect and terminate the stream.

- **`collect(Collector<T, A, R>)`**: Collects the elements into a collection such as a **`List`**, **`Set`**, or **`Map`**
- **`forEach(Consumer<T>)`**: Performs an action for each element of the stream
- **`reduce(BinaryOperator<T>)`**: Performs a reduction on the elements of the stream using an associative accumulation function and returns an Optional

```
// collect
List<String> names = Arrays.asList("Alice", "Bob", "Charlie");
List<String> upperNames =
names.stream().map(String::toUpperCase).collect(Collectors.toList());
System.out.println(upperNames); // Output: [ALICE, BOB, CHARLIE]

// forEach
List<String> names = Arrays.asList("Alice", "Bob", "Charlie");
names.stream().forEach(System.out::println);

// reduce
List<Integer> numbers = Arrays.asList(1, 2, 3, 4, 5);
int sum = numbers.stream().reduce(0, Integer::sum);
System.out.println("Sum: " + sum); // Output: Sum: 15

// findFirst
List<String> names = Arrays.asList("Alice", "Bob", "Charlie");
String firstName = names.stream().findFirst().orElse("No names found");
System.out.println(firstName); // Output: Alice

// count
List<String> names = Arrays.asList("Alice", "Bob", "Charlie");
long count = names.stream().filter(name -> name.length() > 3).count();
System.out.println("Count: " + count); // Output: Count: 2
```

***Figure 3.18:** Terminal Operations*

- **`findFirst()`**: Returns the first element in the stream wrapped in an Optional
- **`count()`**: Returns the number of elements in the stream

# Working with Collectors

**Collectors** is a utility class that provides various built-in collectors to collect stream elements into different collections, or to summarize and group them.

## Common Collectors

- **`toList()`**: Collects elements into a List
- **`toSet()`**: Collects elements into a Set
- **`joining()`**: Concatenates the elements into a single String
- **`groupingBy(Function<T, K>)`**: Groups elements by a classifier function

```
// toList
List<String> names = Stream.of("Alice", "Bob", "Charlie").collect(Collectors.toList());

// toSet
Set<String> uniqueNames = Stream.of("Alice", "Bob", "Alice").collect(Collectors.toSet());

// joining
String joinedNames = Stream.of("Alice", "Bob", "Charlie").collect(Collectors.joining(", "));
System.out.println(joinedNames); // Output: Alice, Bob, Charlie

// groupingBy
Map<Integer, List<String>> namesByLength = Stream.of("Alice", "Bob", "Charlie")
    .collect(Collectors.groupingBy(String::length));
System.out.println(namesByLength);
// Output: {3=[Bob], 5=[Alice], 7=[Charlie]}
```

***Figure 3.19:** Common Collectors*

# Parallel Streams

**Parallel streams** allow parallel processing of data while taking advantage of multi-core processors. Using **`parallelStream()`**, the Stream API can perform operations in parallel to improve performance for large datasets.

**When to Use Parallel Streams**: It is ideal for CPU-intensive operations where the data size is large and the operations are independent.

```
import java.util.Arrays;
import java.util.List;

public class Main {
    public static void main(String[] args) {
        List<Integer> numbers = Arrays.asList(1, 2, 3, 4, 5);

        // Using parallel stream to calculate sum
        int sum = numbers.parallelStream().reduce(0, Integer::sum);
        System.out.println("Sum: " + sum);  // Output: Sum: 15
    }
}
```

***Figure 3.20:*** *Parallel Streams*

# Best Practices for Using Streams

- **Use Streams for Declarative Data Processing**: Use streams to write clean, concise, and readable code for data processing tasks.
- **Prefer `forEach` for Side-Effects**: Use **`forEach`** for side effects, but avoid modifying the underlying collection.
- **Choose the Right Terminal Operations**: Understand the difference between terminal operations (**`collect()`**, **`reduce()`**, **`findFirst()`**) and use them appropriately.
- **Avoid Parallel Streams for Small Data Sets**: Parallel streams add overhead, so use them only when working with large datasets.
- **Understand Lazy Evaluation**: Take advantage of lazy evaluation to improve performance by combining multiple operations efficiently.
- **Use Collectors for Aggregation and Grouping**: Use Collectors to efficiently aggregate and group data.

The **Stream API** in Java provides a powerful and flexible way to process collections and other data sources in a functional style. By leveraging **lambda expressions**, **method references**, and **collectors**, streams allow developers to write more concise, readable, and maintainable code. With its ability to perform parallel processing, the Stream API also offers significant performance advantages for large-scale data processing. Understanding how to effectively use streams, their operations, and the Collectors utility can greatly enhance your ability to manipulate and process data in Java. In the next chapter, we will explore **Concurrency and Multithreading** in Java, building on the foundation laid by streams to create efficient, parallel, and concurrent applications.

# Concurrency and Multithreading

**Concurrency** and **multithreading** are essential concepts in modern software development that enable applications to perform multiple tasks simultaneously, thereby improving efficiency and responsiveness. In Java, concurrency refers to the ability of a program to execute several tasks in overlapping time periods, while **multithreading** allows for concurrent execution of two or more threads within a process. Java provides a rich set of tools and libraries to support concurrency, including threads, synchronization, locks, and the high-level `java.util.concurrent` package. This chapter explores the fundamental concepts of concurrency and multithreading in Java, how to create and manage threads, synchronization mechanisms, and best practices for writing efficient and thread-safe code.

# Understanding Concurrency and Multithreading

Concurrency in programming allows multiple tasks to be executed in overlapping periods, while **multithreading** is a specific form of concurrency that involves multiple threads executing within a single process. Threads are lightweight sub-processes that share the same memory space, allowing for efficient communication but requiring careful management to avoid errors.

## Benefits of Concurrency and Multithreading

- **Improved Performance**: Enables parallel execution of tasks, leveraging multi-core processors
- **Better Resource Utilization**: Allows multiple tasks to make better use of system resources
- **Enhanced Responsiveness**: Keeps applications responsive by performing long-running tasks in the background
- **Simplified Modeling**: Helps in modeling real-world scenarios where multiple tasks occur simultaneously

# Creating and Managing Threads in Java

In Java, a **thread** is an independent path of execution within a program. There are two main ways to create a thread: by extending the `Thread` class and by implementing the Runnable interface.

## Extending the `Thread` Class

The simplest way to create a thread is to extend the Thread class and override its `run()` method.

```
public class MyThread extends Thread {
    @Override
    public void run() {
        System.out.println("Thread is running...");
    }

    public static void main(String[] args) {
        MyThread thread = new MyThread();
        thread.start();  // Starts the thread, calling run() method
    }
}
```

***Figure 3.21:*** *Extending the Thread Class*

## Implementing the `Runnable` Interface

A more flexible way to create a thread is to implement the **`Runnable`** interface, which separates the task from the thread itself.

**Benefits of Implementing `Runnable`**: Allows the same task to be executed by multiple threads and promotes better object-oriented design.

```java
public class MyRunnable implements Runnable {
    @Override
    public void run() {
        System.out.println("Runnable is running...");
    }

    public static void main(String[] args) {
        Thread thread = new Thread(new MyRunnable());
        thread.start();  // Starts the thread, calling run() method
    }
}
```

***Figure 3.22:*** *Implementation of Runnable Interface*

## Using Lambda Expressions for `Runnable`

From Java 8 onwards, you can use lambda expressions to create threads in a more concise manner.

```java
public class Main {
    public static void main(String[] args) {
        Thread thread = new Thread(() -> System.out.println("Lambda Runnable
is running..."));
        thread.start();
    }
}
```

***Figure 3.23:*** *Using Lambda Expressions for Runnable*

# Thread States and Lifecycle

A thread in Java can be in one of several states throughout its lifecycle. Understanding these states is crucial for managing thread execution effectively.

## Thread States

- **`New`**: The thread is created but not yet started (**`new Thread()`**).
- **`Runnable`**: The thread is ready to run and is waiting for CPU time (**`start()`** is called).
- **`Blocked`**: The thread is blocked and waiting for a monitor lock.

- **`Waiting`**: The thread is waiting indefinitely for another thread to perform a specific action (**`wait()`** or **`join()`**).
- **Timed Waiting**: The thread is waiting for a specified period (**`sleep()`** or **`join(long)`**).
- **`Terminated`**: The thread has completed its execution (**`run()`** method has finished).

## Controlling Thread Execution

- **`sleep(long millis)`**: Pauses the current thread for a specified period
- **`join()`**: Waits for another thread to complete
- **`yield()`**: Suggests the scheduler to temporarily pause the execution of the current thread

# Synchronization and Thread Safety

In multithreaded applications, **synchronization** is essential to ensure that multiple threads do not interfere with each other when accessing shared resources. Lack of synchronization can lead to **race conditions**, **deadlocks**, and **inconsistent data states**.

## Synchronized Methods and Blocks

- **Synchronized Methods**: Ensure that only one thread can execute a method at a time
- **Synchronized Blocks**: Provide more granular control over synchronization by locking only specific sections of code

```
// synchronized method
public class Counter {
    private int count = 0;

    public synchronized void increment() {
        count++;
    }

    public synchronized int getCount() {
        return count;
    }
}

// synchronized block
public class Counter {
    private int count = 0;

    public void increment() {
        synchronized (this) {
            count++;
        }
    }
}
```

***Figure 3.24:*** *Synchronized Methods and Blocks*

## The `volatile` Keyword

The **`volatile`** keyword is used to indicate that a variable's value will be modified by different threads, thus ensuring visibility of changes across threads.

```
public class SharedData {
    private volatile boolean flag = true;

    public void updateFlag() {
        flag = false;
    }
}
```

***Figure 3.25:*** *Volatile Keyword*

# High-Level Concurrency Utilities

Java provides a high-level concurrency API in the **`java.util.concurrent`** package that simplifies thread management and synchronization.

## Executors Framework

The **Executors Framework** provides a higher-level replacement for working directly with threads by offering a pool of threads and a mechanism to manage them.

**`ExecutorService`**: An interface that represents a pool of threads to execute submitted tasks.

```
import java.util.concurrent.ExecutorService;
import java.util.concurrent.Executors;

public class Main {
    public static void main(String[] args) {
        ExecutorService executor = Executors.newFixedThreadPool(2);

        executor.submit(() -> System.out.println("Task 1"));
        executor.submit(() -> System.out.println("Task 2"));

        executor.shutdown();
    }
}
```

***Figure 3.26:*** *Executor Service*

## `Future` and `Callable`

- **`Callable<V>`**: A task that returns a result and may throw an exception.
- **`Future<V>`**: Represents the result of an asynchronous computation and allows for checking the status or retrieving the result once it is complete.

```
import java.util.concurrent.Callable;
import java.util.concurrent.ExecutorService;
import java.util.concurrent.Executors;
import java.util.concurrent.Future;

public class Main {
    public static void main(String[] args) throws Exception {
        ExecutorService executor = Executors.newSingleThreadExecutor();
        Callable<Integer> task = () -> 10 + 20;
        Future<Integer> future = executor.submit(task);

        System.out.println("Result: " + future.get()); // Output: Result: 30
        executor.shutdown();
    }
}
```

**Figure 3.27:** Future and Callable

## Locks and `ReentrantLock`

The **`ReentrantLock`** class provides more control over synchronization than the **`synchronized`** keyword, allowing for more complex locking mechanisms.

```
import java.util.concurrent.locks.Lock;
import java.util.concurrent.locks.ReentrantLock;

public class Counter {
    private int count = 0;
    private final Lock lock = new ReentrantLock();

    public void increment() {
        lock.lock();
        try {
            count++;
        } finally {
            lock.unlock();
        }
    }

    public int getCount() {
        return count;
    }
}
```

**Figure 3.28:** Locks

## Synchronizers: `CountDownLatch` and `CyclicBarrier`

- **`CountDownLatch`**: Allows one or more threads to wait until a set of operations being performed in other threads completes

- `CyclicBarrier`: Allows a set of threads to wait for each other to reach a common barrier point

# Best Practices for Multithreading and Concurrency

- **Minimize Use of synchronized**: Use higher-level concurrency utilities like `ReentrantLock` and Executors for better control and scalability.
- **Prefer volatile for Simple Flags**: Use volatile for variables that are shared across threads but do not require full synchronization.
- **Use `ExecutorService` for Managing Threads**: Avoid manually managing threads; use `ExecutorService` to manage thread pools and tasks.
- **Avoid Deadlocks**: Design systems to avoid circular dependencies between locks.
- **Use Future and Callable for Asynchronous Computation**: Use Callable and Future to handle tasks that return results or may throw exceptions.
- **Leverage Synchronizers for Coordination**: Use utilities like `CountDownLatch` and `CyclicBarrier` for complex synchronization scenarios.

Concurrency and multithreading are powerful concepts that can greatly improve the performance and responsiveness of Java applications. By understanding how to create and manage threads, use synchronization effectively, and leverage the high-level concurrency utilities provided by Java, developers can build robust, scalable, and efficient multithreaded applications. The next chapter will delve into **Reflection and Annotations**, which are powerful tools for introspecting classes, methods, and fields at runtime and can be used to build more flexible and dynamic Java applications.

# Reflection and Annotations

**Reflection** and **annotations** are advanced features in Java that have powerful capabilities for inspecting and manipulating classes, methods, fields, and other components at runtime. **Reflection** enables a Java program to analyze or manipulate itself or another program's structure, which is particularly useful in scenarios like frameworks, libraries, and development tools. **Annotations** provide a way to add metadata to Java code that can be processed at compile-time or runtime. Together, reflection and annotations offer flexibility and extensibility, which make them essential tools for advanced Java development.

## Understanding Java Reflection

**The Reflection feature** allows a program to examine or modify the runtime behavior of applications running in the Java Virtual Machine (JVM). Reflection is part of the `java.lang.reflect` package and can be used to inspect classes, interfaces, fields, and methods at runtime without knowing their names at compile-time.

## Key Features of Reflection

- **Inspect Classes and Interfaces**: Retrieve information about classes, interfaces, methods, and fields
- **Create Instances at Runtime**: Instantiate objects dynamically
- **Invoke Methods Dynamically**: Invoke methods on objects at runtime
- **Access and Modify Fields**: Access and modify fields, including private ones, dynamically

# Working with Reflection

The Java Reflection API provides classes like `Class`, `Method`, `Field`, and `Constructor` to represent various elements of a class.

## Getting Class Information

The **Class** class provides methods to inspect the runtime information about a class or an interface. You can obtain an object of the **Class** type using:

- `Class.forName("className")`
- `object.getClass()`
- `ClassName.class`

```
public class ReflectionExample {
    public static void main(String[] args) {
        try {
            // Getting the Class object
            Class<?> clazz = Class.forName("java.util.ArrayList");

            // Printing class name
            System.out.println("Class Name: " + clazz.getName());

            // Printing all methods of the class
            Method[] methods = clazz.getDeclaredMethods();
            for (Method method : methods) {
                System.out.println("Method: " + method.getName());
            }
        } catch (ClassNotFoundException e) {
            e.printStackTrace();
        }
    }
}
```

***Figure 3.29:*** *Reflection Example*

## Creating Instances at Runtime

You can create an instance of a class dynamically using the **newInstance()** method of the **Class** object or the **Constructor** class.

```
public class ReflectionExample {
    public static void main(String[] args) {
        try {
            // Creating an instance dynamically
            Class<?> clazz = Class.forName("java.util.ArrayList");
            Object instance = clazz.getDeclaredConstructor().newInstance();

            System.out.println("Instance created: " + instance);
        } catch (Exception e) {
            e.printStackTrace();
        }
    }
}
```

***Figure 3.30:*** *Creating Instance at Runtime*

## Accessing and Modifying Fields

Reflection allows accessing and modifying private fields of a class using the **`Field`** class.

```
import java.lang.reflect.Field;

public class Person {
    private String name = "John Doe";
}

public class ReflectionExample {
    public static void main(String[] args) {
        try {
            Person person = new Person();
            Class<?> clazz = person.getClass();

            // Accessing private field
            Field field = clazz.getDeclaredField("name");
            field.setAccessible(true);  // Required to access private fields

            System.out.println("Name before change: " + field.get(person));
            field.set(person, "Jane Doe");  // Modifying the field value
            System.out.println("Name after change: " + field.get(person));
        } catch (Exception e) {
            e.printStackTrace();
        }
    }
}
```

***Figure 3.31:*** *Accessing and Modifying Fields*

## Invoking Methods Dynamically

Reflection allows invoking methods on objects dynamically using the **`Method`** class.

```
import java.lang.reflect.Method;

public class Calculator {
    public int add(int a, int b) {
        return a + b;
    }
}

public class ReflectionExample {
    public static void main(String[] args) {
        try {
            Calculator calculator = new Calculator();
            Class<?> clazz = calculator.getClass();

            // Invoking the add method dynamically
            Method method = clazz.getMethod("add", int.class, int.class);
            Object result = method.invoke(calculator, 5, 3);

            System.out.println("Result: " + result);  // Output: Result: 8
        } catch (Exception e) {
            e.printStackTrace();
        }
    }
}
```

***Figure 3.32:*** *Invoking Methods Dynamically*

# Understanding Annotations

**Annotations** provide a way to add metadata to Java code. They are a form of syntactic metadata that can be processed at compile-time, runtime, or by documentation tools. Annotations can be applied to classes, methods, fields, parameters, and other elements.

## Built-in Annotations in Java

Java provides several built-in annotations:

- **`@Override`**: Indicates that a method overrides a method in a superclass
- **`@Deprecated`**: Marks a method or class as deprecated, meaning it should not be used
- **`@SuppressWarnings`**: Instructs the compiler to suppress specific warnings
- **`@FunctionalInterface`**: Marks an interface as a functional interface, which can have only one abstract method
- **`@SafeVarargs`**: Suppresses warnings for **`varargs`** usage

## Custom Annotations

Custom annotations can be defined to add specific metadata to the code. A custom annotation is defined using the **`@interface`** keyword.

**Defining and using a Custom Annotation**

```
import java.lang.annotation.Retention;
import java.lang.annotation.RetentionPolicy;

// Defining a custom annotation
@Retention(RetentionPolicy.RUNTIME) // Specifies that the annotation is available at runtime
public @interface MyAnnotation {
    String value() default "default value";
    int count();
}

// usage
@MyAnnotation(value = "Hello, Annotations!", count = 5)
public class AnnotatedClass {
    // Class code
}
```

***Figure 3.33:*** *Defining and Using a Custom Annotation*

# Processing Annotations with Reflection

You can use reflection to read and process annotations at runtime.

```
import java.lang.annotation.Annotation;
import java.lang.reflect.Method;

// Annotation definition
@Retention(RetentionPolicy.RUNTIME)
@interface MyAnnotation {
    String value() default "default value";
    int count();
}

// Using the annotation
@MyAnnotation(value = "Sample Annotation", count = 3)
public class AnnotatedClass {
    public void display() {
        System.out.println("Display method");
    }
}

public class ReflectionExample {
    public static void main(String[] args) {
        try {
            Class<AnnotatedClass> clazz = AnnotatedClass.class;

            // Checking for the annotation on the class
            if (clazz.isAnnotationPresent(MyAnnotation.class)) {
                Annotation annotation =
clazz.getAnnotation(MyAnnotation.class);
                MyAnnotation myAnnotation = (MyAnnotation) annotation;

                System.out.println("Value: " + myAnnotation.value());
                System.out.println("Count: " + myAnnotation.count());
            }
        } catch (Exception e) {
            e.printStackTrace();
        }
    }
}
```

***Figure 3.34:*** *Processing Annotations with Reflection*

# Common Use Cases of Reflection and Annotations

- **Dependency Injection Frameworks**: Libraries like Spring and Hibernate use reflection and annotations to inject dependencies and manage object lifecycles dynamically.
- **Serialization and Deserialization**: Libraries like Jackson and Gson use reflection to convert Java objects to JSON/XML, and vice versa.
- **Testing Frameworks**: Frameworks like JUnit use annotations (for example, `@Test`) to mark test methods, which are discovered and executed using reflection.
- **Aspect-Oriented Programming (AOP)**: Annotations are used in AOP frameworks to define cross-cutting concerns like logging, security, and transactions.

# Best Practices for Using Reflection and Annotations

- **Avoid Overusing Reflection**: Reflection can result in code that is hard to understand and maintain. Use it judiciously and only when necessary.
- **Be Mindful of Performance**: Reflection is slower than direct method calls because it involves type checking and method resolution at runtime. Avoid using reflection in performance-critical code paths.
- **Use Annotations to Simplify Configuration**: Annotations provide a clean way to configure and extend applications without complex XML or property files.
- **Ensure Annotations Are Documented**: When creating custom annotations, provide clear documentation on their usage and behavior.
- **Combine Reflection with Annotations for Flexibility**: Use reflection to read and process custom annotations, enabling flexible and dynamic behavior in your applications.

Reflection and annotations are powerful tools in Java that provide dynamic capabilities for inspecting, modifying, and configuring code at runtime. By understanding how to effectively use reflection and annotations, developers can create flexible, extensible, and maintainable Java applications. These features are particularly useful in building frameworks, libraries, and tools that require runtime introspection and dynamic behavior. In *Chapter* 4, we will explore **Advanced I/O** in Java, which includes file handling, serialization, and working with streams, to build efficient and robust input/output operations in Java applications.

# Advanced I/O

**Advanced I/O (Input/Output)** in Java involves handling complex input and output operations efficiently, such as file reading and writing, data serialization and deserialization, working with network streams, and non-blocking I/O. The Java I/O (Input/Output) API provides powerful classes and methods for performing these tasks. The `java.io` and `java.nio` packages offer a wide range of tools for managing data streams and file operations.

# Overview of Java I/O Streams

Java I/O is built around the concept of **streams**, which represent an ordered sequence of data. Streams abstract the complexities of data transfer, allowing developers to focus on reading from or writing to a data source or destination.

## Types of Streams

- **Byte Streams**: Handle I/O of raw binary data. These are suitable for all types of file handling (binary files, images, etc.). They use `InputStream` and `OutputStream` classes.
- **Character Streams**: Handle I/O of character data. These are specifically designed for handling character data (text files). They use Reader and Writer classes.

## Common Stream Classes

- `FileInputStream/FileOutputStream`: For reading and writing bytes from/to a file
- `FileReader/FileWriter`: For reading and writing characters from/to a file
- `BufferedReader/BufferedWriter`: For efficient reading and writing of characters, arrays, and lines
- `ObjectInputStream/ObjectOutputStream`: For reading and writing objects, enabling serialization and deserialization

# File I/O with `java.io`

The java.io package provides classes for handling basic file I/O operations, such as reading and writing text and binary files, creating directories, and handling exceptions.

## Reading and Writing Files

To efficiently handle file I/O operations in Java, **`FileReader`** and **`BufferedReader`** are commonly used for reading from files, while **`FileWriter`** and **`BufferedWriter`** are used for writing to files. **`BufferedReader`** enhances the performance of file reading by buffering the input, allowing for a faster reading of characters, arrays, and lines from a file. Similarly, **`BufferedWriter`** improves the efficiency of writing by buffering the output, enabling faster writing of characters, arrays, and lines to a file. Both **`BufferedReader`** and **`BufferedWriter`** are more efficient and effective ways to perform file operations in Java, as they reduce the number of direct read and write operations to the underlying file system.

```
// Reading
import java.io.BufferedReader;
import java.io.FileReader;
import java.io.IOException;

public class FileReadExample {
    public static void main(String[] args) {
        try (BufferedReader reader = new BufferedReader(new FileReader("input.txt"))) {
            String line;
            while ((line = reader.readLine()) != null) {
                System.out.println(line);
            }
        } catch (IOException e) {
            e.printStackTrace();
        }
    }
}

// writing to a file
import java.io.BufferedWriter;
import java.io.FileWriter;
import java.io.IOException;

public class FileWriteExample {
    public static void main(String[] args) {
        try (BufferedWriter writer = new BufferedWriter(new FileWriter("output.txt"))) {
            writer.write("Hello, Advanced I/O!");
        } catch (IOException e) {
            e.printStackTrace();
        }
    }
}
```

***Figure 3.35:*** *Reading and Writing Files*

## Object Serialization and Deserialization

The **`Person`** class implements Serializable to allow its instances to be serialized and deserialized.

- **Serialization** is the process of converting an object's state to a byte stream so that it can be saved to a file or transmitted over a network.
- **Deserialization** is the reverse, where the byte stream is converted back into an object.

```
import java.io.*;

// Serializable class
class Person implements Serializable {
    private static final long serialVersionUID = 1L;
    private String name;
    private int age;

    public Person(String name, int age) {
        this.name = name;
        this.age = age;
    }

    @Override
    public String toString() {
        return "Person{name='" + name + "', age=" + age + "}";
    }
}

public class SerializationExample {
    public static void main(String[] args) {
        Person person = new Person("Alice", 30);

        // Serialization
        try (ObjectOutputStream oos = new ObjectOutputStream(new FileOutputStream("person.ser"))) {
            oos.writeObject(person);
            System.out.println("Object serialized successfully.");
        } catch (IOException e) {
            e.printStackTrace();
        }

        // Deserialization
        try (ObjectInputStream ois = new ObjectInputStream(new FileInputStream("person.ser"))) {
            Person deserializedPerson = (Person) ois.readObject();
            System.out.println("Deserialized Object: " + deserializedPerson);
        } catch (IOException | ClassNotFoundException e) {
            e.printStackTrace();
        }
    }
}
```

***Figure 3.36:*** *Serialization and Deserialization*

# Working with `java.nio` (New I/O)

The **`java.nio`** (New Input/Output) package, introduced in Java 1.4 and further enhanced in Java 7 (NIO.2), provides more efficient and scalable I/O operations. The java.nio package includes **buffers**, **channels**, **selectors**, and **file operations** that are more efficient than the traditional java.io package.

## Buffers and Channels

**`FileChannel`** and **`ByteBuffer`** are used for reading and writing files in an efficient manner.

- **Buffer**: A container for data of a specific primitive type (like **`ByteBuffer`**, **`CharBuffer`**).
- **Channel**: Represents an open connection to an I/O source (like file and socket). Channels can be read from or written to, and they are more flexible than **`InputStream`** and **`OutputStream`**.

```
import java.io.IOException;
import java.nio.ByteBuffer;
import java.nio.channels.FileChannel;
import java.nio.file.Path;
import java.nio.file.StandardOpenOption;

public class NIOExample {
    public static void main(String[] args) {
        Path filePath = Path.of("nio-example.txt");

        // Writing to a file using NIO
        try (FileChannel fileChannel = FileChannel.open(filePath, StandardOpenOption.CREATE,
StandardOpenOption.WRITE)) {
            String content = "Hello, NIO!";
            ByteBuffer buffer = ByteBuffer.allocate(1024);
            buffer.put(content.getBytes());
            buffer.flip(); // Prepare the buffer for writing
            fileChannel.write(buffer);
            System.out.println("Data written to file using NIO.");
        } catch (IOException e) {
            e.printStackTrace();
        }

        // Reading from a file using NIO
        try (FileChannel fileChannel = FileChannel.open(filePath, StandardOpenOption.READ)) {
            ByteBuffer buffer = ByteBuffer.allocate(1024);
            int bytesRead = fileChannel.read(buffer);
            while (bytesRead != -1) {
                buffer.flip(); // Prepare the buffer for reading
                while (buffer.hasRemaining()) {
                    System.out.print((char) buffer.get());
                }
                buffer.clear(); // Clear buffer for the next read
                bytesRead = fileChannel.read(buffer);
            }
        } catch (IOException e) {
            e.printStackTrace();
        }
    }
}
```

***Figure 3.37:*** *Buffers and Channels*

# File Operations with `java.nio.file`

The **`java.nio.file`** package provides a more powerful and flexible API for working with files and directories. It offers methods for common tasks like creating, deleting, copying, moving, and reading files. The **`Files`** class provides static methods for file operations, improving code readability and reducing boilerplate code.

```java
import java.io.IOException;
import java.nio.file.*;

public class FileOperationsExample {
    public static void main(String[] args) {
        Path source = Paths.get("source.txt");
        Path target = Paths.get("target.txt");

        // Copying a file
        try {
            Files.copy(source, target, StandardCopyOption.REPLACE_EXISTING);
            System.out.println("File copied successfully.");
        } catch (IOException e) {
            e.printStackTrace();
        }

        // Moving a file
        try {
            Files.move(target, Paths.get("moved-target.txt"), StandardCopyOption.REPLACE_EXISTING);
            System.out.println("File moved successfully.");
        } catch (IOException e) {
            e.printStackTrace();
        }

        // Deleting a file
        try {
            Files.delete(Paths.get("moved-target.txt"));
            System.out.println("File deleted successfully.");
        } catch (IOException e) {
            e.printStackTrace();
        }
    }
}
```

***Figure 3.38:*** *File Operations*

# Best Practices for Advanced I/O

- **Prefer** Buffered **Streams for Better Performance**: Use `BufferedReader` and `BufferedWriter` for character-based I/O and `BufferedInputStream` and `BufferedOutputStream` for byte-based I/O.
- **Use `java.nio` for High-Performance I/O**: Prefer java.nio for non-blocking and high-performance file and network I/O.
- **Close Streams and Channels**: Always close streams and channels in a finally block or use try-with-resources to prevent resource leaks.
- **Use Serialization Carefully**: Ensure that serialized objects are compatible across different versions and avoid serialization of sensitive information.
- **Handle Exceptions Properly**: Handle `IOException` and other related exceptions properly to ensure that your application is robust and reliable.
- **Use Non-Blocking I/O for Scalability**: Use non-blocking I/O for scalable server applications where handling multiple connections simultaneously is essential.

Advanced I/O in Java enables one to handle complex file, network, and data stream operations efficiently. By leveraging both the classic java.io and modern java.nio packages, developers can build robust, high-performance applications capable of handling various I/O requirements. Understanding how to effectively use buffers, channels, selectors, and advanced file operations allows them to develop more flexible and scalable solutions. In *Chapter 4*, we will explore **Exception Handling** in Java, which provides mechanisms for handling errors and exceptional situations gracefully and ensures robust and error-free code.

# Exception Handling

**Exception Handling** is a critical concept in Java programming that manages runtime errors and unexpected conditions gracefully. Java provides a robust exception handling mechanism to maintain the normal flow of applications even when errors occur.

# Understanding Exceptions

An **exception** is an event that disrupts the normal flow of a program during execution. Exceptions can be caused by various factors such as invalid user input, hardware failures, network issues, or programmatic errors.

## Types of Exceptions

- **Checked Exceptions**: Exceptions that are checked at compile time. Examples include `IOException` and `SQLException`
- **Unchecked Exceptions**: Also known as runtime exceptions, they are not checked at compile time. Examples include `NullPointerException` and `ArrayIndexOutOfBoundsException`.
- **Errors**: Serious problems that a typical application should not attempt to handle. Examples include `OutOfMemoryError` and `StackOverflowError`.

# Basic Exception Handling with `try`, `catch`, and `finally`

The `try-catch-finally` block is the fundamental mechanism for handling exceptions in Java.

## `try-catch` Block

The try block contains code that might throw an exception, while the catch block contains code to handle the exception.

```
public class ExceptionExample {
    public static void main(String[] args) {
        try {
            int result = 10 / 0; // This line throws ArithmeticException
        } catch (ArithmeticException e) {
            System.out.println("Cannot divide by zero: " + e.getMessage());
        }
    }
}
```

**Figure 3.39:** *try-catch Block*

## `finally` Block

The `finally` block always executes after the `try` and `catch` blocks, regardless of whether an exception was thrown or not. It is typically used for resource cleanup.

```
try {
    // Code that may throw an exception
} catch (Exception e) {
    // Handle exception
} finally {
    System.out.println("This block always executes.");
}
```

**Figure 3.40:** *finally Block*

# Throwing and Creating Custom Exceptions

Java allows developers to throw exceptions explicitly using the **`throw`** keyword and define their own exception classes to represent application-specific errors.

```
public class ThrowExample {
    public static void main(String[] args) {
        validateAge(15);
    }

    public static void validateAge(int age) {
        if (age < 18) {
            throw new IllegalArgumentException("Age must be 18 or older.");
        }
    }
}
```

**Figure 3.41:** *Throwing and Creating Custom Exceptions*

## Creating Custom Exceptions

Custom exceptions are created by extending the **`Exception`** class (for checked exceptions), or the **`RuntimeException`** class (for unchecked exceptions).

```
public class InvalidAgeException extends Exception {
    public InvalidAgeException(String message) {
        super(message);
    }
}
```

**Figure 3.42:** *Creating Custom Exceptions*

# Best Practices for Exception Handling

- **Use Specific Exceptions**: Catch specific exceptions instead of using a generic **`Exception`** class.
- **Avoid Empty** catch **Blocks**: Always handle exceptions or log them for debugging.
- **Use** finally **for Resource Cleanup**: Ensure resources like files and network connections are closed properly.
- **Throw Exceptions with Meaningful Messages**: Provide clear, informative messages to help diagnose issues.
- **Avoid Overusing Checked Exceptions**: Consider using unchecked exceptions for non-recoverable errors to reduce boilerplate code.

Exception handling is a vital part of writing robust and reliable Java applications. By understanding the different types of exceptions, using the **`try-catch-finally`** construct effectively, and following best practices, developers can manage errors gracefully and maintain the normal flow of their programs. Proper exception handling helps in debugging and ensures that applications can handle unexpected situations without crashing.

# Java Database Connectivity (JDBC)

**Java Database Connectivity (JDBC)** is a Java API that enables Java applications to interact with a wide range of databases. It provides a standard interface for connecting to relational databases, executing SQL queries, and handling results. JDBC is an essential tool for building data-driven applications in Java.

# JDBC Architecture

JDBC architecture consists of two major components: the **JDBC API** and the **JDBC Driver**.

- **JDBC API**: Defines a set of interfaces and classes to connect to databases, execute SQL queries, and process results
- **JDBC Driver**: A set of classes that implement the JDBC interfaces for a specific database. There are four types of JDBC drivers: Type-1 (JDBC-ODBC Bridge), Type-2 (Native-API), Type-3 (Network Protocol), and Type-4 (Thin Driver)

# Establishing a Database Connection

To interact with a database using JDBC, you must first establish a connection using the **`DriverManager`** class.

## Steps to Connect to a Database

- **Load the JDBC Driver**: Load the database-specific driver class
- **Establish the Connection**: Use the **`DriverManager.getConnection()`** method to connect to the database

```java
import java.sql.Connection;
import java.sql.DriverManager;
import java.sql.SQLException;

public class JDBCExample {
    public static void main(String[] args) {
        String url = "jdbc:mysql://localhost:3306/mydatabase";
        String user = "root";
        String password = "password";

        try (Connection connection = DriverManager.getConnection(url, user, password)) {
            System.out.println("Connected to the database!");
        } catch (SQLException e) {
            e.printStackTrace();
        }
    }
}
```

***Figure 3.43:** JDBC Example*

# Executing SQL Statements

JDBC provides three types of statements for executing SQL queries:

- **`Statement`:** Used for simple SQL queries without parameters
- **`PreparedStatement`:** Used for SQL queries with input parameters, providing better performance and security
- **`CallableStatement`:** Used to call stored procedures in the database

**Executing a Query with `Statement`**

```java
import java.sql.Connection;
import java.sql.DriverManager;
import java.sql.ResultSet;
import java.sql.Statement;

public class JDBCQueryExample {
    public static void main(String[] args) {
        try (Connection connection =
DriverManager.getConnection("jdbc:mysql://localhost:3306/mydatabase", "root", "password");
             Statement statement = connection.createStatement();
             ResultSet resultSet = statement.executeQuery("SELECT * FROM users")) {

            while (resultSet.next()) {
                System.out.println("User ID: " + resultSet.getInt("id"));
                System.out.println("User Name: " + resultSet.getString("name"));
            }
        } catch (Exception e) {
            e.printStackTrace();
        }
    }
}
```

***Figure 3.44:** Executing a Query with Statement*

**Using `PreparedStatement` for Secure SQL Queries**

```
import java.sql.Connection;
import java.sql.DriverManager;
import java.sql.PreparedStatement;
import java.sql.ResultSet;

public class PreparedStatementExample {
    public static void main(String[] args) {
        try (Connection connection =
DriverManager.getConnection("jdbc:mysql://localhost:3306/mydatabase", "root", "password");
             PreparedStatement preparedStatement = connection.prepareStatement("SELECT * FROM users
WHERE id = ?")) {

            preparedStatement.setInt(1, 1); // Set parameter value
            ResultSet resultSet = preparedStatement.executeQuery();

            if (resultSet.next()) {
                System.out.println("User Name: " + resultSet.getString("name"));
            }
        } catch (Exception e) {
            e.printStackTrace();
        }
    }
}
```

***Figure 3.45:*** *Using Prepared Statement*

# Best Practices for Using JDBC

- **Use `PreparedStatement` to Prevent SQL Injection**: Always use **`PreparedStatement`** over Statement to avoid SQL injection vulnerabilities.
- **Close Connections, Statements, and `ResultSets`**: Use try-with-resources to ensure resources are closed automatically.
- **Use Connection Pooling**: Use a connection pool (like HikariCP or Apache DBCP) to manage database connections efficiently.
- **Handle Exceptions Properly**: Catch and handle **`SQLException`** appropriately to ensure that your application can recover from database errors.

JDBC is a fundamental API for connecting Java applications to relational databases. By understanding how to establish connections, execute SQL queries securely, and manage database resources efficiently, developers can build robust, data-driven applications. Following the best practices for JDBC, such as using **`PreparedStatement`** and connection pooling, ensures better performance and security. In *Chapter 4, Understanding Spring Boot Basics*, we will explore **Java Generics**, which provide type safety and reusability, enhancing Java code robustness and flexibility.

# Conclusion

This chapter covered a wide range of advanced Java topics necessary for building robust, scalable, and high-performance applications. **Generics** enable type safety and code reusability, while **Lambda Expressions and Functional Interfaces** allow for more expressive and functional-style programming. The **Java Collections Framework** and **Stream API** provide powerful tools for data manipulation, with streams offering a functional approach to processing collections. **Concurrency and Multithreading** enable efficient parallel execution, crucial for responsive applications, and **Reflection and Annotations** offer dynamic capabilities for introspection and configuration. **Advanced I/O** techniques, such as non-blocking I/O with NIO, enhance file and network operations. **Exception Handling** ensures robust error management, while **JDBC** provides a standard interface for interacting with databases, allowing seamless data integration.

Having mastered these foundational and advanced Java features, we will move on to building modern, production-ready applications using **Spring Boot**. The next chapter, **Understanding Spring Boot Basics**, will introduce the fundamentals of Spring Boot, its architecture, and how it simplifies Java application development by providing auto-configuration, starter dependencies, and embedded servers, which makes it an essential framework for building microservices and RESTful applications.

# Part 2

# Building Weather App with Spring Boot

(Chapters 4–5)

# CHAPTER 4
# Understanding Spring Boot Basics

## Introduction

Spring Boot has revolutionized Java development by simplifying the process of building and deploying Spring applications. In this chapter, you will be introduced to the foundational concepts of Spring Boot, which will enable you to quickly and efficiently create production-ready applications.

We start with an **Introduction to Java Spring Boot**, where you will learn how Spring Boot streamlines the development process by reducing boilerplate code and simplifying configuration. This is followed by an **Overview of Spring Boot Architecture**, which explains the key components and how they interact to provide a cohesive development environment.

Next, we delve into **Understanding Dependencies and Auto-Configuration**, where you will discover how Spring Boot manages dependencies and automatically configures your application based on the libraries you include. We will then introduce pre-configured templates called **Spring Boot Starters**, which further accelerate development by bundling commonly used dependencies.

You will also explore the **Spring Boot Application Properties**, learning how to customize your application's behavior with minimal configuration. The chapter concludes with a hands-on guide to **Building a Simple Hello World Application**, where you will apply what you have learned so far to create and run your first Spring Boot application.

By the end of this chapter, you will have a solid grasp of Spring Boot's basic concepts, setting the stage for more advanced topics in the framework.

## Structure

In this chapter, the following topics will be covered:

- Introduction to Java Spring Boot
- Overview of Spring Boot Architecture
- Understanding Dependencies and Auto-Configuration
- Building a Simple Hello World Application

## Introduction to Java Spring Boot

**Spring Boot** is a powerful, easy-to-use framework that simplifies the development of Java-based enterprise applications. Built on top of the **Spring Framework**, Spring Boot provides a suite of tools, libraries, and features that make it easier to create standalone, production-grade Spring applications. It eliminates much of the boilerplate configuration associated with traditional Spring applications by providing default configurations, embedded servers, and starter dependencies. This chapter introduces the core concepts of Spring Boot, its advantages, and how it revolutionizes Java development.

# Understanding Spring Boot

**Spring Boot** is an open-source Java-based framework developed by **Pivotal** (which is now part of VMware) to simplify the development of Spring applications. It provides an opinionated view of the Spring platform, allowing developers to focus on writing business logic rather than managing complex configurations.

## Key Features of Spring Boot

- **Auto-Configuration**: Automatically configures Spring and third-party libraries based on the dependencies specified in the project
- **Starter POMs**: Simplify dependency management by providing pre-configured starter templates (`spring-boot-starter-web`, `spring-boot-starter-data-jpa`, and so on.)
- **Embedded Servers**: Support embedded servers like **Tomcat**, **Jetty**, and **Undertow**, enabling easy deployment of standalone applications
- **Production-Ready Features**: Offers built-in tools like **Spring Boot Actuator** for monitoring, metrics, health checks, and externalized configuration
- **Opinionated Defaults**: Provides sensible defaults to streamline the development process, which can be customized if needed

# Importance of Spring Boot

Spring Boot addresses several challenges of traditional Spring development, such as extensive XML configuration, complex setup, and lengthy deployment processes. It is designed to help developers build applications more quickly and efficiently.

## Advantages of Spring Boot

- **Rapid Development**: Reduces development time with features like auto-configuration and starter dependencies
- **Less Boilerplate Code**: Eliminates repetitive code and configurations, allowing developers to focus on business logic
- **Easy to Deploy**: Embedded servers make deploying applications as simple as running a Java application
- **Microservices-Ready**: Provides a lightweight, modular architecture ideal for developing microservices-based applications
- **Comprehensive Ecosystem**: Integrates seamlessly with various Spring projects, such as Spring Data, Spring Security, and Spring Cloud

Spring Boot provides a streamlined approach to building Java applications, enabling developers to focus more on business logic than boilerplate code and configurations. With features like auto-configuration, embedded servers, and starter dependencies, Spring Boot simplifies the development of modern, production-ready applications. In the next section, we will explore the **Spring Boot Architecture**, diving deeper into how Spring Boot integrates with various components of the Spring ecosystem, and how it handles auto-configuration and dependency management.

# Overview of Spring Boot Architecture

**Spring Boot** is designed to simplify the development of Java applications by providing a pre-configured framework that eliminates the need for extensive configuration and setup. Its architecture builds on the core **Spring Framework** and integrates seamlessly with various Spring components, offering a streamlined and modular approach to application development. This chapter provides an overview of the **Spring Boot architecture**, its core components such as **Auto-Configuration**, **Starter Dependencies**, **Embedded Servers**, **Spring Boot Actuator**, and how these components work together to provide a cohesive development environment.

# Core Components of Spring Boot Architecture

The Spring Boot architecture is based on several key components that work together to provide a robust and flexible framework for Java development. These components include **Auto-Configuration**, **Starter Dependencies**, **Embedded Servers**, **Spring Boot Actuator**, and **Externalized Configuration**.

## Auto-Configuration

**Auto-Configuration** is a core feature of Spring Boot that automatically configures beans and settings based on the libraries and dependencies present in the **`classpath`**. It significantly reduces the amount of manual configuration needed and allows developers to focus on writing business logic.

- **How It Works**: Spring Boot scans the **`classpath`** for libraries and automatically configures commonly used beans and settings based on predefined conditions. For example, if **`spring-boot-starter-data-jpa`** is included, Spring Boot auto-configures a **`DataSource`**, **`EntityManagerFactory`**, and **`TransactionManager`**.
- **Customization**: Auto-configuration can be customized using **`@Configuration`** classes, properties in **`application.properties`** or **`application.yml`**, and conditional annotations like **`@ConditionalOnMissingBean`**.

## Starter Dependencies

**Starter Dependencies** (or **Starters**) are a set of convenient dependency descriptors that can be added to your project to bring in a curated set of libraries and transitive dependencies for specific functionalities.

**How It Works**: Starters simplify dependency management by providing a single entry point for all dependencies related to a particular feature. For example, spring-boot-starter-web brings in dependencies for building web applications, including Spring MVC, Jackson, and an embedded web server like Tomcat.

- **Common Starters**:
  - **`spring-boot-starter-web`**: For web applications
  - **`spring-boot-starter-data-jpa`**: For JPA and Hibernate
  - **`spring-boot-starter-security`**: For Spring Security
  - **`spring-boot-starter-thymeleaf`**: For **`Thymeleaf`** templating engine

## Embedded Servers

Spring Boot supports **embedded servers** like **Tomcat**, **Jetty**, and **Undertow**, allowing applications to be run independently without needing an external web server.

**How It Works**: When a Spring Boot application is started, it automatically starts the embedded server configured in the `classpath` and deploys the application to it. This feature simplifies deployment and makes it easier to package applications as executable JARs or WARs.

**Benefits:**

- Simplifies deployment by embedding the server within the application
- Ensures consistency across environments (development, testing, production)
- Reduces the complexity of external server management

## Spring Boot Actuator

**Spring Boot Actuator** provides production-ready features such as monitoring, metrics, health checks, and auditing. It exposes various **endpoints** that help manage and monitor the application.

**How It Works**: Actuator endpoints are automatically exposed based on the application's configuration and dependencies. These endpoints provide information about application health (/actuator/health), metrics (/actuator/metrics), environment properties (/actuator/env), and more.

**Key Endpoints:**

- /actuator/health: Shows application health status
- /actuator/info: Displays arbitrary application information
- /actuator/metrics: Provides application metrics
- /actuator/env: Shows environment properties

## Externalized Configuration

Spring Boot provides extensive support for **externalized configuration**, allowing you to manage configuration properties in a flexible and environment-specific manner.

**How It Works**: Configuration properties can be specified in `application.properties` or `application.yml` files, system properties, environment variables, or command-line arguments. The properties are automatically loaded and can be injected into beans using the `@Value` annotation or `@ConfigurationProperties` classes.

**Profiles**: Spring Boot supports **profiles** (for example, `dev`, `test`, `prod`) to allow different configurations for different environments. Profiles can be activated via `application.properties`, environment variables, or command-line arguments.

# Spring Boot's Layered Architecture

Spring Boot follows a **layered architecture** that promotes modular development and separation of concerns. This architecture allows developers to build clean, maintainable, and testable applications.

## Presentation Layer

The **Presentation Layer** is responsible for handling HTTP requests and returning responses to the client. It typically consists of **controllers** in a Spring Boot application.

**Key Components:**

- `@RestController`: Annotates classes that handle RESTful web requests
- `@RequestMapping` and `@GetMapping`: Map HTTP requests to handler methods

- **View Templates**: Used for rendering views in web applications (like Thymeleaf and JSP).

## Service Layer

The **Service Layer** contains business logic and acts as an intermediary between the Presentation Layer and the Data Access Layer.

**Key Components:**

- **`@Service`**: Annotates service classes that contain business logic
- **Transaction Management**: Managed by Spring's declarative transaction management using **`@Transactional`**

## Data Access Layer

The **Data Access Layer** is responsible for interacting with the database and performing CRUD (Create, Read, Update, Delete) operations.

**Key Components:**

- **`@Repository`**: Annotates classes that handle data persistence
- **JPA and Spring Data**: Simplify database operations with **`CrudRepository`**, **`JpaRepository`**, and query methods

## Integration Layer

The **Integration Layer** manages communication with external systems, such as REST APIs, message brokers, or other services.

**Key Components:**

- **`RestTemplate`** and **`WebClient`**: For consuming RESTful services
- **Message Brokers**: Integrate with message brokers like RabbitMQ and Kafka using Spring AMQP or Spring Kafka

# How Spring Boot Handles Dependency Injection

**Dependency Injection (DI)** is a core feature of the Spring Framework, allowing objects to be injected into other objects rather than being created directly. Spring Boot builds on this feature by simplifying dependency management and configuration.

- **`@Autowired` Annotation**: Automatically injects beans based on type
- **`@ComponentScan` Annotation**: Scans the specified package(s) for components, services, and repositories to register them as beans

# How Spring Boot Manages Security

Spring Boot integrates seamlessly with **Spring Security** to provide authentication, authorization, and other security features out-of-the-box.

- **`spring-boot-starter-security`**: A starter that provides security features for Spring Boot applications
- **Default Security Configuration**: Provides a basic HTTP authentication setup for quick security integration
- **Custom Security Configurations**: Can be defined using @EnableWebSecurity and **`WebSecurityConfigurerAdapter`** to customize security settings

# Best Practices for Understanding and Leveraging Spring Boot Architecture

- **Leverage Auto-Configuration**: Use Spring Boot's auto-configuration capabilities to reduce boilerplate code and simplify configuration.
- **Utilize Starter Dependencies**: Choose the right starter dependencies to avoid dependency conflicts and maintain a clean codebase.
- **Monitor with Actuator**: Use Spring Boot Actuator to monitor application health and performance effectively.
- **Separate Concerns with Layers**: Follow a layered architecture to separate concerns and improve maintainability.
- **Externalize Configuration**: Use externalized configuration and profiles to manage environment-specific properties.

Spring Boot's architecture is designed to provide a flexible, modular, and easy-to-use framework that significantly reduces the complexity of Java application development. By understanding its core components like auto-configuration, starter dependencies, embedded servers, and Actuator, developers can harness the full power of Spring Boot to build production-ready applications quickly and efficiently. In the next section, we will delve deeper into **Understanding Dependencies and Auto-Configuration**, exploring how Spring Boot manages dependencies, and automatically configures beans based on the libraries in your project.

# Understanding Dependencies and Auto-Configuration

One of the most powerful features of **Spring Boot** is its ability to automatically configure components based on the libraries present in the classpath and the properties defined in configuration files. This **Auto-Configuration** capability significantly reduces the amount of boilerplate code and manual configuration required for setting up a Spring application. Additionally, **starter dependencies** simplify dependency management, making it easier to add required libraries for specific functionalities. This chapter explores how Spring Boot manages dependencies using **Starter POMs** and how **Auto-Configuration** works behind the scenes to provide a seamless development experience.

**Spring Boot Starters** are a set of convenient dependency descriptors that you can include in your project to get a complete set of dependencies for specific functionalities. These starters simplify Maven or Gradle dependency management by bringing in a curated set of libraries and transitive dependencies.

Starter dependencies are essentially pre-defined Maven or Gradle **POMs** (Project Object Models) that bundle together a group of related libraries. For example, adding spring-boot-starter-web brings in all the dependencies required for building a web application, including **Spring MVC**, **Jackson** for JSON processing, and an embedded **Tomcat** server.

**Commonly Used Starters**

- `spring-boot-starter-web`: For building web applications using Spring MVC, RESTful APIs, and so on
- `spring-boot-starter-data-jpa`: For working with JPA and Hibernate for ORM (Object-Relational Mapping)
- `spring-boot-starter-security`: For adding Spring Security to the application

- **`spring-boot-starter-test`**: For testing applications with libraries like JUnit, Mockito, AssertJ, and others
- **`spring-boot-starter-thymeleaf`**: For using Thymeleaf as a templating engine

**How Starters Simplify Dependency Management**

- **Simplified POM or Build File**: Instead of adding multiple dependencies individually, a single starter dependency can add all the required libraries.
- **Version Compatibility**: Starters ensure compatibility among dependencies, reducing conflicts and simplifying version management.
- **Quick Setup**: Starters allow developers to quickly set up projects without worrying about missing dependencies or version mismatches.

# Understanding Auto-Configuration

**Auto-Configuration** is a key feature of Spring Boot that automatically configures beans and settings based on the libraries and dependencies present in the **`classpath`** and other criteria. It helps developers get started with minimal configuration and allows for easy customization.

**How Auto-Configuration Works**

- **Class Path Detection**: Spring Boot detects the presence of specific libraries on the **`classpath`**. For example, if **`spring-boot-starter-data-jpa`** is present, Spring Boot knows to configure a DataSource bean, an **`EntityManagerFactory`**, and a **`TransactionManager`**.
- **Conditional Annotations**: Auto-configuration classes use annotations like **`@ConditionalOnClass`**, **`@ConditionalOnMissingBean`**, and **`@ConditionalOnProperty`**, to determine whether a particular configuration should be applied.

**Key Annotations for Auto-Configuration**

- **`@EnableAutoConfiguration`**: Automatically configures your Spring application based on the dependencies in the **`classpath`**. This annotation is typically used in the main application class.
- **`@ConditionalOnClass`**: Configures a bean if a specific class is present in the **`classpath`**.
- **`@ConditionalOnMissingBean`**: Configures a bean only if it is not already defined in the application context.
- **`@ConditionalOnProperty`**: Configures a bean based on the value of a specific property defined in **`application.properties`** or **`application.yml`**.

**Example of Auto-Configuration**

- When you add **`spring-boot-starter-data-jpa`** to your project, Spring Boot:
- Checks if **Hibernate** and **Spring Data JPA** are on the **`classpath`**
- Automatically configures a **`DataSource`** bean using the properties defined in **`application.properties`**
- Creates a default **`EntityManagerFactory`** and **`TransactionManager`**

```
# application.properties example
spring.datasource.url=jdbc:mysql://localhost:3306/mydb
spring.datasource.username=root
spring.datasource.password=password
spring.jpa.hibernate.ddl-auto=update
```

# Customizing Auto-Configuration

While Spring Boot provides sensible defaults through auto-configuration, there are times when you need to customize these configurations to suit your application's specific needs.

## Excluding Auto-Configuration

You can exclude specific auto-configuration classes using the **`@EnableAutoConfiguration`** annotation.

```
@SpringBootApplication(exclude = {DataSourceAutoConfiguration.class})
public class MyApplication {
    public static void main(String[] args) {
        SpringApplication.run(MyApplication.class, args);
    }
}
```

***Figure 4.1:*** *Enable Auto Configuration*

## Overriding Auto-Configured Beans

Auto-configured beans can be overridden by defining a custom bean of the same type in your **`@Configuration`** class.

```
import org.springframework.context.annotation.Bean;
import org.springframework.context.annotation.Configuration;

@Configuration
public class CustomDataSourceConfig {
    @Bean
    public DataSource customDataSource() {
        // Custom DataSource configuration
    }
}
```

***Figure 4.2:*** *Overriding Auto Configured Beans*

# Externalized Configuration

Spring Boot supports **externalized configuration**, allowing you to manage environment-specific settings and properties outside your application code.

## Using `application.properties` and `application.yml`

The **`application.properties`** or **`application.yml`** files are the most common ways to define external configuration for a Spring Boot application. They allow you to customize properties for auto-configuration.

**Example:**

```
application.properties:
server.port=8081
spring.application.name=MySpringBootApp
```

## Profiles for Environment-Specific Configuration

Spring Boot supports **profiles** to allow different configurations for different environments (like **dev**, **test**, **prod**).

- **Defining Profiles**: Use **application-{profile}.properties** or **application.yml** files to define environment-specific configurations.
- **Activating Profiles**: Profiles can be activated using the **spring.profiles.active** property, environment variables, or command-line arguments.

## Best Practices for Managing Dependencies and Auto-Configuration

- **Use Starters for Dependency Management**: Leverage starter dependencies to simplify dependency management and avoid conflicts.
- **Customize Auto-Configuration Carefully**: Use exclusions and custom beans judiciously to avoid unnecessary complexity.
- **Leverage @Conditional Annotations**: Use conditional annotations to create flexible and adaptable configurations.
- **Use Externalized Configuration for Flexibility**: Manage environment-specific configurations using externalized configuration files and profiles.
- **Test Configurations Thoroughly**: Ensure that auto-configurations work as expected in all environments, and test any customizations to avoid unexpected behavior.

Understanding dependencies and auto-configuration is key to leveraging the full power of Spring Boot. By using **starter dependencies** and the **auto-configuration** feature, developers can minimize boilerplate code and focus more on business logic. With flexible customization options and support for externalized configuration, Spring Boot provides a robust and scalable platform for modern Java application development.

# Building a Simple Hello World Application

Building a **Hello World** application is a classic way to get started with any new framework or tool. In this chapter, we will guide you through building a simple **Spring Boot** application from scratch. This example will demonstrate how to set up a Spring Boot project, create a RESTful web service, and run it using an embedded server. By the end of this chapter, you will have a basic understanding of how to develop, configure, and run a Spring Boot application.

## Setting Up a Spring Boot Project

To build a Spring Boot application, we first need to set up a project with the necessary dependencies. This can be easily done using **Spring Initializr**, a web-based tool that generates a Spring Boot project with the desired configuration.

## Using `Spring Initializr`

**`Spring Initializr`** is the easiest way to create a Spring Boot project with all required dependencies and configurations.

**Steps to Create a Spring Boot Project:**

1. Go to Spring Initializr
2. Choose **`Project`**: Maven Project or Gradle Project
3. Select **`Language`**: Java
4. Choose the **`Spring Boot Version`**: The latest stable version (for example, 3.1.0)
5. Enter **`Group`**: **`com.example`**
6. Enter **`Artifact`**: hello-world
7. Select **`Dependencies`**: Add **`Spring Web`** to build web applications, including RESTful services
8. Click **`Generate`** to download the project as a ZIP file
9. Extract the ZIP file and import it into your preferred IDE (for example, IntelliJ IDEA, Eclipse)

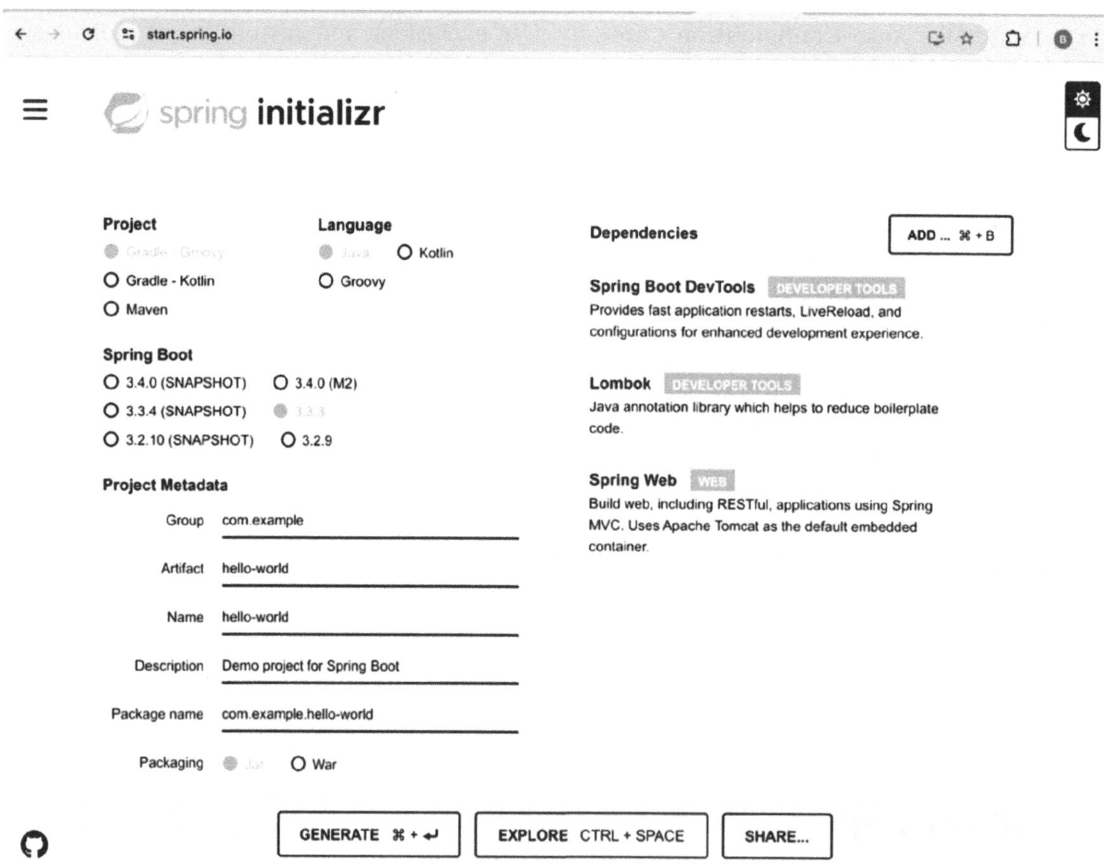


***Figure 4.3:** Spring Initializr*

# Project Structure

Once the project is created and imported into your IDE, you will see a typical Spring Boot project structure:

- **src/main/java**: Contains Java source files
- **com.example.helloworld**: Package containing the main application class and other components
- **src/main/resources**: Contains application configuration files
- **application.properties**: Main configuration file for the Spring Boot application
- **src/test/java**: Contains test cases for the application

# Creating the Main Application Class

The main application class is the entry point of a Spring Boot application. It is annotated with **@SpringBootApplication**, which is a convenience annotation that adds several other annotations:

- **@Configuration**: Marks the class as a source of bean definitions
- **@EnableAutoConfiguration**: Enables Spring Boot's auto-configuration feature
- **@ComponentScan**: Scans for components, configurations, and services in the package

# Writing the Main Application Class

Create a new Java class named **HelloWorldApplication** in the **com.example.helloworld** package.

This class serves as the entry point for the application. The **main()** method uses **SpringApplication.run()** to launch the application.

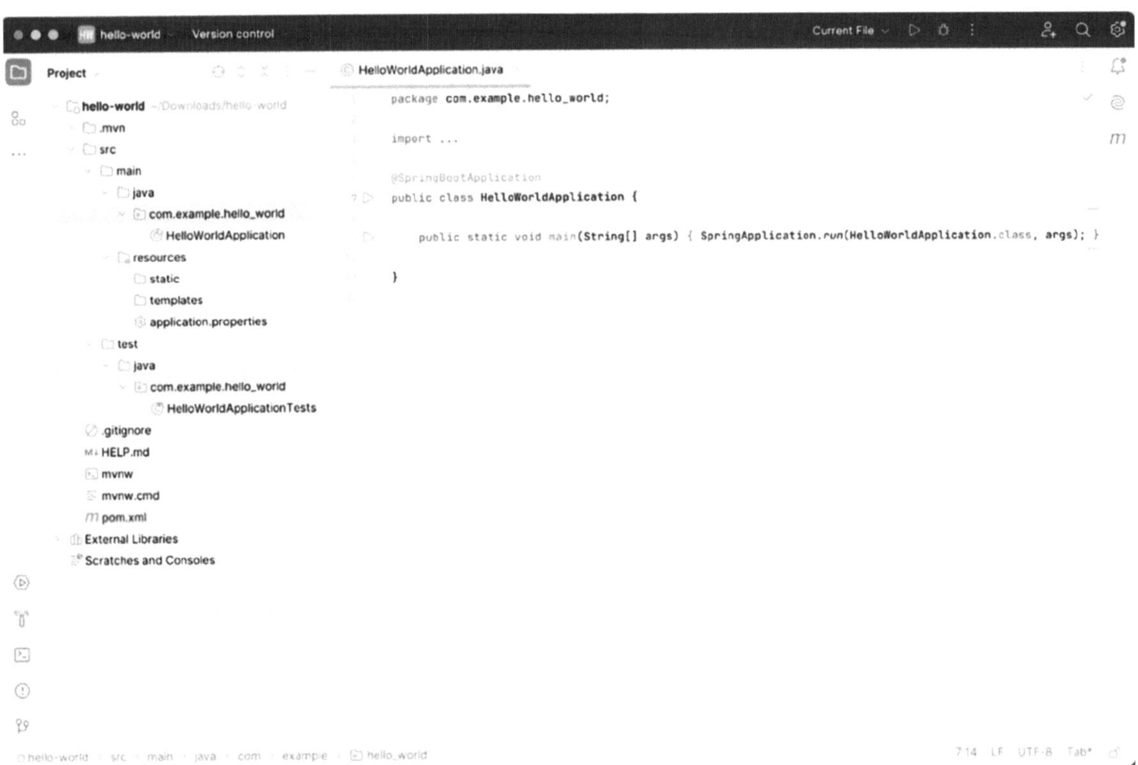


**Figure 4.4:** *Main Application Class*

# Creating a REST Controller

To build a **`Hello World`** web service, we need to create a **REST Controller** that handles HTTP requests and returns a response. Create a new Java class named **`HelloWorldController`** in the **`com.example.helloworld`** package:

**Explanation:**

- **`@RestController`**: This annotation marks the class as a RESTful web service controller.
- **`@GetMapping("/hello")`**: Maps HTTP GET requests to the **`/hello`** URL path to the **`sayHello()`** method.
- **`sayHello()` Method**: Returns a simple "**`Hello, Spring Boot!`**" string response when the **`/hello`** endpoint is accessed.

***Figure 4.5:*** *Hello World Controller*

# Running the Spring Boot Application

Now that we have our main application class and REST controller set up, we can run the Spring Boot application. First, we need to apply the configuration shown in the following figure.

**Using an IDE**: Right-click on the **`HelloWorldApplication`** class and select **`Run`** or **`Debug`**.

**Using the Command Line**:

1. Open a terminal and navigate to the project root directory.
2. Use the following command to build and run the project with Maven:

```
./mvnw spring-boot:run
```

**Figure 4.6:** *Run/Debug Configuration*

Clicking the "**Run**" button at the top right corner starts the application, and you will immediately see the logs streaming in real-time. This indicates that the application is running successfully and has been deployed on port 8080.

**Figure 4.7:** *Running the Application*

# Accessing the Hello World Endpoint

Once the application is running, open a web browser or use a tool like **curl** or **Postman** to access the endpoint:

```
URL: http://localhost:8080/hello
```

You will see the following output: `Hello, Spring Boot!`

# Customizing the Application with `application.properties`

The `application.properties` file allows you to customize the application's behavior. For example, you can change the server port or configure logging.

## Changing the Server Port

To change the default server port (8080), add the following property to `src/main/resources/application.properties`:

```
server.port=9090
```

This property changes the port number to 9090. Restart the application to access it at http://localhost:9090/hello.

# Adding Unit Tests for the REST Controller

Spring Boot provides excellent support for testing, including the `spring-boot-starter-test` starter that comes pre-configured with testing libraries like **JUnit** and **Mockito**.

## Writing a Simple Unit Test

Create a new test class named `HelloWorldControllerTest` in the `src/test/java/com/example/hello_world` package:

The JUnit test `sayHelloShouldReturnDefaultMessage()` verifies that the `/hello` endpoint of the Spring Boot application returns the expected output. If the test is executed successfully, it means that the application is functioning correctly for the particular scenario.

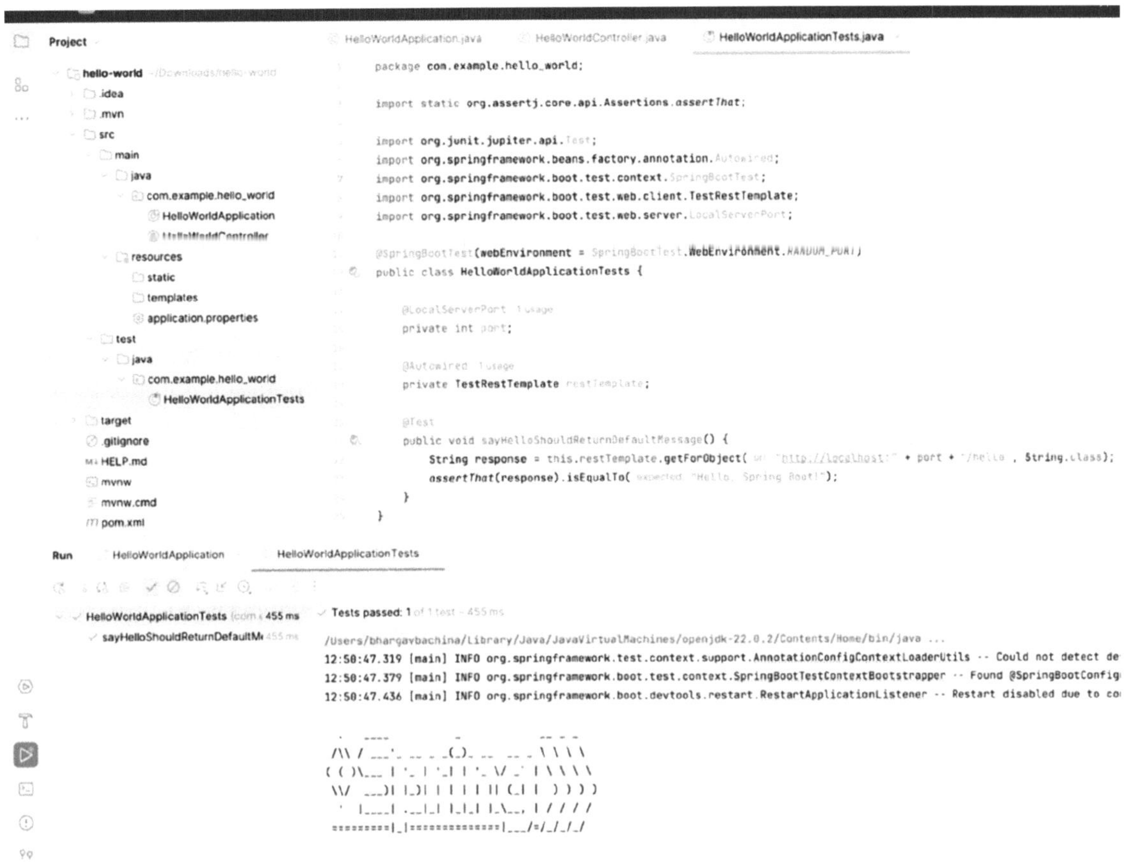

***Figure 4.8:*** JUnit Test

**Explanation**

- `@SpringBootTest`: Loads the full application context for integration testing
- `TestRestTemplate`: A convenient class for making REST calls in tests
- `@Test`: Marks the method as a JUnit test case
- `assertThat()`: Verifies the expected result using AssertJ

# Best Practices for Building Spring Boot Applications

- **Keep the Main Application Class Simple**: The main application class should only contain the `@SpringBootApplication` annotation and the `main()` method.
- **Organize Code by Feature**: Group related classes (controllers, services, repositories) by feature rather than layer.
- **Externalize Configuration**: Use `application.properties` or `application.yml` to manage environment-specific properties.
- **Write Unit and Integration Tests**: Ensure your application is robust by writing tests for controllers, services, and data access layers.
- **Use Spring Boot DevTools**: Leverage **Spring Boot DevTools** for automatic restarts and live reloads during development.

Building a simple `Hello World` application with Spring Boot demonstrates how easy and powerful it is to develop web applications using the framework. By setting up a project, creating a REST controller, customizing configurations, and writing tests, you will gain a solid foundation in Spring Boot development.

# Conclusion

In this chapter, we explored the foundational concepts of **Spring Boot**, starting with an **Introduction to Java Spring Boot**, where we learned how Spring Boot simplifies Java application development through features like auto-configuration, embedded servers, and starter dependencies. We then moved on to an **Overview of Spring Boot Architecture**, which highlighted the key components such as auto-configuration, starter dependencies, and Spring Boot Actuator that work together to provide a streamlined development experience.

Next, we delved into *Understanding Dependencies and Auto-Configuration*, where we saw how Spring Boot intelligently configures application components based on the libraries in the `classpath` and how developers can customize these settings using `@Conditional` annotations and externalized configuration. Finally, we demonstrated these concepts by **Building a Simple Hello World Application**, providing a hands-on experience of setting up a Spring Boot project, creating a RESTful web service, and running it using an embedded server.

With these foundational concepts and skills, you are now well-equipped to build more complex applications using Spring Boot. In the next chapter, we will explore **Database Integration and Weather App Development**, where you will learn how to integrate a relational database with Spring Boot, manage data access using Spring Data JPA, and build a practical weather application that retrieves real-time data from external APIs, providing a more comprehensive understanding of Spring Boot's capabilities.

# CHAPTER 5
# Database Integration and Weather App Development

## Introduction

Integrating a database with a Java application and building a functional, real-time weather app are crucial skills for any modern Java developer. This chapter will hence guide you through the entire process, from setting up a database to deploying a fully functional weather application.

We begin with **Setting Up the MySQL Database**, where you will learn to configure and connect a MySQL database to your Java project. Following this, **Configuring the Java Project for JPA** will introduce you to Java Persistence API (JPA), a key framework for managing database interactions in Java. You will then move on to **Defining and Configuring JPA Entities**, where you will map Java objects to database tables, and **implementing Data Access Operations with JPA**, which covers how to perform CRUD (Create, Read, Update, Delete) operations efficiently.

Next, we will tackle **Database Version Control with Liquibase**, ensuring your database changes are managed effectively and consistently. With your database in place, we shift focus to building the weather application, starting with **Implementing Spring MVC Architecture for a Weather App**, where you will design the application's structure. **Integrating Weather APIs for Real-time Data** will teach you how to fetch live weather data and display it in your app.

On the frontend, **Frontend Development with Thymeleaf** introduces you to using Thymeleaf templates for dynamic content rendering. We will also cover essential aspects like **Exception Handling and Validation in Web Applications** to ensure your app is robust and user-friendly. Finally, you will learn about **Unit Testing with JUnit and E2E Testing with Rest-Assured** to validate your application's functionality and **Building and Managing the Project with Maven** to streamline your development process.

By the end of this chapter, you will be equipped to integrate databases into your Java projects and develop a complete, real-time weather application, which will further reinforce your understanding of both backend and frontend development in Java.

## Structure

This chapter covers the following topics:

- Configuring MySQL Database with JPA
- Defining JPA Entities and Data Access Operations
- Database Version Control with Liquibase

- Integrating Weather APIs for Real-time Data
- Frontend Development with Thymeleaf and Web Exception Handling
- Building and Managing the Project with Maven

# Configuring MySQL Database with JPA

In any modern web application, **persistence** is a critical aspect that allows data to be stored, retrieved, and managed efficiently. **MySQL**, being one of the most widely used relational databases, provides a reliable solution for managing structured data.

Spring Boot simplifies database integration with **Spring Data JPA (Java Persistence API)**, which allows developers to work with relational databases using **object-oriented concepts** rather than writing complex SQL queries manually. In this section, we will **configure MySQL with Spring Boot and JPA**, ensuring seamless data interaction in our **Weather App**.

# Installing and Setting Up MySQL

Before integrating MySQL with our Spring Boot project, we must ensure that MySQL is installed and running on our system. Follow the mentioned steps to do so:

## Installing MySQL

**For Ubuntu/Linux**

```
sudo apt update
sudo apt install mysql-server
sudo systemctl start mysql
sudo systemctl enable mysql
```

**For macOS (Using Homebrew)**

```
brew install mysql
brew services start mysql
```

**For Windows**

You can download and install MySQL from MySQL Official Site and start the MySQL server from the **MySQL Workbench** or **Command Line Client**.

## Creating a Database for the Weather App

Once MySQL is installed, open a terminal and log in to the MySQL shell:

```
mysql -u root -p
```

Then, create a new database for our weather application:

```
sql
CREATE DATABASE weather_db;
USE weather_db;
```

We have now successfully created the **`weather_db`** database to store our weather-related data.

```
bhargavbachina@MacBook-Pro lp % mysql -u root --skip-password
mysql: [Warning] Using a password on the command line interface can be insecure.
Welcome to the MySQL monitor.  Commands end with ; or \g.
Your MySQL connection id is 11
Server version: 9.2.0 Homebrew

Copyright (c) 2000, 2025, Oracle and/or its affiliates.

Oracle is a registered trademark of Oracle Corporation and/or its
affiliates. Other names may be trademarks of their respective
owners.

Type 'help;' or '\h' for help. Type '\c' to clear the current input statement.

mysql>
mysql>
mysql> CREATE DATABASE weather_db;
Query OK, 1 row affected (0.00 sec)

mysql> USE weather_db
Database changed
mysql> select * from weather_db
    ->
    ->
```

**Figure 5.1:** *Setting up mySql*

According to *Figure* 5.1, to build our **Spring Boot Weather Application**, we first generated the project using **Spring Initializr**, a tool to scaffold a Spring Boot application with the necessary dependencies. We selected **Maven** as the build tool, **Java 17** as the programming language, and **Spring Boot 3.4.3** as the framework version. The project metadata was configured with **group ID** **`com.weather`** and **artifact ID** demo. We included essential dependencies such as **Spring Web** for REST API development, **MySQL Driver** for database integration, **Thymeleaf** for frontend rendering, **Spring Boot DevTools** for hot-reloading, and **Lombok** to reduce boilerplate code. After generating the project, we extracted the downloaded **`.zip`** file and opened it in an IDE like **IntelliJ IDEA** or **VS Code** for further development.

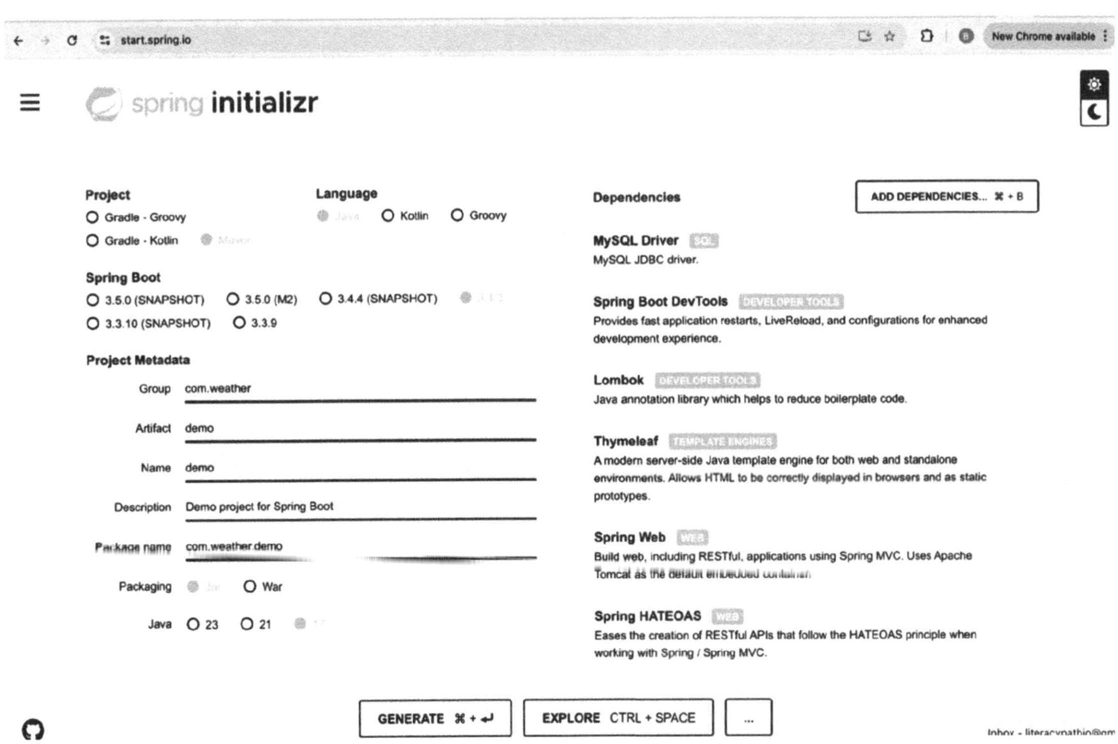


**Figure 5.2:** *Creating a Project*

The generated project structure follows the standard **Spring Boot application setup** and organizes files into different layers for maintainability. The **`src/main/java/com/weather/demo`** directory contains the main application file (**`WeatherApplication.java`**), along with separate packages for **controllers (handling API requests), services (business logic), models (data structures), and repositories (database operations)**. The **`src/main/resources`** directory includes configuration files such as **`application.properties`** for database and server settings. Using this structure, we can efficiently develop a **RESTful Weather Application**, integrating real-time weather data and persisting user information with **MySQL**.

# Adding MySQL and JPA Dependencies

To enable JPA and MySQL support in our Spring Boot project, we need to add the required dependencies in **`pom.xml`**:

The key dependencies are:

- **`spring-boot-starter-data-jpa`**→Provides JPA and Hibernate integration
- **`mysql-connector-java`**→Allows Spring Boot to communicate with MySQL
- **`liquibase-core`**→Helps in database version control and migrations

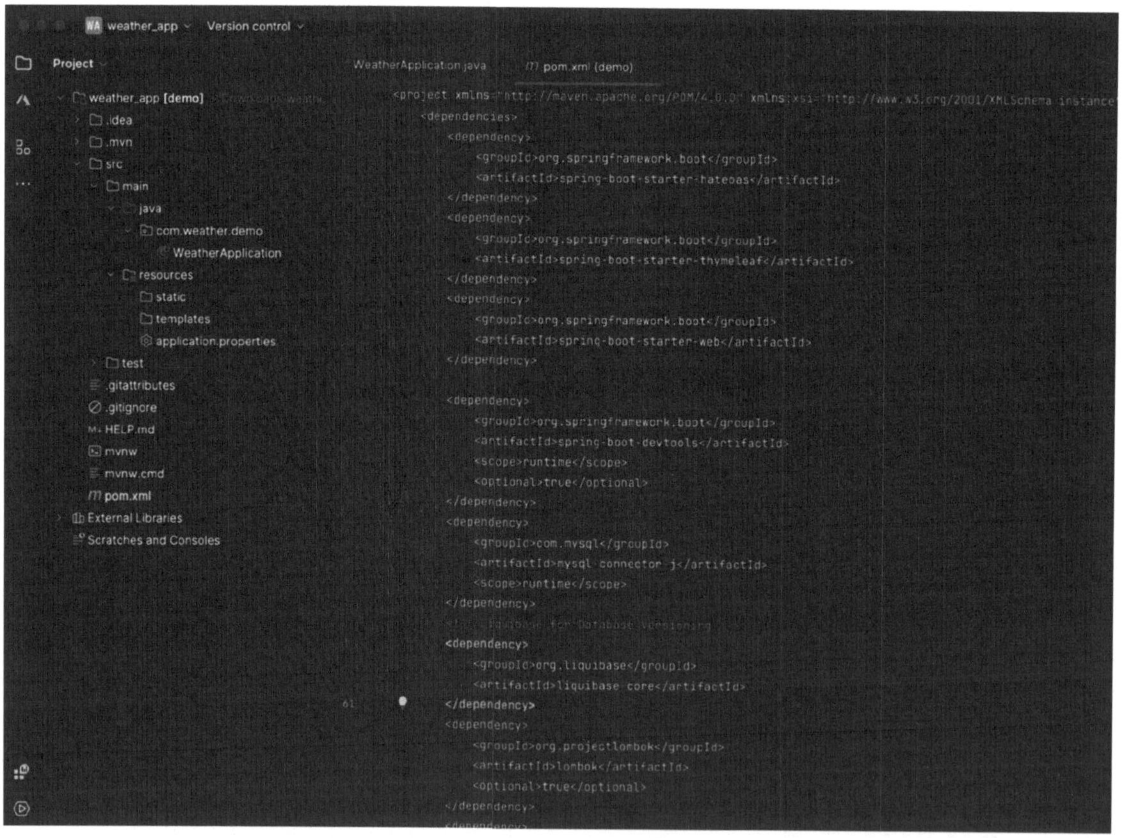


**Figure 5.3:** *pom.xml*

After adding the dependencies, run:

```
mvn clean install
```

This downloads and installs the required dependencies into the project.

# Configuring `application.properties` for MySQL Connection

Spring Boot requires a **database configuration** to establish a connection with MySQL. This is done in the **`src/main/resources/application.properties`** file as shown in the following figures:

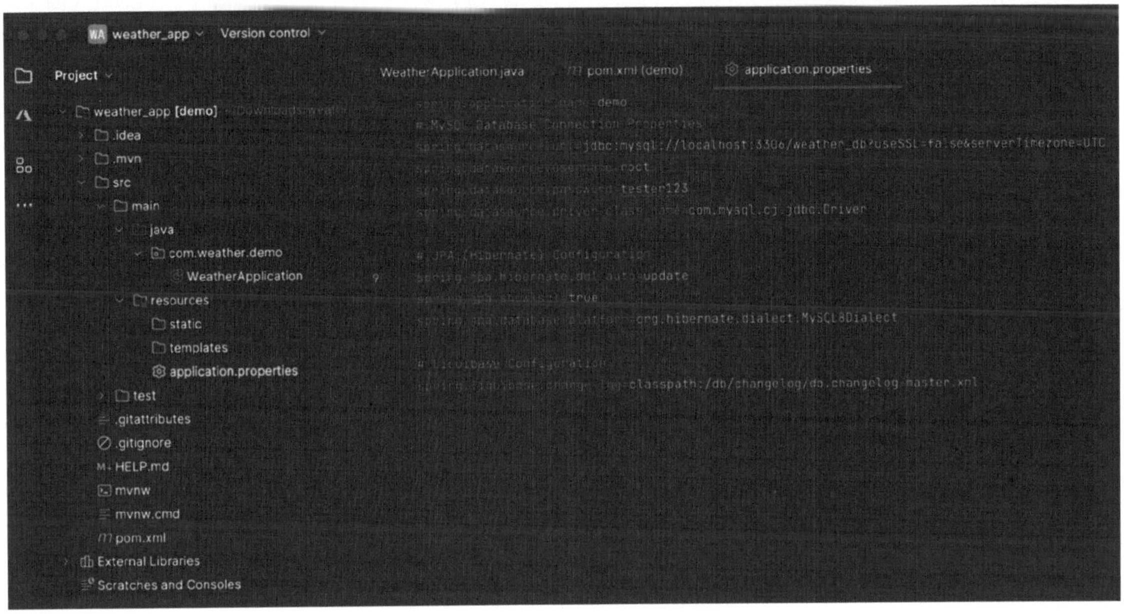


***Figure 5.4:*** *application.properties*

## Explanation of Properties:

1. **`spring.datasource.url`** → Defines the JDBC URL for connecting to MySQL
2. **`spring.datasource.username` and `spring.datasource.password`** → Specify MySQL credentials
3. **`spring.datasource.driver-class-name`** → Specifies the MySQL JDBC driver
4. **`spring.jpa.hibernate.ddl-auto=update`** → Automatically updates database tables based on entity changes
5. **`spring.jpa.show-sql=true`** → Logs SQL queries for debugging
6. **`spring.jpa.database-platform=org.hibernate.dialect.MySQL8Dialect`** → Optimizes Hibernate for MySQL
7. **`spring.liquibase.change-log`** → Points to Liquibase's database migration scripts

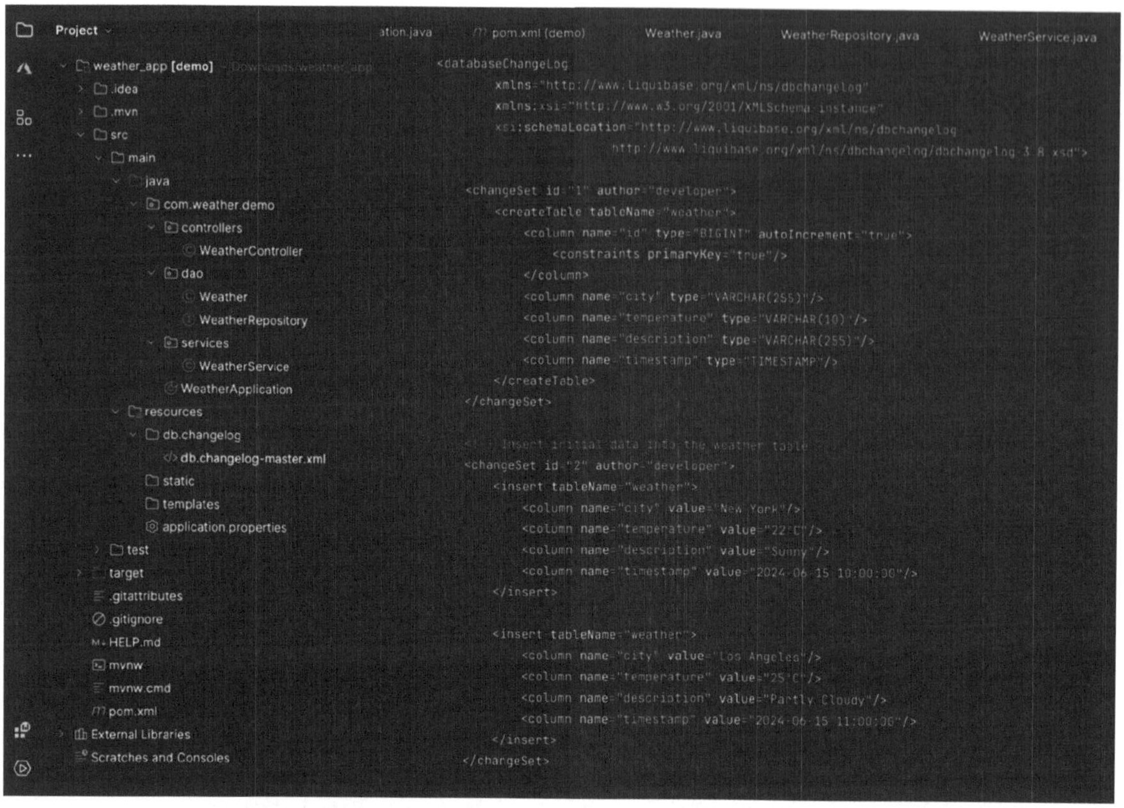


**Figure 5.5:** *Liquibase Config File*

# Testing the MySQL Connection

To verify that MySQL is configured correctly, start the Spring Boot application: We even inserted a couple of records through **liquibase xml**.

```
mvn spring-boot:run
```

```
mysql> use weather_db
Reading table information for completion of table and column names
You can turn off this feature to get a quicker startup with -A

Database changed
mysql>
mysql>
mysql>
mysql>
mysql>
mysql> SELECT * FROM weather;
+----+-------------+-------------+---------------+---------------------+
| id | city        | temperature | description   | timestamp           |
+----+-------------+-------------+---------------+---------------------+
|  1 | New York    | 22°C        | Sunny         | 2024-06-15 10:00:00 |
|  2 | Los Angeles | 25°C        | Partly Cloudy | 2024-06-15 11:00:00 |
+----+-------------+-------------+---------------+---------------------+
2 rows in set (0.00 sec)

mysql>
mysql>
```

**Figure 5.6:** *Testing Connection*

If the connection is successful, the application will start without errors, and you will see logs indicating that Hibernate has successfully initialized the database.

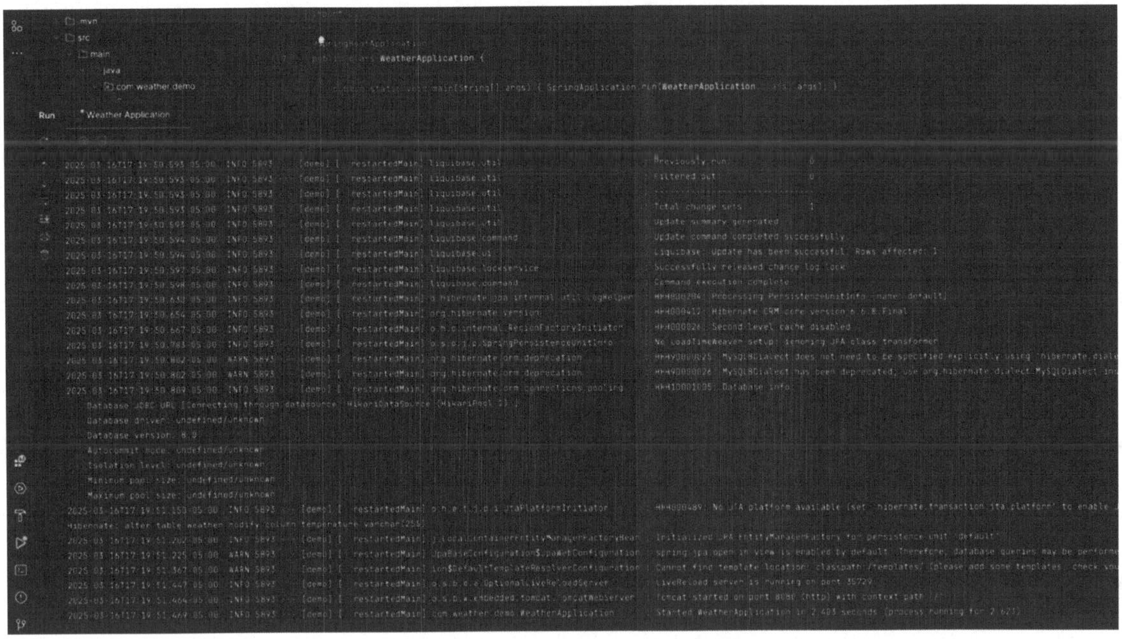

**Figure 5.7:** *Starting the Application*

# Defining JPA Entities and Data Access Operations

The Weather.java class is a JPA entity that represents the weather table in a MySQL database and is used for persisting weather-related data. It uses Lombok annotations such as **`@Data`** for automatic getter and setter generation and **`@AllArgsConstructor`** for a constructor with all fields. The class includes fields for id, city, temperature, description, and timestamp, with **`@JsonProperty`** annotations to control JSON field names when it is serializing objects to JSON responses. The id field is marked with **`@Id`** and **`@GeneratedValue(strategy = GenerationType.IDENTITY)`**, allowing MySQL to auto-generate unique IDs. The timestamp field is formatted with **`@JsonFormat(pattern = "yyyy-MM-dd HH:mm:ss")`** to ensure correct date-time serialization. Additionally, a no-argument constructor is explicitly defined to prevent JSON deserialization issues. This entity is essential for managing weather data in a Spring Boot application that integrates with a relational database.

```
pom.xml (demo)    Weather.java    WeatherRepository.java    WeatherService.java    WeatherController.java

import com.fasterxml.jackson.annotation.JsonProperty;
import jakarta.persistence.*;
import lombok.AllArgsConstructor;
import lombok.Data;

import java.time.LocalDateTime;

@Data  10 usages
@AllArgsConstructor
@Entity
@Table(name = "weather")
public class Weather {

    @Id
    @GeneratedValue(strategy = GenerationType.IDENTITY)
    @JsonProperty("id")
    private Long id;

    @JsonProperty("city")
    private String city;

    @JsonProperty("temperature")
    private String temperature;

    @JsonProperty("description")
    private String description;

    @JsonFormat(pattern = "yyyy-MM-dd HH:mm:ss")
    private LocalDateTime timestamp;

    public Weather() {}  no usages

    public Weather(String city, String temperature, String description, LocalDateTime timestamp) {  no usages
        this.city = city;
        this.temperature = temperature;
        this.description = description;
        this.timestamp = timestamp;
    }

}
```

***Figure 5.8:*** *Defining an Entity Class*

The **`WeatherRepository.java`** interface extends **`JpaRepository<Weather, Long>`**, allowing it to perform CRUD operations on the weather table without requiring explicit SQL queries. Marked with the **`@Repository`** annotation, this interface acts as the data access layer in the application and interacts with the database through Spring Data JPA. The method **`findByCity(String city)`** is a derived query method that automatically retrieves weather records based on the city name, leveraging Spring Data JPA's query method conventions. This eliminates the need for manually writing queries, making data retrieval efficient and readable. The repository integrates seamlessly with the **`WeatherService`**, ensuring that weather data is fetched and processed correctly before being returned to the controller for JSON serialization.

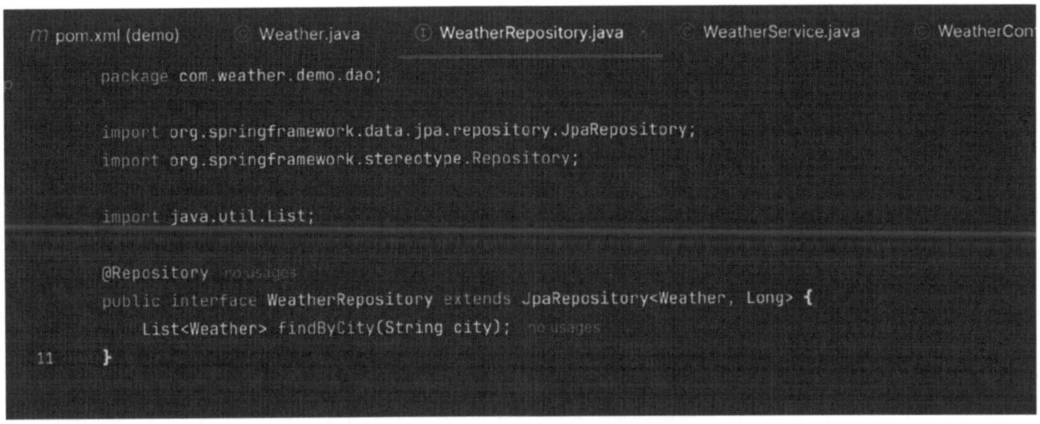


**Figure 5.9:** *Repository*

The **`WeatherService.java`** class follows the Service Layer Pattern, which acts as an intermediary between the controller and repository layers, ensuring separation of concerns and better maintainability. Annotated with **`@Service`**, this class encapsulates the business logic for retrieving, saving, and processing weather data. The **`WeatherRepository`** is injected using **`@Autowired`**, enabling seamless database access without explicitly instantiating the repository. The method **`getWeatherByCity(String city)`** fetches weather records for a specific city by delegating the query execution to the repository, while **`getWeatherData()`** retrieves all stored weather records. Additionally, **`saveWeather(Weather weather)`** persists a new weather entry into the database, leveraging Spring Data JPA's **`save()`** method. This service layer ensures that data retrieval and persistence operations are well-structured and promotes scalability and maintainability in the microservices architecture.

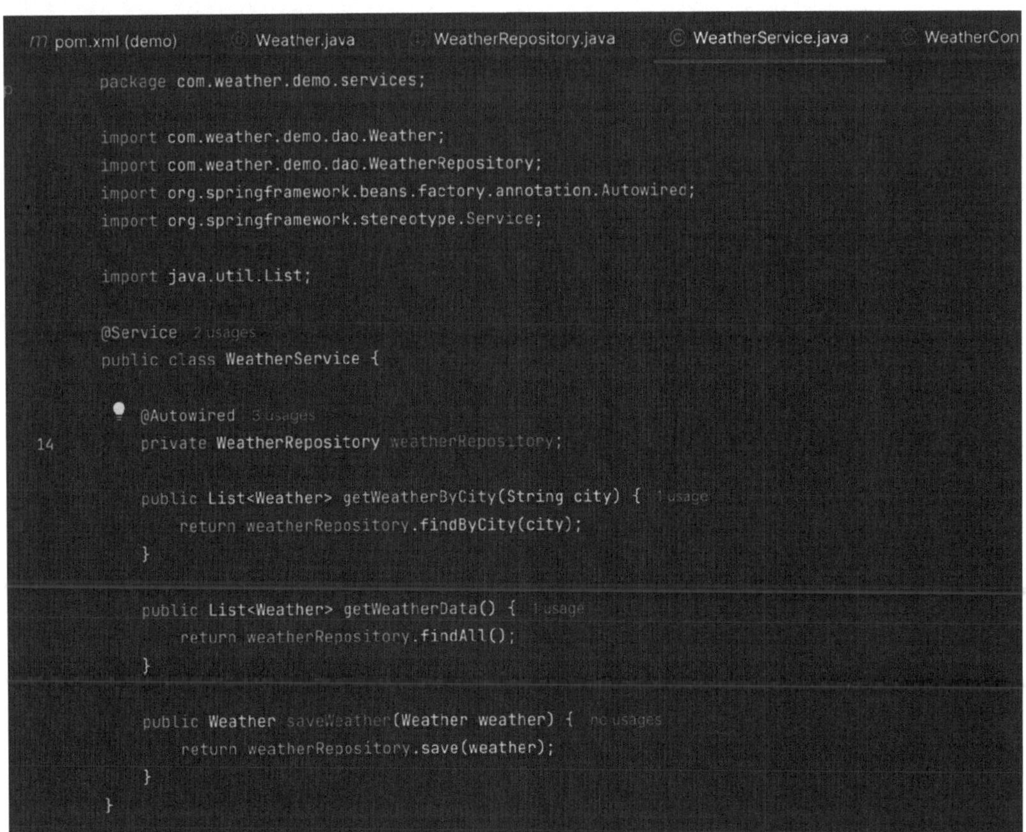


**Figure 5.10:** *Service*

The WeatherController.java class serves as the entry point for handling HTTP requests related to weather data, following the **Controller Layer Pattern** in Spring Boot's MVC architecture. Annotated with **@RestController**, it exposes RESTful endpoints under the base URL **/api/weather** using **@RequestMapping**. The controller is injected with the **WeatherService** using **@Autowired**, allowing it to delegate business logic execution to the service layer. The **getWeather(@PathVariable String city)** method maps GET requests to **/api/weather/{city}**, fetching weather data for a specific city by calling **weatherService.getWeatherByCity(city)**. Similarly, the **getWeatherData()** method, mapped to **/api/weather**, retrieves all stored weather records. This layered architecture ensures a clear separation of concerns, where the controller handles HTTP interactions, the service layer processes business logic, and the repository interacts with the database while making the application modular, maintainable, and scalable.

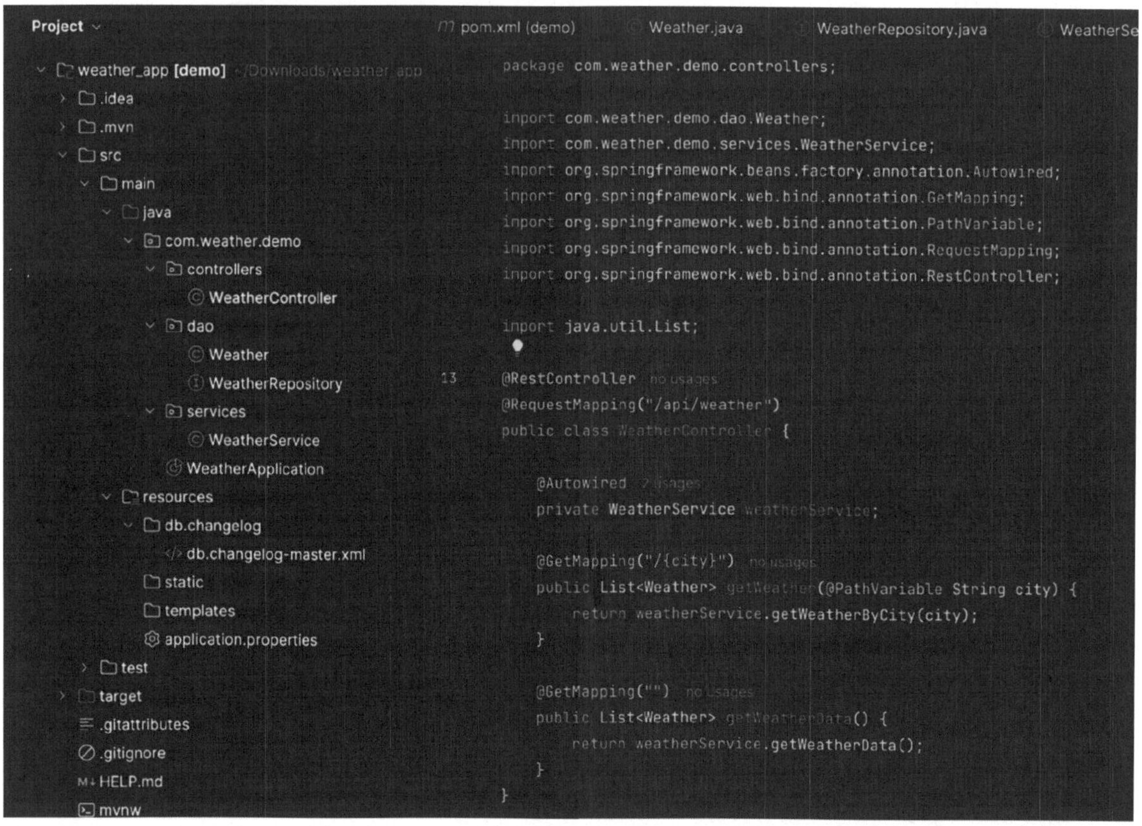


**Figure 5.11:** *Controller*

The screenshot displays the JSON response from the **Weather API**, accessed via the **/api/weather** endpoint in a web browser. The response consists of an array of **weather records**, each containing fields such as id, city, temperature, description, and timestamp. This confirms that the **Spring Boot application** is successfully fetching data from the **MySQL database**, processing it through the **service layer**, and serializing it into JSON format via the **REST controller**. The structured and properly formatted response indicates that **Spring Boot's Jackson integration is working correctly**, ensuring seamless object-to-JSON conversion. The timestamps are formatted in "**yyyy-MM-dd HH:mm:ss**", as specified in the entity class, providing clarity for time-based weather data.

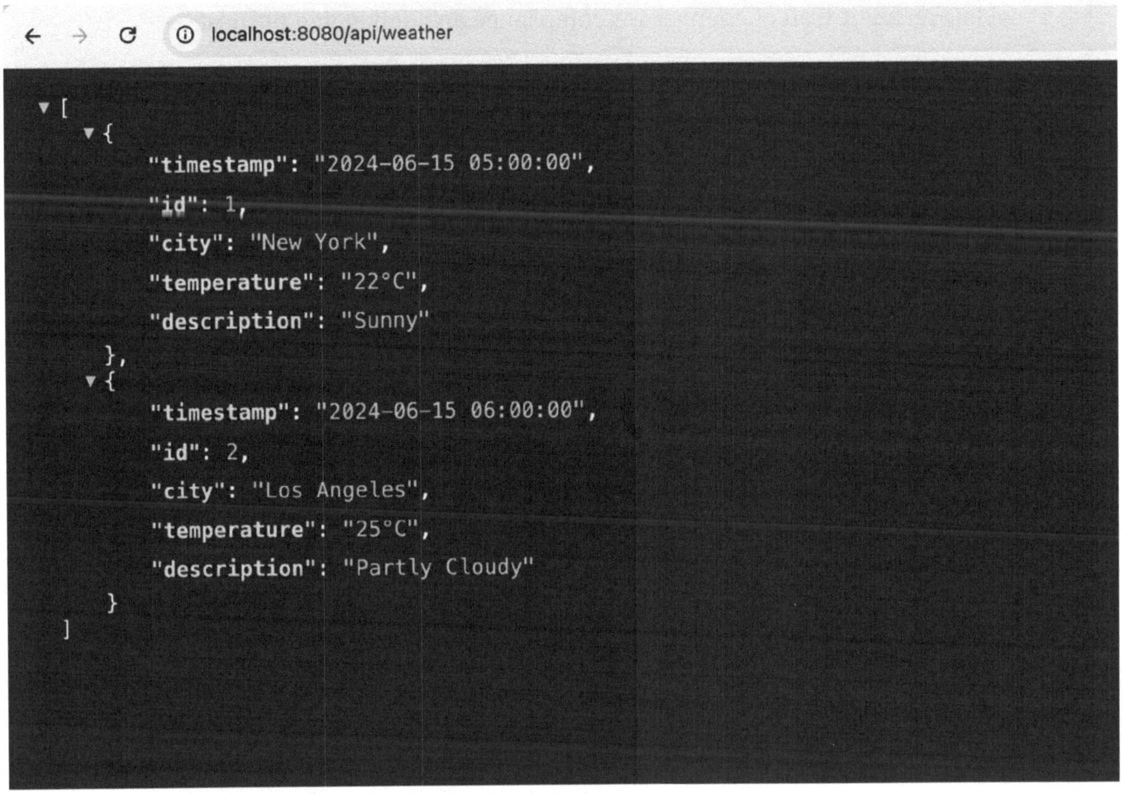


***Figure 5.12:*** *Testing the API*

This section demonstrated the end-to-end functionality of a Spring Boot-based Weather API, covering database configuration, entity mapping, repository interaction, service-layer processing, and RESTful API exposure. The successful JSON response validates that all components–from database interactions to API response serialization–are working as intended. With this foundation in place, the next step involves enhancing the application with additional features such as API security, error handling, and real-time data updates to further improve its reliability and scalability in a microservices architecture.

# Database Version Control with Liquibase

In modern application development, managing database schema changes efficiently is as critical as managing application code. Liquibase is a powerful open-source database version control tool that allows developers to track, version, and deploy database changes seamlessly. In our Weather API, we are using Liquibase to manage table creation, insert initial data, and ensure consistency across different environments. This section extends the previous discussion where we inserted two records into the weather table and further explores how Liquibase helps in version-controlling the database schema.

## Understanding Database Version Control with Liquibase

When working with relational databases, schema evolution is a common challenge. With manual SQL scripts, tracking changes, rolling back incorrect modifications, and ensuring different environments are in sync becomes complex. **Liquibase solves these issues by:**

- Maintaining a **history of database changes** using XML, YAML, JSON, or SQL-based changelogs
- Enabling **automated schema migration** during application deployment
- Supporting **rollback operations**, allowing developers to undo changes if needed

- Providing an **audit trail** of changes for compliance and debugging purposes

## Extending Liquibase Configuration for Weather Application

In our previous example, we created the **weather** table and inserted two records. Now, let us extend this by:

- Adding an **index** to optimize queries
- Introducing **rollback functionality** for safe database modifications

```
<!-- Adding an Index to Improve Query Performance -->
<changeSet id="3" author="developer">
    <createIndex indexName="idx_city" tableName="weather">
        <column name="city"/>
    </createIndex>
</changeSet>

<!-- Rollback Support for Safety -->
<changeSet id="4" author="developer">
    <addColumn tableName="weather">
        <column name="humidity" type="VARCHAR(10)"/>
    </addColumn>
    <rollback>
        <dropColumn tableName="weather" columnName="humidity"/>
    </rollback>
</changeSet>
```

***Figure 5.13:*** *Extending the Liquibase Configuration*

## Explanation of New Changes

- **ChangeSet id="3":** Introduces an **index (idx_city) on the city column** to optimize query performance, particularly for searches by city
- **ChangeSet id="4":**
  a. Adds a **new column humidity** to the **weather** table
  b. Implements a **rollback operation** so that if we need to **revert** the change, the **humidity** column will be **dropped**

## Applying and Testing the Changes

After modifying the Liquibase changelog file, apply the changes by running:

```
mvn liquibase:update
```

To verify that the changes have been applied, run the following SQL queries in MySQL:

```
mysql>
mysql>
mysql> SELECT * FROM weather;
+----+-------------+-------------+---------------+---------------------+
| id | city        | temperature | description   | timestamp           |
+----+-------------+-------------+---------------+---------------------+
|  1 | New York    | 22°C        | Sunny         | 2024-06-15 10:00:00 |
|  2 | Los Angeles | 25°C        | Partly Cloudy | 2024-06-15 11:00:00 |
+----+-------------+-------------+---------------+---------------------+
2 rows in set (0.00 sec)

mysql> SELECT * FROM weather;
+----+-------------+-------------+---------------+---------------------+----------+
| id | city        | temperature | description   | timestamp           | humidity |
+----+-------------+-------------+---------------+---------------------+----------+
|  1 | New York    | 22°C        | Sunny         | 2024-06-15 10:00:00 | NULL     |
|  2 | Los Angeles | 25°C        | Partly Cloudy | 2024-06-15 11:00:00 | NULL     |
+----+-------------+-------------+---------------+---------------------+----------+
2 rows in set (0.00 sec)
```

**Figure 5.14**: *Updating the Liquibase*

## Benefits of Using Liquibase

By integrating Liquibase into our Spring Boot Weather API, we ensure:

- **Consistent database structure** across environments (dev, QA, production)
- **Automated versioning** prevents schema drift and allows controlled database evolution
- **Rollback capability** provides a safety net for accidental schema modifications
- **Performance improvements** by applying indexes and schema optimizations systematically

In this section, we extended our **Liquibase-powered database version control** by adding **indexes for optimization**, **new columns for additional data**, and **rollback functionality** for safer migrations. With this setup, our Weather API ensures a **structured, version-controlled, and easily maintainable database**. In the next section, we will explore how to implement the **Spring MVC architecture for the Weather App**, connecting the database with a user-facing API for real-time weather data retrieval.

# Integrating Weather APIs for Real-Time Data

Now that we have successfully implemented the **Spring MVC architecture** for our **Weather App**, the next step is to **integrate real-time weather data** from an external API. This will enhance our application by providing **live weather updates** instead of relying solely on manually stored weather records in the database.

In this section, we will:

1. Select an appropriate **Weather API provider**
2. Configure **Spring Boot** to fetch weather data dynamically
3. Implement a **`service` class** to consume the API
4. Update our **controller** to return real-time weather data alongside stored records
5. Test the integration using **Postman or cURL**

# Choosing a Weather API Provider

Several public weather APIs provide real-time weather data, including:

- **OpenWeatherMap** (openweathermap.org)
- **WeatherAPI** (weatherapi.com)
- **WeatherStack** (weatherstack.com)

For this implementation, we will use **OpenWeatherMap**, which provides a **free-tier API** that allows fetching current weather data based on **city names, coordinates, or ZIP codes.**

# Configuring API Access in application.properties

To access the **OpenWeatherMap API**, we first need an **API key**. You can sign up for a free API key at **OpenWeatherMap**.

Once you get the **API key**, add it to **application.properties**:

```
spring.application.name=demo
# MySQL Database Connection Properties
spring.datasource.url=jdbc:mysql://localhost:3306/weather_db?useSSL=false&serverTimezone=UTC
spring.datasource.username=root
spring.datasource.password=tester123
spring.datasource.driver-class-name=com.mysql.cj.jdbc.Driver

# JPA (Hibernate) Configuration
spring.jpa.hibernate.ddl-auto=update
spring.jpa.show-sql=true
spring.jpa.database-platform=org.hibernate.dialect.MySQL8Dialect

# Liquibase Configuration
spring.liquibase.change-log=classpath:/db/changelog/db.changelog-master.xml

weather.api.url=https://api.openweathermap.org/data/2.5/weather
weather.api.key=your_api_key_here
weather.api.units=metric  # Use 'imperial' for Fahrenheit
```

***Figure 5.15:*** *Configuring API Access*

# Implementing the Weather API Service

The **WeatherAPIService** will handle API calls to **OpenWeatherMap** and retrieve real-time weather data.

**Explanation:**

1. Uses **Spring Boot's RestTemplate** to call **OpenWeatherMap** API
2. Constructs the API **URL dynamically** with the city name, API key, and units
3. Parses the JSON response using **Jackson's JsonNode**
4. Returns relevant weather data such as **temperature, humidity, wind speed, and description**

```
@Service
public class WeatherAPIService {

    @Value("${weather.api.url}")
    private String weatherApiUrl;

    @Value("${weather.api.key}")
    private String apiKey;

    @Value("${weather.api.units}")
    private String units;

    private final RestTemplate restTemplate = new RestTemplate();

    public Map<String, Object> getRealTimeWeather(String city) {
        String url = UriComponentsBuilder.fromHttpUrl(weatherApiUrl)
                .queryParam("q", city)
                .queryParam("appid", apiKey)
                .queryParam("units", units)
                .toUriString();

        JsonNode response = restTemplate.getForObject(url, JsonNode.class);

        if (response == null || response.has("cod") && response.get("cod").asInt() != 200) {
            throw new RuntimeException("Failed to fetch weather data for city: " + city);
        }

        Map<String, Object> weatherData = new HashMap<>();
        weatherData.put("city", city);
        weatherData.put("temperature", response.get("main").get("temp").asText() + "°C");
        weatherData.put("description", response.get("weather").get(0).get("description").asText());
        weatherData.put("humidity", response.get("main").get("humidity").asText() + "%");
        weatherData.put("wind speed", response.get("wind").get("speed").asText() + "m/s");

        return weatherData;
    }
}
```

***Figure 5.16:*** *Implementation of Weather Service*

# Updating the Controller to Fetch Live Weather

Now, we will **update `WeatherController`** to fetch both **stored weather records and real-time data**.

```java
@RestController
@RequestMapping("/api/weather")
public class WeatherController {

    @Autowired
    private WeatherService weatherService;

    @Autowired
    private WeatherAPIService weatherAPIService;

    @GetMapping("/{city}")
    public Map<String, Object> getWeather(@PathVariable String city) {
        return weatherAPIService.getRealTimeWeather(city);
    }

    @GetMapping("")
    public List<Weather> getWeatherData() {
        return weatherService.getWeatherData();
    }
}
```

***Figure 5.17:*** *Updating the Controller*

Integrating real-time weather data into our **Spring Boot Weather App** using the **`OpenWeatherMap`** **One Call API 3.0** has fetched us live weather updates dynamically. By using **latitude and longitude**, we now have a more precise and flexible approach to retrieving weather information compared to using static city names. The implementation of a **dedicated service layer (`WeatherAPIService`)** ensures modularity, making it easy to extend or switch API providers in the future.

With the proper **API key configured**, users can now query real-time weather data by simply providing latitude and longitude. To test this functionality, you can **use Postman, a web browser, or cURL** to send a request to our REST API and receive live weather details, including **temperature, humidity, wind speed, and a weather description**. If the API key is incorrect or expired, the application will return an error message, thereby ensuring a smooth user experience.

By successfully implementing real-time data retrieval, our Weather App is now dynamic and up-to-date. In the upcoming section, we will focus on **frontend integration using Thymeleaf**, where we will display the fetched weather data in a structured and user-friendly format.

# Frontend Development with Thymeleaf and Web Exception Handling

Now that we have developed the backend APIs to handle weather data using Spring Boot and exposed them through RESTful endpoints, it is time to bring the data to life on the frontend. In this section, we will explore how to use Thymeleaf, a modern server-side Java template engine, to build a clean and interactive user interface (UI) for our weather application. Additionally, we will implement web exception handling to gracefully manage and display error messages in the UI when something goes wrong.

## Integrating Thymeleaf for UI Rendering

Thymeleaf integrates seamlessly with Spring Boot and supports natural HTML templates that can be rendered directly in browsers. It allows you to dynamically inject model attributes from the controller into your HTML pages without requiring a separate frontend framework. This is especially useful for applications that do not require complex front-end logic.

To begin, create an **`index.html`** file under **`src/main/resources/templates`**:

```
<!DOCTYPE html>
<html xmlns:th="http://www.thymeleaf.org">
<head>
    <title>Weather Dashboard</title>
</head>
<body>
<h1>Weather Information</h1>
<form th:action="@{/weather}" method="get">
    <label for="city">Enter City:</label>
    <input type="text" name="city" id="city">
    <button type="submit">Get Weather</button>
</form>

<div th:if="${weatherList != null}">
    <h2>Results:</h2>
    <table border="1">
        <tr>
            <th>City</th>
            <th>Temperature</th>
            <th>Description</th>
            <th>Timestamp</th>
        </tr>
        <tr th:each="weather : ${weatherList}">
            <td th:text="${weather.city}"></td>
            <td th:text="${weather.temperature}"></td>
            <td th:text="${weather.description}"></td>
            <td th:text="${weather.timestamp}"></td>
        </tr>
    </table>
</div>
</body>
</html>
```

**Figure 5.18:** *Integrating Thymeleaf*

In your controller, return the model and view:

```
@GetMapping("/weather")
public String viewWeather(@RequestParam String city, Model model) {
    List<Weather> weatherList = weatherService.getWeatherByCity(city);
    model.addAttribute("weatherList", weatherList);
    return "index";
}s
```

**Figure 5.19:** *Returning the Model View*

This approach allows us to collect input from the user, send it to the backend, and render a dynamic table of weather data, all from a single HTML page.

# Implementing Web Exception Handling

To improve user experience and system robustness, it is important to handle exceptions that may occur during execution, such as when a city is not found or the API call fails. Instead of returning technical error messages, we can use Spring Boot's exception handling capabilities to show user-friendly messages on the UI.

Create a global exception handler class:

```
@ControllerAdvice
public class GlobalExceptionHandler {

    @ExceptionHandler(Exception.class)
    public String handleGeneralException(Exception ex, Model model) {
        model.addAttribute("errorMessage", "Something went wrong: " +
ex.getMessage());
        return "error";
    }

    @ExceptionHandler(NoSuchElementException.class)
    public String handleNoSuchElementException(NoSuchElementException ex,
Model model) {
        model.addAttribute("errorMessage", "City not found. Please try
again.");
        return "error";
    }
}
```

**Figure 5.20:** *Implementing Web Exception Handling*

Create a simple **error.html** template:

```
<!DOCTYPE html>
<html xmlns:th="http://www.thymeleaf.org">
<head>
    <title>Error</title>
</head>
<body>
<h1>Error</h1>
<p th:text="${errorMessage}"></p>
<a th:href="@{/}">Go Back</a>
</body>
</html>
```

**Figure 5.21:** *Error.html*

With this in place, any exception thrown during controller execution will be intercepted and rendered on a user-friendly error page. This not only helps developers during debugging but also guides end users with informative feedback.

By combining **Thymeleaf** for frontend rendering with **Spring Boot's global exception handling**, we have established a solid foundation for a well-structured and user-friendly web application. Thymeleaf enables us to build dynamic HTML pages that respond to user input and display real-time data from our backend services. It bridges the gap between server-side logic and client-side presentation by allowing developers to inject data directly into HTML templates. This makes it easier to keep the UI and backend tightly integrated, especially for Java developers who prefer full-stack development within a single framework.

Meanwhile, Spring's global exception handling mechanism ensures that unexpected errors, such as data not being found or backend failures, are gracefully managed and communicated to the user. Rather than exposing raw stack traces or confusing error codes, the application can redirect users to friendly error pages with meaningful messages. This improves user experience and also adds a layer of professionalism and trust to your application.

Now that you have seen how to implement a basic weather dashboard with search functionality, this is a great point to **experiment further and enhance the UI**. You can try adding new pages that display additional details like humidity, wind speed, or forecasts for multiple days. You can also build a landing page, a historical data view, or a city favorites list that stores commonly searched locations. These enhancements will make your application more useful while providing you valuable experience in working with Thymeleaf templates, controller routing, and Spring MVC patterns.

As we move to the next section, we will connect the application to **real-time weather APIs** to dynamically fetch and display current weather information based on user input. This will bring the project to life, allowing it to go beyond static or preloaded data and interact with external data providers, taking your Spring Boot application to the next level.

# Building and Managing the Project with Maven

As your Spring Boot weather application grows in complexity and size, managing builds, dependencies, and project structure becomes increasingly important. Apache Maven is a powerful build automation tool used extensively in the Java ecosystem to simplify these tasks. In this section, we will explore how Maven helps in managing our Spring Boot project, from resolving dependencies to building and packaging the application for deployment.

**What is Maven and Why Should We Use It?**

Maven is a project management and build tool that follows a standardized project layout. It uses an XML file (`pom.xml`) to describe the structure and dependencies of a Java project. It abstracts many repetitive tasks such as compiling source code, running tests, packaging the application into JAR or WAR files, and managing external libraries.

One of Maven's key benefits is dependency management. Instead of manually downloading and referencing external libraries; you can simply declare them in the `pom.xml` file, and Maven will automatically download the correct versions from central repositories. This ensures consistent builds across environments and makes it easier to manage updates or conflicts.

## The `pom.xml` File

Your Spring Boot project comes with a `pom.xml` file, which is the core configuration file for Maven. Here is a simplified breakdown of what it typically includes:

```xml
<dependencies>
    <!-- Spring Boot Starter Web -->
    <dependency>
        <groupId>org.springframework.boot</groupId>
        <artifactId>spring-boot-starter-web</artifactId>
    </dependency>

    <!-- Spring Data JPA -->
    <dependency>
        <groupId>org.springframework.boot</groupId>
        <artifactId>spring-boot-starter-data-jpa</artifactId>
    </dependency>

    <!-- MySQL Driver -->
    <dependency>
        <groupId>mysql</groupId>
        <artifactId>mysql-connector-java</artifactId>
        <scope>runtime</scope>
    </dependency>

    <!-- Thymeleaf -->
    <dependency>
        <groupId>org.springframework.boot</groupId>
        <artifactId>spring-boot-starter-thymeleaf</artifactId>
    </dependency>
</dependencies>
```

***Figure 5.22:*** *Dependencies*

Each **`<dependency>`** tag defines a library that your application needs. Maven will download these libraries automatically and include them during the build process.

# Building the Project

To compile and build your Spring Boot project using Maven, you can run the following command from the terminal:

```
mvn clean install
```

- **`clean`**: Deletes the **`target/`** directory to ensure a fresh build
- **`install`**: Compiles the source code, runs tests, and packages the project into a deployable JAR file

After a successful build, you will find the output JAR file in the **`target/`**directory, which can be executed with:

```
java -jar target/demo-0.0.1-SNAPSHOT.jar
```

# Running the Application

You can also run the application directly using Maven without explicitly building the JAR:

```
mvn spring-boot:run
```

This command compiles your code and launches the embedded Tomcat server with your loaded application.

## Managing Profiles and Environments

Maven allows you to define profiles to manage different configurations for environments such as **dev**, **test**, and **prod**. You can activate profiles from the command line:

```
mvn spring-boot:run -Dspring-boot.run.profiles=dev
```

In conjunction with Spring's **application-dev.properties** and **application-prod.properties**, this paves the way for environment-specific configurations without changing the core codebase.

**Best Practices with Maven**

- **Keep your dependencies up to date**, but avoid unnecessary additions that bloat your build.
- **Use dependency scopes** (**compile**, **runtime**, **test**) appropriately.
- **Use plugins** like the Spring Boot Maven Plugin for easy builds and deployment.
- **Document your build process** and maintain a consistent project structure.

# Conclusion

In modern Java development, especially with Spring Boot applications, Apache Maven is an indispensable tool. It brings structure and consistency to the entire project lifecycle–right from compiling source code and managing dependencies, to running tests and producing deployable artifacts. By relying on Maven, developers avoid the pitfalls of manual dependency handling, configuration mismatches, and inconsistent builds across environments.

Through the **pom.xml** configuration, Maven not only declares what your application needs but also controls how it is built, tested, and deployed. Whether you are managing multiple environments, integrating third-party libraries, or collaborating with a team, Maven provides the standardization and automation necessary to maintain quality and efficiency. Integrating it with tools like Spring Boot, Docker, and CI/CD systems such as Jenkins or GitHub Actions makes it a cornerstone of any scalable development pipeline.

As we move forward in our application journey into areas like containerization with Docker and orchestration using Kubernetes, Maven will continue to serve as the foundation for packaging and distributing our microservices. It will automate tasks, streamline deployment processes, and support production-ready builds. Learning to use Maven today will pay dividends later as your projects scale in size, complexity, and sophistication.

With Maven providing the build foundation, we will now focus on constructing a fully functional, real-time chat application in Java. In the next chapter, you will learn how to architect scalable systems, implement real-time messaging with WebSockets, build secure backend services, design modern frontend interfaces, and integrate conversational AI using OpenAI's APIs. By the end of it, you will have a production-ready, intelligent chat application and a deep understanding of how to combine microservices, messaging protocols, and AI for powerful communication experiences.

# Part 3

# Advancing Further with Java Project Development

(Chapters 6–7)

# CHAPTER 6
# Building a Chat Application with Java

## Introduction

In today's digital world, chat applications have become indispensable for enabling real-time communication across the globe. This chapter will walk you through the end-to-end development of a modern, intelligent chat application using Java–from the foundational setup to integrating conversational AI.

We will begin by **designing and architecting the chat application** while focusing on establishing a scalable structure and message flow to ensure long-term maintainability. Next, we will dive into **implementing real-time communication using WebSockets**, enabling instant bi-directional messaging that forms the core of any chat experience.

We will then move on to **developing the backend and implementing a secure user management system**, covering message handling, persistence, authentication, and access control. Once the server side is in place, we will focus on **building the frontend interface** to craft a responsive and intuitive UI that users can engage with seamlessly.

In the second half of the chapter, we will explore **integrating OpenAI APIs and applying prompt engineering techniques** to enhance conversational capabilities and empower the chat app to deliver meaningful, contextual responses. Finally, we will touch upon **ethical AI usage**, addressing privacy, personalization, and responsible deployment practices.

By the end of this chapter, you will have the tools and techniques needed to build a fully functional, secure, and AI-powered chat application with Java, and will be ready to support both real-time messaging and intelligent interaction.

## Structure

This chapter addresses the following topics:

- Designing and Architecting the Chat Application
- Implementing Real-Time Communication with WebSockets
- Developing the Backend and Security Layer
- Building the Frontend Interface
- Integrating OpenAI APIs and Prompt Engineering
- Ensuring Responsible AI Usage

## Designing and Architecting the Chat Application

Designing a modern chat application is a multifaceted challenge that requires careful consideration of scalability, fault tolerance, security, real-time performance, and adaptability to evolving user needs. This section explores each architectural decision point in depth, providing the foundational knowledge for building a robust, production-ready chat system.

# Core Architectural Components

A scalable chat application is typically built on a distributed, client-server architecture that separates concerns and enables independent scaling as well as maintenance of each subsystem.

## Client-Server Model

At its heart, the chat application uses a client-server paradigm where:

- Clients (web browsers, mobile apps, desktop clients) interact with the backend via APIs and persistent connections (WebSockets) for real-time updates.
- The server manages business logic, message routing, authentication, and integration with databases and other services.

This separation ensures that as the user base grows, both the client and server components can be scaled independently to meet the demand.

## Microservices Architecture

Modern chat applications benefit from a microservices approach, where each core function is encapsulated in its own service. Typical microservices include:

- **Authentication Service:** Manages user registration, login, OAuth2/JWT token issuance, and multi-factor authentication
- **Messaging Service:** Handles message delivery, storage, and real-time communication via WebSockets or similar protocols
- **Notification Service:** Sends push notifications or in-app alerts for new messages, mentions, or system events
- **Media Service**: Manages file uploads, image processing, and secure storage (for example, AWS S3, GCP Cloud Storage)
- **Presence Service:** Tracks user online/offline status and delivers present updates to contacts

This modularization allows teams to develop, deploy, and scale each service independently, improving fault isolation and maintainability.

## Database Layer

A hybrid database strategy is often employed to balance performance, flexibility, and consistency:

- **Relational Database (example, PostgreSQL):** Stores structured data such as user profiles, group memberships, and access control lists
- **NoSQL Database (example, MongoDB):** Stores chat messages and conversation history, benefiting from schema flexibility and high write throughput
- **In-Memory Store (example, Redis):** Caches active sessions, user presence, and frequently accessed metadata for low-latency access

Data partitioning (sharding) is used to distribute chat history across multiple database nodes, often by user region or chat room, to reduce latency and improve scalability.

# Application Server

The application server is the central orchestrator and executes business logic, handles API requests, and manages real-time communication channels. It is stateless to support horizontal scaling, meaning that any server instance can handle any request and user state is stored in external systems (such as databases or caches).

# Scalability and Fault Tolerance

**Horizontal Scaling:** To handle spikes in user activity (such as during major events), chat servers are deployed as stateless containers or VMs behind a load balancer (like NGINX and AWS ALB). This allows the system to elastically scale up or down based on demand, thus optimizing resource usage and cost.

**Redundancy and High Availability**

- **Multi-Region Deployment:** Infrastructure is distributed across multiple geographic regions to ensure high availability, even if a data center or region fails.
- **Redundant Services:** Each microservice runs on multiple instances, so if one fails, others can seamlessly take over the workload.
- **Message Brokers (like RabbitMQ, Kafka):** Decouple message producers from consumers, enabling reliable message delivery and processing, even during failures or spikes in traffic.

**Data Integrity and Consistency**

- **Message Ordering:** Use sequence numbers or timestamps to preserve the order of messages, especially in distributed systems.
- **Exactly-Once Delivery:** Implement mechanisms to prevent duplicate message delivery, such as idempotent message IDs and deduplication logic.
- **Event Sourcing:** Log all message events for auditability and replay in case of system recovery.

**Dynamic Elasticity:** The system must be able to automatically add or remove capacity in real time, responding to traffic fluctuations without manual intervention. This is achieved via container orchestration platforms (Kubernetes, Docker Swarm) and cloud auto-scaling features.

# Security and Compliance

Security is a non-negotiable aspect of chat application architecture:

- **End-to-End Encryption (E2EE):** Ensures that only intended recipients can read messages, protecting against eavesdropping, even from the server itself
- **Transport Layer Security (TLS):** All communications between clients and servers are encrypted using the latest TLS protocols to prevent man-in-the-middle attacks
- **Authentication and Authorization:** Uses secure token-based authentication (OAuth2, JWT), role-based access control (RBAC), and enforce strong password policies and multi-factor authentication
- **Data Protection:** Encrypts sensitive data at rest (AES-256), enforce data retention and deletion policies, and comply with regulations such as GDPR
- **Input Sanitization:** Prevents XSS and injection attacks by sanitizing user-generated content and applying content security policies
- **DDoS Protection:** Employs rate limiting, IP reputation checks, and cloud-based DDoS mitigation services (Cloudflare, AWS Shield) to maintain service availability under attack

## Monitoring, Logging, and Observability

A production-grade chat application must include:

- **Centralized Logging:** Aggregate logs from all services for real-time monitoring and forensic analysis (ELK stack, Splunk)
- **Metrics and Health Checks:** Use Prometheus, Grafana, or similar tools to monitor system health, latency, error rates, and resource utilization
- **Alerting:** Set up alerts for abnormal patterns (such as message delivery failures, unauthorized access attempts) to enable rapid response

## Key Architectural Patterns and Best Practices

To ensure scalable, decoupled, and resilient architecture, modern systems often incorporate the following foundational patterns and principles:

- **Pub/Sub Messaging:** Use publish/subscribe patterns for message distribution, enabling efficient, scalable, and decoupled communication between components
- **Statelessness:** Design services to be stateless wherever possible, storing session and user state externally to maximize scalability and resilience
- **Multi-Tenancy:** Architect for multi-tenancy of supporting multiple organizations, ensuring data isolation and access control at every layer
- **API-First Design:** Expose well-documented APIs for all client interactions, enabling extensibility and integration with third-party service

## Example: End-to-End Message Flow

A typical end-to-end message flow in a real-time chat application involves the following sequential steps:

1. The user sends a message from the client app.
2. WebSocket connection transmits the message to the backend messaging service.
3. Message broker (for example, Kafka) queues the message for delivery and persistence.
4. Messaging service stores the message in MongoDB, and updates user presence in Redis.
5. Notification service triggers push notifications to recipients.
6. Clients receive the message via WebSocket, updating the UI in real time.

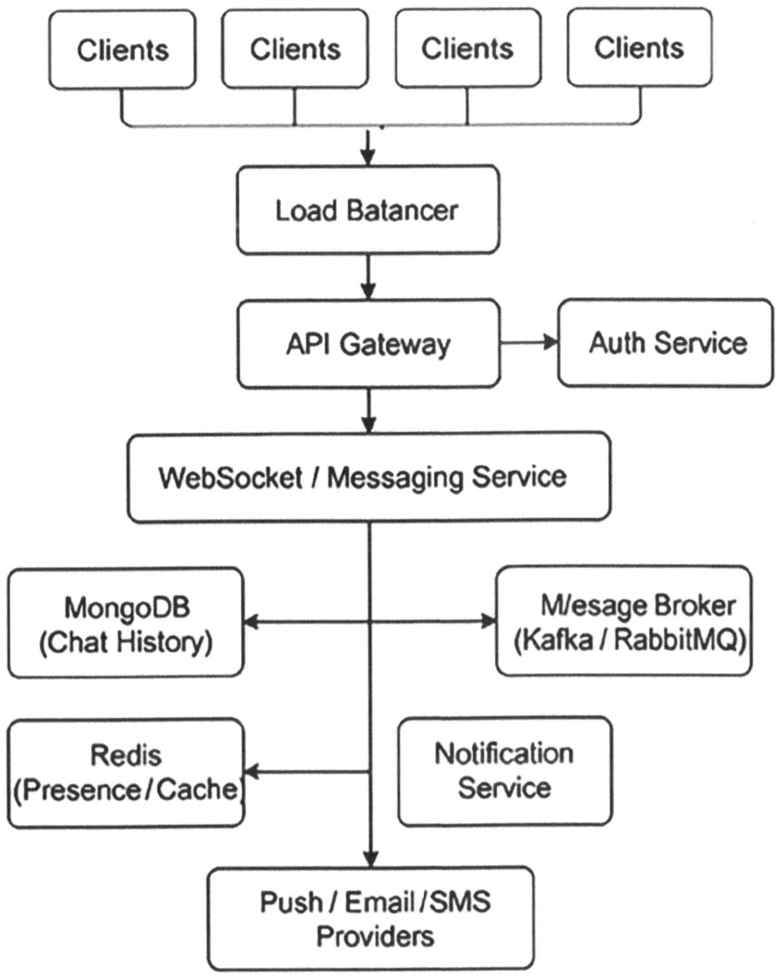


**Figure 6.1:** *End to End Message Flow*

A well-architected chat application is the result of thoughtful design choices that balance scalability, fault tolerance, security, and user experience. By leveraging a microservices architecture, hybrid data storage, robust security practices, and dynamic scaling, developers can build chat systems that are responsive, reliable, and ready for millions of concurrent users. As user expectations and technologies evolve, this architectural foundation ensures that the chat application can adapt, scale, and deliver real-time communication at a global scale.

# Implementing Real-Time Communication with WebSockets

WebSockets enable bidirectional, low-latency communication between clients and servers, making them ideal for chat applications, live notifications, and collaborative tools. The following is a detailed implementation guide for Java, covering both raw WebSocket APIs and Spring Boot integrations, with best practices from industry standards.

## WebSocket Basics in Java

The Java API for WebSocket (JSR 356) provides annotations and classes to create endpoints.

## Server Endpoint Example

The **ChatEndpoint** class is a Java WebSocket server endpoint that enables real-time communication between multiple clients. Annotated with **@ServerEndpoint("/chat")**, it listens for WebSocket connections at the **/chat** URI. The class maintains a synchronized set of active client sessions, adding new sessions when clients connect and removing them on disconnect. When a client sends a message, the **@OnMessage** method broadcasts that message to all other connected clients, enabling group chat functionality. Error handling is provided via the **@OnError** method, ensuring that any connection or messaging issues are logged for troubleshooting. This example demonstrates the core mechanics of a chat server using Java's standard WebSocket API.

```
import javax.websocket.*;
import javax.websocket.server.ServerEndpoint;
import java.io.IOException;
import java.util.Collections;
import java.util.HashSet;
import java.util.Set;

@ServerEndpoint("/chat")
public class ChatEndpoint {
    private static final Set<Session> clients =
        Collections.synchronizedSet(new HashSet<>());

    @OnOpen
    public void onOpen(Session session) {
        clients.add(session);
        System.out.println("Client connected: " + session.getId());
    }

    @OnClose
    public void onClose(Session session) {
        clients.remove(session);
        System.out.println("Client disconnected: " + session.getId());
    }

    @OnMessage
    public void onMessage(String message, Session sender) throws IOException {

        // Broadcast message to all clients except sender
        for (Session client : clients) {
            if (!client.equals(sender)) {
                client.getBasicRemote().sendText(message);
            }
        }
    }

    @OnError
    public void onError(Session session, Throwable error) {
        error.printStackTrace();
    }
}
```

***Figure 6.2:*** *Server Endpoint Example*

## Client Implementation

The **ChatClient** class illustrates how a Java application can act as a WebSocket client to connect and interact with the chat server. Marked with **@ClientEndpoint**, it defines a method to handle incoming messages from the server and simply prints them to the console. The main method uses a **WebSocketContainer** to establish a connection to the server endpoint at **ws://localhost:8080/chat**.

Once connected, the client can send and receive messages in real time, participating in the group chat managed by the server. This straightforward implementation provides the foundation for building interactive chat clients in Java, which can be extended with user input, authentication, and advanced message handling as needed.

```
import javax.websocket.*;
import java.net.URI;

@ClientEndpoint
public class ChatClient {
    @OnMessage
    public void onMessage(String message) {
        System.out.println("Received: " + message);
    }

    public static void main(String[] args) throws Exception {
        WebSocketContainer container =
ContainerProvider.getWebSocketContainer();
        container.connectToServer(
            ChatClient.class,
            URI.create("ws://localhost:8080/chat")
        );
        System.out.println("Connected to server");
    }
}
```

**Figure 6.3:** *Client Implementation*

# Spring Boot and STOMP over WebSocket

WebSocket enables full-duplex communication between clients and servers, while Simple Text Oriented Messaging Protocol (STOMP) adds structure to messages with headers and destinations. Spring Boot simplifies this integration with annotations and auto-configuration.

# Configuration

**Dependencies:**

```
Include spring-boot-starter-websocket in pom.xml:
<dependency>
    <groupId>org.springframework.boot</groupId>
    <artifactId>spring-boot-starter-websocket</artifactId>
</dependency>
```

**WebSocket `Configuration` Class:**

- **`@EnableWebSocketMessageBroker`**: Enables STOMP broker relay and WebSocket handling
- **`registerStompEndpoints`**:
  - Defines **`/ws`** as the WebSocket endpoint
  - **`withSockJS()`** adds fallback support for browsers without WebSocket

- `configureMessageBroker`:
  - `/topic`: Messages sent to destinations prefixed with `/topic` are broadcast to all subscribed clients
  - `/app`: Routes messages to `@MessageMapping`-annotated methods

```
@Configuration
@EnableWebSocketMessageBroker
public class WebSocketConfig implements WebSocketMessageBrokerConfigurer {

    @Override
    public void registerStompEndpoints(StompEndpointRegistry registry) {
        registry.addEndpoint("/ws").withSockJS(); // WebSocket endpoint
    }

    @Override
    public void configureMessageBroker(MessageBrokerRegistry registry) {
        registry.enableSimpleBroker("/topic"); // Broker for broadcasting
        registry.setApplicationDestinationPrefixes("/app"); // Prefix for
client-to-server
    }
}
```

***Figure 6.4:*** *Websocket Configuration*

**Message Handling Controller:**

- `@MessageMapping("/send")`: Maps incoming messages sent to `/app/send` (due to the `/app` prefix in `config`)
- `@SendTo("/topic/messages")`: Sends the return value to all subscribers of `/topic/messages`

```
@Controller
public class ChatController {

    @MessageMapping("/send")
    @SendTo("/topic/messages")
    public Greeting sendMessage(HelloMessage message) {
        return new Greeting("Hello, " + message.getName() + "!");
    }
}
```

***Figure 6.5:*** *Websocket Configuration*

# Client-Side Implementation

- `SockJS`: Handles WebSocket connection with fallbacks
- `stompClient.subscribe()`: Listens for messages on `/topic/messages`
- `stompClient.send()`: Sends messages to `/app/send`, triggering the controller method

```
const socket = new SockJS('/ws');
const stompClient = Stomp.over(socket);

stompClient.connect({}, () => {
    // Subscribe to topic
    stompClient.subscribe('/topic/messages', (message) => {
        console.log('Received:', JSON.parse(message.body));
    });

    // Send message to server
    stompClient.send('/app/send', {}, JSON.stringify({ name: 'Alice' }));
});
```

***Figure 6.6:*** *Client Side Implementation*

Spring Boot's STOMP over WebSocket provides a robust framework for real-time applications. By leveraging destinations, brokers, and Spring's annotation-driven model, developers can efficiently implement features such as chat, notifications, and live updates. For production, it is advisable to always secure connections, use external brokers, and plan for horizontal scaling.

# Best Practices for Spring Boot with STOMP over WebSocket

To build secure, reliable, and maintainable chat applications using Spring Boot and STOMP over WebSocket, these best practices should be followed:

- **Secure All Connections**: Always use encrypted WebSocket connections (`wss://`) to protect data in transit. Configure SSL/TLS on your server and ensure clients connect securely.
- **Enable Heartbeat Monitoring**: Configure heartbeat intervals between client and server to detect and close stale or dead connections, preventing resource leaks and improving reliability.
- **Implement Robust Error Handling**: Set up centralized error handling for your WebSocket controllers to gracefully manage exceptions and provide meaningful feedback to clients.
- **Throttle and Limit Connections**: Apply rate limiting and connection throttling to prevent abuse, denial-of-service attacks, and ensure fair resource allocation among users.
- **Manage User Sessions Effectively**: Track active user sessions and clean up disconnected or idle sessions promptly to optimize server resource usage and maintain accurate presence information.
- **Authenticate and Authorize WebSocket Connections**: Integrate your WebSocket endpoints with your authentication and authorization mechanisms (such as JWT or session-based auth) to ensure only authorized users can connect and interact.
- **Use Appropriate Message Destinations**: Organize your message routing using clear and consistent destination prefixes (such as `/app` for inbound and `/topic` for outbound messages) to keep your messaging architecture maintainable and scalable.
- **Plan for Scalability and Clustering**: For high-traffic applications, use external message brokers (such as RabbitMQ or Kafka) and session clustering (with Redis or similar) to synchronize messages and sessions across multiple server instances.

- **Monitor and Log WebSocket Activity**: Implement comprehensive logging and monitoring for all WebSocket events, which includes connections, disconnections, errors, and message traffic, to facilitate troubleshooting and performance tuning.
- **Test WebSocket Endpoints Thoroughly**: Develop automated tests for your WebSocket endpoints to ensure reliability, correct message routing, and resilience under load. Include both unit and integration tests in your CI/CD pipeline.

By following these best practices, you can build a secure, reliable, and scalable real-time communication system using Spring Boot and STOMP over WebSocket, suitable for production-grade chat, notification, and collaboration applications.

# Developing the Backend and Security Layer

A robust backend and security architecture is the cornerstone of any production-grade chat application. This layer ensures reliability, scalability, and protection against evolving threats while maintaining seamless real-time communication. Here is a detailed breakdown of critical components and best practices:

# Authentication and Authorization

WebSocket connections, unlike traditional HTTP, do not inherently support authentication. To secure access:

- **Token-Based Authentication (JWT)**: Issue JSON Web Tokens (JWT) during user login and validate them during `ebSocket` handshakes. Tokens can be passed via query parameters (like `wss://chat.example.com?token=JWT`) or cookies
- **Ticket-Based Systems**: For enhanced security, use a two-step process:
    a. Clients request a short-lived, signed "`ticket`" from an HTTP endpoint after initial login.
    b. The ticket (containing user ID, IP, and expiration) is validated during WebSocket connection establishment. This prevents token leakage and ensures sessions are tied to specific clients.
- **Role-Based Access Control (RBAC)**: Assign roles (like `user`, `admin`, `moderator`) to limit access to sensitive channels or actions. For example, only admins can delete messages or ban users.

# Data Security

To safeguard user data and ensure secure communication in real-time chat applications, it is essential to implement the following data security best practices:

**Encryption:**

- In Transit: Use WebSocket Secure (`wss://`) with TLS 1.3 to encrypt all data, preventing man-in-the-middle attacks.
- At Rest: Encrypt sensitive data (e.g., messages, user details) using AES-256. For end-to-end encryption (E2EE), ensure messages are encrypted client-side before transmission, with the keys never being exposcd to the server.

**Input Sanitization:**

- Prevent XSS/Code Injection: Sanitize user-generated content using libraries such as DOMPurify or framework-specific escaping (such as React's JSX `{}` syntax).

- Schema Validation: Validate message payloads against strict schemas to reject malformed or malicious data.

# Securing Communication Protocols

To ensure the integrity, confidentiality, and trustworthiness of real-time data exchange, it is necessary to secure the communication channels between clients and servers using the following strategies:

- **WebSocket Over TLS (WSS)**: Enforce TLS for all WebSocket connections to protect against eavesdropping and tampering.
- **Frame Masking**: While built into WebSocket clients, ensure masking is enabled to prevent cache poisoning in intermediaries.
- **Cross-Origin Resource Sharing (CORS)**: Restrict WebSocket endpoints to trusted domains to mitigate cross-site WebSocket hijacking.

# Rate Limiting and DDoS Mitigation

- **Throttle Connections**: Limit new WebSocket connections per IP (like 100 connections/minute) using tools such as Redis or NGINX.
- **Message Rate Limits**: Restrict users to sending 10-20 messages/second to prevent spamming.
- **Cloud-Based Protection**: Deploy services such as Cloudflare or AWS Shield to absorb volumetric DDoS attacks before they reach your infrastructure.

# Session Management and Monitoring

Session management and real-time monitoring are vital components of a resilient architecture and are instrumental in maintaining stable, efficient, and observable WebSocket communication at scale. The following best practices help ensure reliable session tracking and proactive system visibility:

- **Stateful Sessions**: Track active WebSocket sessions using in-memory stores (like Redis) to manage reconnects and detect stale connections.
- **Heartbeat Checks**: Implement WebSocket ping/pong frames to identify and close inactive connections, freeing server resources.
- **Real-Time Monitoring**: Use tools such as Prometheus and Grafana to track metrics (such as active connections, message throughput) and set alerts for anomalies.

# Compliance and Audits

To build trust and meet regulatory obligations, modern chat applications must incorporate comprehensive compliance mechanisms and audit capabilities. The following practices ensure that data privacy standards are upheld and systems remain secure through ongoing scrutiny:

- **Data Privacy**: Comply with regulations such as GDPR and CCPA by anonymizing logs, enabling data deletion requests, and limiting data retention periods.
- **Audit Trails**: Log all critical actions (like logins, message deletions) with timestamps and user IDs for forensic analysis.
- **Penetration Testing**: Conduct regular security audits to identify vulnerabilities (such as insecure WebSocket handshakes, and weak encryption).

## Architectural Best Practices

Designing a scalable, resilient, and secure chat application requires thoughtful architectural decisions that prioritize modularity, fault tolerance, and performance. The following best practices help ensure that your system remains robust under real-world operational demands:

- **Microservices Isolation**: Decouple authentication, messaging, and notification services to limit blast radius during breaches.
- **Message Brokers**: Use Kafka or RabbitMQ to buffer and reliably deliver messages during traffic spikes or failures.
- **Stateless Design**: Avoid storing session data on servers; use JWTs or external stores (Redis) for scalability.

A secure backend layer balances performance with protection. By combining token-based authentication, end-to-end encryption, and robust monitoring, developers can create chat applications that withstand both technical and regulatory challenges. Regular updates, adherence to OWASP guidelines, and leveraging battle-tested frameworks (like Spring Security, Centrifugo) further fortify the system against emerging threats.

# Building the Frontend Interface

Designing the frontend of a chat application is a multifaceted process that requires balancing usability, real-time responsiveness, accessibility, and visual appeal. The user interface (UI) serves as the bridge between users and the underlying real-time infrastructure, and its quality directly impacts user engagement and satisfaction. This section will explore the essential considerations, structural components, and best practices for building a modern chat frontend.

## User-Centric Design

A chat app is inherently interactive, so the UI must prioritize clarity and intuitiveness. Start by structuring the interface into clear segments: a message header (with user or group info, avatars, and status), a chat box displaying the message history, and an input area for composing new messages. Responsive design is crucial-ensure layouts adapt seamlessly to desktops, tablets, and mobile devices using CSS Flexbox and media queries. Accessibility should be a core principle: implement keyboard navigation, screen reader support, and sufficient color contrast to comply with WCAG guidelines, making the app usable for everyone. Micro-interactions, such as subtle animations when sending messages or receiving notifications, enhance engagement and provide immediate feedback.

## Real-Time Performance and State Management

Seamless real-time communication is the heart of any chat application. Use WebSockets to enable low-latency, bidirectional messaging between the client and server, ensuring that messages, typing indicators, and presence updates appear instantly. For older browsers, implement HTTP long polling as a fallback. Efficient state management is vital for performance and scalability; libraries such as Redux or Zustand (in React) help synchronize message histories, user lists, and unread counts across the interface. To handle long or busy chat threads, use rendering optimizations such as virtualization (for example, react-window) to avoid UI slowdowns. Throttle frequent updates like typing indicators to prevent unnecessary re-renders and network congestion.

## Core UI Components

A well-structured chat interface typically includes:

- **Message Header**: Displays user or group names, avatars, and status (like online, last seen).
- **Chat Box**: Shows incoming and outgoing messages, each with timestamps and sender avatars. Outgoing messages are usually aligned right, incoming left, and time breaks are inserted to group messages by date for readability.
- **Input Area**: Contains a text field for composing messages and a **send** button. Enhance this with features such as emoji pickers, file attachments, and quick reply suggestions.
- **Typing Indicators**: Show when another user is typing, providing real-time feedback and fostering engagement.
- **Message Statuses**: Indicate sent, delivered, and read states with icons or tooltips, helping users track message delivery.
- **Responsive Layout**: Use CSS media queries to ensure the layout adapts gracefully to various screen sizes, maintaining usability on both desktop and mobile devices.

## Enhancing User Experience

Modern chat UIs benefit from features that streamline conversations and increase engagement. Implement dynamic message suggestions or quick replies to help users respond efficiently. Use avatars and fallback initials for user identification, and display tooltips or icons for message statuses. Insert time breaks automatically to visually organize conversations by day or session, improving readability. For accessibility, ensure all interactive elements are reachable via keyboard and provide descriptive ARIA labels.

## Integration with Real-Time Data

The frontend should be tightly integrated with real-time data streaming services. Bind chat components to live data sources so that new messages, typing indicators, and presence updates are reflected instantly. This integration ensures that the chat experience is dynamic and engaging, matching user expectations for immediacy in modern messaging platforms.

## Best Practices

To deliver a seamless and inclusive user experience in real-time applications, it is essential to incorporate design and engineering best practices that balance usability, performance, and feedback-driven iteration. The following guidelines serve as a foundation for building engaging and reliable interfaces:

- Prioritize usability and accessibility from the outset
- Optimize for performance using efficient state management and rendering techniques
- Ensure real-time responsiveness with WebSockets and appropriate fallbacks
- Test across devices and browsers to guarantee a consistent experience
- Continuously gather user feedback and iterate on the interface to address pain points and enhance satisfaction

By following these principles and leveraging modern frontend frameworks and libraries, you can build a chat interface that is not only visually appealing and easy to use but also robust, scalable, and ready to support real-time communication at scale.

# Integrating OpenAI APIs and Prompt Engineering

Enhancing your Java chat application with OpenAI's capabilities transforms it into an intelligent platform capable of generating dynamic responses, summarizing conversations, translating languages, and even assisting with code. The following is a detailed, step-by-step guide to integrate OpenAI while maintaining security, performance, and scalability-with explanations for each part.

# Setting Up OpenAI API Integration in Java

To connect a Java application to OpenAI's API, you typically use the standard Java HTTP client or a third-party library such as OkHttp or Apache HttpClient. Begin by securely storing your OpenAI API key (using environment variables or a secrets manager), as you will need to include it in the Authorization header for each API request.

**Example: Sending a Prompt to OpenAI with Java's HttpClient**

This example demonstrates how to send a prompt to the OpenAI API and print the response. For production, handle exceptions, timeouts, and rate limits gracefully.

```
import java.net.URI;
import java.net.http.HttpClient;
import java.net.http.HttpRequest;
import java.net.http.HttpResponse;

public class OpenAIClient {
    private static final String API_KEY = System.getenv("OPENAI_API_KEY");
    private static final String ENDPOINT =
"https://api.openai.com/v1/chat/completions";

    public static void main(String[] args) throws Exception {
        String prompt = "Write a Java function that reverses a string.";
        String requestBody = """
            {
                "model": "gpt-4",
                "messages": [{"role": "user", "content": "%s"}]
            }
            """.formatted(prompt);

        HttpRequest request = HttpRequest.newBuilder()
            .uri(URI.create(ENDPOINT))
            .header("Content-Type", "application/json")
            .header("Authorization", "Bearer " + API_KEY)
            .POST(HttpRequest.BodyPublishers.ofString(requestBody))
            .build();

        HttpClient client = HttpClient.newHttpClient();
        HttpResponse<String> response = client.send(request,
HttpResponse.BodyHandlers.ofString());

        System.out.println(response.body());
    }
}
```

**Figure 6.7:** *Sending a Prompt*

# Prompt Engineering Best Practices for Java Developers

Prompt engineering is the art and science of crafting input prompts that yield the most relevant and accurate AI responses. In Java applications, prompts are often dynamically generated based on user input, business logic, or data context.

**Best Practices:**

- **Be Explicit and Contextual**: Provide clear instructions and necessary context in your prompt. For example, "*Summarize the following Java code in plain English:*" followed by the code snippet.
- **Structure Prompts for Consistency**: Use delimiters or templates to separate instructions from data, ensuring that the model interprets your intent correctly.
- **Iterate and Test**: Experiment with different phrasings, temperature, and max tokens to optimize response quality.
- **Role-Based Prompts**: For conversational AI, use system and user roles to guide the model's persona and response style.

**Example: Dynamic Prompt Construction in Java**

```
String userCode = "..."; // Java code from user input
String prompt = "You are a senior Java developer. Review the following code
and suggest improvements:\n\n" + userCode;
```

***Figure 6.8:*** *Dynamic Prompt Construction*

This approach helps the model generate more targeted and useful feedback.

# Production Considerations

- **Security**: Never expose your API key in client-side code. Store it securely on the server and use environment variables or a secrets manager.
- **Error Handling**: Implement robust error handling for network issues, API rate limits, and invalid responses.
- **Performance**: Cache frequent queries and consider batching requests to optimize throughput and reduce costs.
- **Compliance**: If handling sensitive data, anonymize inputs and avoid logging Personally Identifiable Information (PII).

# Integrating with Java Frameworks

Java's rich ecosystem includes frameworks such as Spring Boot, Quarkus, and Micronaut, which can simplify API integration and dependency management. For example, you can encapsulate OpenAI API calls in a Spring `@Service`, inject configuration via `@Value`, and expose endpoints for frontend consumption.

# Example Use Cases in Java Applications

Integrating AI-powered capabilities into Java applications opens up a wide range of possibilities across several domains. From enhancing user interactions to automating development workflows, here are some practical examples of how these innovations can be applied:

- **Chatbots:** Enhance customer support with AI-driven chat interfaces
- **Code Review Tools:** Automatically review and comment on Java code submissions
- **Content Generation:** Generate documentation, summaries, or test cases from code or requirements
- **Data Analysis:** Summarize or interpret large text datasets in enterprise applications

Thus, by integrating OpenAI APIs into Java applications and applying prompt engineering best practices, developers can unlock powerful AI-driven features while maintaining Java's strengths in security, scalability, and maintainability. Whether building chatbots, code assistants, or intelligent content generators, Java offers a stable foundation for production-ready AI solutions.

# Ensuring Responsible AI Usage

Responsible AI usage is essential to building trust, minimizing harm, and ensuring that artificial intelligence systems deliver positive, ethical, and equitable outcomes for individuals and society. As organizations increasingly deploy AI in critical applications, a clear framework for responsible AI helps manage risks such as bias, privacy violations, lack of transparency, and security vulnerabilities. The following key principles and actionable steps ensure responsible AI usage informed by leading industry standards and expert guidance.

## Fairness and Bias Mitigation

AI systems must be designed and operated to treat all individuals and groups without any discrimination based on race, gender, age, or other protected characteristics. This begins with using diverse and representative training data, regularly auditing algorithms for biased outcomes, and implementing mathematical fairness techniques. Organizations should test AI models for fairness using various demographic slices and adjust models or data as needed to address any disparities.

**Example:** A recruitment AI tool should be tested to ensure it does not favor candidates of a particular gender or background, and its training data should reflect the diversity of the job-seeking population.

## Transparency and Explainability

Transparency means making AI systems understandable to both technical and non-technical stakeholders. This includes clear documentation of how models are trained, what data is used, and how decisions are made. Explainability goes further, providing accessible reasons for specific AI outputs so users and regulators can understand, trust, and challenge decisions when necessary.

**Example:** In a loan approval scenario, the AI system should be able to provide applicants with clear reasons for denial, such as insufficient credit history, rather than opaque model outputs.

## Accountability and Human Oversight

Accountability ensures that there are clear lines of responsibility for the design, deployment, and monitoring of AI systems. Human oversight is crucial-AI should augment, not replace, human judgment. Organizations must establish processes for reviewing AI decisions, handling exceptions, and addressing unintended consequences. This includes maintaining audit trails and designating responsible individuals and teams for AI governance.

**Example:** A healthcare AI system that flags potential diagnoses should always allow a medical professional to review and override the AI's recommendation.

# Privacy and Data Protection

Respecting user privacy is fundamental. AI systems should comply with data protection laws (such as GDPR), use only the data necessary for their purpose, and implement strong data governance and security practices. Data should be anonymized wherever possible and users should have control over how their data is collected, used, and retained.

**Example:** An AI-powered customer support chatbot should not store or process sensitive personal information beyond what is needed to resolve the customer's inquiry.

# Security and Robustness

AI systems must be resilient against cyber threats, adversarial attacks, and data breaches. This involves implementing robust security protocols, regular vulnerability assessments, and monitoring for unusual behavior. Systems should be designed to fail safely and recover from errors or attacks.

**Example:** A fraud detection AI in banking should be protected against adversarial inputs designed to trick the model, and the system should immediately alert the administrators to any suspicious activity.

# Safety and Ethical Use

AI should be deployed in ways that prioritize the safety, well-being, and rights of individuals and communities. Organizations must avoid harmful applications of AI, assess the potential societal impact, and align with ethical standards and regulations. This includes environmental considerations and sustainability in AI operations.

**Example**: Facial recognition AI should not be used in ways that violate civil liberties, or enable mass surveillance without oversight and clear public benefits.

# Continuous Monitoring and Improvement

Responsible AI is an ongoing commitment. Organizations should continuously monitor AI systems for performance, fairness, and compliance, adapting to new risks, regulations, and societal expectations. Feedback loops, regular audits, and user education are key to maintaining responsible AI over time.

**Example:** A company using AI for content moderation should regularly review flagged content, update models based on emerging trends, and provide users with clear appeal processes.

# Inclusivity and Accessibility

AI should be designed to be accessible and beneficial to people of all backgrounds, abilities, and communities. Engaging diverse stakeholders in the design and evaluation process helps identify and mitigate potential ethical concerns and ensures a broader positive impact.

**Example:** Voice recognition AI should be trained and tested with speakers of different accents and dialects to ensure accessibility for all users.

## Vendor and Partner Diligence

When using third-party AI tools or data providers, organizations must ensure that those partners also adhere to responsible AI principles. This includes due diligence during selection and ongoing oversight throughout the partnership.

## Documentation and Legal Compliance

Maintain thorough documentation of AI design decisions, data sources, model training, and risk assessments. Ensure that all AI activities comply with applicable laws and industry regulations, and be prepared to demonstrate compliance to regulators and stakeholders.

Ensuring responsible AI usage is not a one-time task, but a continuous process that spans the entire AI lifecycle-from data collection and model development to deployment, monitoring, and improvement. By embedding fairness, transparency, accountability, privacy, security, and inclusivity into every stage, organizations can harness the benefits of AI while minimizing risks and building trust with users and society.

# Conclusion

In this chapter, we explored the essential building blocks of a modern chat application, beginning with scalable and resilient architecture that leverages microservices, hybrid databases, and real-time communication through WebSockets. We delved into backend best practices, emphasizing robust security with encryption, authentication, and role-based access control, as well as frontend strategies for creating responsive, accessible, and engaging user interfaces. The integration of OpenAI APIs and thoughtful prompt engineering was highlighted as a way to introduce intelligent, context-aware features while ensuring that the system remains performant and user-friendly.

We also underscored the importance of responsible AI usage by embedding fairness, transparency, privacy, and human oversight into every stage of development and deployment. Developers can build chat applications that not only deliver seamless, real-time communication and advanced AI-driven interactions but also foster trust and inclusivity for all users by combining technical rigor with ethical considerations.

As we turn our focus to the next critical area of secure application development, we will dive into *Implementing Symmetric Encryption in Java*. In this upcoming chapter, you will deepen your understanding of how to protect sensitive data using robust encryption techniques. From the foundational concepts of symmetric encryption to working with initialization vectors and Java-based encryption APIs, you will gain the necessary skills to implement strong, performant, and compliant security mechanisms, which is an essential step for any production-grade system handling personal or confidential data.

CHAPTER 7

# Implementing Symmetric Encryption in Java

## Introduction

In an age where data security is paramount, understanding and implementing encryption techniques is a crucial skill for any developer. This chapter will thus introduce you to the fundamentals of symmetric encryption and guide you through the process of securing data in your Java applications.

We will begin with an **Introduction** to the concept of encryption, emphasizing its importance in protecting sensitive information. You will then dive deeper into **Understanding Symmetric Encryption**, exploring how this method uses a single key for both encryption and decryption, making it a fast and effective way to secure data.

Next, we will cover **Setting Up the Java Environment** to ensure you have the necessary tools to implement encryption. Following this, the core of the chapter, **Implementing Symmetric Encryption in Java**, will walk you through the process of coding and applying encryption techniques within your Java programs.

Working with **Initialization Vectors** is also covered, highlighting their role in enhancing security by ensuring that the same plaintext encrypts differently each time. The chapter will also take up **Best Practices and Security Considerations**, offering guidance on how to implement encryption securely and effectively and avoid common pitfalls.

Finally, you will reinforce your learning with **Practical Examples and Exercises**, allowing you to apply what you have learned and gain hands-on experience in implementing symmetric encryption in Java.

By the end of this chapter, you will be well-equipped with the knowledge and skills to protect data in your Java applications using symmetric encryption, ensuring that your projects meet modern security standards.

## Structure

This chapter will cover the following topics:

- Foundations of Secure Java Applications
- Understanding Symmetric Encryption
- Implementing Symmetric Encryption in Java
- Working with Initialization Vectors
- Best Practices and Security Considerations

## Foundations of Secure Java Applications

Data security is a critical aspect of modern software development, especially in applications where sensitive information is transmitted, processed, or stored. Encryption plays a pivotal role in protecting such data from unauthorized access. Among the various types of encryption, **symmetric encryption** is one of the most widely used methods due to its simplicity, efficiency, and speed. It relies on a single, shared key for both encryption and decryption processes, making it ideal for scenarios where secure key management is feasible.

Symmetric encryption ensures that data remains confidential and secure by transforming plaintext into ciphertext using a shared secret key. Only entities with access to this key can decrypt the data back into its original form. This makes symmetric encryption a cornerstone in securing communications, file storage, and databases in enterprise and personal applications.

In this chapter, we will delve into the fundamental concepts of symmetric encryption, its advantages, and its limitations. We will also explore how symmetric encryption fits into the broader cryptographic landscape and its common use cases in software development. By the end of this chapter, you will have a comprehensive understanding of symmetric encryption and be equipped to implement it securely and effectively in your Java applications.

# The Importance of Symmetric Encryption

As the digital world continues to grow, so does the risk of data breaches, cyberattacks, and unauthorized access to sensitive information. Symmetric encryption is a practical and efficient tool to address these challenges. Unlike asymmetric encryption, which uses a pair of public and private keys, symmetric encryption uses a single key for both encryption and decryption. This makes it faster and less resource-intensive, making it suitable for encrypting large datasets or real-time communications.

Symmetric encryption is used in a variety of applications, including:

- **Securing Communications**: Protocols like TLS and SSL use symmetric encryption for secure communication between clients and servers.
- **Data Storage**: Files, databases, and backups are often encrypted using symmetric algorithms to protect against unauthorized access.
- **Payment Systems**: Symmetric encryption secures credit card information and transactions in compliance with standards like PCI-DSS.
- **Media Encryption**: Video streaming services use symmetric encryption to protect content from unauthorized distribution.

# Key Features of Symmetric Encryption

- **Single Shared Key**: A single key is used for both encrypting and decrypting the data.
- **Speed and Efficiency**: Symmetric encryption algorithms are computationally faster compared to asymmetric encryption, making them suitable for bulk data encryption.
- **Common Algorithms**:
    - **AES (Advanced Encryption Standard)**: A widely used standard for secure encryption, offering 128-bit, 192-bit, or 256-bit key sizes.
    - **DES (Data Encryption Standard)**: An older standard, now largely replaced by AES due to vulnerabilities.
    - **Triple DES (3DES)**: An extension of DES that applies encryption three times for added security.
    - **Blowfish**: A fast and secure algorithm, particularly for applications with low processing power.
- **Deterministic Encryption**: Given the same key and plaintext, the output ciphertext will always be the same.

## Challenges and Considerations

While symmetric encryption is effective, it comes with certain challenges, particularly concerning key management. Since the same key is used for both encryption and decryption, securely distributing and storing it is critical. If the key is compromised, the confidentiality of the encrypted data is lost. Other considerations include:

- **Key Distribution**: Securely sharing the key between sender and receiver without interception
- **Scalability**: Managing keys in large systems or for many users can become complex
- **Replay Attacks**: Without additional mechanisms, encrypted messages might be intercepted and replayed without detection

Symmetric encryption remains a fundamental and efficient method for securing data in a variety of applications. While its simplicity and speed are advantageous, proper implementation and key management are critical to maintaining its effectiveness. As we proceed through this chapter, we will explore how to use symmetric encryption in Java, from setting up the environment to implementing robust encryption solutions. Whether you are securing communications, protecting files, or safeguarding sensitive user data, the knowledge in this section will equip you with the skills to apply symmetric encryption effectively in your projects.

# Understanding Symmetric Encryption

Symmetric encryption is one of the foundational techniques in cryptography, widely used for securing sensitive information. Its defining characteristic is the use of a single, shared key for both encrypting and decrypting data. This makes it simpler and faster compared to asymmetric encryption, which relies on a pair of public and private keys. In this section, we will explore the key concepts, advantages, limitations, and common algorithms associated with symmetric encryption.

## Symmetric Encryption

Symmetric encryption is a cryptographic technique where the same key is used for both the encryption of plaintext and the decryption of ciphertext. It ensures that only those with access to the shared secret key can interpret the encrypted information.

**How It Works**

- **Encryption**: The sender encrypts the plaintext data using a shared secret key and a symmetric encryption algorithm. This process transforms the plaintext into unreadable ciphertext.
- **Transmission**: The encrypted data (ciphertext) is sent over a communication channel.
- **Decryption**: The receiver uses the same secret key to decrypt the ciphertext back into readable plaintext.

**Example**

- **Plaintext**: `Hello, World!`
- **Key**: `s3cr3tk3y`
- **Ciphertext** (after encryption): `uY9fhw2b8o3Jr5g`
- Using the same key, the ciphertext is decrypted to reveal the original plaintext.

## Advantages of Symmetric Encryption

- **Simplicity:** Symmetric encryption is conceptually straightforward. It uses a single key for both encryption and decryption, which makes implementation and understanding easier for developers and security architects.

- **High Performance:** Because it relies on less complex mathematical operations compared to asymmetric encryption, symmetric algorithms are significantly faster. This makes them ideal for encrypting large volumes of data efficiently.
- **Low Resource Consumption:** Due to its simpler computations, symmetric encryption consumes fewer system resources (CPU and memory), making it suitable for performance-critical applications such as real-time communication, streaming, and embedded systems.
- **Broad Adoption and Maturity:** Symmetric encryption algorithms like AES (Advanced Encryption Standard) are industry-standard and battle-tested. They are widely supported across programming languages, platforms, and hardware, ensuring interoperability and long-term support.
- **Ideal for Secured Environments:** In environments where secure key exchange can be guaranteed, such as internal microservice communication or encrypted databases, symmetric encryption provides a secure and performant choice without the Public-Key Infrastructure (PKI) overhead.

# Limitations of Symmetric Encryption

While symmetric encryption is highly effective, it has certain limitations that must be managed carefully:

- **Key Management**: Securely distributing and storing the shared key is a challenge. If the key is compromised, the entire encryption system is at risk.
- **Scalability**: In systems with multiple parties, managing a unique key for every pair of users becomes increasingly complex.
- **No Built-in Authentication**: Symmetric encryption does not verify the sender's identity, thereby making it vulnerable to certain attacks such as **man-in-the-middle attacks**.

## Key Concepts in Symmetric Encryption

Here are the key concepts of Symmetric Encryption:

- The **key** is a string of characters used to encrypt and decrypt data.
- The security of symmetric encryption depends entirely on the secrecy of the key.
- **Key Length**: Longer keys provide stronger encryption but require more computational resources.

# Initialization Vectors (IVs)

- An **Initialization Vector (IV)** is a random or pseudo-random value used to ensure that the same plaintext encrypted multiple times with the same key will produce different ciphertexts.
- IVs add randomness to encryption, enhancing security.

# Modes of Operation

Symmetric encryption algorithms are often used with different **modes of operation** to enhance their functionality:

- **Electronic Codebook (ECB):**
  - Simplest mode; encrypts each block of plaintext independently
  - **Limitation**: Produces the same ciphertext for identical plaintext blocks, making it insecure for most use cases

- **Cipher Block Chaining (CBC):**
  - Encrypts each block of plaintext by combining it with the ciphertext of the previous block
  - Requires an IV to encrypt the first block
- **Galois/Counter Mode (GCM):**
  - Provides both encryption and integrity verification
  - Popular in secure communication protocols like TLS

## Common Symmetric Encryption Algorithms

Several symmetric encryption algorithms are widely used in cryptography and are mentioned as follows:

**Advanced Encryption Standard (AES)**

- **Description**: AES is the most commonly used symmetric encryption algorithm today. It supports key sizes of 128, 192, or 256 bits.
- **Advantages**:
  - Strong security
  - Highly efficient for both hardware and software implementations
- **Applications:**
  - SSL/TLS protocols, secure file storage, and data encryption for databases

**Data Encryption Standard (DES)**

- **Description**: An older encryption standard that uses a 56-bit key
- **Limitation**: Vulnerable to brute-force attacks due to its short key length
- **Replacement**: Largely replaced by AES

**Triple DES (3DES)**

- **Description**: Enhances DES by applying encryption three times with different keys
- **Applications**: Still used in some legacy systems

**Blowfish**

- **Description**: A fast block cipher with variable key lengths (32 – 448 bits)
- **Applications**: Secure file transfers and password management systems

**ChaCha20**

- **Description**: A modern stream cipher known for its speed and security
- **Applications**: Often used in mobile and IoT applications due to its efficiency

Symmetric encryption remains a cornerstone of modern cryptography, offering a balance between simplicity and efficiency. Its reliance on a shared key makes it highly efficient for securing large datasets and real-time communications. However, secure key management is critical to its success. In the next section, we will discuss **setting up the Java environment** to implement symmetric encryption, preparing the necessary libraries, tools, and dependencies to begin building secure encryption solutions in Java.

# Implementing Symmetric Encryption in Java

Symmetric encryption is a key technique for securing data in various applications. In this section, we will explore how to implement symmetric encryption in Java, step by step. Using the **Java**

**Cryptography Architecture (JCA)**, we will perform encryption and decryption operations with popular algorithms like **AES**. By the end of this section, you will have a clear understanding about how to integrate symmetric encryption into your Java applications. including aspects like key generation, encryption, and decryption processes.

## Setting Up the Java Environment

Before implementing symmetric encryption, ensure that your development environment is configured:

- **JDK**: Install the latest JDK (Java Development Kit). Java 8 or higher is recommended
- **IDE**: Use a preferred IDE like IntelliJ IDEA, Eclipse, or Visual Studio Code
- **Dependencies**: The `javax.crypto` and `java.security` packages are included in the JDK, so no additional libraries are required.

## Key Concepts for Implementation

- **Algorithm**: Choose a secure algorithm like AES. For this section, we will use AES with a key size of 128 bits.
- **Key**: The shared secret key for encryption and decryption. It must be securely stored or exchanged.
- **Cipher**: A cryptographic engine that performs encryption and decryption using a specified algorithm and key.

# Steps to Implement Symmetric Encryption in Java

**Key Generation:** To encrypt and decrypt data, we need a shared secret key. Java provides the **`KeyGenerator`** class for generating keys.

```
import javax.crypto.KeyGenerator;
import javax.crypto.SecretKey;

public class KeyGenerationExample {

    public static SecretKey generateKey() throws Exception {
        KeyGenerator keyGenerator = KeyGenerator.getInstance("AES");
        keyGenerator.init(128); // Key size: 128, 192, or 256 bits
        return keyGenerator.generateKey();
    }
}
```

***Figure 7.1:*** *keyGeneration Example*

**Encrypting Data:** The **`Cipher`** class in the **`javax.crypto`** package handles encryption and decryption. To encrypt data:

- Initialize the cipher in **encryption mode** with the secret key
- Provide plaintext as input, and the cipher will generate ciphertext

```
import javax.crypto.Cipher;
import javax.crypto.SecretKey;
import java.util.Base64;

public class EncryptionExample {

    public static String encrypt(String plainText, SecretKey key) throws
Exception {
        Cipher cipher = Cipher.getInstance("AES");
        cipher.init(Cipher.ENCRYPT_MODE, key);
        byte[] encryptedBytes = cipher.doFinal(plainText.getBytes());
        return Base64.getEncoder().encodeToString(encryptedBytes);
    }
}
```

***Figure 7.2:*** *Encrypting Data*

**Decrypting Data:** To decrypt data, initialize the cipher in **decryption mode** using the same secret key. Pass the ciphertext as input to retrieve the original plaintext.

```
import javax.crypto.Cipher;
import javax.crypto.SecretKey;
import java.util.Base64;

public class DecryptionExample {

    public static String decrypt(String cipherText, SecretKey key) throws
Exception {
        Cipher cipher = Cipher.getInstance("AES");
        cipher.init(Cipher.DECRYPT_MODE, key);
        byte[] decryptedBytes =
cipher.doFinal(Base64.getDecoder().decode(cipherText));
        return new String(decryptedBytes);
    }
}
```

***Figure 7.3:*** *Decrypting Data*

Implementing symmetric encryption in Java is straightforward, thanks to the powerful **Java Cryptography Architecture (JCA)** and built-in libraries. By using secure algorithms like AES, you can encrypt and decrypt data efficiently and securely. In the next section, we'll explore the role of **Initialization Vectors (IVs)** in symmetric encryption, understanding how they add randomness to encryption and protect against replay attacks.

# Working with Initialization Vectors

In symmetric encryption, **IVs** play a critical role in enhancing security by ensuring that the same plaintext encrypted with the same key produces different ciphertexts. This randomness prevents patterns from emerging in the encrypted data, which could otherwise be exploited by attackers. In this chapter, we will explore what IVs are, why they are essential, how they are used in various encryption modes, and how to implement them in Java.

# Initialization Vector

An **Initialization Vector (IV)** is a random or pseudo-random value that is used along with a secret key during the encryption process. The IV adds randomness to the encryption, ensuring that even if the same plaintext is encrypted multiple times with the same key, the resulting ciphertext will be different.

**Key Characteristics of IVs:**

- **Length**: The IV size is typically equal to the block size of the encryption algorithm (for example, 16 bytes for AES).
- **Uniqueness**: Each IV should be unique for every encryption operation to prevent replay attacks or ciphertext analysis.
- **Non-secret**: Unlike the encryption key, the IV does not need to be kept secret. However, it must be transmitted or stored securely along with the ciphertext.

# Importance of IVs

IVs are critical for maintaining the security of symmetric encryption in certain modes of operation. They provide the following benefits:

- **Prevents Pattern Recognition**: Without an IV, identical plaintexts encrypted with the same key would produce identical ciphertexts, revealing patterns that attackers could exploit.
- **Adds Randomness**: The IV introduces entropy into the encryption process, making the ciphertext more resistant to cryptanalysis.
- **Enhances Security in Chaining Modes**: In encryption modes like CBC (Cipher Block Chaining), the IV ensures that each encryption operation is independent of previous ones.

# Encryption Modes That Use IVs

IVs are used in specific modes of operation for block ciphers. Some common modes include:

**Cipher Block Chaining (CBC)**

- **Description**: In the CBC mode, each plaintext block is XORed with the previous ciphertext block before encryption. The IV is used for the first block.
- **Benefits**: Prevents identical plaintext blocks from producing identical ciphertext blocks
- **Usage**: Commonly used in file encryption

**Counter (CTR)**

- **Description**: CTR mode uses an IV as a counter, which is incremented for each block. This ensures that each block is encrypted with a unique value.
- **Benefits**: Parallelizable and efficient for large datasets
- **Usage**: Commonly used in streaming data encryption

**Galois/Counter Mode (GCM)**

- **Description**: GCM combines CTR mode with authentication, using the IV for both encryption and integrity checks.
- **Benefits**: Provides confidentiality and data integrity

- **Usage**: Widely used in secure communication protocols like TLS

# Generating and Using IVs in Java

**Generating a Random IV:** Java provides the **`SecureRandom`** class for generating cryptographically strong random numbers, which can be used to create IVs.

```
import javax.crypto.Cipher;
import javax.crypto.KeyGenerator;
import javax.crypto.SecretKey;
import javax.crypto.spec.IvParameterSpec;
import java.security.SecureRandom;

public class IVExample {

    public static byte[] generateIV(int blockSize) {
        byte[] iv = new byte[blockSize];
        SecureRandom secureRandom = new SecureRandom();
        secureRandom.nextBytes(iv);
        return iv;
    }
}
```

**Figure 7.4:** *Generating a Random IV*

**Using IVs in Encryption:** To use an IV during encryption, you need to initialize the **`Cipher`** instance with both the secret key and the IV. The IV is specified using the **`IvParameterSpec`** class.

```
import javax.crypto.Cipher;
import javax.crypto.spec.IvParameterSpec;
import javax.crypto.SecretKey;

public class EncryptionWithIV {

    public static byte[] encrypt(String plainText, SecretKey key, byte[] iv)
throws Exception {
        Cipher cipher = Cipher.getInstance("AES/CBC/PKCS5Padding");
        IvParameterSpec ivSpec = new IvParameterSpec(iv);
        cipher.init(Cipher.ENCRYPT_MODE, key, ivSpec);
        return cipher.doFinal(plainText.getBytes());
    }
}
```

**Figure 7.5:** *Using IV in Encryption*

**Using IVs in Decryption:** The same IV used during encryption must be provided during decryption.

```
public class DecryptionWithIV {

    public static String decrypt(byte[] cipherText, SecretKey key, byte[] iv)
throws Exception {
        Cipher cipher = Cipher.getInstance("AES/CBC/PKCS5Padding");
        IvParameterSpec ivSpec = new IvParameterSpec(iv);
        cipher.init(Cipher.DECRYPT_MODE, key, ivSpec);
        byte[] plainTextBytes = cipher.doFinal(cipherText);
        return new String(plainTextBytes);
    }
}
```

**Figure 7.6:** *Using IV in Decryption*

# Complete Example: Encrypting and Decrypting with IVs

Here is a complete example that demonstrates how to generate an IV, use it during encryption, and then decrypt the ciphertext using the same IV.

```
import javax.crypto.Cipher;
import javax.crypto.KeyGenerator;
import javax.crypto.SecretKey;
import javax.crypto.spec.IvParameterSpec;
import java.security.SecureRandom;
import java.util.Base64;

public class SymmetricEncryptionWithIV {

    public static void main(String[] args) {
        try {
            // Step 1: Generate Secret Key and IV
            KeyGenerator keyGenerator = KeyGenerator.getInstance("AES");
            keyGenerator.init(128);
            SecretKey secretKey = keyGenerator.generateKey();
            byte[] iv = generateIV(16);

            // Step 2: Encrypt the Plaintext
            String plainText = "Hello, IV!";
            Cipher cipher = Cipher.getInstance("AES/CBC/PKCS5Padding");
            cipher.init(Cipher.ENCRYPT_MODE, secretKey, new
IvParameterSpec(iv));
            byte[] encryptedBytes = cipher.doFinal(plainText.getBytes());
            String encryptedText =
Base64.getEncoder().encodeToString(encryptedBytes);

            System.out.println("Encrypted Text: " + encryptedText);

            // Step 3: Decrypt the Ciphertext
            cipher.init(Cipher.DECRYPT_MODE, secretKey, new
IvParameterSpec(iv));
            byte[] decryptedBytes =
cipher.doFinal(Base64.getDecoder().decode(encryptedText));
            String decryptedText = new String(decryptedBytes);

            System.out.println("Decrypted Text: " + decryptedText);

        } catch (Exception e) {
            e.printStackTrace();
        }
    }

    private static byte[] generateIV(int blockSize) {
        byte[] iv = new byte[blockSize];
        SecureRandom secureRandom = new SecureRandom();
        secureRandom.nextBytes(iv);
        return iv;
    }
}
```

**Figure 7.7:** Complete Example

## Best Practices for Using IVs

1. **Generate IVs Randomly**: Always use a secure random number generator to create unique IVs.
2. **Do Not Reuse IVs**: Reusing IVs with the same key weakens the encryption and can lead to data compromise.
3. **Transmit IVs Securely**: Include the IV with the ciphertext but ensure it is not tampered with during transmission (such as, by using encryption or authentication).
4. **Use Appropriate Block Size**: The IV size should match the block size of the encryption algorithm (such as, 16 bytes for AES).

## Use Cases of IVs

- **Secure Communication**: TLS and other protocols use IVs to encrypt multiple messages securely.
- **File Encryption**: Each file block is encrypted with a unique IV to prevent patterns from emerging.
- **Database Security**: Databases encrypt rows with unique IVs to ensure data confidentiality.

Initialization Vectors (IVs) are essential for maintaining the security of symmetric encryption. By introducing randomness, IVs prevent patterns in ciphertext and protect against cryptanalysis. Proper implementation of IVs in Java, as demonstrated in this chapter, ensures robust and secure encryption for a variety of use cases. In the next section, we will explore **Best Practices and Security Considerations** for symmetric encryption, focusing on key management, algorithm selection, and common pitfalls to avoid.

# Best Practices and Security Considerations

While **symmetric encryption** provides an efficient way to **secure data**, improper implementation can introduce **security vulnerabilities**. Simply applying encryption without considering **key management, algorithm selection, or potential attacks** can leave sensitive information exposed. To ensure **strong encryption practices**, developers must follow established **best practices** and consider the broader security implications when implementing **symmetric encryption in Java**.

## Choosing the Right Encryption Algorithm

Not all encryption algorithms are equally secure. It is crucial to use **modern and standardized encryption algorithms** to prevent known vulnerabilities.

**Recommended Algorithm: AES**

- AES is **widely accepted and highly secure** for symmetric encryption. It is supported in Java's built-in `Cipher` class and offers **strong cryptographic protection**.
- **AES-GCM (Galois/Counter Mode)** provides **integrity protection** and is **highly recommended** over ECB (Electronic Codebook Mode).

**Avoid Deprecated Algorithms**

- **DES (Data Encryption Standard)**: Weak and vulnerable to brute-force attacks
- **RC4 (Rivest Cipher 4)**: Insecure due to significant vulnerabilities

## Key Management Best Practices

Since **symmetric encryption relies entirely on the secrecy of the encryption key**, **proper key management is critical**. If a key is exposed, the encrypted data is no longer secure.

**Key Storage Recommendations**

- Use a Secure Key Vault – Store encryption keys securely using Key Management Systems (KMS) such as:
    - AWS KMS
    - Google Cloud KMS
    - HashiCorp Vault
- Use Environment Variables for Loading Keys
- Rotate Encryption Keys Periodically – Regularly update encryption keys to mitigate risks

**Avoid the Following Practices**

- Hardcoding encryption keys in source code
- Storing keys in database fields without encryption
- Checking keys into version control repositories (such as GitHub and GitLab)

## Using Secure Initialization Vectors (IVs)

An **Initialization Vector (IV)** adds **randomness** to encryption, ensuring that the same plaintext encrypts to different ciphertexts each time.

**Best Practices for IVs**

- Use a Unique IV for Every Encryption Operation
- Generate IVs Securely Using Java's `SecureRandom`
- **Include IVs Alongside Ciphertext**: IVs are not secret but must be transmitted with the encrypted data for decryption.

**Avoid Reusing IVs**

- Reusing IVs allows attackers to **correlate encrypted messages**, making cryptanalysis easier.

## Implementing Proper Padding Techniques

When encrypting plaintext that is not a multiple of the block size, **padding** is required.

**Recommended Padding Schemes**

- Use PKCS5Padding or PKCS7Padding for Block Ciphers
- For Stream Ciphers or AEAD, Use NoPadding

**Avoid ECB Mode (Electronic Codebook Mode)**

- ECB produces **identical ciphertext for identical plaintext**, making it vulnerable to pattern analysis.

## Ensuring Data Integrity with Authentication (AEAD)

Standard encryption methods **do not protect against data tampering**. Attackers may modify encrypted messages **without knowing their contents**, leading to corrupted or malicious data.

**Recommended: Authenticated Encryption with AEAD**

- **Use AES-GCM or AES-CCM Mode:** These provide both **encryption and integrity protection**.

**Use Message Authentication Codes (MACs)**

- If using **CBC mode**, add an **HMAC-SHA256 checksum** to verify integrity.

**Avoid Encryption Without Integrity Checks**

- Attackers can alter encrypted data if it lacks integrity protection.

## Securing Transmission of Encrypted Data

Even encrypted data must be **securely transmitted** to prevent **man-in-the-middle (MITM) attacks**.

**Best Practices for Secure Transmission**

- Use TLS (Transport Layer Security) for API and network communication
- Encrypt data before sending over unsecured channels
- Sanitize input to prevent padding oracle attacks

**Implementing Strong Access Controls**

- **Restrict Access to Encrypted Data:** Only authorized users or services should be able to decrypt sensitive information.
- **Use Role-Based Access Control (RBAC) and Multi-Factor Authentication (MFA)** for added security.

**Regular Security Audits and Testing**

- **Perform Penetration Testing:** Simulate attacks to identify vulnerabilities
- **Use Static Code Analysis Tools:** Scan for **hardcoded keys and weak encryption**
- **Keep Java and Cryptographic Libraries Updated:** Stay up-to-date with the latest security patches

# Conclusion

In this chapter, we explored the best practices for implementing symmetric encryption in Java, emphasizing the importance of using strong encryption algorithms, secure key management, proper initialization vectors, and data integrity mechanisms. By following these guidelines, developers can ensure that sensitive data remains protected from unauthorized access and cryptographic vulnerabilities. Encryption alone is not enough–proper storage, secure transmission, and access control must also be enforced to maintain robust security in enterprise applications. Regular audits and security testing further strengthen the encryption implementation, ensuring compliance with industry standards and best practices.

**Looking Ahead: Java Microservices**

While encryption secures data at rest and in transit, modern applications require more than just data protection, they need scalability, flexibility, and efficient communication between distributed services. In the next chapter, we will transition to Java Microservices, exploring how to design and develop microservices-based architectures using Spring Boot, API Gateways, Service Discovery, and Secure Communication. This shift will provide a deeper understanding of building resilient, high-performance applications that can scale in cloud environments.

# PART 4
# Building Microservices

(CHAPTERS 8–14)

# CHAPTER 8
# From MicroServices Foundations to Your First Application

## Introduction

Microservices architecture has transformed how modern applications are built while enabling greater flexibility, scalability, and maintainability. This chapter is designed to introduce you to the core concepts of microservices and guide you through the process of developing your first microservice-based application.

We will start with the **Fundamentals of Microservices Architecture and Its Advantages**, where you will learn why microservices have become the preferred approach for many developers and organizations. You will explore the key benefits, such as modularity, easier deployment, and improved fault isolation, which make microservices ideal for large-scale, complex applications.

Next, we will examine the **Differences Between Microservices and Monolithic Architectures**, highlighting the contrasts between these two approaches to help you understand the reasons and occasions to choose microservices over traditional monolithic designs.

Once the theoretical foundation is laid, we will move on to **Setting Up the Development Environment for Microservices**, ensuring you have the tools and environment configured to start building microservices. We will then introduce you to the **Key Components and Tools for Microservices Development**, including essential technologies like Spring Boot, Docker, and Kubernetes, which play a critical role in the microservices ecosystem.

The chapter culminates in **Building and Testing Your First Spring Boot Microservice**, where you will apply what you have learned to create a simple, functional microservice. You will also learn how to test and deploy your microservice, setting the stage for more complex projects in the future.

By the end of this chapter, you will have a solid understanding of microservices architecture and the practical experience needed to begin developing microservice-based applications.

## Structure

This chapter will cover the following topics:

- Fundamentals of Microservices Architecture and Its Advantages
- Monolithic vs. Microservices Architecture: A Strategic Perspective
- Setting Up the Development Environment for Microservices
- Key Components and Tools for Microservices Development
- Building and Testing Your First Spring Boot Microservice

# Fundamentals of Microservices Architecture and Its Advantages

Microservices architecture is a **software development approach** that structures an application as a **collection of small, independent services** that work together to deliver business functionality. Each microservice is responsible for a specific feature or capability and can be developed, deployed, and scaled independently. Unlike traditional **monolithic architectures**, where all components of an application are tightly integrated and must be deployed together, microservices provide a **modular approach** that enhances flexibility and efficiency.

Each microservice typically:

1. Runs in its **own process**
2. Communicates with other services via **well-defined APIs**, usually using RESTful HTTP, gRPC, or messaging protocols like Kafka and RabbitMQ
3. Has its **own database** or persistent storage to ensure **loose coupling**
4. Can be developed and maintained **by independent teams**

By embracing **decentralization**, microservices enable organizations to build and maintain large-scale applications more effectively, accommodating continuous integration and deployment strategies.

# How Microservices Differ from Monolithic Architecture

As organizations transition to modern software architectures, it is crucial to understand the fundamental differences between **microservices** and **monolithic architectures**. While monolithic applications bundle all functionalities into a single unit, microservices decompose applications into independent, loosely coupled services. This section explores the key contrasts between these two approaches, their advantages, challenges, and the best use cases to help you determine when and why to choose microservices over traditional monolithic designs.

| Feature | Monolithic Architecture | Microservices Architecture |
|---|---|---|
| **Structure** | Single, unified application | Modular, loosely coupled services |
| **Scalability** | Difficult, scales entire app | Scales individual services independently |
| **Deployment** | Must redeploy entire app for changes | Each service can be deployed independently |
| **Fault Isolation** | A failure can bring down the entire system | Easier to maintain and update due to modularity |
| **Technology** | Uses a single tech stack | Allows multiple technologies for different services |
| **Development Speed** | Slower due to interdependencies | Faster as teams work on different services simultaneously |
| **Maintenance** | Easier to maintain and update due to modularity | Easier to maintain and update due to modularity |

***Table 8.1:*** *Monolithic vs Microservices Architecture*

# Key Characteristics of Microservices Architecture

Microservices architecture exhibits the following fundamental characteristics that make it distinct and beneficial for modern applications:

## Independence

Each microservice is developed, tested, deployed, and scaled **independently** without affecting other services. This reduces development bottlenecks and brings about **continuous deployment**.

**Example:** In an e-commerce application, the "`Order Processing`" service can be updated separately from the "`User Authentication`" service.

## Single Responsibility Principle (SRP)

Microservices follow **SRP**, meaning that each service **performs only one business function**. This improves code maintainability and makes each service easier to understand.

Example: A "`Payment Service`" should only handle payment processing, while an "`Inventory Service`" should manage stock levels.

## Decentralized Data Management

Unlike monolithic applications, where a **single database** is shared across all modules, microservices often use **dedicated databases** per service. This prevents **tight coupling** between services and results in **flexible data storage solutions**.

**Example**: A "`Customer Service`" may use **PostgreSQL**, while an "`Analytics Service`" might prefer **MongoDB** for handling large-scale data.

## Resilience

Microservices enhance **fault tolerance** because a failure in one service does **not** crash the entire application. Mechanisms like **circuit breakers** (e.g., Resilience4J, Hystrix) and **fallback methods** ensure graceful degradation.

**Example**: If the "`Recommendation Service`" in a shopping app fails, the system can continue working without personalized recommendations.

## Scalability

Each microservice can scale **independently**, optimizing infrastructure usage and **reducing costs**. Services that experience heavy traffic can be scaled separately without overloading the entire system.

**Example**: A "`Search Service`" in a marketplace might require **10 instances**, while an "`Admin Panel Service`" might only need **1 instance**.

## Technology Agnostic

Different microservices can be built using **different programming languages, databases, and frameworks** based on what is best suited for their functionality.

**Example**: A "`Machine Learning Service`" might be built in **Python**, while a "`Web API Service`" might use **Java Spring Boot**.

# Advantages of Microservices Architecture

Microservices offer several advantages that make them the preferred choice for **scalable, high-performance applications**:

## Scalability

Microservices allow teams to **scale individual components** based on demand, thus optimizing resource usage and performance.

**Example**: A **video streaming service** can scale the "`Video Encoding Service`" separately from the "`User Management Service`", ensuring smooth playback during peak traffic.

## Fault Isolation

Failures in **one microservice do not impact** the entire system, leading to **higher availability** and resilience.

**Example**: If the "`Notifications Service`" fails, users can still place orders and make payments in an e-commerce system.

## Faster Development and Deployment

Microservices allow **parallel development** as teams work on different services independently. This speeds up feature delivery and supports **Continuous Integration or Continuous Deployment (CI/CD)**.

**Example**: A **travel booking app** can have separate teams developing "`Flight Booking`", "`Hotel Reservation`", and "`User Reviews`" concurrently.

## Better Maintainability

With **smaller, modular codebases**, microservices are easier to maintain, update, and debug.

**Example**: If a bug is found in the "`Billing Service`", developers can fix and redeploy it without affecting the "`User Profile Service`".

## Technology Flexibility

Microservices are **technology-agnostic**, meaning different services can be developed using different technologies, **best suited for their needs**.

**Example**: A "`Real-time Chat Service`" in a social media app can use **Node.js**, while the "`Content Management Service`" can run on **Spring Boot**.

# Challenges of Microservices (Trade-offs to Consider)

Despite its advantages, microservices also present the following **challenges**:

- **Complex Deployment and Management:** Managing multiple microservices requires sophisticated tools like **Docker, Kubernetes, and CI/CD pipelines** to automate deployment.
- **Increased Network Latency:** As microservices communicate over the network, API calls introduce **latency**, which may impact performance if not optimized.
- **Distributed Data Management:** Handling **data consistency** across multiple databases and services is **challenging**. Techniques like **Eventual Consistency** and the **Saga Pattern** help address these issues.

- **Security Risk:** More exposed APIs mean **increased security concerns**. Best practices include using **OAuth2, JWT authentication, API Gateways**, and **Zero Trust Security Models**.

Microservices architecture **breaks down complex applications** into independent services, enabling better **scalability, maintainability, and resilience**. By leveraging **service independence, decentralized data management, and technology flexibility**, microservices help organizations build **robust, scalable** systems.

However, the trade-offs like increased complexity and security concerns require careful planning and **best practices** to implement successfully. In the next sections, we will explore how to set up a **microservices development environment**, compare it with **monolithic architectures**, and guide you through building your **first Spring Boot microservice**.

# Monolithic vs. Microservices Architecture: A Strategic Perspective

Software architecture has evolved significantly over the years, with organizations moving from **monolithic applications** to **microservices-based systems** to meet the growing demands for scalability, flexibility, and rapid deployment. While monolithic architectures are rather simple in the early stages of development, they become increasingly challenging to maintain as applications grow. In contrast, microservices address these challenges by **breaking down applications into independently managed and deployed services**.

Instead of looking at just the technical differences, this section explores **why organizations transition from monolithic to microservices, the trade-offs involved, and the real-world considerations when making this shift**.

## Monolithic Architecture: A Practical Choice for Certain Use Cases

Despite its limitations, monolithic architecture **remains a viable approach** for specific use cases. Many startups and small-scale applications begin as monolithic due to its **simplicity and ease of deployment**.

**Strengths of Monolithic Architecture**

- **Rapid Initial Development**: With all components in a single codebase, developers can quickly build and launch applications without complex service orchestration.
- **Consistent Performance**: Since all modules run within the same process, monolithic applications often avoid inter-service communication overhead.
- **Easier Debugging and Testing**: Developers can run and debug the entire system locally without the complexities of distributed environments.

**Challenges That Arise over Time**

- **Scalability Bottlenecks**: As applications grow, certain components may require more resources than others, leading to inefficient scaling.
- **Slow Development Cycles**: Any update requires rebuilding and deploying the entire application, slowing down release cycles.
- **Operational Complexity**: A large monolithic codebase becomes harder to maintain, especially as multiple teams work on it.

**Monolithic Architecture works best during the following occasions:**

- Small to medium-sized applications with a clear and stable feature set.

- Projects with a single development team where communication overhead is minimal.
- Applications that require low latency without the need for inter-service calls.

# Microservices: A Solution for Scalability and Agility

Microservices architecture **emerges as a natural progression** when applications require greater flexibility, independent scaling, and decentralized development. Instead of compiling them in a single codebase, microservices **divide applications into loosely coupled services**, where each is responsible for a distinct business capability.

**Why Organizations Move to Microservices**

- **Independent Scaling**: Services can scale individually, optimizing infrastructure costs and improving performance under high loads.
- **Faster Feature Releases**: Teams can work on different services in parallel, reducing dependencies and accelerating development cycles.
- **Technology Freedom**: Different services can be built using the most appropriate technology stack, rather than being restricted to a single language or framework.
- **Resilience and Fault Tolerance**: Failures are contained within specific services, ensuring that one issue does not take down the entire system.

**Challenges and Trade-Offs in Microservices**

- **Increased Complexity**: Unlike monolithic applications, microservices introduce **service discovery, API gateways, and distributed data management**, which require additional expertise.
- **Network Latency**: Communication between services over HTTP or message brokers introduces **network overhead**, which needs to be optimized.
- **Security Concerns**: With multiple APIs exposed, **authentication, authorization, and data encryption** become more critical.

**When Microservices Work Best:**

- Large-scale applications with frequent updates and new feature rollouts.
- Organizations with multiple development teams working on different parts of the system.
- Applications requiring modular design, where independent services handle different business functions (like payments, authentication, and analytics)

# Strategic Decision-Making: Choosing the Right Approach

Many organizations do not start with microservices immediately; instead, they transition from monolithic to microservices **as their needs evolve**. The decision should be **business-driven**, considering factors like **team size, scalability requirements, and operational complexity**.

## The Strangler Pattern: Gradual Migration from Monolithic to Microservices

For companies running large monolithic systems, **rewriting the entire application is often impractical**. Instead, a gradual approach like the **Strangler Pattern** is recommended to:

- **Identify modules** in the monolithic system that can be extracted as microservices
- **Develop new features** as microservices instead of adding them to the monolith

- **Gradually replace monolithic components** with microservices over time

This approach **reduces risk, maintains business continuity, and allows teams to adapt gradually** to the microservices paradigm.

# Beyond the Technology: Organizational and Cultural Shifts

Adopting microservices is not just a technical shift—it requires **organizational and cultural changes**:

- **Cross-functional Teams**: Microservices development requires close collaboration between **developers, operations, and security teams**.
- **DevOps Practices**: CI/CD pipelines, containerization (like Docker, Kubernetes), and automated testing become essential for managing microservices.
- **Service Ownership**: Each microservice should have a **dedicated team** responsible for its lifecycle, from development to monitoring.

Organizations like **Netflix, Amazon, and Uber** successfully scaled their platforms by **adopting a microservices mindset** while enabling **continuous innovation and operational efficiency**.

While **monolithic architecture** offers simplicity and ease of development, it struggles with **scalability and maintainability** in the long run. **Microservices architecture** solves these challenges by breaking applications into independent, scalable services, but at the cost of increased **complexity and operational overhead**.

Choosing between these architectures **depends on the project's scope, team expertise, and business requirements**. For small-scale applications, monolithic architecture may be the right choice, whereas for large, evolving systems, **microservices enable long-term agility and resilience**.

In the next section, we will **set up the development environment for microservices**, equipping you with the tools and frameworks required to build a scalable, cloud-native application.

# Setting Up the Development Environment for Microservices

Before diving into microservices development, it is crucial to set up the right development environment to ensure seamless coding, testing, and deployment. Microservices involve multiple services running independently, often requiring tools for containerization, orchestration, database management, service communication, and API testing. In this section, we will walk through the prerequisites for developing microservices and how to set up a Spring Boot microservice project.

## Prerequisites

### Java Development Kit (JDK) 17 or Later

Java is one of the most commonly used programming languages for building microservices. Spring Boot, a leading microservices framework, is built on Java and requires a **Java Development Kit (JDK)** for compilation and execution.

- **Download JDK 17 or Later**:
  - From **Oracle**: JDK Downloads
  - From **OpenJDK**: OpenJDK Downloads

**Verify JDK Installation**: `java -version`

**Spring Boot**

Spring Boot simplifies **microservices development** by providing an opinionated framework with built-in configurations, dependency management, and embedded servers like Tomcat.

**Installing Spring Boot:**

1. Use **`Spring Initializr`** to generate a Spring Boot project
2. Choose **Maven** or **Gradle** as the build tool
3. Add required dependencies (covered later in the chapter)
4. **Verify Spring Boot Installation**: `spring --version`

**Build Tools: Maven or Gradle**

Microservices projects typically use **Maven** or **Gradle** for dependency management and project builds.

- **Maven (Apache Maven)**: Preferred for Java-based projects
    a. **Install Maven** from Maven Downloads
    b. **Verify Installation**: `maven -version`
- **Gradle:** An alternative to Maven, offering better performance in large projects
    a. **Install Gradle** from Gradle Downloads
    b. **Verify Installation**: `gradle -version`

**Docker**

Docker is an essential tool for **containerizing microservices**, allowing them to run in isolated environments with all dependencies included.

a. **Install Docker**: Docker Official Site

b. **Verify Docker Installation**: `docker -version`

**Why Use Docker for Microservices?**

- Ensures consistency across development, testing, and production
- Provides lightweight, portable containers for microservices
- Works well with **Kubernetes** for orchestration

**Postman or cURL for API Testing**

Since microservices communicate via RESTful APIs, testing APIs is crucial.

- **Postman:**
    - A GUI-based API testing tool
    - Download from Postman
- **cURL:**
    - A command-line tool for sending HTTP requests
    - Pre-installed on most Unix-based systems
    - Example API Request: **`curl -X GET`** http://localhost:8080/hello

**Kubernetes (Optional, for Orchestration)**

For production-level microservices, Kubernetes manages containerized applications.

- **Install Kubernetes via Minikube**: `Minikube Installation`

**Why Kubernetes?**

- Automates deployment and scaling of microservices
- Manages networking and load balancing
- Self-healing capabilities ensure high availability

**Database (MySQL or PostgreSQL) for Data Storage**

Each microservice often requires its own **database** for data persistence.

**Install MySQL:**

a. Download from MySQL Official Site

b. **Verify Installation**: `mysql -version`

**Why Use a Separate Database for Each Microservice?**

- Prevents **tight coupling** between services
- Allows microservices to use **different database technologies**
- Enables **scalability** and **fault tolerance**

**Message Broker (Kafka or RabbitMQ) for Inter-Service Communication**

For asynchronous communication between microservices, **message brokers** like Kafka or RabbitMQ are used.

**Apache Kafka (For Event-Driven Architecture)**

a. Download from Kafka Official Site

**Why Use a Message Broker?**

- Enables **asynchronous processing**
- Improves **resilience** by decoupling services
- Supports **event-driven microservices**

# Setting Up a Spring Boot Project

With all prerequisites in place, we can now set up a **Spring Boot microservice**.

1. **Using Spring Initializr**

   a. Open **Spring Initializr**

   b. Choose **Maven** or **Gradle**

   c. Select **Spring Boot version (latest stable release)**

   d. Add required dependencies

2. **Required Dependencies**

   Include the following dependencies based on the microservice requirements:

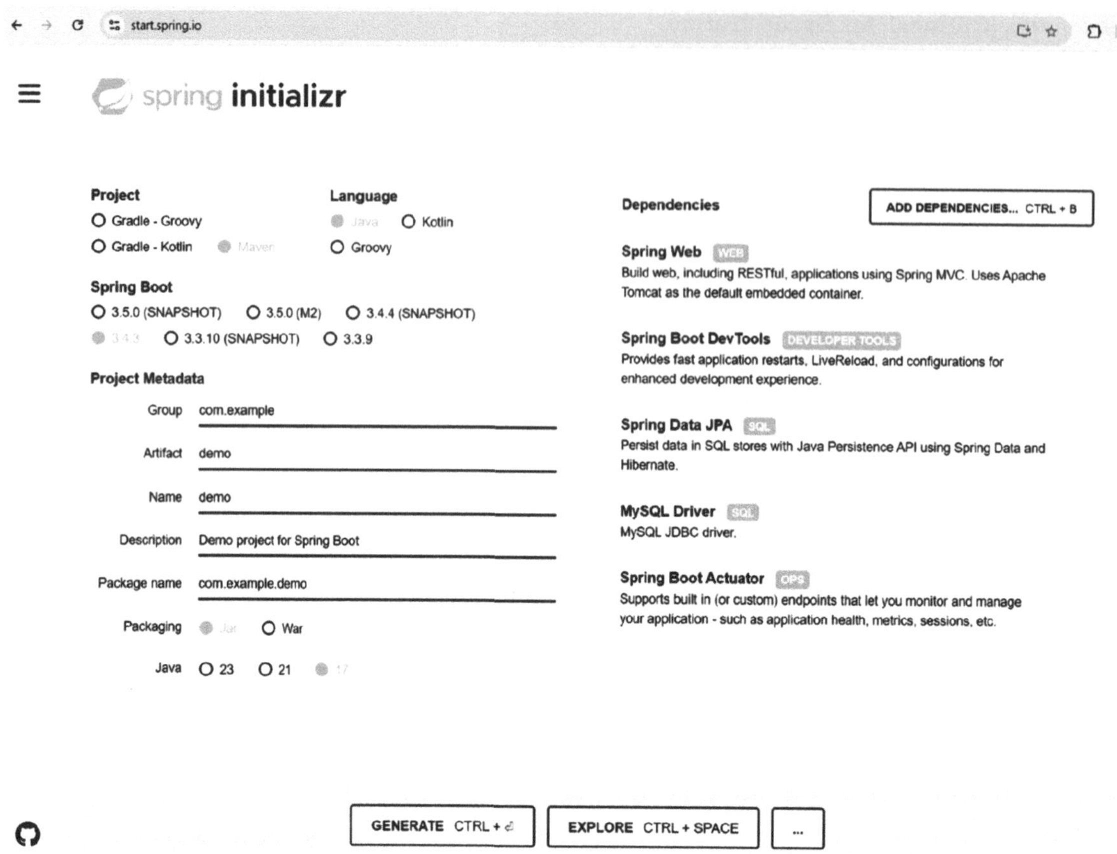


***Figure 8.1:*** *Spring Initialzr*

| Dependency | Purpose |
|---|---|
| Spring Web | Enables REST API development |
| Spring Boot DevTools | Provides live reload and enhanced development experience |
| Spring Data JPA | Simplifies database interactions |
| MySQL Driver | Enables MySQL database connectivity |
| Spring Boot Actuator | Adds monitoring and observability features |

***Table 8.2:*** *Purpose of Each Dependency*

Click **`Generate`**, **`download`**, and extract the project.

1. **Import the Project into an IDE**
    a. Open **IntelliJ IDEA**, **Eclipse**, or **VS Code**
    b. Select **"`Open Project`"**, then choose the extracted folder
    c. Build the project using: **`mvn clean install`**
2. Run the Spring Boot Application

Once the project is set up, run the main application. The following image shows a **Spring Boot** application running in **IntelliJ IDEA**, successfully starting on **port 8081** with an embedded **Tomcat server**. The logs indicate that **Spring Boot Actuator** is enabled, exposing an endpoint at **`/actuator/`**. However, there are warnings related to **HikariCP and Hibernate**, suggesting missing or undefined

**database connection settings**. Despite this, the application has started successfully in **3.858 seconds** and is ready to handle requests.

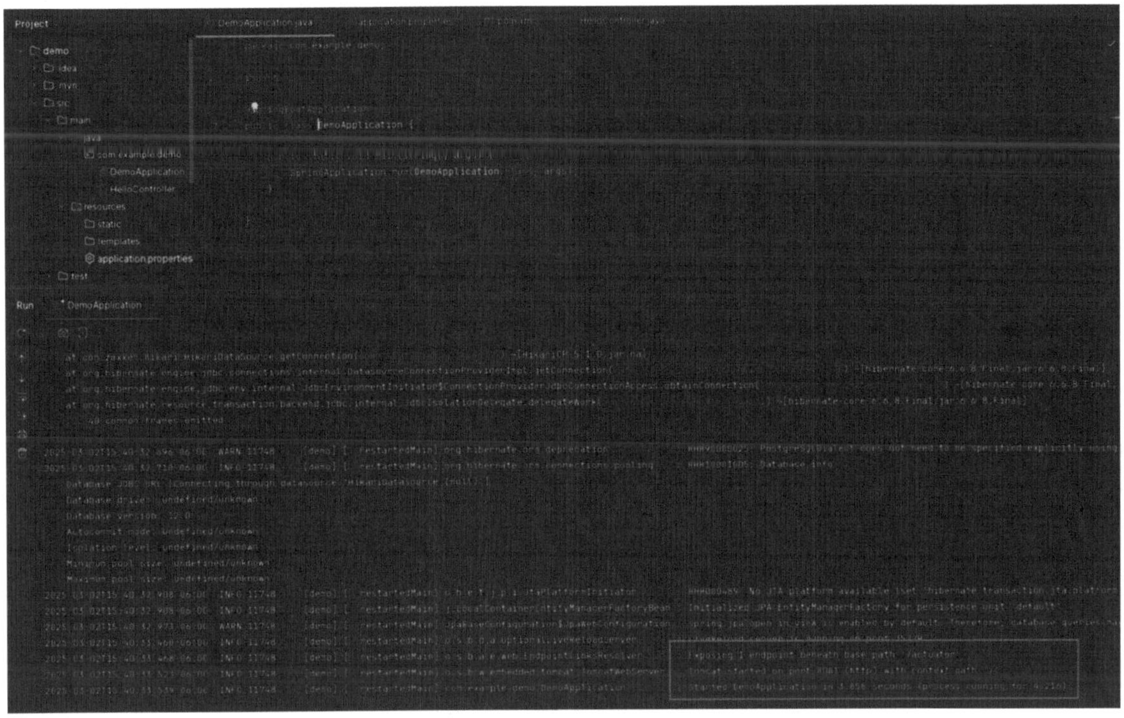

***Figure 8.2:*** *Running the Spring Boot Application*

Setting up the right **development environment** is essential for microservices development. We covered the necessary tools, including **JDK, Spring Boot, Docker, Kubernetes, databases, and message brokers**. We also walked through **creating a Spring Boot microservice** using Spring Initializr.

With this foundation in place, we are now ready to move on to **understanding the key components and tools required for microservices development**, such as API gateways, service discovery, and load balancing.

# Key Components and Tools for Microservices Development

Microservices architecture is built upon a set of core **components and tools** that enable efficient development, deployment, and management of distributed systems. Unlike monolithic applications, where all functionalities are tightly coupled, microservices require specialized tools to handle **API management, service discovery, load balancing, inter-service communication, configuration management, logging, and container orchestration**.

This section explores these key components and the technologies that facilitate microservices development.

## API Gateway

**Tool:** Spring Cloud Gateway, Zuul

**Purpose:** Routes requests to appropriate microservices and handles authentication, rate limiting, and logging.

In a microservices ecosystem, clients (such as frontend applications or mobile apps) should not interact directly with each microservice. Instead, an **API Gateway** acts as a **reverse proxy**, routing incoming requests to the appropriate microservice, while also handling **authentication, security, rate limiting, and logging**.

**Key Responsibilities of an API Gateway:**

- **Request Routing:** Directs client requests to the correct microservice
- **Load Balancing:** Distributes traffic across multiple instances of a microservice
- **Security & Authentication:** Implements OAuth, JWT, and API Key-based authentication
- **Rate Limiting:** Controls request frequency to prevent overloading
- **Protocol Translation:** Converts between REST, gRPC, and WebSockets

**Popular API Gateway Tools**

- **Spring Cloud Gateway:** A modern gateway built on Spring Boot
- **Netflix Zuul:** A legacy API Gateway solution that provides filtering, routing, and security

# Service Discovery

**Tool:** Eureka, Consul, or Kubernetes Service Discovery

**Purpose:** Keeps track of available microservices and their network locations

In a microservices system, services **dynamically scale up and down**, making it impractical to hardcode service locations. **Service Discovery** automates this process, allowing services to **register** and **discover** each other.

**Types of Service Discovery:**

- **Client-Side Discovery:** Services query the discovery tool to find other services (such as Ribbon + Eureka).
- **Server-Side Discovery:** The gateway (like Kubernetes) routes requests dynamically without requiring the client to handle discovery.

**Popular Service Discovery Tools**

1. **Eureka (Netflix OSS):** A registry-based discovery service for Spring Boot applications
2. **Consul (HashiCorp):** A distributed service mesh that provides DNS-based discovery
3. **Kubernetes Service Discovery:** Uses built-in DNS to automatically resolve service endpoints

# Load Balancer

**Tool:** Ribbon, Nginx

**Purpose:** Distributes incoming traffic evenly across instances of a microservice

Load balancing is **crucial** in microservices to ensure traffic is evenly distributed among instances. This prevents **overloading a single service instance** and ensures high availability.

**Types of Load Balancing:**

- **Client-Side Load Balancing:** The client decides which instance of the service to call.

  **Example**: **Spring Cloud Ribbon** (used with Eureka)

- **Server-Side Load Balancing:** A gateway or load balancer distributes traffic.

  **Example: Nginx, Kubernetes Ingress, AWS ELB**

**Popular Load Balancing Tools**

- **Ribbon (Spring Cloud):** Works with Eureka for client-side discovery and load balancing
- **Nginx:** A reverse proxy for routing traffic to multiple instances
- **Kubernetes Ingress Controller:** Provides HTTP-based load balancing for Kubernetes clusters

# Inter-Service Communication

Inter-service communication refers to the ways in which individual microservices within a distributed system interact with each other to complete business workflows. Since microservices are typically small, autonomous, and focused on a single responsibility, they often need to collaborate with other services to handle complex tasks.

Here is a breakdown of the key concepts, styles, and considerations involved:

- **Synchronous (RESTful APIs):** Spring Web, Feign Client
- **Asynchronous (Event-driven):** Kafka, RabbitMQ

Microservices communicate with each other using either **synchronous** or **asynchronous** methods.

**Synchronous Communication (RESTful APIs)**

- Microservices interact via **HTTP requests**
- **Tools:**
  - **Spring Web:** Provides RESTful API support
  - **Feign Client:** A declarative REST client for making API calls between microservices

**Asynchronous Communication (Event-Driven Architecture)**

- Instead of direct API calls, services exchange **messages via a message broker**
- **Tools:**
  - **Apache Kafka:** A distributed event-streaming platform for real-time processing
  - **RabbitMQ:** A lightweight message broker for queue-based communication

**Choosing the Right Communication Strategy**

| Feature | Synchronous (REST) | Asynchronous (Kafka/Rabbit MQ) |
|---|---|---|
| Response Time | Faster, immediate response | Delayed processing |
| Decoupling | Tightly coupled | Loosely coupled |
| Use Case | CRUD operations, APIs | Event-driven applications, high scalability |

***Table 8.3:*** *Choosing the Right Communication Strategy*

# Configuration Management

**Tool:** Spring Cloud Config Server, HashiCorp Vault

**Purpose:** Centralized management of configurations across microservices

Microservices require **centralized configuration management** to maintain consistency across environments.

**Why Use Configuration Management?**

- **Consistency:** Avoids hardcoding configurations in services
- **Dynamic Updates:** Allows real-time configuration changes without restarting services
- **Security:** Encrypts sensitive configurations (for instance, database credentials and API keys)

**Popular Tools**

- **Spring Cloud Config Server:** Centralized configuration management for Spring Boot microservices
- **HashiCorp Vault:** Securely stores secrets and credentials

# Logging and Monitoring

**Tool:** ELK Stack (Elasticsearch, Logstash, Kibana), Prometheus, Grafana

**Purpose:** Collect and analyze logs for performance monitoring

With multiple microservices running independently, **centralized logging and monitoring** are critical to identifying issues, tracking errors, and improving performance.

**Logging Tools**

- **ELK Stack (Elasticsearch, Logstash, Kibana):**
    - **Elasticsearch**: Stores and indexes logs
    - **Logstash**: Processes and ships logs
    - **Kibana**: Visualizes logs in dashboards

**Monitoring Tools**

- **Prometheus:** Monitors system metrics, microservices health, and alerts
- **Grafana:** Provides real-time dashboards for application performance

**Why Logging and Monitoring Matter?**

- **Detect failures** before they impact the system
- **Identify performance bottlenecks**
- **Improve debugging** across distributed services

# Containerization and Orchestration

Containerization and Orchestration are foundational concepts in building, deploying, and scaling modern cloud-native applications, particularly in a microservices architecture. Together, they enable portability, consistency, automation, and scalability across different cloud environments.

Containerization is the practice of packaging an application along with its dependencies, libraries, and configuration into a standardized unit, which is also called **a container**. Unlike virtual machines, containers are lightweight and share the host system's kernel, enabling faster startup times and lower resource usage.

Orchestration refers to the automated management of containers at scale, which includes deployment, scheduling, monitoring, networking, scaling, and self-healing of containerized applications.

**Tool: Docker, Kubernetes**

**Purpose: Deploy and manage microservices at scale.**

Microservices require containerization to **ensure consistency across different environments**. Orchestration tools like Kubernetes manage these containers efficiently.

**Containerization with Docker**

- Packages microservices **along with dependencies** into lightweight containers
- Allows services to run **independently across multiple environments**

**Orchestration with Kubernetes**

- **Automates deployment, scaling, and management** of microservices
- Provides **service discovery, load balancing, and fault recovery**

**Popular Container and Orchestration Tools**

- **Docker:** Packages microservices into containers
- **Kubernetes:** Manages containerized microservices at scale
- **Docker Compose:** Manages multi-container applications locally

Developing microservices requires an ecosystem of **specialized tools** to manage service communication, discovery, load balancing, configuration, logging, and deployment. By leveraging tools like **Spring Cloud Gateway, Eureka, Kafka, Docker, and Kubernetes**, teams can build **scalable, fault-tolerant, and maintainable microservices**.

In the next section, we will explore **Building and Testing Your First Spring Boot Microservice**, guiding you through the process of creating a functional microservice from scratch.

# Building and Testing Your First Spring Boot Microservice

Building a microservice involves several key steps, from setting up the development environment to writing, testing, and deploying the service. This section walks through creating a **Spring Boot-based microservice**, running and testing it, and finally deploying it in a **Docker container** for scalability.

By the end of this section, you will have a fully functional **Spring Boot microservice** that handles a simple request and responds accordingly. You will also learn how to **write unit tests** to validate the functionality and **containerize the application using Docker**.

## Step 1: Create a Simple Microservice

A microservice consists of:

a. A **main application class** that initializes Spring Boot

b. A **REST controller** that exposes an API endpoint

c. A **build tool** (Maven/Gradle) to manage dependencies

d. A **testing framework** to verify functionality

### Define the Main Class

The entry point for a Spring Boot application is the main class, which is annotated with `@SpringBootApplication`. This automatically enables **Spring Boot's configuration, component scanning**, and **auto-configuration features**.

```java
import org.springframework.boot.SpringApplication;
import org.springframework.boot.autoconfigure.SpringBootApplication;

@SpringBootApplication
public class DemoServiceApplication {
    public static void main(String[] args) {
        SpringApplication.run(DemoServiceApplication.class, args);
    }
}
```

**Figure 8.3:** *SpringBootApplication*

**`@SpringBootApplication`** marks this class as a **Spring Boot application**.

**`SpringApplication.run()`** launches the microservice.

# Create a Simple REST Controller

A REST controller defines the **API endpoint** that clients can call. Here, we will create a simple **`HelloController`** that responds with a greeting:

Create `HelloController.java`

a. **`@RestController`** marks this class as a Spring REST Controller

b. **`@GetMapping("/hello")`** maps the **`/hello`** endpoint to this method

c. **`@RequestParam(defaultValue = "World")`** allows passing a name parameter, defaulting to "**`World`**" if none is provided

```java
import org.springframework.web.bind.annotation.GetMapping;
import org.springframework.web.bind.annotation.RequestParam;
import org.springframework.web.bind.annotation.RestController;

@RestController
public class HelloController {

    @GetMapping("/hello")
    public String sayHello(@RequestParam(defaultValue = "World") String name) {
        return "Hello, " + name;
    }
}
```

**Figure 8.4:** RestController

# Step 2: Writing Unit Tests

Testing is essential for ensuring microservices work correctly before deployment. Spring Boot supports **JUnit** for unit testing.

## Writing a Basic Unit Test

We will write a simple **JUnit test** to check whether the microservice loads correctly.

Create **`DemoServiceApplicationTests.java`**

- **`@SpringBootTest`** tells Spring Boot to **load the application context** for testing
- **`contextLoads()`** checks if the microservice starts correctly

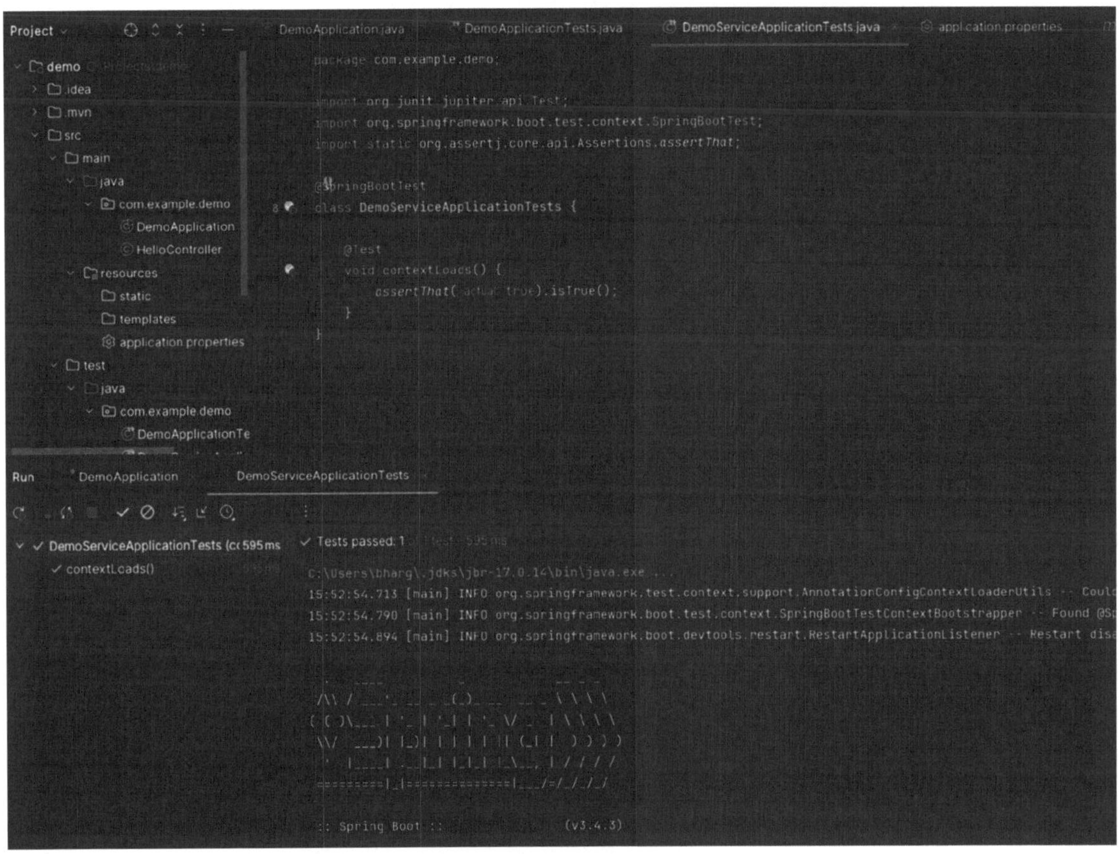


***Figure 8.5:*** *All Tests Passed*

If everything is set up correctly, the output should confirm **all tests passed**.

# Step 4: Deploying with Docker

Once the microservice is tested, we can **containerize it using Docker**. This ensures that the microservice can run **consistently across different environments**.

## Create a Dockerfile

A **`Dockerfile`** specifies how to **package the microservice into a Docker image**.

**Create a `Dockerfile` in the project root:**

- **`FROM openjdk:17`** Uses Java 17 base image
- **`COPY target/demo-service.jar demo-service.jar`** Copies the JAR file into the container
- **`ENTRYPOINT ["java", "-jar", "demo-service.jar"]`** Runs the application when the container starts

## Build the Docker Image

First, **package the microservice as a JAR file**:

```
docker build -t demo-service
```

## Run the Microservice in a Docker Container

Once the image is built, start a container:

```
docker run -p 8080:8080 demo-service
```

Now, the microservice is running inside **a Docker container** and can be accessed at:

```
http://localhost:8080/hello?name=Docker
```

# Conclusion

In this chapter, we took our first step towards **microservices development** by building, testing, and deploying a simple **Spring Boot microservice**. Through a structured approach, we covered **core aspects** of microservices, such as setting up a development environment and containerizing the application for scalable deployment.

The journey into microservices development began with a deep dive into the core components and tools necessary to build scalable and maintainable systems. We explored critical technologies including API Gateways, Service Discovery mechanisms, Load Balancers, Configuration Management, Logging frameworks, and Container Orchestration platforms. Each of these plays a foundational role in shaping a resilient, production-grade microservices architecture. With these concepts in place, we proceeded to build our first Spring Boot microservice, while defining its entry point, exposing a RESTful API, verifying behavior through unit tests, and containerizing it with Docker for seamless deployment across environments.

Successfully running this microservice represents a pivotal milestone, but it also highlights an important reality: microservices are not meant to exist in isolation. In real-world systems, services must locate and communicate with one another, even as they scale dynamically or move across infrastructure. This complexity introduces the need for robust service discovery mechanisms. Without them, other services or clients would struggle to find the correct endpoints, especially in containerized or cloud-native deployments where instances are ephemeral.

In the next phase of this journey, we will focus on Service Discovery and Registration. This chapter will explore how tools like **Eureka**, **Consul**, and **Kubernetes Service Discovery** help track and manage ever-changing service endpoints. You will learn how dynamic registration, health checks, and self-healing systems enable microservices to communicate reliably, even under shifting loads and failures. By integrating Service Discovery into our architecture, we will begin transforming isolated components into a fully interconnected, responsive ecosystem capable of scaling and recovering autonomously.

# CHAPTER 9

# Service Discovery and Registration

## Introduction

In a microservices architecture where services are numerous and dynamic, managing the interactions between them becomes a complex challenge. This chapter will thus focus on how services in a microservices environment can communicate with each other without hard-coded configurations, while ensuring scalability and resilience.

We will begin with an **Introduction to Service Discovery Patterns**, where you will learn about the different approaches to service discovery, including client-side and server-side discovery. These patterns are important as they help us to understand how microservices locate each other in a distributed system.

Next, you will set up a **Eureka Server for Service Registry**, a key component in the Spring Cloud ecosystem, which acts as a centralized registry where services can register themselves and discover other services. Following this, we will guide you through **Configuring Microservices with Eureka Client**, enabling your microservices to communicate with the Eureka Server and automatically register themselves.

We then explore the **Self-registration Pattern**, explaining how services can register themselves with the discovery server and why this pattern is widely used in modern microservices architectures. Finally, the chapter wraps up with **Testing Service Discovery and Registration**, where you will verify that your microservices can successfully register with the Eureka Server and discover other services.

By the end of this chapter, you will have a thorough understanding of service discovery and registration mechanisms, equipped to implement these patterns in your own microservices projects to enhance scalability and flexibility.

## Structure

We will cover the following topics in this chapter:

- Introduction to Service Discovery Patterns
- Building and Deploying Three Java Microservices in Kubernetes
- Setting Up Istio for Service Discovery in Kubernetes
- Configuring Microservices for Dynamic Service Discovery in Istio
- Implementing Service Mesh-Based Traffic Routing
- Testing and Observability in Istio

# Introduction to Service Discovery Patterns

In a monolithic architecture, service communication is relatively simple because all components exist within the same application. However, in a **microservices architecture** where multiple independent services interact across a network, managing communication between these services becomes a **complex challenge**.

Microservices are designed to be **scalable and dynamic**, which means:

- New service instances can be created or terminated based on demand.
- Services may run on different hosts or cloud environments.
- IP addresses and ports of services are not fixed.
- Manual configuration of service locations is impractical.

To address these challenges, **Service Discovery** mechanisms are implemented to allow services to dynamically locate and communicate with one another **without hard-coded configurations**. Instead of relying on fixed URLs or manually maintaining service addresses, **service discovery automates** the registration and lookup of services.

**Key Benefits of Service Discovery**

- **Dynamic Service Registration**: Services automatically register and deregister when they start or shut down
- **Eliminates Hard-Coded Endpoints**: No need to manually configure service locations
- **Enhances Scalability**: New service instances can be added seamlessly
- **Improves Fault Tolerance**: If a service instance goes down, traffic is redirected to available instances
- **Supports Load Balancing**: Distributes requests among multiple instances of a service

# Types of Service Discovery Patterns

There are two primary patterns for **service discovery**:

- **Client-Side Service Discovery**
- **Server-Side Service Discovery**

Each pattern has its own advantages and trade-offs. The choice of pattern depends on factors like network complexity, infrastructure, and load balancing requirements.

## Client-Side Service Discovery

In **Client-Side Service Discovery**, the client is responsible for locating available service instances and routing requests accordingly. This means that the client directly interacts with a **Service Registry**, retrieves service information, and chooses which service instance to communicate with.

**How It Works**

1. **A microservice (service provider) starts and registers itself with a Service Registry** (like Eureka, Consul, or Zookeeper)
2. **A client service (consumer) queries the registry** to get a list of available service instances
3. **The client selects an instance** using a load balancing algorithm (like round-robin)
4. The request is sent directly to the chosen service instance

#### Example with Eureka and Ribbon

- The client queries **Eureka Server** to discover available instances
- A **Load Balancer (Ribbon)** selects an instance and sends the request

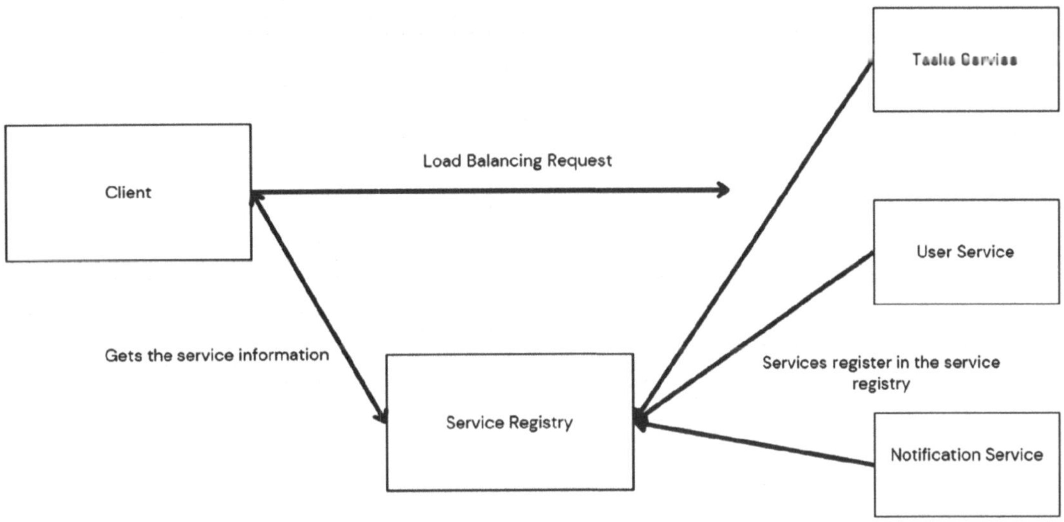


***Figure 9.1:*** *Example with Eureka and Ribbon*

#### Pros of Client-Side Discovery

- **Efficient:** No additional hop is needed between the client and service
- **Flexible Load Balancing:** Clients can implement custom load-balancing logic
- Works well with microservices frameworks like Spring Cloud Eureka

#### Cons of Client-Side Discovery

- **Clients Must Implement Discovery Logic:** Every client needs to be aware of the service registry
- **Tight Coupling:** Changes in discovery logic require updates to clients

## Server-Side Service Discovery

In **Server-Side Service Discovery**, the client does **not** need to query a Service Registry. Instead, a **load balancer** or API Gateway acts as an intermediary between clients and services.

#### How It Works

- **A service registers itself with a Service Registry** (like Eureka, Consul, or Kubernetes Service Discovery).
- **A client sends a request to an API Gateway or Load Balancer**, without knowing the exact service location
- **The API Gateway queries the Service Registry** to determine the available service instances.
- The request is routed to the appropriate service instance.

#### Example with Kubernetes Service Discovery

- The client calls a **Kubernetes Service** (like `my-service`).
- **Kubernetes Ingress Controller or a Load Balancer** directs traffic to a healthy service instance.

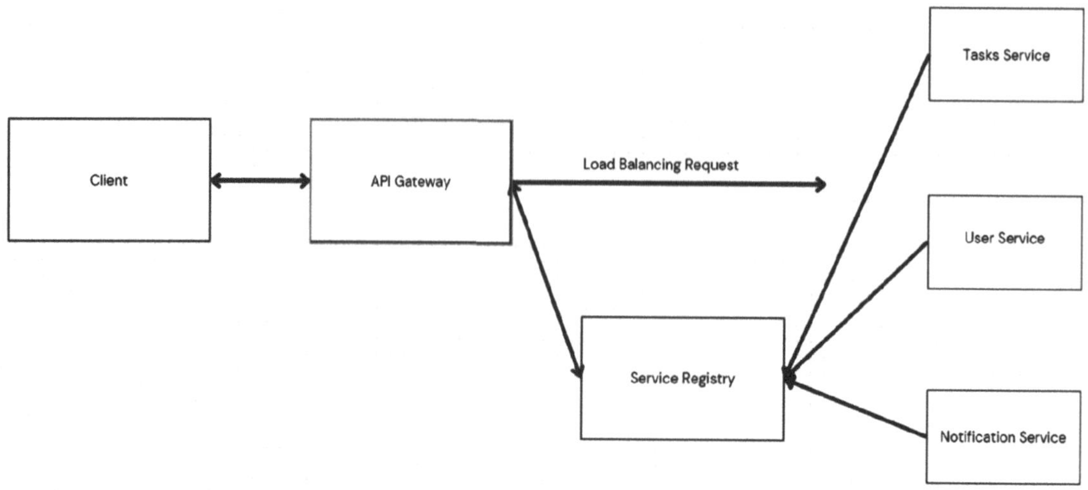


***Figure 9.2:*** *Example with Kubernetes Service Discovery*

**Pros of Server-Side Discovery**

- **Clients Remain Simple:** No need to handle service discovery logic.
- **Centralized Routing and Load Balancing:** The server controls request distribution.
- **More Scalable:** Works well with cloud environments (AWS ELB, Kubernetes, and more).

**Cons of Server-Side Discovery**

- **Additional Network Hop:** Requests go through an intermediary before reaching the destination service.
- **Requires Extra Infrastructure:** Load balancers or API gateways need to be managed.

# Comparison of Client-Side vs. Server-Side Service Discovery

When designing a **service discovery mechanism** for a microservices architecture, it is crucial to choose between **client-side** and **server-side service discovery**. Each approach has its own advantages and trade-offs and impacts factors such as **latency, scalability, and complexity**. The following comparison highlights the key differences between these two discovery patterns to help you determine the most suitable option based on your system's needs:

| **Feature** | **Client-Side Discovery** | **Server-Side Discovery** |
|---|---|---|
| Who Resolves the Service Location? | Client | Load Balancer / API Gateway |
| Complexity on the Client? | Yes | No |
| Load Balancing | Performed by the client (such as Ribbon) | Managed centrally (such as Kubernetes Ingress) |
| Flexibility | Customizable per client | More centralized management |
| Scalability | May require additional logic for large-scale deployments | Works well for dynamic scaling |

***Table 9.1:*** *Client-Side Discovery vs Server-Side Discovery*

# Other Service Discovery Mechanisms

Besides the traditional client-side and server-side discovery patterns, the following additional mechanisms can enhance service discovery:

**DNS-Based Service Discovery**

- Instead of using a dedicated **Service Registry**, microservices can **register themselves as DNS records**.
- Clients resolve service locations using **DNS lookups**.
- **Example**: Kubernetes Service Discovery uses **Cluster DNS** to map service names to IP addresses.

**Service Mesh-Based Discovery (Istio, Linkerd)**

- A **Service Mesh** is a dedicated layer that manages service-to-service communication **without requiring services to handle it themselves**.
- **How it works**: Services do not directly discover each other; instead, a **sidecar proxy** (e.g., Envoy in Istio) handles discovery, security, and observability.
- **Best for**: Large-scale microservices architectures requiring **advanced security, observability, and traffic control**.

# Choosing the Right Service Discovery Pattern

Choosing the right **service discovery pattern** depends on the following application requirements:

| Use Case | Recommended Pattern |
|---|---|
| Small to Medium Microservices Deployment | Client-Side Discovery (Eureka, Consul) |
| Large-Scale Deployments with Many Services | Server-Side Discovery (API Gateway, Kubernetes) |
| Cloud-Native Microservices | Kubernetes Service Discovery |
| Advanced Security & Observability Needed | Service Mesh (Istio, Linkerd) |

***Table 9.2:*** *Choosing the Right Service Discovery Pattern*

Service Discovery is an essential component of **scalable and dynamic microservices architectures**. By automating the process of service registration and lookup, **Service Discovery eliminates the need for hardcoded configurations** and enables **seamless communication between microservices**.

As we move forward, we will implement **a microservices gateway using Istio and Kubernetes**, leveraging **Istio's powerful service mesh capabilities** for **traffic management, security, and observability**. Unlike traditional API gateways, **Istio provides advanced service discovery, load balancing, and security policies at the infrastructure level**, thereby eliminating the need for application-level service registry solutions like **Spring Cloud Eureka**.

In the next section, we will set up **Istio as a Service Mesh in Kubernetes**, enabling microservices to **dynamically register, discover, and securely communicate** with each other while applying traffic routing, monitoring, and security policies at scale.

# Building and Deploying Three Java Microservices in Kubernetes

In this sample architecture, we have three independent Spring Boot microservices: Task Service, User Service, and Notification Service. Each service is a standalone application responsible for a specific domain (tasks, users, and notifications respectively). All services register with a central service registry (such as Eureka or Consul) so that they can discover each other. The client first enquires the service registry to get the location of a service and then sends requests to the appropriate microservice (often via load balancing if multiple instances exist). All microservices use MongoDB as their database to store data, and each service interacts only with its own collection/data in MongoDB. We will deploy these services on Kubernetes, which will run the service containers and service discovery within the cluster (for simplicity, we are not covering Istio or any service mesh in this section).

# Building the Task Service Microservice

Let us start by building the Task Service as an example microservice. This service will be a Spring Boot application that manages "Task" data in a MongoDB database. We will use Spring Boot starters for Web (to create a REST API) and MongoDB (to interact with MongoDB). The Task Service will consist of the following components:

- **Task model**: A Java class representing the Task entity (to be stored in MongoDB)
- **Task repository**: A Spring Data repository interface for CRUD operations on Task data
- **Task service layer:** A service class (business logic layer) that uses the repository to perform operations
- **Task REST controller:** A controller exposing RESTful endpoints (for example, to create a task or fetch tasks)

We will ensure the Spring Data MongoDB dependency is included, and configure the MongoDB connection (for example, via an application property like **spring.data.mongodb.uri=mongodb://<host>:27017/<database>** or an environment variable). The following are the simplified implementations of each component of the Task Service:

To build our microservice, we will first visit Spring Initializr, where we generate a basic project template by selecting the required configurations such as language (Java), build tool (Maven), Spring Boot version, project metadata, and necessary dependencies like Spring Web, Spring Data MongoDB, and Lombok. Once the setup is complete, we can download and import the generated project into our preferred IDE (such as IntelliJ IDEA or Eclipse) to start developing.

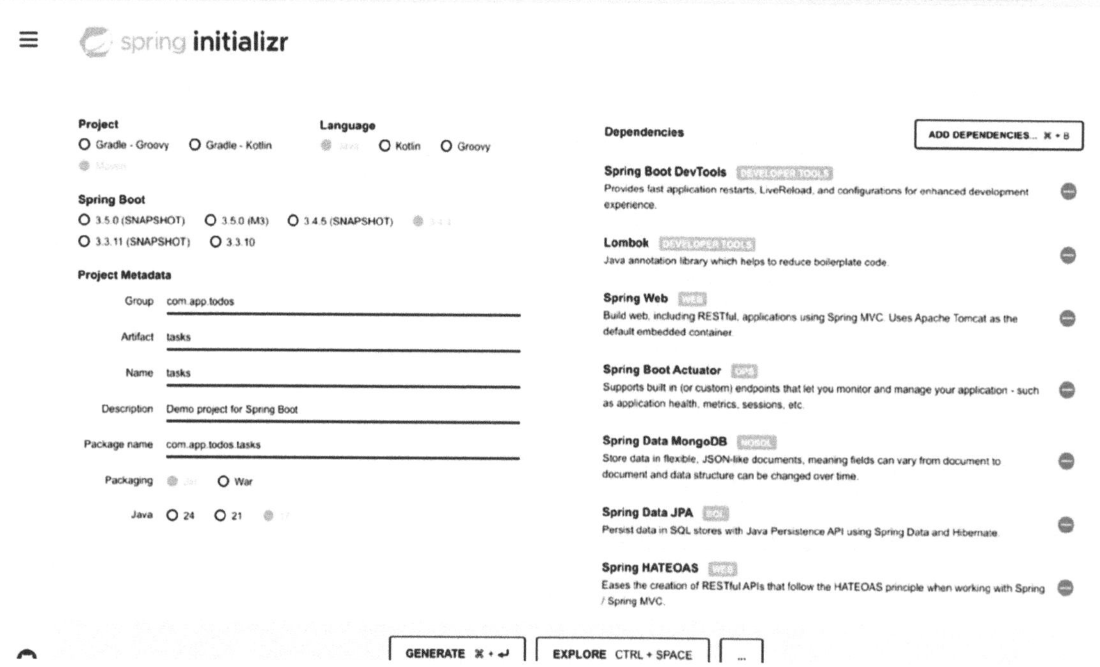


***Figure 9.3**: Building Microservice*

We ensure that the Spring Data MongoDB dependency is included, and configure the MongoDB connection (for example, via an application property like **spring.data.mongodb.**

**uri=mongodb://<host>:27017/<database>** or an environment variable). Below are simplified implementations of each component of the Task Service:

In the below model, **@Document(collection = "tasks")** marks this class to be stored in the tasks collection in MongoDB, and **@Id** marks the primary key field. Next, we define a repository interface to allow CRUD operations on Task documents:

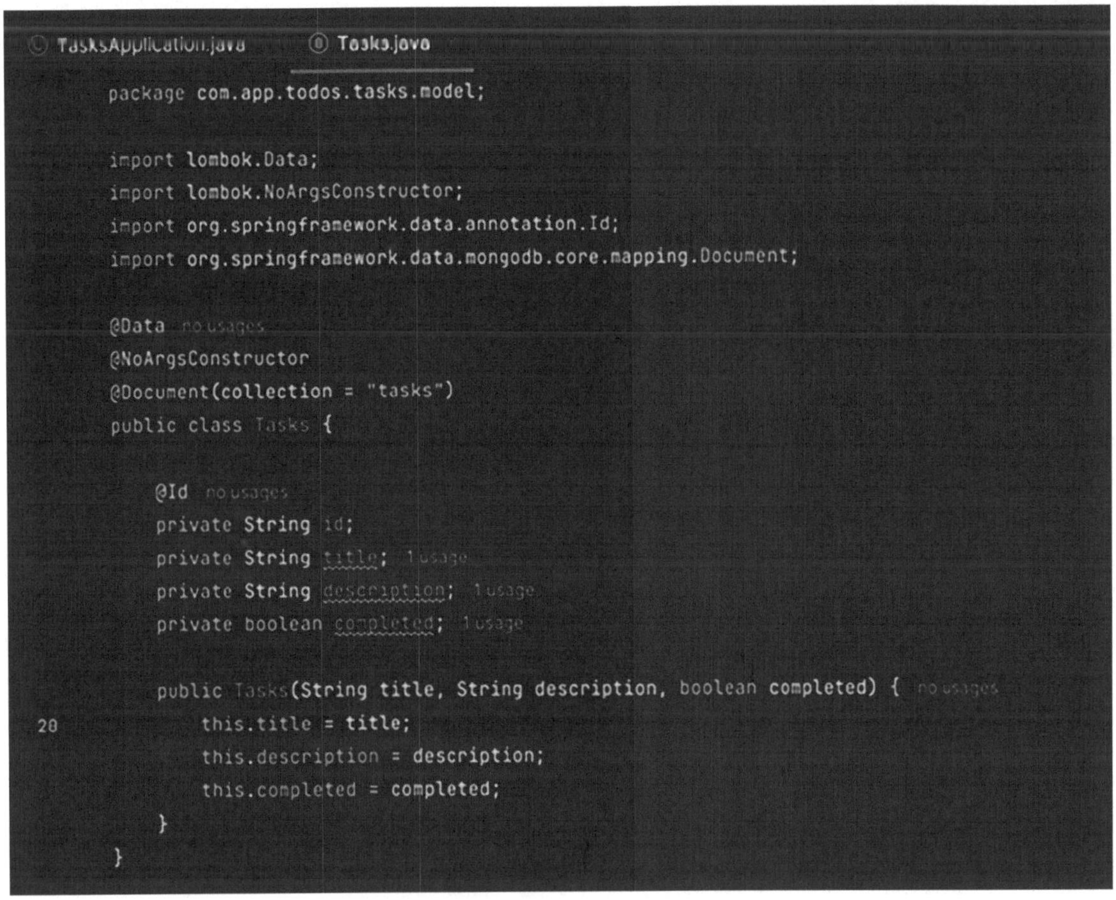

```
package com.app.todos.tasks.model;

import lombok.Data;
import lombok.NoArgsConstructor;
import org.springframework.data.annotation.Id;
import org.springframework.data.mongodb.core.mapping.Document;

@Data
@NoArgsConstructor
@Document(collection = "tasks")
public class Tasks {

    @Id
    private String id;
    private String title;
    private String description;
    private boolean completed;

    public Tasks(String title, String description, boolean completed) {
        this.title = title;
        this.description = description;
        this.completed = completed;
    }
}
```

***Figure 9.4:*** *Tasks.java*

By extending **MongoRepository<Task, String>**, we inherit common methods to save, find, and delete Task objects. The repository will automatically be implemented by Spring at runtime.

We will also create a service layer to encapsulate business logic (this can be light if we are just delegating to the repository, but it aids in separation of concerns):

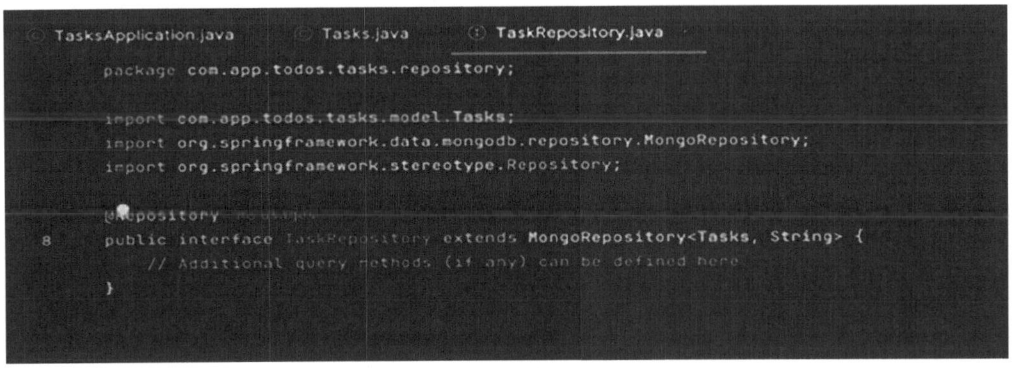

```
package com.app.todos.tasks.repository;

import com.app.todos.tasks.model.Tasks;
import org.springframework.data.mongodb.repository.MongoRepository;
import org.springframework.stereotype.Repository;

@Repository
public interface TaskRepository extends MongoRepository<Tasks, String> {
    // Additional query methods (if any) can be defined here
}
```

***Figure 9.5:*** *TaskRepository.java*

By extending **`MongoRepository<Task, String>`**, we can inherit common methods to save, find, and delete Task objects. The repository will automatically be implemented by Spring at runtime.

We can also create a service layer to encapsulate business logic (this can be light if we are just delegating to the repository, but it helps in separating concerns):

```
TasksApplication.java   Tasks.java   TaskRepository.java   TaskService.java

package com.app.todos.tasks.services;

import com.app.todos.tasks.model.Tasks;
import com.app.todos.tasks.repository.TaskRepository;
import org.springframework.beans.factory.annotation.Autowired;
import org.springframework.stereotype.Service;
import java.util.List;
import java.util.Optional;

@Service
public class TaskService {
    @Autowired
    private TaskRepository taskRepository;

    public List<Tasks> getAllTasks() {
        return taskRepository.findAll();
    }
    public Optional<Tasks> getTaskById(String id) {
        return taskRepository.findById(id);
    }
    public Tasks createTask(Tasks task) {
        return taskRepository.save(task);
    }
}
```

***Figure 9.6:*** *TaskService.java*

Finally, we will expose REST endpoints via a controller. Using Spring MVC annotations, we will map HTTP requests to service calls:

```java
package com.app.todos.tasks.controllers;

import com.app.todos.tasks.model.Tasks;
import com.app.todos.tasks.services.TaskService;
import org.springframework.beans.factory.annotation.Autowired;
import org.springframework.http.ResponseEntity;
import org.springframework.web.bind.annotation.*;

import java.util.List;

@RestController
@RequestMapping("/tasks")
public class TaskController {
    @Autowired
    private TaskService taskService;

    @GetMapping
    public List<Tasks> getAllTasks() {
        // Retrieve all tasks from the service
        return taskService.getAllTasks();
    }

    @GetMapping("/{id}")
    public ResponseEntity<Tasks> getTaskById(@PathVariable String id) {
        // Retrieve a task by its ID, or return 404 if not found
        return taskService.getTaskById(id)
                .map(ResponseEntity::ok)
                .orElse(ResponseEntity.notFound().build());
    }

    @PostMapping
    public Tasks createTask(@RequestBody Tasks task) {
        // Create a new task (the task ID is generated by MongoDB)
        return taskService.createTask(task);
    }
}
```

*Figure 9.7: TaskController.java*

This controller defines endpoints under the base path **`/tasks`**. For example:

- **`GET /tasks`** returns a list of all tasks
- **`GET /tasks/{id}`** returns a single task by ID (or 404 if not found)
- **`POST /tasks`** creates a new task from the JSON body of the request

At this point, the Task Service application can be run (e.g., using **`mvn spring-boot:run`** or by running the built JAR). It will connect to MongoDB (using the configuration provided) and listen for HTTP requests on its port (default 8080). Next, we will package this service into a Docker container for deployment.

# Dockerizing the Task Service

To deploy our Task Service on Kubernetes, we first need to containerize it with Docker. The following steps outline how to create a Docker image for the Task Service:

1. **Build the Spring Boot application jar:** Use Maven or Gradle to package the application. For example, with Maven: **`mvn clean package`**
2. *This should produce a JAR file (for instance,* **`task-service-0.0.1-SNAPSHOT.jar`** *in the* **`target`** *directory).*
3. **Create a Dockerfile:** *In the project directory, create a file named Dockerfile with the following content to define the image:*

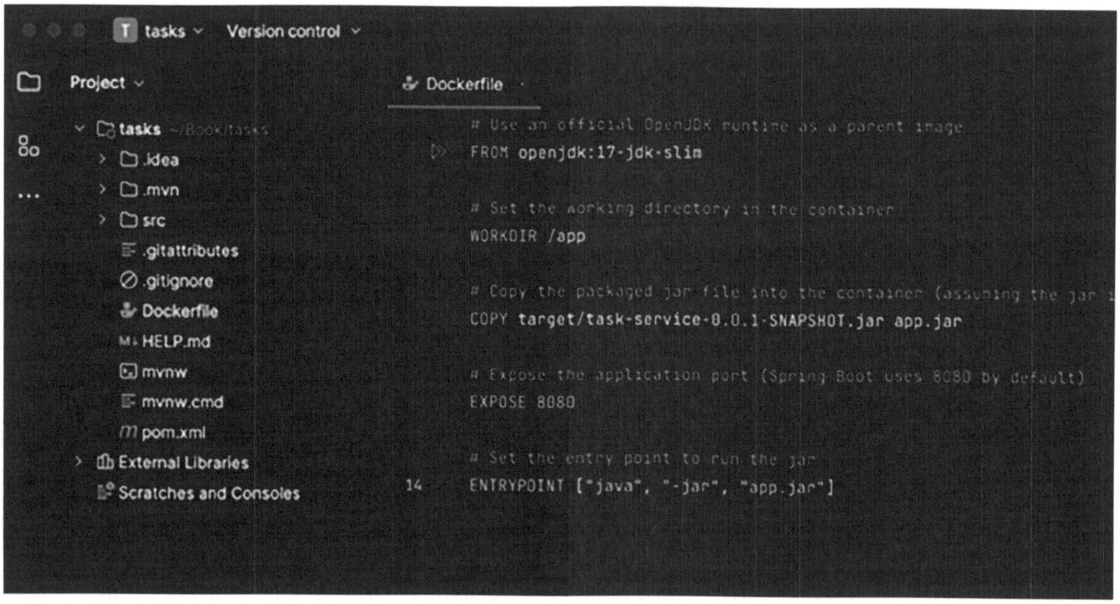


***Figure 9.8:*** *Dockerfile*

This Dockerfile uses a lightweight OpenJDK 17 base image. It copies the Spring Boot fat jar into the container image and sets the entrypoint to run the jar. Make sure the JAR file name in the Dockerfile matches the actual built file (You can also use a generic name like app.jar as shown in the figure).

**Build the Docker image locally:** Run the Docker build command in the same directory as the Dockerfile. For example:

```
docker build -t myorg/task-service:1.0
```

This command builds an image tagged **`myorg/task-service:1.0`** using the Dockerfile in the current directory (`.`). You can choose any repository/name and tag for your image. After a successful build, you have a Docker image of the Task Service. (You can test it by running **`docker run -p 8080:8080 myorg/task-service:1.0`** and hitting the endpoints, assuming it can reach a MongoDB instance.)

With the Task Service containerized, we are ready to deploy it to Kubernetes. We will write Kubernetes manifest files for deployment, and then apply them to our cluster.

# Deploying to Kubernetes

In Kubernetes, we will create separate resources to run the Task Service and make it accessible:

- A **Deployment** to run one or more pods of the Task Service container

- A **Service** (Kubernetes Service) to expose the Task Service pods on a stable network endpoint within the cluster (and optionally to the outside world)
- An **Ingress** (optional) to route external HTTP requests to the Task Service (requires an ingress controller in the cluster)

Let us prepare the Kubernetes YAML manifests for the Task Service:

**Deployment manifest:** Create a file (e.g., `task-service-deployment.yaml`) for the Deployment:

In this Deployment spec, we run a single replica of the Task Service. The container uses the image we built (`myorg/task-service:1.0`). We also set an environment variable `SPRING_DATA_MONGODB_URI` to tell the application how to connect to MongoDB (in this case pointing to a Mongo instance service at hostname "`mongo`" on default port 27017, using a database named `tasksdb`). It is assumed that a MongoDB service is available in the cluster (for example, you might deploy MongoDB as another Deployment/Service named "`mongo`"). The label `app: task-service` is used to match the pod with the Deployment selector and also will be used by the Service.

```yaml
apiVersion: apps/v1
kind: Deployment
metadata:
  name: task-service
  labels:
    app: task-service
spec:
  replicas: 1
  selector:
    matchLabels:
      app: task-service
  template:
    metadata:
      labels:
        app: task-service
    spec:
      containers:
      - name: task-service
        image: myorg/task-service:1.0  # use the image built for Task Service
        ports:
        - containerPort: 8080
        env:
        - name: SPRING_DATA_MONGODB_URI
          value: "mongodb://mongo:27017/tasksdb"
```

***Figure 9.9:** Deployment*

**Service manifest:** Create a file (like `task-service-service.yaml`) for the Kubernetes Service that exposes the Task Service pods:

```yaml
apiVersion: v1
kind: Service
metadata:
  name: task-service
spec:
  selector:
    app: task-service     # targets pods with this label
  ports:
  - port: 80              # the port on the Service (cluster IP)
    targetPort: 8080      # forwards to container's port 8080
    protocol: TCP
  type: ClusterIP         # default type, service only inside cluster
```

***Figure 9.10:*** *Service*

This **Service** will route traffic from port 80 to our pod's port 8080. Within the cluster, other services can reach the Task Service by using the DNS name **task-service** (for example, **http://task-service:80/tasks**). If we only need internal communication (service-to-service), a **ClusterIP** is sufficient. The selector ties the Service to the pods with label **app: task-service** (set in the Deployment).

**Ingress manifest (optional):** If we want external clients to reach the Task Service through HTTP, we can set up an Ingress. Create a file (like **task-service-ingress.yaml**):

```yaml
apiVersion: networking.k8s.io/v1
kind: Ingress
metadata:
  name: task-service-ingress
spec:
  rules:
  - host: example.com  # domain name for ingress (use your domain or localhost for testing)
    http:
      paths:
      - path: /tasks
        pathType: Prefix
        backend:
          service:
            name: task-service
            port:
              number: 80
```

***Figure 9.11:*** *Ingress*

In this example, the Ingress routes requests hitting **http://example.com/tasks** to the Task Service. The path **/tasks** (and anything under it, due to **Prefix** matching) will be forwarded to the **task-service** Service on port 80. In a real setup, you would replace **example.com** with your domain or omit the host for a catch-all. Note that for the Ingress to work, an Ingress Controller (such as NGINX Ingress

Controller) must be installed in the cluster. Covering Ingress setup is beyond our scope here, so this manifest is a placeholder to show how you'd expose the service externally.

**Apply the manifests:** Once you have these YAML files, you can deploy them to Kubernetes using **`kubectl`**. For example, to apply all manifests:

```
kubectl apply -f task-service-deployment.yaml
kubectl apply -f task-service-service.yaml
kubectl apply -f task-service-ingress.yaml
```

Kubernetes will create the Deployment to start the Task Service container in a pod, the Service which maps to the pod, and the Ingress, if it is configured. You can check the status with commands like **`kubectl get pods`**, **`kubectl get svc`**, and **`kubectl describe ingress`**. If everything is set up correctly (and MongoDB is accessible to the pod), the Task Service should be running in the cluster. The microservice can then be accessed by other services in the cluster via the service name (for instance, **`http://task-service/tasks`**), or by external clients via the Ingress (like **`http://example.com/tasks`**) if applicable.

# Applying to Other Services

We built and deployed the Task Service in detail; the **User Service** and **Notification Service** can be created following the same pattern. Each of these is a separate Spring Boot application with its own data model and endpoints, but the structure is identical:

- **User Service:** Could manage user data with a **`User`** model (fields like id, name, email, etc.), a **`UserRepository`** (extending MongoRepository), a service layer, and a REST controller exposing endpoints such as **`GET /users`**, **`GET /users/{id}`**, **`POST /users`** to manage user profiles.
- **Notification Service:** Could manage notifications with a **`Notification`** model (fields like id, message, recipient, etc.), a **`NotificationRepository`**, service layer, and controller with endpoints like **`POST /notifications`** (to send or save a notification) and **`GET /notifications/{id}`**.

Each service will use its own MongoDB collection (for example, a "**`users`**" collection for User Service, and "**`notifications`**" collection for Notification Service). The implementation code layout (model, repository, controller) and the process to Dockerize and deploy are the same as we did for Task Service. You would create a Dockerfile for each service (producing images like **`myorg/user-service:1.0`** and **`myorg/notification-service:1.0`**), and write similar Kubernetes Deployment and Service YAMLs (just changing names, container images, and perhaps the environment variables/database names). If exposed via Ingress, you can add rules for **`/users`** and **`/notifications`** paths (or use separate Ingress resources) pointing to each service's Kubernetes Service.

By following this approach, we will end up with three independent Java microservices running in Kubernetes. They are registered in the service registry for discovery (if using one), and within Kubernetes they can discover each other via service names. Each microservice can be scaled or updated independently. In summary, we have built a robust foundation where the Task, User, and Notification services are all up and running in containers, backed by MongoDB, and accessible via RESTful APIs in our Kubernetes cluster.

# Setting Up Istio for Service Discovery in Kubernetes

In a microservices architecture, service discovery, traffic management, observability, and security are critical concerns. While Kubernetes provides basic capabilities for service discovery through **`ClusterIP`** Services and DNS-based lookup, it lacks built-in features like retries, timeouts, telemetry, mutual TLS, and advanced routing. This is where Istio, a powerful open-source service mesh, comes in.

Istio enhances service-to-service communication in Kubernetes without requiring changes to the application code. It provides an abstracted layer that enables intelligent routing, load balancing, secure communication, and observability between services.

**Definition: Istio** is a service mesh that manages how microservices share data with one another. It uses a **sidecar proxy model** (based on Envoy) to intercept and control all traffic to and from services. This enables features such as:

- **Automatic service discovery** using Kubernetes Services
- **Advanced traffic control** including A/B testing, canary releases, and circuit breaking
- **Zero-trust security** through mutual TLS authentication
- **Comprehensive observability** with metrics, logs, and distributed tracing

With Istio, services do not need to know about the network or handle communication concerns themselves as everything is handled by the sidecar proxies.

# Installing Istio on Kubernetes

To get started, we need a running Kubernetes cluster (such as, using Minikube, Kind, or a cloud provider like GKE/EKS/AKS). Follow these steps to install Istio:

**Download Istio CLI:**

```
curl -L https://istio.io/downloadIstio | sh -
cd istio-*/bin
export PATH=$PWD:$PATH
```

**Install Istio with the demo profile (good for learning and testing):**

```
istioctl install --set profile=demo -y
```

**Verify installation:**

```
kubectl get pods -n istio-system
```

You should see Istio components such as:

- `istiod` (the control plane)
- `istio-ingressgateway`
- `istio-egressgateway`

# Enabling Automatic Sidecar Injection

Istio works by injecting an **Envoy sidecar** into each pod to intercept traffic. You can enable **automatic sidecar injection** in a namespace like this:

```
kubectl label namespace default istio-injection=enabled
```

This tells Istio to automatically inject sidecar proxies into all pods deployed in the `default` namespace (or whichever namespace you choose). All services deployed after this label is applied will be part of the mesh and benefit from Istio's features.

# Deploying Services with Istio

Once the namespace is labeled, you can deploy your microservices as usual using above Kubernetes `Deployment` and `Service` YAML files.

After deployment, Istio will automatically inject the sidecar proxy into each pod. All traffic to and from these services will now be managed by Istio.

## Verifying Service Discovery

Once your services are running in the mesh, you can verify that communication is routed through Envoy proxies and controlled by Istio.

**Use `istioctl proxy-status` to verify proxy health:**

```
istioctl proxy-status
```

1. **Monitor traffic using Kiali or Prometheus (installed with demo profile):**
    - Run `kubectl port-forward svc/kiali -n istio-system 20001:20001`

      Open `http://localhost:20001` in your browser
2. **Use `istioctl analyze` to detect configuration issues:**

   ```
   istioctl analyze
   ```

## Benefits of Istio Service Discovery

By using Istio for service discovery, you unlock a wide range of advanced capabilities beyond what native Kubernetes provides:

- **Resilient communication**: With retries, timeouts, circuit breakers, and fault injection
- **Secure service-to-service traffic**: Using mutual TLS encryption
- **Traffic routing and control**: A/B testing, staged rollouts, and request mirroring
- **Visibility and observability**: With detailed metrics, logs, and traces
- **Policy enforcement and access control**: To restrict which services can talk to each other

Setting up **Istio** for service discovery transforms your Kubernetes cluster into a more powerful, observable, and secure environment for microservices. Unlike native Kubernetes, which provides only basic discovery and load balancing, Istio introduces intelligent traffic routing, fine-grained control, and deep visibility–all without touching your application code.

Now that your microservices are integrated into the Istio service mesh, you are ready to explore more advanced features such as **traffic shaping**, **security policies**, and **telemetry dashboards**. In upcoming sections, we will continue to build on this foundation and demonstrate how Istio supports a production-grade microservices architecture.

# Configuring Microservices for Dynamic Service Discovery in Istio

Once Istio is installed and the sidecar injection is enabled, microservices can seamlessly participate in dynamic service discovery. In Istio, service discovery leverages Kubernetes DNS and internal service routing, but enhances it through sidecar proxies that intercept and manage all incoming and outgoing traffic.

To configure microservices for service discovery in Istio:

1. **Label the Namespace**: Ensure the namespace where your services reside is labeled for Istio injection:

   ```
   kubectl label namespace default istio-injection=enabled
   ```

2. **Deploy Services Normally**: Define your **`Deployment`** and **`Service`** YAMLs as you would in Kubernetes. No special Istio configuration is required for basic discovery. For example:

```
apiVersion: v1
kind: Service
metadata:
  name: user-service
spec:
  selector:
    app: user-service
  ports:
  - port: 80
    targetPort: 8080
```

***Figure 9.12:*** *Service*

3. **Access via DNS**: Services can communicate using their Kubernetes DNS names (like **`http://user-service`**). Istio routes the traffic through sidecars, enabling telemetry, retries, and security by default.

**Destination Rules (Optional)**: To define subsets for advanced routing:

```
apiVersion: networking.istio.io/v1beta1
kind: DestinationRule
metadata:
  name: user-service
spec:
  host: user-service
  subsets:
  - name: v1
    labels:
      version: v1
  - name: v2
    labels:
      version: v2
```

***Figure 9.13:*** *DestinationRule*

# Implementing Service Mesh-Based Traffic Routing

One of Istio's powerful features is its ability to perform intelligent traffic routing without changing application code. This enables scenarios such as A/B testing, canary deployments, and gradual rollouts.

To implement advanced traffic routing:

**Use `VirtualService` to Control Routing**:

```
apiVersion: networking.istio.io/v1beta1
kind: VirtualService
metadata:
  name: user-service
spec:
  hosts:
  - user-service
  http:
  - route:
    - destination:
        host: user-service
        subset: v1
      weight: 90
    - destination:
        host: user-service
        subset: v2
      weight: 10
```

***Figure 9.14:*** *VirtualService*

This configuration sends 90% of traffic to version `v1` and 10% to version `v2` of the User Service.

**Enable Fault Injection (Optional)**: You can simulate failures to test service resilience:

```
fault:
  delay:
    percentage:
      value: 100
    fixedDelay: 5s
```

***Figure 9.15:*** *Enabling Fault Injection*

**Header-Based Routing**: Route traffic based on user agent, auth header, or custom metadata for targeted testing.

Routing rules defined in **`VirtualService`** are enforced by the Envoy proxies sidecars, offering granular control at runtime.

# Testing and Observability in Istio

Istio provides built-in observability tools to monitor microservices communication, performance, and failures without modifying code. This is made possible by sidecar proxies that collect metrics and traces.

Key components and steps to enable observability:

1. **Install Addons**: If using the demo profile, Istio already includes Prometheus, Grafana, Jaeger, and Kiali. Otherwise, you can install them manually:

   `kubectl apply -f samples/addons`

2. **Access Observability Dashboards**:
   - **Kiali (Service Graph)**:
     ```
     kubectl port-forward svc/kiali -n istio-system 20001:20001
     ```
     Navigate to **`http://localhost:20001`**
   - **Prometheus** for metrics: **`http://localhost:9090`**
   - **Grafana** for dashboards: **`http://localhost:3000`**
   - **Jaeger** for tracing: **`http://localhost:16686`**
3. **Generate Traffic**: Use tools like **`curl`**, **`Postman`**, or browser to hit endpoints and generate observable traffic.
4. **Visualize Traffic and Errors**:
   - Kiali shows service-to-service connections
   - Jaeger displays request trace timelines
   - Prometheus + Grafana monitor request latency, success rates, and resource usage

These tools provide a real-time view into your microservices and help you detect bottlenecks, trace failures, and improve system resilience. Observability is a core pillar of Istio that ensures transparency and debuggability in complex distributed systems.

# Conclusion

In this chapter, we explored the foundational principles and practical implementation of service discovery and traffic management in a microservices ecosystem. We began by understanding the importance of service discovery in distributed systems and walked through common patterns, highlighting the limitations of basic client-side and server-side discovery in Kubernetes.

We then built and deployed three independent Spring Boot microservices—Task, User, and Notification Services—using MongoDB as the database backend. These services were containerized using Docker and deployed into a Kubernetes cluster, providing a scalable and maintainable architecture.

To extend the native capabilities of Kubernetes, we introduced Istio, a powerful service mesh that brings advanced features such as traffic control, observability, security, and fault tolerance. We configured our services for dynamic discovery through Istio's sidecar model, implemented traffic routing strategies using **`VirtualService`** and **`DestinationRule`** configurations, and enabled detailed observability through built-in tools like Kiali, Prometheus, Grafana, and Jaeger.

Together, these practices elevate our microservices architecture from a collection of isolated services to a resilient, intelligent, and observable system, capable of adapting to changes in traffic, user load, and failure conditions without compromising stability or security.

Now that our services are discoverable and managed efficiently, the next step is to focus on **how microservices communicate**. In the upcoming chapter, we will dive into the **differences between synchronous and asynchronous communication**, explore REST clients like **RestTemplate**, **WebClient**, and **Feign**, and examine how **Kafka** enables reliable event-driven communication. This understanding is critical for designing microservices that are both responsive and scalable in real-world distributed environments.

# CHAPTER 10
# Microservices Communication

## Introduction

In a microservices architecture, effective communication between services is crucial for maintaining the overall functionality and performance of the system. This chapter delves into the various methods and tools that enable microservices to interact with each other, ensuring seamless data flow and coordination.

We start with an **Overview of Synchronous vs. Asynchronous Communication**, where you will learn the differences between these two communication styles and understand when to use each based on the requirements of your application. This foundational knowledge is key to designing efficient and responsive microservices.

Next, we explore **implementing a RESTful Client with RestTemplate and WebClient**, two of the most commonly used tools in Spring Boot for making synchronous REST API calls. Following this, you will be introduced to **Feign Client for Declarative REST Calls**, which simplifies the process of making HTTP requests by allowing you to define them in a more declarative way.

As the chapter progresses, we shift focus to **Understanding Message Brokers and Event-Driven Architecture**, where you will learn about the role of message brokers like RabbitMQ and Kafka in facilitating asynchronous communication between services. We will then guide you through **Implementing Asynchronous Communication with RabbitMQ or Kafka**, equipping you with the skills to build systems that can handle large volumes of messages and events efficiently.

By the end of this chapter, you will have a comprehensive understanding of the different communication strategies in microservices and how to implement them using various tools and frameworks, enabling you to build more resilient and scalable applications.

## Structure

This chapter covers the following topics:

- Overview of Synchronous vs. Asynchronous Communication
- Implementing RESTful Client with `RestTemplate` and `WebClient`
- Introduction to Feign Client for Declarative REST Calls
- Understanding Message Brokers and Event-Driven Architecture
- Implementing Asynchronous Communication with Kafka

# Overview of Synchronous vs. Asynchronous Communication

In a microservices architecture, services often need to communicate with each other to exchange data, coordinate tasks, and ensure seamless operations. Choosing the right communication strategy is crucial for maintaining scalability, reliability, and performance.

There are two primary communication patterns in microservices:

- **Synchronous Communication**: The sender waits for a response before continuing execution.
- **Asynchronous Communication**: The sender does not wait for an immediate response, allowing for non-blocking operations.

Both approaches have their own advantages, challenges, and use cases. This section explores how each method works, the differences between them, and when to use them to build resilient and efficient microservices.

# Synchronous Communication

Synchronous communication follows a **request-response** model, where a service sends a request to another service and waits for a response before proceeding. This is similar to how traditional client-server applications interact over HTTP.

How It Works

1. **Service A** sends a request (for example, an HTTP API call) to **Service B**.
2. **Service B** processes the request and returns a response.
3. **Service A** waits until it receives the response before continuing execution.

**Example: Synchronous REST API Call**

A microservice calls another service using **`RestTemplate`** in Spring Boot:

```
RestTemplate restTemplate = new RestTemplate();
String response = restTemplate.getForObject("http://user-service/users/123",
String.class);
System.out.println("Response: " + response);
```

***Figure 10.1:*** *RestTemplate Example*

The call to "**`http://user-service/users/123`**" **blocks** execution until the user service responds.

## Common Technologies for Synchronous Communication

To implement synchronous communication in microservices, various technologies enable **direct, real-time interactions between services**. These technologies provide structured methods for **request-response communication** and ensure immediate feedback.

- **HTTP/RESTful APIs** (Spring Boot RestTemplate, WebClient, Feign Client)
- **gRPC** (for high-performance, strongly-typed RPC communication)
- **SOAP Web Services** (used in legacy systems)
- **Database Queries** (SQL-based interactions)

## Advantages of Synchronous Communication

Synchronous communication offers several benefits, particularly for applications requiring **immediate responses and structured workflows**.

- **Simple and Easy to Implement:** Works well for direct service-to-service interactions
- **Consistent and Reliable:** Provides an immediate response, making error handling straightforward
- **Easier Debugging and Monitoring:** Logs and tracing are more structured

## Challenges of Synchronous Communication

Despite its benefits, synchronous communication introduces challenges, especially in **scalability and fault tolerance**.

- **Tightly Coupled Services:** If a dependent service is down, the request fails, affecting availability
- **Increased Latency:** Waiting for a response introduces network delays
- **Scalability Issues:** Handling multiple synchronous requests requires efficient load balancing

### When to Use Synchronous Communication

Choosing **synchronous communication** depends on the use case, system requirements, and the nature of service interactions.

- **When immediate responses are required** (for example, authentication services)
- **For small-scale applications** where service interdependencies are minimal
- **For CRUD operations,** where real-time feedback is necessary (for example, retrieving user details)

# Asynchronous Communication

Asynchronous communication follows an **event-driven** model, where a service sends a request without waiting for an immediate response. Instead, the request is processed independently, and the sender continues execution.

### How It Works

1. **Service A** sends a message or event to a **message broker** (for example, Kafka, RabbitMQ).
2. **Service B** listens to the message broker and processes the event when available.
3. **Service A** does not wait; it continues executing other tasks.

### Example: Asynchronous Event Processing with Kafka

A microservice **produces an event** to Kafka and another microservice **listens for the event** and processes it. The sender **does not** wait for a response, allowing it to process other tasks.

```
// Sending an Event
KafkaTemplate<String, String> kafkaTemplate;
kafkaTemplate.send("task-events", "Task Created: ID 456");

// listening to an event
@KafkaListener(topics = "task-events", groupId = "task-group")
public void consume(String message) {
    System.out.println("Received event: " + message);
}
```

**Figure 10.2:** *KafkaListener Example*

**Common Technologies for Asynchronous Communication**

Asynchronous communication facilitates event-driven, non-blocking interactions between microservices, allowing them to process requests independently and at different times. This approach is essential for high-performance, loosely coupled architectures. Several technologies facilitate asynchronous messaging and event streaming in microservices environments and are mentioned as follows:

- **Message Brokers**: RabbitMQ, Apache Kafka, AWS SQS
- **Event-Driven Architectures**: Kafka Streams, AWS EventBridge
- **WebSockets and gRPC Streams** (for real-time updates)
- **Reactive Programming**: Spring WebFlux (for non-blocking HTTP calls)

**Advantages of Asynchronous Communication**

Asynchronous communication offers several benefits that enhance scalability, resilience, and responsiveness in microservices systems.

- **Loose Coupling:** Services operate independently, reducing interdependencies
- **Better Scalability:** Multiple consumers can process messages in parallel
- **Improved Fault Tolerance:** The sender does not fail if the receiver is temporarily unavailable
- **Handles High-Volume Data Streams:** Best for real-time processing of large datasets

**Challenges of Asynchronous Communication**

While powerful, asynchronous communication comes with complexities that require careful handling.

- **Complex Debugging and Monitoring:** Since processing happens independently, tracing requests across services is harder.
- **Delayed Processing:** There is no immediate feedback after sending a message.
- **Event Ordering and Consistency Issues:** Messages might not be processed in the same order they were sent.

**When to Use Asynchronous Communication**

Asynchronous communication is well-suited for event-driven, scalable microservices architectures where services need to function independently and handle high traffic loads.

- **Event-Driven Workflows** (for example, sending notifications when an order is placed)
- **High Throughput Systems** (for example, logging systems, payment processing)

- **Scalable Microservices,** where independent processing is beneficial (for example, streaming analytics)

# Comparison: Synchronous vs. Asynchronous Communication

When designing a microservices architecture, choosing between **synchronous** and **asynchronous communication** is critical to achieve the right balance between **performance, scalability, and reliability**. While synchronous communication ensures **immediate responses and structured workflows**, asynchronous communication enhances **scalability and fault tolerance** by decoupling services. The following table provides a side-by-side comparison to help determine the best approach for different scenarios.

| Feature | Synchronous Communication | Asynchronous Communication |
|---|---|---|
| Request Handling | Immediate response | Processes independently |
| Latency | Higher due to waiting | Lower as the sender does not wait |
| Service Coupling | Tightly coupled | Loosely coupled |
| Scalability | Limited by synchronous calls | Scales better with event-driven systems |
| Fault Tolerance | Prone to failures if dependent services are down | More resilient due to message queuing |
| Use Case | API calls, database queries | Event-driven architectures, logging, background processing |

***Table 10.1:*** *Synchronous vs Asynchronous Communication*

Choosing the Right Communication Pattern

- Use **synchronous communication** when **immediate feedback is required** (for example, login validation, fetching user details)
- Use **asynchronous communication** when dealing with **high-volume, loosely coupled systems** (for example sending emails, processing transactions)

# Hybrid Approach: Combining Synchronous and Asynchronous Communication

Many real-world microservices **combine both synchronous and asynchronous approaches** to achieve **optimal performance and reliability**.

**Example: E-Commerce Application**

1. **Synchronous:** When a user places an order, the Order Service immediately validates payment using a REST API call.
2. **Asynchronous:** After payment confirmation, an event is published to **Kafka**, notifying the **Shipping Service** to process the order asynchronously.

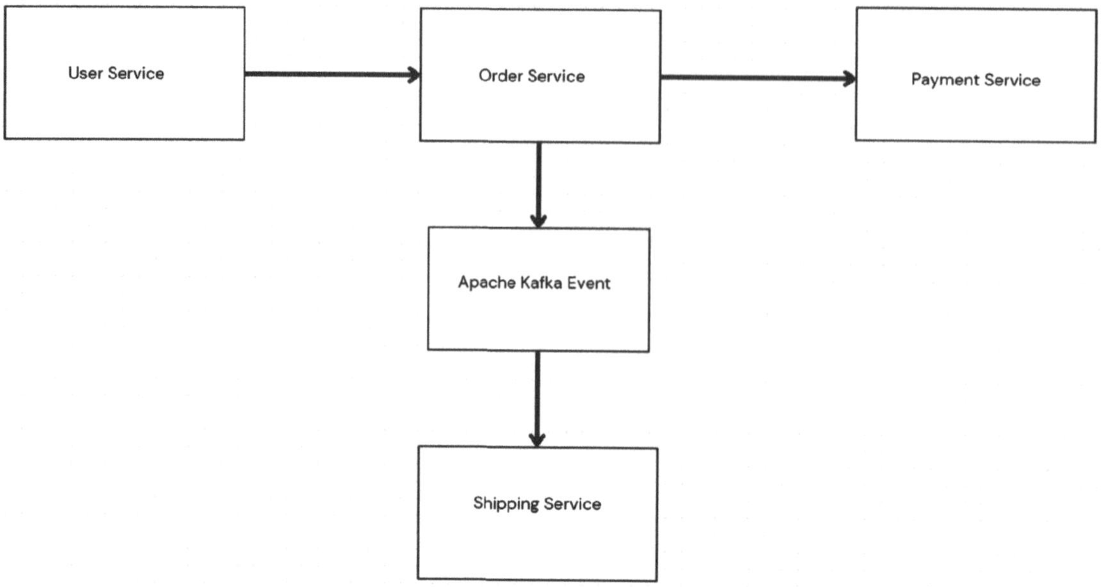


***Figure 10.3:*** *Example Application*

This approach ensures:

- **Immediate payment validation** using a synchronous REST API call
- **Decoupled order processing** using an asynchronous event-driven system

In this section, we explored **synchronous vs. asynchronous communication** in microservices, highlighting their differences, benefits, and use cases.

- **Synchronous communication** is **simple and reliable**, but **tightly couples services** and introduces **latency issues.**
- **Asynchronous communication** improves **scalability and fault tolerance**, but comes with **increased complexity and debugging challenges**.
- Many real-world applications **combine both approaches**, ensuring a balance between **performance and reliability**.

In the next section, we will **implement synchronous communication using RESTful clients** in Spring Boot while leveraging tools like **`RestTemplate`** and **`WebClient`** to facilitate efficient service-to-service interaction.

# Implementing RESTful Client with `RestTemplate` and `WebClient`

Modern microservices often need to communicate with each other over HTTP. In Java-based microservices, this is typically done using RESTful APIs. Spring provides two powerful HTTP client tools: **`RestTemplate`** (traditional, blocking) and **`WebClient`** (modern, non-blocking). In this section, we will explore how to use both clients to interact with RESTful endpoints effectively.

## `RestTemplate`: The Traditional Approach

**`RestTemplate`** is a synchronous HTTP client introduced in Spring 3. It simplifies communication with HTTP servers and enforces RESTful principles. Although it has been officially deprecated in favor of **`WebClient`** in Spring 5, it is still widely used in legacy applications.

**Adding Dependencies**

If you are using Spring Boot, **`RestTemplate`** comes with the **`spring-boot-starter-web`** dependency:

```
<dependency>
    <groupId>org.springframework.boot</groupId>
    <artifactId>spring-boot-starter-web</artifactId>
</dependency>
```

**Configuration**

You can create a **`RestTemplate`** bean in your configuration class:

```
@Configuration
public class AppConfig {
    @Bean
    public RestTemplate restTemplate() {
        return new RestTemplate();
    }
}
```

***Figure 10.4***: *Configuration*

**Usage Example**

Assume that another microservice exposes an endpoint **`GET /users/{id}`**. You can call it using **`RestTemplate`** like this:

```
@Service
public class UserService {

    @Autowired
    private RestTemplate restTemplate;

    public User getUserById(String id) {
        String url = "http://user-service/users/" + id;
        return restTemplate.getForObject(url, User.class);
    }
}
```

***Figure 10.5***: *Usage Example*

This approach blocks the thread until a response is received, which can be a drawback under high load or in reactive applications.

# `WebClient`: The Reactive Approach

**`WebClient`** is the non-blocking, reactive HTTP client introduced in Spring 5 as part of the WebFlux framework. It provides a more flexible and functional API and is the recommended way to make HTTP calls in modern Spring applications.

**Adding Dependencies**

For **WebClient**, include the following dependency:

```
<dependency>
    <groupId>org.springframework.boot</groupId>
    <artifactId>spring-boot-starter-webflux</artifactId>
</dependency>
```

**Configuration**

Define a **WebClient.Builder** bean for reuse across your application:

```
@Configuration
public class WebClientConfig {
    @Bean
    public WebClient.Builder webClientBuilder() {
        return WebClient.builder();
    }
}
```

***Figure 10.6***: *WebClient Builder*

**Usage Example**

Here is how to use **WebClient** to call an external service:

```
@Service
public class UserWebClientService {

    @Autowired
    private WebClient.Builder webClientBuilder;

    public Mono<User> getUserById(String id) {
        return webClientBuilder.build()
                .get()
                .uri("http://user-service/users/{id}", id)
                .retrieve()
                .bodyToMono(User.class);
    }
}
```

***Figure 10.7***: *Webclient Example*

This returns a **Mono<User>**, which is a part of the Project Reactor's reactive programming model. You can subscribe to it asynchronously or integrate it into a reactive flow.

**Advantages of WebClient**

- Non-blocking and asynchronous
- More efficient under heavy load

- Supports reactive streams, backpressure, and error handling
- Suitable for both REST and streaming APIs (WebSockets, SSE)

# Choosing between `RestTemplate` and `WebClient`

Before deciding which client to use in your application, it is essential to understand the fundamental differences between **`RestTemplate`** and **`WebClient`**, especially in terms of performance, threading model, and development style.

| **Feature** | **`RestTemplate`** | **`WebClient`** |
|---|---|---|
| API Style | Imperative | Reactive (Fluent, Functional) |
| Threading | Blocking (Synchronous) | Non-Blocking (Asynchronous) |
| Performance | Lower Under load | High Throughput |
| Use Case | Simple REST Calls | Reactive, High Concurrency apps |
| Spring Recommendation | Depreciated (Spring 5+) | Modern Web Development |

***Table 10.2**: RestTemplate vs WebClient*

For modern microservices and cloud-native systems, **`WebClient`** is strongly recommended due to its performance and flexibility. However, if you are maintaining or integrating with legacy systems, **`RestTemplate`** may still be appropriate.

In this section, we explored two primary ways to make HTTP calls from a Spring Boot application: **`RestTemplate`** and **`WebClient`**. While **`RestTemplate`** is easy to use and suitable for simpler use cases, **`WebClient`** is the future-proof option that supports reactive and non-blocking programming. As microservices become more distributed and event-driven, adopting **`WebClient`** aligns better with the performance and scalability demands of cloud-native applications.

In the next section, we will further simplify REST communication using Feign Client, which offers a declarative approach to defining HTTP clients with minimal boilerplate code.

# Introduction to Feign Client for Declarative REST Calls

In microservices architecture, services often need to communicate with one another using REST APIs. Traditional approaches, such as using **`RestTemplate`** or **`WebClient`**, require manual configuration and code for every API call, which can become verbose and error-prone as the application scales. Feign Client, developed by Netflix and integrated into the Spring Cloud ecosystem, offers a declarative approach to writing REST clients, thus reducing the boilerplate code dramatically.

Feign allows developers to define interfaces with annotations that describe HTTP requests. Behind the scenes, Feign generates the implementation at runtime, enabling you to invoke REST endpoints as if calling local service methods.

**Advantages of Feign Client**

- **Declarative Syntax**: Write clean, interface-based HTTP clients
- **Tight Integration with Spring Boot**: Seamless support for Spring Cloud, Eureka, Ribbon, and Hystrix
- **Reduced Boilerplate**: No need to manually configure and write repetitive code for REST calls
- **Pluggable and Extensible**: Supports custom encoders, decoders, error handling, and logging

# Setting Up Feign in a Spring Boot Project

**Step 1: Add Dependencies**

Ensure that the following dependencies are included in your `pom.xml`:

```
<dependency>
    <groupId>org.springframework.cloud</groupId>
    <artifactId>spring-cloud-starter-openfeign</artifactId>
</dependency>
```

Also, include the Spring Cloud BOM for version management:

```
<dependencyManagement>
    <dependencies>
        <dependency>
            <groupId>org.springframework.cloud</groupId>
            <artifactId>spring-cloud-dependencies</artifactId>
            <version>2022.0.3</version> <!-- Choose your preferred version -->
            <type>pom</type>
            <scope>import</scope>
        </dependency>
    </dependencies>
</dependencyManagement>
```

**Step 2: Enable Feign Clients**

Enable Feign in your main application class by using the `@EnableFeignClients` annotation:

```
@SpringBootApplication
@EnableFeignClients
public class Application {
    public static void main(String[] args) {
        SpringApplication.run(Application.class, args);
    }
}
```

**Figure 10.8**: *Enabling Feign Clients*

# Creating a Feign Client Interface

Let us say you have a microservice **`user-service`** exposing **`GET /users/{id}`**. You can create a Feign client as follows:

```
@FeignClient(name = "user-service")
public interface UserClient {

    @GetMapping("/users/{id}")
    User getUserById(@PathVariable("id") String id);
}
```

**Figure 10.9**: *Creating a Feign Client Interface*

You can now autowire **UserClient** in your services:

```
@Service
public class TaskService {

    @Autowired
    private UserClient userClient;

    public void performTask(String userId) {
        User user = userClient.getUserById(userId);
        // Process user
    }
}
```

***Figure 10.10**: TaskService*

Feign automatically handles the HTTP request execution, response parsing, and error propagation.

# Feign with Eureka and Load Balancing

Feign integrates smoothly with **Spring Cloud Netflix Eureka** for service discovery. When used with Eureka, the **name** attribute in **@FeignClient** maps to the registered service name.

Additionally, Feign clients work with **Ribbon** for client-side load balancing, distributing traffic across instances.

**Example**: If you have multiple instances of **user-service**, Feign + Ribbon will automatically balance requests among them.

# Error Handling and Fallbacks

Feign allows for custom error handling using **@ControllerAdvice** or through Hystrix fallback methods (if enabled):

```
@FeignClient(name = "user-service", fallback = UserClientFallback.class)
public interface UserClient {
    @GetMapping("/users/{id}")
    User getUserById(@PathVariable("id") String id);
}

@Component
class UserClientFallback implements UserClient {
    public User getUserById(String id) {
        return new User("N/A", "Fallback User");
    }
}
```

***Figure 10.11**: Error Handling and Fallbacks*

This ensures service resilience during partial outages.

## Feign Configuration Tips

- Use **custom configurations** for timeouts and encoders.
- Combine Feign with **Spring Retry** for automatic retries.
- Integrate **OpenFeign Logging** for request/response inspection:

Feign simplifies REST client development by transforming REST calls into simple Java method invocations. It improves readability, maintainability, and integration across microservices. When combined with Spring Cloud and tools like Eureka and Ribbon, it becomes a powerful tool for building resilient and scalable microservice architectures.

In the next section, we will shift our focus to **asynchronous communication** using **message brokers** and explore the benefits of **event-driven architecture** using tools like Kafka.

# Understanding Message Brokers and Event-Driven Architecture

In traditional request-response-based communication, microservices interact synchronously, expecting immediate replies from one another. Although this approach is straightforward, it creates tight coupling, introduces latency, and impacts scalability when services depend on one another to respond quickly. As systems scale and become more complex, a shift toward asynchronous and event-driven architectures becomes essential. The following section will explore the fundamentals of event-driven design and the critical role of message brokers in enabling such architectures.

## Understanding Event-Driven Architecture (EDA)

**Event-Driven Architecture (EDA)** is a software design pattern in which services communicate by producing and consuming events. Instead of calling each other directly, microservices emit events when something significant happens (for example, "`UserCreated`" or "`OrderPlaced`") and when other services interested in those events act upon them.

**Key Components of EDA**

1. **Producer:** The service that generates and publishes events
2. **Consumer:** The service that listens for and reacts to events
3. **Event:** A message that describes a change in state
4. **Event Bus/Message Broker:** A middleware system that routes events between producers and consumers

**Benefits of EDA**

- **Loose Coupling:** Services do not need to know about each other.
- **Scalability:** Events can be consumed by multiple services in parallel.
- **Resilience:** Services are less likely to fail due to synchronous dependencies.
- **Flexibility:** New consumers can be added without modifying producers.

## Introduction to Message Brokers

A **message broker** is a software component that enables services to exchange information in the form of messages. In an event-driven system, it acts as an intermediary that manages the transmission, routing, and persistence of messages.

**Popular Message Brokers**

1. **Apache Kafka:** A distributed streaming platform designed for high throughput and fault tolerance
2. **RabbitMQ:** A lightweight message queue with strong delivery guarantees and plugin support
3. **Amazon SQS/SNS:** Managed messaging services provided by AWS
4. **Azure Service Bus/Event Grid:** Microsoft's cloud-native messaging and eventing solutions

**Key Features of Message Brokers**

- **Decoupling:** Producers and consumers operate independently
- **Asynchronous Messaging:** Enables non-blocking communication
- **Durability:** Messages are stored until consumed
- **Retry and Dead Letter Queues:** Handle failed delivery attempts
- **Topic-Based Routing:** Send messages to specific consumers using topics or routing keys

# Event Types and Messaging Models

There are two primary messaging models used in event-driven architectures, and understanding their distinctions is the key to choosing the right design for your system. Depending on your application's requirements—whether you need messages to be consumed by one or many consumers—you can adopt a point-to-point or publish-subscribe model. In the following paragraphs, we will explore both models and their typical use cases.

1. **Point-to-Point (Queues)**
   - A single producer sends a message to a queue
   - One consumer receives and processes the message
   - Ensures **one-to-one** communication

**Example:** A billing service reads payment tasks from a queue.

2. **Publish-Subscribe (Topics)**
   - A producer sends messages to a topic
   - Multiple subscribers receive the same event
   - Supports **one-to-many** communication

**Example:** An order placed event is sent to inventory, notification, and analytics services.

# Use Cases for Event-Driven Architecture

Event-driven architecture is especially powerful when systems need to react to changes in state or trigger downstream processes without being tightly coupled. Below are some practical use cases that illustrate how events can be utilized to build scalable, decoupled microservices ecosystems.

- **User Signup Workflow:** User service emits a `UserRegistered` event; notification and onboarding services consume it
- **Order Fulfillment:** Order service emits `OrderPlaced;` shipping, billing, and inventory services react independently
- **Audit Logging:** Services emit domain events that are persisted for auditing

- **Real-time Analytics:** Stream processing services subscribe to events and generate metrics or insights

## Challenges of Event-Driven Systems

While EDA has many advantages, it also introduces the following complexities:

- **Event Ordering:** Ensuring the correct sequence of events
- **Data Consistency:** Achieving eventual consistency across services
- **Message Duplication:** Handling the same event more than once
- **Error Handling:** Managing failed or unprocessable messages
- **Debugging and Monitoring:** Tracing events across asynchronous flows

Best practices such as idempotent event handling, schema validation, and proper use of dead-letter queues can help address these issues.

## Event Streaming vs. Messaging

While both involve passing data between services, event streaming platforms like **Kafka** are optimized for continuous data flow and real-time processing. Messaging systems like **RabbitMQ** are better suited for discrete messages and command processing.

**Kafka:**

- Ideal for high-throughput logging and analytics
- Supports message replay, retention policies, and event versioning

**RabbitMQ:**

- Ideal for task-based workflows
- Supports message acknowledgments, retries, and routing

Event-driven architecture and message brokers enable modern distributed systems to be decoupled, scalable, and reactive. By shifting communication from direct calls to asynchronous events, systems become more flexible and resilient. Whether you use **Kafka** for high-volume streaming or **RabbitMQ** for lightweight task processing, understanding how message brokers work is foundational to building robust microservices.

In the next section, we will explore how to **implement asynchronous communication in practice** using **Apache Kafka**, including setup, producing, consuming, and integrating Kafka into your Spring Boot microservices.

# Implementing Asynchronous Communication with Kafka

In this section, we will explore how to implement asynchronous communication in a microservices architecture using **Apache Kafka**. **Kafka** is a distributed, partitioned, and replicated commit log service that provides a robust foundation for building event-driven and reactive systems. Its high throughput, scalability, and fault-tolerant capabilities make it an ideal choice for microservices that need to communicate asynchronously.

## Significance of Kafka

Kafka allows services to publish and subscribe to streams of records in real-time. It decouples producers and consumers, allowing them to scale independently and communicate without being aware of each other's existence.

**Key Benefits:**

- High throughput and low latency
- Horizontal scalability with partitioned topics
- Persistent message storage
- Fault tolerance and message replay
- Integration with stream processing tools

# Setting Up Kafka Locally

To get started with Kafka, you need to install **Apache Kafka** and **Zookeeper**. If you are using Docker, here is a simple way to set them up:

```
version: '2'
services:
  zookeeper:
    image: confluentinc/cp-zookeeper:latest
    environment:
      ZOOKEEPER_CLIENT_PORT: 2181
      ZOOKEEPER_TICK_TIME: 2000

  kafka:
    image: confluentinc/cp-kafka:latest
    ports:
      - "9092:9092"
    environment:
      KAFKA_BROKER_ID: 1
      KAFKA_ZOOKEEPER_CONNECT: zookeeper:2181
      KAFKA_ADVERTISED_LISTENERS: PLAINTEXT://localhost:9092
      KAFKA_OFFSETS_TOPIC_REPLICATION_FACTOR: 1
```

***Figure 10.12**: Setting up Kafka Locally*

Run with: **`docker-compose up -d`**

# Spring Boot Integration with Kafka

To use Kafka with Spring Boot, add the following dependency:

```
<dependency>
  <groupId>org.springframework.kafka</groupId>
  <artifactId>spring-kafka</artifactId>
</dependency>
```

# Creating a Kafka Producer

One of the first steps in setting up asynchronous communication is creating a Kafka producer. Producers are responsible for sending messages (events) to Kafka topics. In the context of a Spring

Boot application, this involves configuring the necessary properties and defining a service class that uses the **KafkaTemplate** to send messages.

**Configuration:**

```
spring:
  kafka:
    bootstrap-servers: localhost:9092
    producer:
      key-serializer: org.apache.kafka.common.serialization.StringSerializer
      value-serializer: org.apache.kafka.common.serialization.StringSerializer
```

***Figure 10.13**: Configuration*

**Producer Class:**

```
@Service
public class KafkaProducerService {

    @Autowired
    private KafkaTemplate<String, String> kafkaTemplate;

    private static final String TOPIC = "user-events";

    public void sendMessage(String message) {
        kafkaTemplate.send(TOPIC, message);
    }
}
```

***Figure 10.14**: Producer Class*

# Creating a Kafka Consumer

After a producer sends messages to a Kafka topic, consumers are responsible for retrieving and processing those messages. Kafka consumers subscribe to one or more topics and continuously poll for new data. In a Spring Boot application, you can implement a consumer using **@KafkaListener** to automatically listen to incoming messages and handle them asynchronously.

**Configuration**

```
spring:
  kafka:
    consumer:
      group-id: my-group
      key-deserializer:
org.apache.kafka.common.serialization.StringDeserializer
      value-deserializer:
org.apache.kafka.common.serialization.StringDeserializer
      auto-offset-reset: earliest
```

***Figure 10.15**: Configuration*

**Consumer**

```
@Service
public class KafkaConsumerService {

    @KafkaListener(topics = "user-events", groupId = "my-group")
    public void consume(String message) {
        System.out.println("Received message: " + message);
        // Process message asynchronously
    }
}
```

***Figure 10.16**: Kafka Consumer*

# Sending and Receiving Domain Events

In a real-world microservices application, communication is often more than just strings of text—it involves sharing structured data. To achieve this, domain events are typically represented as Java objects and serialized into a format like JSON for transmission via Kafka. This approach ensures that rich, typed data can be shared between services in a standardized way, maintaining clarity and data integrity.

In a real application, you would typically serialize a domain object into JSON:

**Model Class**: Start by defining a domain model class that represents the structure of your event. This could include fields relevant to the business logic, such as **`userId`**, **`action`**, timestamps, or metadata.

```
public class UserEvent {
    private String userId;
    private String action;
    // Getters and setters
}
```

## Use Jackson for Serialization

Before sending the event, you need to convert the Java object into a JSON string. Jackson's **`ObjectMapper`** can serialize the object, ensuring that the data sent over Kafka maintains the original structure and field values.

```
ObjectMapper objectMapper = new ObjectMapper();
String json = objectMapper.writeValueAsString(userEvent);
kafkaTemplate.send("user-events", json);
```

## And Deserialize in the Consumer

When the consumer receives a JSON message, it should convert the JSON string back into the original domain object. This deserialization enables the consuming service to work directly with structured Java objects, making downstream processing more intuitive and reliable.

```
UserEvent event = objectMapper.readValue(message, UserEvent.class);
```

# Common Use Cases for Kafka

Kafka's versatility makes it suitable for a wide range of real-time and asynchronous use cases. We have mentioned some of the most common scenarios where Kafka can enhance the robustness and responsiveness of your microservices architecture:

- **Activity/Event Logging**: Kafka can capture every user action or system change as an event and persist it to enable real-time analysis, audits, or replaying historical data for debugging and compliance.
- **User Notifications**: Microservices can emit events like `OrderPlaced` or `PasswordChanged`, which Kafka routes to a notification service that sends emails, push notifications, or SMS messages to users.
- **Audit Trails**: Kafka helps log sensitive system interactions such as data modifications or login attempts. These immutable logs serve as an authoritative audit source for security and regulatory reviews.
- **Order/Payment Workflows**: In e-commerce systems, services like order processing, inventory, billing, and shipping can coordinate via Kafka events, enabling each component to act asynchronously and reliably.
- **Data Ingestion Pipelines**: Kafka excels at ingesting high-volume streaming data (for example IoT sensor data, logs, social media feeds) and routing it to storage systems or real-time analytics engines like Apache Flink or Spark.

Kafka is a powerful tool for implementing asynchronous communication in distributed systems. By decoupling producers and consumers, it enables scalable and fault-tolerant communication patterns. In this chapter, we integrated Kafka with Spring Boot, created producers and consumers, and demonstrated how to send and receive structured events.

In the next chapter, we will explore how to implement API gateways and edge services to manage, secure, and route communication between internal microservices and external clients.

# Conclusion

In this chapter, we explored the fundamental communication strategies used in microservices architecture–synchronous and asynchronous communication–and learned how each influences system design and scalability.

We began by examining the key differences between the two approaches, understanding when to use each depending on responsiveness, resilience, and real-time requirements. We then implemented synchronous communication using `RestTemplate`, `WebClient`, and the more modern `Feign Client`, showcasing how declarative REST calls simplify inter-service communication in Spring Boot applications.

Next, we transitioned into the world of event-driven architecture, discussing how message brokers like Kafka play a central role in enabling asynchronous, decoupled service communication. We provided a thorough explanation of Kafka concepts, set up a local environment, and demonstrated how to implement producers and consumers within a Spring Boot microservices ecosystem. Real-world examples such as user notifications, audit logging, and order workflows illustrated the power of asynchronous messaging.

Together, these tools and strategies form the backbone of robust, scalable microservice systems. In the next chapter, we will take this communication model even further by exploring API Gateways and Edge Services. You will learn how to manage cross-cutting concerns like routing, rate limiting, and security, while exposing a unified entry point for your microservices to the outside world.

# CHAPTER 11
# API Gateway and Edge Services

## Introduction

In a microservices architecture, managing and securing the flow of requests between clients and backend services is critical. This chapter will thus explore the essential role of API gateways in streamlining and safeguarding communication in a distributed system.

We begin by examining the **Role of API Gateways in Microservices**, where you will learn how API gateways act as a single entry point for client requests, managing and routing them to the appropriate microservices. This section will also highlight the importance of API gateways in handling cross-cutting concerns like security, load balancing, and monitoring.

Next, we will move on to **Configuring Spring Cloud Gateway**, a powerful tool for implementing API gateways in a Spring Boot environment. You will learn how to set up and customize Spring Cloud Gateway to suit your application's needs.

We will then delve into **Implementing Rate Limiting and Circuit Breaker Patterns**, essential techniques for protecting your services from overload and ensuring system resilience in the face of failures.

Finally, the chapter concludes with **Securing Microservices with JWT and OAuth2**, where you will learn how to implement robust security measures using JSON Web Tokens (JWT) and OAuth2 to protect your microservices from unauthorized access.

By the end of this chapter, you will have a solid understanding of how to implement and configure API gateways and edge services to enhance the performance, security, and reliability of your microservices-based applications.

## Structure

This chapter will address the following topics:

- Role of API Gateways in Microservices
- Configuring Spring Cloud Gateway
- Integrating Spring Cloud Gateway with Istio
- Implementing Rate Limiting and Circuit Breaker Patterns
- Securing Microservices with JWT and OAuth2

## Role of API Gateways in Microservices

In a microservices architecture, multiple independent services handle different business functionalities, and clients interact with them over a network. However, exposing each microservice directly to clients introduces complexity, security risks, and operational challenges.

This is where an API Gateway plays a crucial role. It acts as a single entry point for external clients, managing request routing, security, load balancing, monitoring, and response aggregation. By centralizing these concerns, API gateways simplify communication between clients and microservices while enhancing the security, performance, and manageability of the system.

# API Gateway

An **API Gateway** is a **reverse proxy** that receives all incoming client requests and directs them to the appropriate microservice. It acts as a **middleware** layer that abstracts away the complexity of interacting with multiple services, ensuring that clients do not need to know the internal structure of the microservices system.

**Key Responsibilities of an API Gateway**

- **Request Routing and Load Balancing:** Directs requests to the appropriate microservice instance, balancing traffic across multiple instances to avoid overloading
- **Security Enforcement:** Implements authentication and authorization mechanisms using **JWT, OAuth2, API keys, or token-based authentication**
- **Rate Limiting and Throttling:** Prevents abuse by restricting the number of requests a client can make within a certain timeframe
- **Response Aggregation:** Combines responses from multiple microservices into a single response, reducing multiple client-side requests
- **Logging and Monitoring:** Captures detailed logs and metrics to track API usage, failures, and performance bottlenecks
- **Protocol Translation:** Converts different communication protocols (like **HTTP, gRPC**, and **WebSockets**) to provide a consistent client experience

# Using an API Gateway in Microservices

In a traditional **monolithic application**, all functionalities are a part of the same system, and communication between different modules happens internally. However, in a **microservices architecture**, different services handle different business functionalities and communicate over a network. This introduces **several challenges** mentioned in the following table:

| Challenge | Solution with API Gateway |
|---|---|
| Direct exposure of microservices to clients | API Gateway abstracts microservices and provides a unified endpoint |
| Security risks with multiple exposed endpoints | Centralized authentication and authorization with JWT/OAuth2 |
| Complexity in client-side request handling | API Gateway aggregates multiple microservices responses |
| Load balancing issues | API Gateway distributes traffic efficiently across instances |
| High traffic can overload microservices | Implements rate limiting and request throttling |
| Monitoring and logging across multiple services | API Gateway captures logs and provides performance analytics |

***Table 11.1:** Use Cases of API Gateway*

By addressing these challenges, API gateways **enhance system security, improve scalability,** and **simplify microservices management**.

# How API Gateways Work in Microservices

To understand the role of an API Gateway in a microservices architecture, it is essential to examine how it handles client requests and routes them to the appropriate backend services. The API Gateway acts as an intermediary between clients and microservices, ensuring secure, efficient, and controlled communication. Here is a step-by-step breakdown of how an API Gateway processes requests and responses in a microservices ecosystem:

1. **Client Requests API Gateway**
   a. A client (mobile app, web app, or another service) sends a request to the API Gateway instead of directly calling individual microservices.
2. **API Gateway Processes the Request**
   a. The gateway **validates authentication tokens** (JWT/OAuth2).
   b. It applies **rate limiting and security policies**.
   c. Finally, it routes the request to the appropriate **microservice**.
3. **Microservice Responds to API Gateway**
   a. The microservice processes the request and sends a response back to the gateway.
4. **API Gateway Modifies and Sends the Response to the Client**
   a. The gateway **aggregates responses** (if needed), applies transformations, and sends the final result back to the client.

# Popular API Gateway Tools

Several **API Gateway solutions** are available, each offering unique features tailored for **microservices communication, security enforcement, traffic management**, and **observability**. The choice of an API Gateway depends on factors such as **ease of integration, scalability, cloud compatibility,** and **enterprise requirements**.

An API Gateway must be **reliable, flexible, and efficient** to handle high volumes of incoming traffic while ensuring **low latency** and **security**. The following is an overview of some of the most widely used API Gateway solutions in modern microservices architectures.

| API Gateway | Key Features |
|---|---|
| Spring Cloud Gateway | Built for Spring Boot, supports dynamic routing, filters, and security |
| Netflix Zuul | Open-source, used for intelligent routing and request filtering |
| Kong API Gateway | Cloud-native, offers security, analytics, and plugins for API management |
| NGINX API Gateway | High-performance, supports reverse proxy and load balancing |
| AWS API Gateway | Fully managed solution for serverless applications in AWS. |
| Azure API Management | Provides enterprise-grade security and monitoring for Azure microservices |

*Table 11.2: Popular Gateway Tools*

# Appropriate Use Cases for an API Gateway

API Gateways **should be implemented in most microservices architectures**, but they are especially useful in the following scenarios:

- **Microservices with multiple APIs:** To unify multiple services under a single endpoint
- **Securing APIs from direct client exposure:** Protect backend services with authentication

- **Load balancing and traffic management:** Distribute requests among service instances
- **Simplifying client-side interactions:** Reduce complexity by aggregating responses
- **Monitoring & logging request flows:** Track API performance and errors

API Gateways play a **fundamental role** in microservices by acting as a **centralized entry point** for managing requests, security, load balancing, and monitoring. They **simplify communication between clients and backend services** while **enhancing security, scalability,** and **resilience**.

In the next section, we will **configure Spring Cloud Gateway**, a powerful and flexible API gateway solution for Spring Boot microservices.

# Configuring Spring Cloud Gateway

While Istio is ideal for Kubernetes-native environments, Spring Cloud Gateway is a powerful, code-first API Gateway suitable for Spring Boot applications and service-to-service routing outside of Kubernetes clusters. It provides dynamic routing, path rewriting, rate limiting, circuit breaking, and integration with service discovery tools like Eureka.

This section walks through setting up and configuring Spring Cloud Gateway for managing and routing traffic in a microservices architecture.

# Reason to Use Spring Cloud Gateway

Spring Cloud Gateway is built on top of Spring WebFlux and offers a non-blocking, reactive API gateway solution. It acts as a reverse proxy and provides:

- Dynamic routing to backend services
- Request/response filtering
- Path rewriting and header transformation
- Circuit breaker and retry logic
- Integration with Spring Security, Resilience4j, and Netflix OSS tools

# Adding Dependencies

To use Spring Cloud Gateway, add the following dependencies to your pom.xml:

```
<dependency>
  <groupId>org.springframework.boot</groupId>
  <artifactId>spring-boot-starter-webflux</artifactId>
</dependency>
<dependency>
  <groupId>org.springframework.cloud</groupId>
  <artifactId>spring-cloud-starter-gateway</artifactId>
</dependency>
```

**Figure 11.1:** *Adding Dependencies*

Also include the Spring Cloud BOM:

```
<dependencyManagement>
  <dependencies>
    <dependency>
      <groupId>org.springframework.cloud</groupId>
      <artifactId>spring-cloud-dependencies</artifactId>
      <version>2022.0.3</version> <!-- Choose appropriate version -->
      <type>pom</type>
      <scope>import</scope>
    </dependency>
  </dependencies>
</dependencyManagement>
```

**Figure 11.2:** *Spring Cloud BOM*

# Basic Routing Example

In Spring Cloud Gateway, routing rules determine how incoming requests are matched and forwarded to backend services. Each route is defined by an **`id`**, a **`uri`** that points to the backend service, and one or more **`predicates`** that determine when the route should be applied. Below is an example configuration that sets up basic routing for two microservices.

This configuration tells Spring Cloud Gateway to forward any request matching **`/users/**`** to a service running at **`http://localhost:8081`**, and any request matching **`/orders/**`** to **`http://localhost:8082`**. This makes the gateway act as a reverse proxy, routing traffic based on the URL path.

Configure routing rules in **`application.yml`** as follows:

```
spring:
  cloud:
    gateway:
      routes:
        - id: user-service
          uri: http://localhost:8081
          predicates:
            - Path=/users/**
        - id: order-service
          uri: http://localhost:8082
          predicates:
            - Path=/orders/**
```

**Figure 11.3:** *Configure Routing Rules*

# Adding Filters

Spring Cloud Gateway allows you to apply filters to routes. Filters can manipulate the request before it is sent to the backend or the response before it is sent back to the client. Filters are useful for adding headers, rewriting URLs, modifying request/response bodies, and implementing policies.

Filters allow you to modify requests and responses like in the following figure:

```
filters:
  # Adds a custom header to every request that passes through the gateway
  # This is useful for tracing or debugging

  - AddRequestHeader=X-Request-ID, demo-header
  - RewritePath=/api/(?&lt;segment&gt;.*), /${segment}  # Strips '/api' prefix from the request path, forwarding only the segment
```

***Figure 11.4:*** *Adding Filters*

# Circuit Breaker and Retry

In distributed systems, service failures are inevitable due to transient faults, network issues, or temporary unavailability of downstream services. To maintain system resilience and improve user experience, Spring Cloud Gateway supports two crucial fault tolerance mechanisms: **circuit breakers** and **automatic retries**.

## Circuit Breaker

A circuit breaker monitors the health of downstream services and stops forwarding requests when a service is consistently failing. This prevents the gateway from overwhelming a failing service and allows time for recovery. When the circuit is '**open**', all requests are redirected to a fallback URI defined by the developer.

In the example below, any request routed through this path is monitored by a **`CircuitBreaker`** named **`myCircuitBreaker`**. If the destination service fails beyond a threshold, the request is redirected to **`/fallback`**, which can be another route that returns a cached or default response.

```
filters:
  - name: CircuitBreaker
    args:
      name: myCircuitBreaker
      fallbackUri: forward:/fallback
  # Retry filter automatically re-attempts failed requests based on the number of retries and status codes specified
  - name: Retry
    args:
      retries: 3
      statuses: BAD_GATEWAY
```

***Figure 11.5:*** *Circuit Breaker*

## Retry Filter

The **`Retry`** filter automatically re-attempts failed requests. This is particularly useful when dealing with intermittent network issues or services that temporarily fail under load. The **`retries`** argument specifies the number of retry attempts, and **`statuses`** defines which HTTP response codes should trigger a retry.

Together, these filters provide a robust mechanism for handling failure gracefully. By limiting retries and triggering fallback responses, you can ensure higher availability and a smoother user experience even when parts of your system are degraded. Spring Cloud Gateway supports resilience patterns such as circuit breakers and automatic retries using Resilience4j. These patterns protect your application from cascading failures and improve reliability.

## Service Discovery Integration

Spring Cloud Gateway can dynamically discover and route to services registered with Eureka or other service discovery mechanisms. When the **`discovery.locator.enabled`** flag is set to true, it automatically creates routes for all registered services using their service IDs.

If you are using **Eureka**, Spring Cloud Gateway can auto-register services in the following manner:

```yaml
spring:
  cloud:
    gateway:
      discovery:
        locator:
          enabled: true
          lowerCaseServiceId: true
```

***Figure 11.6:*** *Using Eureka*

With this setup, there is no need to manually define routes for each service. You can simply access your services using a pattern like **`http://gateway/SERVICE-NAME/path`**, and the gateway will resolve and forward the request to the appropriate Eureka-registered service.

Spring Cloud Gateway is a versatile option for microservices routing in Spring Boot environments. It provides essential API gateway features and integrates smoothly with the Spring Cloud ecosystem. While it is more suitable for monolithic-to-microservices transitions or non-Kubernetes deployments, it remains a popular choice for projects requiring Spring-native, reactive, and pluggable gateway support.

In Kubernetes environments, however, Istio offers a more infrastructure-centric and policy-driven approach. Depending on your architecture, Spring Cloud Gateway and Istio can even co-exist to serve different roles in your microservices journey.

# Integrating Spring Cloud Gateway with Istio

In many real-world microservices deployments, especially those transitioning to Kubernetes or requiring hybrid-cloud environments, it is common to see **Spring Cloud Gateway** and **Istio** coexisting within the same architecture. Each serves different layers of the system and complements the other when applied strategically.

**Why Use Both?**

- **Spring Cloud Gateway** is excellent for **application-level routing** and customization. It is ideal when you need fine-grained request/response transformations, developer-centric customization, or integration with Spring ecosystems.
- **Istio**, on the other hand, operates at the **infrastructure level** in Kubernetes. It is better suited for traffic management, security (such as mTLS and JWT), observability, and policy enforcement without modifying application code.

By combining both, you can leverage the flexibility of Spring Cloud Gateway at the app edge while relying on Istio for mesh-level control and observability.

# Common Integration Patterns

- Istio as External Gateway, Spring Gateway as Internal Entry Point
  - Use **Istio IngressGateway** to expose the application to external traffic.
  - Forward specific paths to a Spring Cloud Gateway service running inside the mesh.
  - Spring Cloud Gateway performs application-specific routing or filtering.

**Use Case:** You want to control cross-cutting policies like mTLS, retries, and metrics with Istio but still benefit from Spring Cloud Gateway's filter mechanisms for request transformations or header enrichment.

- Spring Cloud Gateway as External Gateway, Istio for Internal Routing
  - Use Spring Cloud Gateway as the external API gateway (such as when the edge service exposed via LoadBalancer or Ingress).
  - Forward traffic into the Kubernetes service mesh where Istio manages internal routing between services.

**Use Case:** You already have a Spring Cloud Gateway-based ecosystem and are migrating backend services into Istio gradually.

- Gateway Chaining with Sidecars
  - Deploy Spring Cloud Gateway as a service **with an Istio sidecar proxy**.
  - Traffic entering Spring Gateway is still observable and controllable via Istio policies.
  - This enables full monitoring, security, and tracing capabilities.

**Use Case:** You want to retain Spring Gateway logic but benefit from Istio's telemetry stack (like Kiali, Prometheus, and Jaeger).

# Configuring the Integration

Here is a high-level setup if you are using Istio to route traffic into Spring Cloud Gateway.

## Gateway

The **Gateway** resource in Istio defines how incoming traffic is allowed to enter the mesh. It is essentially the ingress controller for Istio, specifying the ports, protocols, and hosts that should be exposed externally. In this example, the gateway is listening for HTTP traffic on port 80 for the specified host.

```yaml
apiVersion: networking.istio.io/v1beta1
kind: Gateway
metadata:
  name: spring-gateway-gw
spec:
  selector:
    istio: ingressgateway
  servers:
  - port:
      number: 80
      name: http
      protocol: HTTP
    hosts:
    - "your-domain.com"
```

**Figure 11.7:** *Gateway Resource*

## VirtualService

The **VirtualService** resource defines the routing logic for the traffic that passes through the Istio gateway. It specifies the destination service, path matching rules, and the gateway through which the traffic should be routed. In the given configuration, it routes all the requests that start with **/api** to the internal Spring Cloud Gateway service and effectively bridges external requests into the application layer inside the Kubernetes cluster.

```yaml
apiVersion: networking.istio.io/v1beta1
kind: VirtualService
metadata:
  name: route-to-spring-gateway
spec:
  hosts:
  - "your-domain.com"
  gateways:
  - spring-gateway-gw
  http:
  - match:
    - uri:
        prefix: "/api"
    route:
    - destination:
        host: spring-cloud-gateway.default.svc.cluster.local
        port:
          number: 8080
```

***Figure 11.8:*** *VirtualService*

This will allow the traffic entering through the Istio ingress gateway to be routed to your Spring Cloud Gateway pod inside the cluster.

Using **Spring Cloud Gateway and Istio together** provides the best of both worlds. Spring Cloud Gateway empowers developers with application-level control and seamless Spring integration, while Istio offers Kubernetes-native networking, observability, and policy enforcement. Whether you choose to place Spring Cloud Gateway inside the mesh or at the edge, this layered gateway approach can help bridge the gap between application and infrastructure in your microservices architecture.

# Implementing Rate Limiting and Circuit Breaker Patterns

In distributed microservices architecture, ensuring that services remain resilient under heavy load or when downstream services fail is essential. Two powerful resilience patterns–Rate Limiting and Circuit Breakers–play a crucial role in maintaining system reliability and performance. When deploying in Kubernetes, especially with a combination of Istio for mesh-level traffic management and Spring Cloud Gateway for application-layer control, these patterns can be implemented with great flexibility and clarity.

## Significance of Rate Limiting and Circuit Breaker

Before we dive into the implementation, it is important to understand the critical role that rate limiting and circuit breaking play in modern microservices architecture. These patterns are essential to protect individual services from being overwhelmed and maintain overall system health and user experience, especially in a cloud-native deployment environment like Kubernetes, where dynamic scaling and service discovery are common.

- **Rate Limiting** protects services from being overwhelmed by excessive or abusive traffic. It allows administrators to define thresholds, beyond which requests are throttled or rejected.
- **Circuit Breakers** prevent cascading failures by stopping requests to downstream services that are consistently failing, giving them time to recover and avoiding unnecessary load.

Both these mechanisms serve as the first line of defense in distributed systems, improving fault tolerance, service isolation, and user experience.

# Implementing Rate Limiting with Istio

Istio provides advanced traffic management features, including rate limiting, which can be applied at the service mesh level without requiring changes to application code. This makes it especially useful in Kubernetes environments where policy enforcement and service protection must be handled externally and uniformly across all services.

Istio provides native support for rate limiting through **Envoy filters** or **Istio's extension provider API** integrated with external tools like **Redis** or **Istio WASM filters**.

## Envoy Rate Limiting via Istio `ExtensionProvider` (Redis Backend)

To implement rate limiting with Istio, we use an external rate-limiting service such as Envoy's integrated extension backed by Redis. This service intercepts requests at the Envoy proxy level and decides whether to allow or block them based on pre-defined policies.

**Deploy Redis and Istio Rate Limit Service**

To enable rate limiting in Istio using Envoy's extension mechanism, you must first deploy a Redis instance to act as the backend store and a compatible rate limit service that integrates with Envoy. You can deploy Redis using Helm or a Kubernetes manifest, and the rate limit service using open-source implementations like Envoy's **`ratelimit`** component.

**Deploy Redis**

Redis is used as a backend store because it provides a fast, in-memory data store that supports atomic operations and expiration policies, which is ideal for counting and tracking requests. In the context of rate limiting, Redis helps store token buckets, counters, or sliding window data structures for each client or service.

Its low-latency and high-throughput capabilities make Redis an excellent choice for real-time rate-limiting decisions across distributed services. Moreover, Redis's built-in support for key expiration enables the automatic cleanup of request counters, reducing memory usage and ensuring rate limits reset correctly over time.

Use Helm to quickly install Redis as demonstrated:

```
helm repo add bitnami https://charts.bitnami.com/bitnami
helm install redis bitnami/redis --set auth.enabled=false
```

**Deploy Rate Limit Service**

You can clone the official Envoy rate limit GitHub repo and deploy it with the accompanying Kubernetes manifests:

```
git clone https://github.com/envoyproxy/ratelimit.git
cd ratelimit/kube/
kubectl apply -f .
```

Ensure the service is running:

```
kubectl get svc -n default | grep rate-limit-service
```

This setup enables the rate limit service to respond to requests from the Envoy proxy (used by Istio) and apply logic based on Redis-backed rules. These rules are defined in configuration files and can be tailored per service, per user, or per endpoint using descriptors.

**Define the `RateLimitService` provider in Istio mesh config**:

```
apiVersion: install.istio.io/v1alpha1
kind: IstioOperator
spec:
  meshConfig:
    extensionProviders:
    - name: redis-rate-limit
      envoyExtAuthzHttp:
        service: rate-limit-service.default.svc.cluster.local
        port: 8081
```

***Figure 11.9:*** *IstioOperator*

**Configure the Envoy Filter to apply rate limits to specific paths**:

```
apiVersion: networking.istio.io/v1alpha3
kind: EnvoyFilter
metadata:
  name: rate-limit-filter
spec:
  configPatches:
    - applyTo: HTTP_FILTER
      match:
        context: GATEWAY
        listener:
          portNumber: 80
          filterChain:
            filter:
              name: envoy.filters.network.http_connection_manager
      patch:
        operation: INSERT_BEFORE
        value:
          name: envoy.filters.http.ext_authz
          typed_config:
            "@type":
type.googleapis.com/envoy.extensions.filters.http.ext_authz.v3.ExtAuthz
            http_service:
              server_uri:
                uri: http://rate-limit-service.default.svc.cluster.local:8081
                cluster: outbound|8081||rate-limit-
service.default.svc.cluster.local
```

***Figure 11.10:*** *EnvoyFilter*

This setup allows you to define granular rate-limiting rules, such as 100 requests per minute per client IP or based on JWT claims.

# Implementing Rate Limiting with Spring Cloud Gateway

Spring Cloud Gateway offers a simple and elegant way to apply rate limiting policies on a per-route basis. It does so by leveraging a token-bucket algorithm implemented using Redis, which is used to persist the counters for different consumers such as users, IPs, or API keys. This makes it a great choice when rate limiting needs to be more dynamic, tenant-aware, or tied to application-level business logic.

Spring Cloud Gateway rate limiting is especially effective in cloud-native environments, where application teams want direct control over service-level throttling behavior while still integrating with Spring's robust ecosystem. The configuration is highly declarative and customizable through YAML, allowing developers to set up throttling rules quickly and with minimal boilerplate code.

Unlike Istio, Spring Cloud Gateway implements rate limiting at the application layer. It uses Redis as a distributed store to track request counts per client, route, or token. This approach is helpful when rate-limiting logic needs to be dynamic, route-specific, or based on user roles or API keys.

Spring Cloud Gateway allows you to define rate limits per route using Redis as a backing store.

```
<dependency>
  <groupId>org.springframework.boot</groupId>
  <artifactId>spring-boot-starter-data-redis-reactive</artifactId>
</dependency>
```

## Configuration

The following example demonstrates how to configure rate limiting for the **/users/**** route. The **replenishRate** indicates how many requests are allowed per second, while **burstCapacity** defines the maximum number of requests that can be made in a short burst before you enforce throttling. This provides a balance between steady traffic and short spikes:

```
spring:
  cloud:
    gateway:
      routes:
      - id: user-service
        uri: http://user-service
        predicates:
          - Path=/users/**
        filters:
          - name: RequestRateLimiter
            args:
              redis-rate-limiter.replenishRate: 10
              redis-rate-limiter.burstCapacity: 20
```

**Figure 11.11:** *Routing Configuration*

This configuration sets a soft limit of 10 requests per second, allowing short bursts of up to 20 requests. If a client exceeds this threshold, the request is automatically rejected with a **429 Too**

`Many Requests` status code. This is useful for protecting backend services from misuse or accidental overload by limiting the frequency of incoming calls.

# Implementing Circuit Breakers

Circuit breakers are a defensive programming pattern designed to protect services from continued interaction with downstream systems that are failing or underperforming. When a service call fails repeatedly, the circuit breaker opens and halts further attempts to access the failing service for a predetermined recovery period. This prevents resource exhaustion and allows the failing system time to recover.

Circuit breakers act as failure guards by detecting service degradation and temporarily halting calls to problematic services. This pattern not only prevents overloading failing services, but also improves response time for users by serving fallback responses instead of waiting for timeouts.

## With Istio

Istio uses **`DestinationRule`** to configure circuit breaking at the network level. These rules can define limits for concurrent connections, pending requests, and retries. Additionally, Istio's outlier detection monitors the health of service instances and automatically removes unhealthy pods from the routing pool, ensuring more resilient service-to-service communication.

Istio's implementation of circuit breakers relies on connection and outlier detection settings defined in **`DestinationRule`**. These configurations control how traffic is handled and when to eject unhealthy service instances from the load balancer pool.

Istio implements circuit breaking using **`DestinationRules`**, which is demonstrated as follows:

```
apiVersion: networking.istio.io/v1beta1
kind: DestinationRule
metadata:
  name: user-service-dr
spec:
  host: user-service.default.svc.cluster.local
  trafficPolicy:
    connectionPool:
      tcp:
        maxConnections: 1
      http:
        http1MaxPendingRequests: 1
        maxRequestsPerConnection: 1
    outlierDetection:
      consecutive5xxErrors: 3
      interval: 10s
      baseEjectionTime: 30s
      maxEjectionPercent: 100
```

**Figure 11.12:** DestinationRule

This rule monitors the number of 5xx responses from service instances and removes (or ejects) any instance that exceeds the defined threshold of 3 errors within 10 seconds. Once ejected, traffic is no longer routed to that instance for a recovery period of 30 seconds. This allows healthy instances to continue serving traffic while giving the failed ones a chance to recover.

## With Spring Cloud Gateway

At the application layer, Spring Cloud Gateway provides integration with Resilience4j to implement circuit breakers that wrap around service calls. These circuit breakers offer granular control at the route level, and can include fallback logic, timeouts, retry mechanisms, and custom failure thresholds.

Spring Cloud Gateway uses `Resilience4j` to implement circuit breakers at the route level. These circuit breakers are ideal for applying application-level logic, defining custom fallback URIs, and tuning service-specific failure policies directly within Spring Boot configurations.

Spring Cloud Gateway integrates with `Resilience4j` to implement circuit breakers.

```
<dependency>
  <groupId>io.github.resilience4j</groupId>
  <artifactId>resilience4j-spring-boot2</artifactId>
</dependency>
```

**Configuration**

```yaml
spring:
  cloud:
    gateway:
      routes:
        - id: user-service
          uri: http://user-service
          predicates:
            - Path=/users/**
          filters:
            - name: CircuitBreaker
              args:
                name: userCircuitBreaker
                fallbackUri: forward:/fallback
```

***Figure 11.13:*** *Configuring Routing*

This configuration defines a circuit breaker named `userCircuitBreaker` that monitors the availability of the `user-service`. If failures exceed a predefined threshold (configured elsewhere in Resilience4j settings), the breaker opens and automatically redirects the traffic to `/fallback`, ensuring that users receive a graceful response even during outages. This approach improves user experience and reduces the load on failing components.

Implementing **rate limiting and circuit breaker patterns** is essential for building resilient microservices. **Istio** provides powerful, infrastructure-level support for both, while **Spring Cloud Gateway** allows application-level policies to be enforced with full Spring ecosystem integration. When used together in a Kubernetes environment, they offer a comprehensive fault tolerance strategy, thereby protecting both the platform and application layers from overloads and cascading failures.

# Securing Microservices with JWT and OAuth2

In modern microservices architectures, security is a critical pillar. As services grow in number and complexity, managing authentication and authorization across these services becomes increasingly challenging. Istio provides a robust and scalable way to implement security policies like JWT authentication and OAuth2-based authorization at the service mesh level without altering application code. This section explores how to secure microservices in a Kubernetes environment using Istio's built-in features.

# Istio Usage for Authentication and Authorization

Unlike application-level security implementations, Istio offloads security enforcement to the service mesh layer. This provides several key advantages:

- Decouples security from application logic
- Centralizes access policies for easier management
- Supports standard protocols like JWT, OAuth2, and mTLS
- Applies policies uniformly across services, regardless of the underlying tech stack

# JWT Authentication in Istio

JSON Web Token (JWT) is a compact and self-contained way to transmit user identity information between parties. Istio can validate JWTs at the gateway or service proxy level using **`AuthorizationPolicies`** and **`RequestAuthentication`**.

**Step 1: Define the `RequestAuthentication` Resource**

```
apiVersion: security.istio.io/v1beta1
kind: RequestAuthentication
metadata:
  name: jwt-authentication
  namespace: default
spec:
  selector:
    matchLabels:
      app: weather-api
  jwtRules:
  - issuer: "https://auth.example.com"
    jwksUri: "https://auth.example.com/.well-known/jwks.json"
```

***Figure 11.14:*** *JWT Authentication in Istio*

This resource tells Istio to accept and validate JWTs issued by **`https://auth.example.com`**. The **`jwksUri`** points to the public keys used for token signature verification.

**Step 2: Apply an `AuthorizationPolicy` to Enforce Authentication**

This policy only allows requests that include a valid JWT token issued by the specified identity provider.

```yaml
apiVersion: security.istio.io/v1beta1
kind: AuthorizationPolicy
metadata:
  name: jwt-authz
  namespace: default
spec:
  selector:
    matchLabels:
      app: weather-api
  action: ALLOW
  rules:
  - from:
    - source:
        requestPrincipals: ["https://auth.example.com/*"]
```

***Figure 11.15:*** *AuthorizationPolicy*

# Integrating OAuth2 with Istio Gateway

Although Istio does not natively support full OAuth2 flows (like authorization code exchange), it can integrate with external OAuth2 proxies such as **OAuth2-Proxy** or **Keycloak Gatekeeper**.

## OAuth2-Proxy Architecture

1. User requests a service via Istio IngressGateway.
2. The request is routed through an **OAuth2 Proxy** container (deployed alongside or in front of your services).
3. OAuth2 Proxy redirects the user to a login screen (handled by providers like Google, GitHub, or Keycloak).
4. After it successfully implementing the above steps, it attaches a JWT token and sends the request to the application via Istio.

## Example Istio `VirtualService` Routing OAuth2

In this example, we will demonstrate how to configure Istio's **`VirtualService`** resource to route all incoming traffic through the OAuth2 Proxy before arriving at the intended backend service. This is especially important for enforcing login and token issuance flows before access to sensitive microservices is granted.

The configuration defines a **`VirtualService`** that matches all requests coming to **`app.example.com`** and forwards them to the OAuth2 Proxy service. The OAuth2 Proxy is typically configured to authenticate users with an external identity provider (such as Keycloak, Google, and GitHub) and inject a valid JWT into the request headers.

By intercepting all incoming traffic at the ingress gateway and sending it to the proxy running on port **`4180`**, this setup ensures that unauthorized or unauthenticated requests are redirected to the login screen before ever reaching any internal service. Once authenticated, the OAuth2 proxy forwards the original request with a valid token to the application, which can be validated further by Istio if JWT policies are applied downstream.

This pattern is commonly used when organizations want to support centralized login portals for all services while offloading session and token management to a dedicated and scalable proxy layer.

```
apiVersion: networking.istio.io/v1beta1
kind: VirtualService
metadata:
  name: oauth2-protected-service
spec:
  hosts:
    - app.example.com
  gateways:
    - istio-ingressgateway
  http:
    - match:
        - uri:
            prefix: /
      route:
        - destination:
            host: oauth2-proxy.default.svc.cluster.local
            port:
              number: 4180
```

***Figure 11.16:*** *VirtualService*

This ensures that all unauthenticated users are intercepted by the OAuth2 proxy.

# Fine-Grained Access Control with Claims

JWTs can include custom claims (such as **`role`**, **`email`**, and **`department`**). Istio can use these fields in **`AuthorizationPolicy`** for fine-grained access control.

```
rules:
- when:
  - key: request.auth.claims["role"]
    values: ["admin"]
```

***Figure 11.17:*** *Fine Grained Access Control*

This rule restricts access to users with the `admin` role claim in their JWT.

## Best Practices

To maximize the effectiveness of Istio-based security and ensure long-term maintainability, it is essential to follow industry-proven best practices. The following guidelines can help you mitigate common security risks, simplify policy management, and improve observability across your microservices landscape:

- Always use **HTTPS** when communicating with identity providers.
- Rotate and manage **JWKS keys** securely.
- Enable **mTLS** to protect service-to-service communication.

- Deploy OAuth2 Proxy with proper timeout, cookie, and session management policies.
- Monitor and audit traffic using tools like **Kiali**, **Prometheus**, and **Grafana**.

By leveraging Istio for JWT validation and OAuth2 integration, microservices can offload complex authentication logic from individual applications. This not only enhances security and maintainability, but also promotes consistency across services. With centralized enforcement, developers can focus on business logic while operators ensure compliance and resilience at the mesh layer.

# Conclusion

In this chapter, we explored the pivotal role of API gateways in managing traffic flow, enhancing security, and simplifying service-to-service communication in a microservices architecture. We began with an overview of API gateways and progressed into hands-on configurations using both Spring Cloud Gateway and Istio and highlighted how they can coexist to offer both application-level flexibility and mesh-level control.

You learned how to configure essential features like routing, rate limiting, and circuit breakers to maintain system stability under load. Furthermore, we secured our services using robust identity protocols like JWT and OAuth2, which can leverage Istio's declarative policy enforcement to decouple security from application logic.

Together, these tools form a strong foundation for building secure, resilient, and manageable microservices at scale. As systems scale, managing configurations across dozens or hundreds of services becomes complex and error-prone. In the next chapter, we will explore how to centralize and streamline configuration using Spring Cloud Config Server. You will learn how to externalize configuration properties, refresh them dynamically, and secure sensitive information, thereby empowering your teams with consistency and agility across environments.

# CHAPTER 12
# Configuring Centralized Configuration

## Introduction

Managing configuration settings across multiple microservices can become complex and error-prone, especially as your system scales. This chapter will thus focus on the importance of centralizing configuration management to ensure consistency, flexibility, and ease of maintenance in a microservices architecture.

We will begin with an **Introduction to Centralized Configuration**, where you will learn why centralizing configuration is crucial for maintaining coherence and control over your microservices environment. This section will highlight the benefits of centralized configuration, such as reducing redundancy and simplifying updates.

Next, we will guide you through **Setting Up Spring Cloud Config Server**, server-side and client-side support tool for externalized configuration in a distributed system. You will learn how to set up and configure the Spring Cloud Config Server to manage your microservices' configurations centrally.

The chapter also covers **Refreshing Configuration Properties at Runtime**, which will explain how to update configuration properties without restarting your microservices, ensuring minimal downtime and disruption. Finally, we will discuss **Securing Configuration Information**, focusing on protecting sensitive data such as passwords and API keys stored in your configuration files.

By the end of this chapter, you will have a comprehensive understanding of how to implement and manage centralized configuration in a microservices environment, which will further ensure that your applications remain consistent, secure, and easy to maintain as they grow.

## Structure

This chapter covers the following topics:

- Introduction to Centralized Configuration
- Setting Up Spring Cloud Config Server
- Using Vault and Centralized Configuration Alternatives
- Refreshing Configuration Properties at Runtime
- Securing Configuration Information

## Introduction to Centralized Configuration

In a **microservices architecture**, different services run independently, with each requiring a distinct set of **configuration properties** like database connections, API keys, environment variables, and security credentials. **Manually configuring each service** can become inefficient, error-prone, and difficult to maintain as the system scales.

**Centralized Configuration** addresses this challenge by **storing and managing all configurations in a central location**. This ensures **consistency, flexibility,** and **dynamic updates** across all microservices without requiring code changes or redeployment.

# Understanding Centralized Configuration Important

Without a centralized configuration mechanism, microservices **must store their configurations individually**, often within their **local property files**. This approach leads to **several challenges mentioned in the next section**.

## Challenges of Decentralized Configuration

- **Configuration Duplication:** Each microservice has its own configuration, leading to inconsistencies.
- **Difficult Maintenance**: Updating a single configuration requires modifying multiple services.
- **Environment-Specific Complexity:** Managing configurations for development, testing, and production is cumbersome.
- **Security Risks:** Sensitive information (for example, database credentials, API keys) might be hardcoded in multiple locations.

To solve these problems, a **Centralized Configuration Management System** allows microservices to **retrieve their configuration from a single source**, improving **scalability, maintainability,** and **security**.

# How Centralized Configuration Works

The **Centralized Configuration approach** involves a **Configuration Server** that acts as a **repository** where all microservices fetch their configurations dynamically.

## Steps in Centralized Configuration Management

- **The Configuration Server stores global configurations** for all microservices.
- **Microservices fetch their configuration at startup** (or periodically) from the Configuration Server.
- **If a configuration changes**, services can dynamically refresh their settings **without requiring redeployment**.
- **Security and access controls** ensure that only authorized services can fetch sensitive configurations.

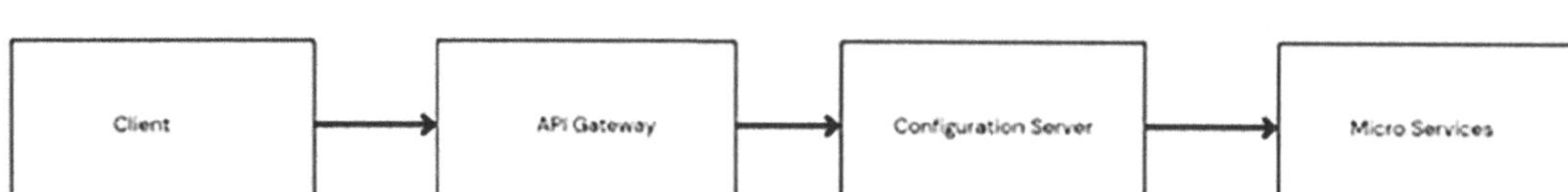


***Figure 12.1:*** *Centralized Configuration*

Each microservice **queries the Configuration Server** at runtime to fetch its settings. Developers update configurations in **one central location**, and all services receive the changes dynamically.

# Key Benefits of Centralized Configuration

Managing configurations across multiple microservices can quickly become **complex and error-prone**, especially when dealing with **environment-specific settings, security credentials,** and **frequent updates**. A **Centralized Configuration System** helps resolve these challenges by providing a **single, structured source** for managing configurations efficiently. Below are the key benefits of adopting **centralized configuration** in a microservices architecture.

# Consistency across Microservices

One of the biggest challenges in microservices is ensuring **configuration consistency** across all services. With a **centralized approach**, all microservices fetch their configuration from a **single, authoritative source**, eliminating inconsistencies caused by **misconfigured or outdated local properties**.

**Why is this important?**

- In a distributed system, **services running in different environments** (like `staging`, `production`) need **separate configurations** while maintaining **structural uniformity**.
- Without centralized configuration, different teams might accidentally use **outdated settings**, leading to **unexpected failures and debugging challenges**.

**Example:** A **payment service** in a monolithic application might have a hardcoded database URL, whereas in a microservices environment, different instances need **separate database credentials** for **testing and production**. A centralized configuration ensures each instance pulls the **correct** database URL dynamically.

# Simplified Configuration Management

In traditional systems, updating configurations requires **modifying multiple microservices manually**, which is a time-consuming and error-prone process. A **Centralized Configuration System** simplifies this by allowing **global configuration updates** from a **single location**.

**Why is this beneficial?**

- Instead of updating individual service configuration files and redeploying them, teams can **modify settings centrally** and all microservices fetch the latest version automatically.
- Changes **propagate dynamically, reducing downtime and deployment overhead**.

**Example:** Imagine an **API Gateway rate-limiting policy** needs to be changed from **100 requests per second to 200**. With **Centralized Configuration**, this update can be applied globally, and **all microservices inherit the new rule without requiring a restart**.

# Secure Storage of Sensitive Information

Security is **paramount** in a distributed microservices architecture. **API keys, database credentials, encryption keys, and access tokens** should **never** be hardcoded within microservices or stored in version control repositories.

A **Centralized Configuration System** provides **secure storage** and **access control mechanisms** for sensitive data. **Only authorized services** can retrieve these credentials, ensuring **data protection** and **compliance with security policies**.

**Security Benefits:**

- **Encryption & Role-Based Access Control (RBAC):** Only authorized microservices or users can access specific configurations.
- **Eliminates Hardcoded Secrets:** Secrets are retrieved dynamically, preventing accidental **exposure in public repositories** (such as **GitHub leaks**).
- **Prevents Configuration Drift:** Keeps a **consistent security policy** across all services.

**Example:** A **Spring Boot microservice** needs a **database password**. Instead of storing it in **`application.yml`**, it retrieves the password securely from **Spring Cloud Config Server with encryption** or **HashiCorp Vault**.

## Dynamic Configuration Updates

One of the most **powerful** benefits of centralized configuration is **real-time adaptability**. Microservices **can automatically reload configurations** when updates are made, without requiring a restart or redeployment.

**Why is this beneficial?**

- Reduces **downtime** by eliminating the need to manually restart services for configuration updates
- Allows **rapid response** to changing requirements (such as modifying API rate limits and enabling/disabling features dynamically)
- Supports **feature flags** and **progressive rollouts** for new functionality

**Example:** If an **email notification service** needs a new SMTP server configuration, it can dynamically retrieve the updated value **without being restarted**, using **Spring Boot's `@RefreshScope` annotation**.

## Version Control and Auditability

Configuration changes should be **trackable, reversible, and auditable**. A **Centralized Configuration System** enables **version control**, making it easy to:

- Track changes over time
- Roll back to previous configurations if an update introduces **unexpected issues**
- Maintain an **audit trail** for security and compliance

**Why is this important?**

- If an accidental configuration change **breaks the system**, the previous version can be **restored immediately**.
- Helps in **compliance with security and audit regulations**, as all changes are logged.
- Ensures **team collaboration**, as multiple developers can work on configuration files without conflicts.

**Example:** Using **Spring Cloud Config Server with Git**, configuration updates are **automatically versioned**, and previous versions can be retrieved using Git rollback commands.

# Technologies for Centralized Configuration

Several tools enable **centralized configuration management** for microservices:

| Tool | Description |
|---|---|
| Spring Cloud Config Server | A dedicated configuration server for **Spring Boot** microservices |
| HashiCorp Vault | Manages secrets and securely stores sensitive credentials |
| Kubernetes ConfigMaps & Secrets | Native Kubernetes approach for managing configurations in containerized environments |
| Consul | A service mesh tool that includes **configuration management and service discovery** |
| AWS Systems Manager Parameter Store | A managed AWS service for **storing configuration parameters securely** |

***Table 12.1:*** *Technologies for Centralized Configuration*

Each of these tools provides **dynamic configuration management, security enforcement,** and **environment-based configurations.**

# Best Practices for Centralized Configuration

To ensure **efficient, secure, and scalable** centralized configuration management in a microservices architecture, it is essential to follow **best practices** that enhance reliability, security, and performance. Managing configurations properly not only prevents **misconfigurations and security breaches,** but also ensures that microservices remain **resilient and adaptable** to changing business needs. Below are some key best practices for implementing **Centralized Configuration effectively**:

- **Use Environment-Specific Configuration Files:** Store configurations separately for **`dev`**, **`qa`**, **`prod`**, and **`staging`** environments.
- **Secure Sensitive Data with Secrets Management:** Use **HashiCorp Vault, AWS Secrets Manager, or Kubernetes Secrets** to encrypt credentials.
- **Implement Configuration Caching:** Microservices should cache configurations to reduce unnecessary API calls to the Configuration Server.
- **Enable Dynamic Configuration Reloading:** Use **`@RefreshScope`** in Spring Boot to enable **real-time configuration updates.**
- **Monitor Configuration Changes:** Implement logging to **track configuration updates and prevent misconfigurations.**

In this section, we explored the importance of **Centralized Configuration** in microservices and how it helps **manage configurations dynamically, improve security, and simplify maintenance.**

Key takeaways:

- **Microservices should avoid hardcoded configurations** and rely on a **centralized source.**
- **Spring Cloud Config Server** and **Kubernetes ConfigMaps** are powerful tools for managing configurations.
- **Secrets should be stored securely** using **HashiCorp Vault or Kubernetes Secrets.**
- **Dynamic configuration reloading** enhances flexibility and minimizes downtime.

In the next section, we will set up **Spring Cloud Config Server** to manage centralized configurations dynamically, providing a practical implementation for your microservices architecture.

# Setting Up Spring Cloud Config Server

This section provides a step-by-step guide to deploying a Spring Cloud Config Server in a Kubernetes cluster. The server will pull configuration data from a Git repository and serve it to client applications over HTTP. The clients can fetch their config dynamically and use Spring's native support for configuration binding in a Hybrid Istio Environment.

In a microservices ecosystem, especially while using Spring Boot, managing application-level configuration centrally is essential for consistency, maintainability, and rapid deployment. While Istio excels at service mesh-level configuration such as traffic routing, retries, and authentication policies, it does not manage application-level configuration properties like database URLs, feature flags, or environment-specific behavior. This is where Spring Cloud Config Server complements Istio in a hybrid configuration architecture.

# Understanding Spring Cloud Config Server

Spring Cloud Config Server allows you to serve configuration properties to Spring Boot applications in a centralized and consistent way. Instead of hardcoding values like database URLs, API keys, and environment-specific flags inside each service, you store them in a remote Git repository. The Config Server reads these values and serves them over HTTP to each application during startup or even at runtime, if refresh is enabled.

This enables easy version control of configuration, seamless environment switching, and greater separation between configuration and code.

Spring Cloud Config Server is a central place to manage external configuration for applications across all environments. It supports version-controlled configuration from Git, filesystem, or Vault, and can serve properties to applications on demand. Using it prevents duplication and hardcoding configuration across microservices.

# Using Spring Cloud Config Server with Istio

In Kubernetes environments where Istio is deployed for service mesh functionality (such as traffic shaping and security policies), Spring Cloud Config Server complements Istio by handling application-level configuration that Istio does not manage.

For example, use Spring Cloud Config to define things like database hostnames, cache expiration settings, or feature flags that change across environments. Meanwhile, use Istio to enforce JWT authentication, circuit breaking, and service-to-service authorization. This separation keeps the mesh secure and performant, while letting developers fine-tune their application behavior independently.

You should consider integrating Spring Cloud Config Server in an Istio-based architecture when:

- Your microservices are based on **Spring Boot**.
- You want to keep configuration logic decoupled from containers.
- You want to manage **application-specific properties**, not mesh policies.
- You require a hot-reload **of configuration** using **`@RefreshScope`** and Spring Actuator.

# Setting Up Spring Cloud Config Server

**Create a Git Repository with Configuration Files**

Your Git repo acts as the configuration source for the entire application landscape. Each YAML or properties file should be named after the service it belongs to (like **`user-service.yml`**) or represent global/shared settings (**`application.yml`**). You can also use profile suffixes (**`-dev`**, **`-prod`**) to represent environment-specific settings. Organize your properties using service names and profiles as shown here:

```
/config-repo
├── application.yml
├── user-service.yml
├── weather-service-dev.yml
├── weather-service-prod.yml
```

**Create a Spring Boot Config Server**

Build a new Spring Boot application and include the Config Server starter. The **`@EnableConfigServer`** annotation activates the config serving capabilities. This server listens on a configurable port (typically 8888) and responds to requests like **`/weather-service/dev`** with the corresponding config from Git. Create a new Spring Boot project with the following dependencies:

```
<dependency>
  <groupId>org.springframework.cloud</groupId>
  <artifactId>spring-cloud-config-server</artifactId>
</dependency>
```

Add the **`@EnableConfigServer`** annotation:

```
@SpringBootApplication
@EnableConfigServer
public class ConfigServerApplication {
    public static void main(String[] args) {
        SpringApplication.run(ConfigServerApplication.class, args);
    }
}
```

***Figure 12.2:*** *Enabling Config Server*

Configure **`application.yml`** to point to your Git repo:

```
server:
  port: 8888
spring:
  cloud:
    config:
      server:
        git:
          uri: https://github.com/your-org/config-repo
          searchPaths: config-repo
```

***Figure 12.3:*** *Spring Cloud Configuration*

**Configure Your Client Microservices**

Each client microservice should declare its **`spring.application.name`** to match its config file in Git. The **`config.import`** directive tells the app to load configuration from the config server at startup. You can route these HTTP calls through Istio if the services are mesh-enabled, enabling observability and policy enforcement. In each Spring Boot client (such as weather-service):

```
spring:
  application:
    name: weather-service
  config:
    import: optional:configserver:http://config-server:8888
```

***Figure 12.4:*** *Configuring Client Microservices*

Make sure to expose **config-server** as a Kubernetes service, or use Istio's **VirtualService** and **DestinationRule** to route internal requests.

**Enable Auto-Refresh (Optional)**

By annotating beans with **@RefreshScope**, you enable them to be refreshed at runtime when config changes. This is helpful for live feature flagging or reconfiguring external integrations without restarting services. Actuator's **/refresh** endpoint is used to trigger the refresh manually or via webhook (such as from GitHub). Enable dynamic refresh using Spring Actuator:

```
<dependency>
  <groupId>org.springframework.boot</groupId>
  <artifactId>spring-boot-starter-actuator</artifactId>
</dependency>
And annotate your beans:
@RefreshScope
@RestController
public class WeatherController { ... }
```

Then refresh via:

```
curl -X POST http://weather-service/actuator/refresh
```

# Securing Config Server in Istio

To avoid exposing sensitive config data, it is important to enforce access control on your config server. With Istio, you can define JWT-based authorization policies and enable mutual TLS (mTLS) for secure communication. This ensures that only authenticated services can fetch configuration, and traffic is encrypted across the mesh.

Follow these steps to secure the config server:

1. Add JWT and TLS policies to the config-server deployment using Istio's **AuthorizationPolicy**
2. Apply **mTLS** in the mesh to ensure secure service-to-service communication
3. Use Istio **DestinationRule** with retry/timeouts to make config server highly available

```yaml
apiVersion: security.istio.io/v1beta1
kind: AuthorizationPolicy
metadata:
  name: config-server-auth
spec:
  selector:
    matchLabels:
      app: config-server
  rules:
  - from:
    - source:
        requestPrincipals: ["https://auth.example.com/*"]
```

***Figure 12.5***: *Authorization Policy*

## Observability and Troubleshooting

Monitor configuration fetches using Spring Boot Actuator and Istio's telemetry stack. Tools like Kiali, Grafana, and Jaeger allow you to trace calls to the config server, see request latencies, and detect startup failures due to missing or misconfigured values. This visibility maintains resilience as your service landscape grows. Use Spring Boot Actuator endpoints (`/health`, `/env`, `/refresh`) for diagnostics. Additionally, you can leverage Istio observability tools like **Kiali**, **Prometheus**, and **Jaeger** to trace configuration calls and detect failures during app boot or refresh cycles.

Spring Cloud Config Server and Istio serve distinct but complementary roles in a cloud-native microservices setup. While Istio enforces platform-level policies, the config server handles the application-specific properties developers need to fine-tune behavior across environments. By combining both, you gain secure, observable, and maintainable configuration delivery across your entire system.

In a hybrid cloud-native environment, combining **Istio** for mesh-wide policies and **Spring Cloud Config Server** for application-specific configuration creates a powerful, scalable, and secure microservices architecture. This separation of concerns enables developers to manage feature toggles and environment settings while platform teams manage networking, security, and resiliency, thereby ensuring both agility and stability at scale.

# Using Vault and Centralized Configuration Alternatives

While Spring Cloud Config Server is ideal for managing Git-backed configuration files, there are scenarios, especially involving sensitive information, where using a dedicated secrets management solution like HashiCorp Vault is more appropriate.

## Why Use Vault?

Vault provides a central location to store and access secrets securely, which is essential when working with distributed systems like microservices. In contrast to static configuration files stored in Git, Vault encrypts sensitive values at rest, enforces access policies at a granular level, and supports short-lived dynamic credentials (like database login and access tokens). This ensures that microservices always access the latest and most secure version of a secret, minimizing the risks of exposure or unauthorized use.

The need for Vault becomes more pronounced when:

- You want to avoid hardcoded credentials in Git repositories or Docker images.
- You want to rotate secrets automatically without service restarts.
- You require secure access logs for compliance and auditing purposes.

Vault can also be integrated with various identity providers (like Kubernetes, AWS IAM and LDAP), making authentication seamless across environments.

Vault is a tool for securely accessing secrets such as API keys, credentials, and certificates. It supports fine-grained access control, dynamic secrets, and built-in auditing capabilities. When combined with Spring Cloud, Vault becomes a powerful solution for managing secure configuration in microservices.

Use Vault when:

- You want to avoid storing sensitive data in source control (such as Git).
- You need dynamic secrets (like short-lived database credentials).
- You require strong audit trails for compliance.

# Integrating Spring Boot with Vault

Spring Cloud Vault provides first-class integration for pulling secure values from Vault into your Spring Boot applications. These values are injected into your application's environment at runtime and can be used like any other configuration property.

This integration enables applications to retrieve sensitive values (such as database credentials or API tokens) on demand, without developers needing to see or store those values during development or deployment.

To use Vault with Spring Boot, follow these steps:

1. **Add Dependencies**

```
<dependency>
  <groupId>org.springframework.cloud</groupId>
  <artifactId>spring-cloud-starter-vault-config</artifactId>
</dependency>
```

2. **Configure Bootstrap Properties**

```
spring:
  cloud:
    vault:
      uri: http://vault.default.svc.cluster.local:8200
      authentication: TOKEN
      token: your-vault-token
      kv:
        enabled: true
        backend: secret
        default-context: application
```

**Figure 12.6:** *Bootstrap Properties*

This configuration tells Spring Boot to fetch values from Vault's **`secret/application`** path.

Below is a basic Java example that shows how to use a property retrieved from Vault inside a Spring Boot application:

# Java Example: Reading Vault Secrets in Spring Boot

Assuming you have a Vault secret like:

```
secret/weather-app
  api-key = abc123xyz
```

You can access this value in your application by using **@Value** or by mapping it into a configuration class.

**Option 1: Using @Value Annotation**

```java
import org.springframework.beans.factory.annotation.Value;
import org.springframework.web.bind.annotation.GetMapping;
import org.springframework.web.bind.annotation.RestController;

@RestController
public class WeatherController {

    @Value("${api-key}")
    private String apiKey;

    @GetMapping("/apikey")
    public String getApiKey() {
        return "API Key from Vault: " + apiKey;
    }
}
```

**Figure 12.7:** Reading Configuration Properties

**Option 2: Using @ConfigurationProperties**

```java
import org.springframework.boot.context.properties.ConfigurationProperties;
import org.springframework.stereotype.Component;

@Component
@ConfigurationProperties(prefix = "weather")
public class WeatherConfig {
    private String apiKey;

    public String getApiKey() {
        return apiKey;
    }

    public void setApiKey(String apiKey) {
        this.apiKey = apiKey;
    }
}
```

**Figure 12.8:** Another Option of Reading Configuration

And in your **application.yml**:

weather:

```
api-key: ${api-key}
```

This example illustrates how Vault-managed secrets can be accessed in code just like any other Spring property, making integration both secure and developer-friendly. first-class integration for pulling secure values from Vault into your Spring Boot applications. These values are injected into your application's environment at runtime and can be used like any other configuration property.

This integration enables applications to retrieve sensitive values (such as database credentials or API tokens) on demand, without developers needing to see or store those values during development or deployment.

# Other Centralized Configuration Alternatives

While Vault is excellent for secret management, other centralized configuration tools exist to handle non-sensitive application settings. Choosing the right tool depends on your operational requirements, cloud environment, and preferred integration models.

## Kubernetes ConfigMaps and Secrets

Kubernetes offers two native resources–**ConfigMaps** for general configuration values and Secrets for sensitive data. These resources can be mounted as files in pods or exposed as environment variables.

While this method is simple and Kubernetes-native, it lacks versioning and does not support dynamic reload of values out-of-the-box. If changes are made to a **ConfigMap** or Secret, pods typically need to be restarted for the updated values to take effect.

Use them when:

- You need a lightweight solution that works well with Kubernetes.
- You prefer infrastructure-as-code for your configuration values.
- You do not require dynamic updates or encryption at rest (for **ConfigMaps**). These are the native ways of managing configuration and secrets in Kubernetes. They can be mounted as volumes or exposed as environment variables.

**Pros:**

- Built-in to Kubernetes
- Supports both plain configuration and encrypted secrets

**Cons:**

- Static by nature (no versioning or refresh)
- Manual updates required

## Consul as a Configuration Store

HashiCorp Consul provides both a distributed key-value store and service discovery capabilities. When used with Spring Cloud Consul, applications can fetch configuration properties from the Consul's key-value backend, just like they did with Vault.

Consul excels in multi-data center deployments and supports service health checks, dynamic updates, and integrations with both Vault and Nomad. This makes it an attractive choice for teams already using HashiCorp's ecosystem.

Use Consul when:

- You want to manage both configuration and service discovery in one tool.
- You require dynamic config refresh with support for watches and subscriptions.
- You are deploying across multiple regions or clusters. HashiCorp Consul can also serve as a configuration and service discovery tool. It integrates with Spring via Spring Cloud Consul.

Use when:

- You need a distributed key-value store for service metadata.
- You also require service registry and health checks.

Vault and other centralized configuration tools such as Kubernetes Secrets or Consul provide secure, scalable, and production-grade alternatives or complements to Spring Cloud Config Server. Choosing the right tool depends on your need for dynamic secrets, auditability, and operational complexity. In many modern microservice systems, especially those running in Kubernetes with Istio, a hybrid approach using Vault for secrets and Config Server or **`ConfigMaps`** for application settings provides the ideal balance of flexibility, security, and control.

By configuring each microservice as a config client, you decouple application behavior from environment-specific properties. This promotes clean separation of concerns, centralized control, and easier scaling across environments. When combined with Istio's traffic policies and observability stack, Spring Cloud Config Server provides a powerful mechanism for managing microservice configurations consistently and securely.

# Refreshing Configuration Properties at Runtime

In dynamic microservices environments, configuration changes must often be applied without restarting services. Spring Boot and related ecosystems such as Spring Cloud Config, Vault, and Kubernetes-native configurations each offer mechanisms for runtime updates, though with varying degrees of flexibility. This section explores all the common approaches to refreshing configuration properties at runtime.

## Spring Cloud Config with `@RefreshScope`

Spring Cloud Config enables applications to externalize and dynamically refresh properties stored in a Git-backed config server. For this to work:

- Beans must be annotated with **`@RefreshScope`**
- Spring Boot Actuator must be enabled with the **`/refresh`** endpoint exposed

**Example:**

```
@RefreshScope
@RestController
public class FeatureFlagController {
    @Value("${feature.enabled}")
    private boolean isFeatureEnabled;

    @GetMapping("/feature")
    public String featureStatus() {
        return "Feature is " + (isFeatureEnabled ? "ENABLED" : "DISABLED");
    }
}
```

***Figure 12.9:*** *Refreshing at Runtime*

**Triggering a Refresh:**

```
curl -X POST http://localhost:8080/actuator/refresh
```

This rebinds **`@RefreshScope`** beans and updates their values from the config server.

# Vault with Spring Cloud Vault

Secrets retrieved from Vault are typically injected at application startup. However, Spring Cloud Vault can be combined with **`@RefreshScope`** and the **`/refresh`** actuator endpoint for runtime updates.

**Note**: *Vault integration requires that secrets are updated in Vault before refreshing the beans.*

**Limitations:**

- No auto-reload mechanism—requires manual **`/refresh`** call
- No native "**`watcher`**" support like Kubernetes volumes

# Kubernetes ConfigMap/Secrets + Volume Mount

Kubernetes **`ConfigMaps`** and Secrets can be mounted as volumes into pods. When values change, Kubernetes updates the volume, but not the running application.

To reflect changes:

- Use a **`ConfigMap`** reload sidecar (for instance, Reloader and K8s Sidecar Injector)
- Write a custom file watcher to rebind configs

This approach is less flexible without custom logic.

# Spring Cloud Consul + Dynamic Refresh

If using HashiCorp Consul as a key-value store with Spring Cloud, you can:

- Enable watches using Spring Cloud Bus or Consul auto-refresh
- Configure dynamic refresh with polling

This allows apps to automatically pick up changed config values from Consul KV.

**Example Configuration:**

```
spring:
  cloud:
    consul:
      config:
        watch:
          enabled: true
          delay: 1000
```

***Figure 12.10**: Example Configuration*

This polls every second for updated keys and refreshes the application context accordingly.

## Spring Cloud Bus with AMQP/Kafka

To propagate refresh signals to multiple services (especially in distributed systems), use Spring Cloud Bus:

- Works with RabbitMQ or Kafka
- Automatically broadcasts **`/refresh`** events across instances

**Example:**

Trigger a global refresh:

```
curl -X POST http://config-client-1:8080/actuator/bus-refresh
```

All services listening to the bus will update their context accordingly.

Refreshing configuration at runtime is essential for zero-downtime updates and responsive service tuning. Spring provides multiple levels of support—from simple Actuator-based refresh, to advanced event-driven updates via Spring Cloud Bus. Choose the strategy that aligns best with your operational requirements, security standards, and deployment model. In most modern Kubernetes and Istio-enabled environments, combining Git-based Spring Cloud Config with Spring Cloud Bus or Vault-backed secrets with manual refresh offers the best blend of control, security, and flexibility.

# Securing Configuration Information

In a microservices architecture, configuration often contains sensitive information, such as database credentials, API keys, encryption secrets, and service tokens. Securing this configuration is critical to protecting both the integrity of services and the confidentiality of data. In this section, we cover best practices, tools, and patterns to ensure that configuration data is securely managed across your microservices.

## Avoid Hardcoding Sensitive Data

Hardcoding secrets like database credentials or access tokens directly into application source code, Dockerfiles, or configuration files within Git repositories is a common mistake that introduces serious security vulnerabilities. If source code repositories are shared with multiple developers or made public (accidentally or otherwise), those secrets can easily be exposed and misused by malicious actors.

Instead, externalize all configurations that may change between environments or contain sensitive values. Use tools like Spring Cloud Config, Vault, or Kubernetes Secrets to store and manage these values securely. This separation of concerns enhances security and allows you to rotate secrets without redeploying code. such as API keys or passwords directly in source code or Docker images. These artifacts are often widely shared, and exposing secrets here makes them vulnerable to leakage.

**Use Externalized Configuration:**

- Spring Cloud Config Server
- Vault or AWS Secrets Manager
- Kubernetes Secrets

Externalization ensures that sensitive data can be managed, rotated, and audited independently of the application lifecycle.

# Encrypt Sensitive Properties

Even when configuration is externalized, the values may still be stored in plaintext in Git or other version control systems. This creates a vulnerability if the repository is compromised. To mitigate this, use encryption mechanisms, such as Jasypt or Spring Cloud Config's encryption support.

Spring Cloud Config allows you to encrypt values using a symmetric or asymmetric key that is stored securely in the Config Server. At runtime, the server decrypts the values before delivering them to the client. This means that secrets can remain safe even if the Git repository is read-only shared.

Be sure to secure the encryption key or keystore used by the Config Server, ideally through integration with Vault or cloud-managed KMS solutions. (like in Spring Cloud Config), encrypt sensitive values using tools like Jasypt or Spring Cloud Config's built-in encryption support.

**Example using symmetric encryption in `application.yml`:**

```
spring:
  datasource:
    password: '{cipher}AQB+Y4hzds...=='
```

The **`Config Server`** can decrypt this value at runtime using a configured encryption key or keystore.

# Use Secure Secrets Management Tools

Secrets management tools are purpose-built to handle sensitive configuration in a secure and scalable manner. These tools store secrets encrypted at rest, enforce access controls, support automatic rotation, and offer audit trails.

## HashiCorp Vault

Vault is widely used in microservice environments for its advanced security features. It supports dynamic secrets, which are generated on-demand and have short lifetimes, limiting exposure in case of compromise. Vault can integrate with identity systems like Kubernetes, LDAP, and cloud IAM roles to authenticate service identities without relying on hardcoded tokens.

## Cloud Secrets Managers

Providers like AWS Secrets Manager, Azure Key Vault, and Google Secret Manager offer managed secret lifecycle capabilities such as automatic rotation, access logging, and IAM-based access policies. These services are ideal for cloud-native workloads and simplify compliance with regulatory frameworks like PCI-DSS and HIPAA. A secure store that encrypts secrets at rest and allows tight access control using policies. It supports dynamic secrets and automatic rotation.

## AWS/GCP/Azure Secrets Manager

Managed solutions that offer fine-grained access control, encryption, and audit logging out of the box.

These tools are highly recommended when working in a cloud-native or Kubernetes environment.

# Limit Access with RBAC and Policies

One of the most important principles in securing configuration is the principle of least privilege. Services should have access only to the secrets they require and nothing more. This limits the impact in case of a breach or misconfiguration.

Using role-based access control (RBAC), you can define who (or what) has access to which secrets. For example, Vault's policy language allows you to define precise capabilities (read, write, and delete) per secret path. In Kubernetes, RBAC rules can restrict access to Secrets to specific service accounts. This level of granularity ensures tighter security and minimizes lateral movement in the event of compromise., Kubernetes Secrets, or a cloud secret manager, always:

- Defines **least privilege** access using RBAC
- Creates **fine-grained access policies** per service or namespace
- Uses **separate credentials per service** to reduce blast radius

**Example: In Vault, restrict access with ACL policies:**

```
path "secret/data/weather-service/*" {
  capabilities = ["read"]
}
```

# Protect Configuration in Transit and at Rest

It is not enough to store secrets securely, it also matters how they are transmitted between services. All communication between microservices, config servers, and secret managers should be encrypted in transit using TLS or mTLS. Istio, for example, provides automatic mTLS encryption between pods within the mesh.

Similarly, secrets and configuration files should be encrypted at rest in your databases, config repositories, or volume mounts. Vault encrypts secrets before storage, and cloud secret managers also handle encryption automatically. Ensure that encryption keys are stored in secure key management systems and rotated regularly to maintain strong cryptographic hygiene between config clients and servers is encrypted using TLS.

- Use HTTPS for Config Server endpoints
- Use mTLS inside Istio mesh
- Ensure encryption at rest for any database or file store

Vault and most cloud secret managers encrypt secrets by default. Verify encryption settings are enabled and keys are rotated regularly.

# Monitor and Audit Access to Secrets

Keeping track of who accessed which secret, when, and how is crucial for detecting breaches and ensuring compliance. All major secret management tools support auditing features such as:

- Vault generates detailed audit logs for each request.
- Kubernetes can be configured with audit policies to track API access to Secrets.
- AWS, GCP, and Azure offer cloud-native audit logs and integration with SIEM systems.

Use this data to establish alerts, detect anomalies (like access from unauthorized services), and generate compliance reports during security audits.

- Vault provides full audit trails.
- Kubernetes Secrets access can be logged with audit policies.
- Cloud providers offer event logging for secret access.

Set up alerts for unexpected access patterns or privilege escalations.

## Use Environment Variables Cautiously

Environment variables are a common method for injecting secrets into applications, but they come with risks. They are visible to any process running in the same container or namespace and can be leaked in logs or diagnostic dumps.

Use them sparingly and only for non-sensitive values. When you must use environment variables for secrets, restrict access to the container, and disable verbose logging of environment context. Better alternatives include mounting secrets as files through Kubernetes volumes, or using sidecar injection tools that dynamically inject secrets securely into the running application memory. These are visible to any process within the container or node. However, it is useful to consider a few best practices while using them:

- Avoid printing them in logs
- Prefer mounted secrets when using Kubernetes
- Use tools like Doppler or Chamber to scope environment secrets tightly

Securing configuration is foundational to building trustworthy and resilient microservices. By combining encryption, secret management tools, RBAC, TLS, and audit logging, you ensure that sensitive data is protected throughout its lifecycle. As part of a broader DevSecOps strategy, these practices also help meet regulatory compliance and reduce the surface area of security vulnerabilities in your cloud-native applications.

# Conclusion

Securing configuration is foundational to building trustworthy and resilient microservices. In this chapter, we explored how to safeguard sensitive information throughout the configuration lifecycle using tools like Spring Cloud Config, Vault, Kubernetes Secrets, and cloud secret managers. We examined strategies such as encrypting properties, implementing RBAC policies, securing communication with TLS/mTLS, and enabling audit logging. Each technique contributes to a layered security approach that minimizes risk and maximizes operational confidence in cloud-native deployments.

When applied effectively, these practices help prevent accidental exposures, unauthorized access, and potential breaches, all while streamlining compliance with security standards and regulations. Whether you choose Git-based config management, a secrets manager like Vault, or a hybrid approach, securing the configuration layer is key to modern DevSecOps practices.

With centralized and secure configuration in place, your microservices architecture is well-equipped to handle sensitive information and maintain integrity across environments. But in a distributed system, failures are as possible as they are inevitable. Building trustworthy and resilient microservices requires more than just protecting secrets. It involves designing systems that gracefully handle outages, overload, and unexpected conditions without degrading user experience. In the next chapter, we shift focus to understanding and implementing resilience patterns such as circuit breakers, bulkheads, retries, fallbacks, and observability practices. These tools and strategies empower your services to stay responsive and recover quickly in the face of real-world disruptions, thus completing the foundation for a scalable, reliable, and secure cloud-native system.

# CHAPTER 13
# Microservices Resilience and Fault Tolerance

## Introduction

In a distributed microservices architecture, ensuring that your system remains resilient and can tolerate faults is critical to maintain service reliability and user satisfaction. This chapter will thus explore the strategies and patterns that help build robust and fault-tolerant microservices.

We begin with **Understanding Resilience in Microservices**, where you will learn about the core concepts of resilience and why it is essential in a microservices architecture. This section will provide insights into how microservices can be designed to withstand failures and continue operating smoothly under adverse conditions.

Next, we will delve into **Implementing Circuit Breaker Pattern with Resilience4j**, which is a key technique for preventing cascading failures by monitoring service interactions and breaking the circuit when a service fails repeatedly. This helps to protect the system from being overwhelmed by persistent faults.

The chapter then covers **Configuring Bulkhead, RateLimiter,** and **Retry Mechanisms**, which are additional resilience patterns that isolate failures, limit the rate of requests, and provide mechanisms for retrying failed operations. These patterns collectively enhance the robustness of your microservices by controlling resource consumption and improving service availability.

We also explore **Understanding and Implementing Fallback Methods**, where you will learn how to define alternative execution paths when primary services fail, ensuring that your application can gracefully degrade its functionality rather than fail entirely.

Finally, the chapter concludes with **Monitoring and Logging with Spring Boot Actuator**, which teaches you how to implement effective monitoring and logging strategies to detect, diagnose, and respond to faults in real-time, further enhancing the resilience of your microservices.

By the end of this chapter, you will have a comprehensive understanding of how to build resilient and fault-tolerant microservices that can handle failures gracefully and maintain consistent service levels.

## Structure

The chapter addresses the following topics:

- Understanding Resilience in Microservices
- Implementing Circuit Breaker Pattern with Resilience4j
- Configuring Bulkhead, RateLimiter, and Retry Mechanisms
- Understanding and Implementing Fallback Methods
- Monitoring and Logging

# Understanding Resilience in Microservices

Resilience in microservices refers to the system's ability to remain functional and recover gracefully in the face of failures, overloads, or unexpected conditions. In a distributed environment, where services communicate over unreliable networks, resilience is a key architectural concern. This section explores what resilience means in practice, why it is crucial, and how to approach it using Java Spring Boot and Istio.

## Why Resilience Matters in Microservices

Microservices bring about flexibility and scalability by decomposing applications into smaller, independently deployable components. However, this decomposition comes at a cost–inter-service communication over networks introduces latency and failure risks. Unlike monolithic applications where failure in one module may still be recoverable within the same process, a microservice might rely on multiple other services across the network, each of which may fail independently.

Failures might occur due to:

- Temporary service unavailability due to deployment or restarts
- Network partitions or DNS resolution issues
- Overloaded downstream systems that result in timeouts
- Unexpected spikes in traffic or resource exhaustion

Without proper resilience strategies, such failures can cascade and bring down entire systems. Building resilient microservices ensures that services fail gracefully and continue to serve users with reduced or default functionality, improving system robustness and customer trust due to their distributed nature. However, failures might occur because of:

- Network latency and timeouts
- Downstream service unavailability
- Infrastructure crashes
- Configuration or deployment errors

A resilient system absorbs these failures and continues to operate at a reduced capacity instead of crashing completely. This enhances system reliability, maintains service quality, and improves user trust.

# Resilience in Java Spring Boot

Spring Boot, through its support for the Resilience4j library, provides robust resilience patterns that developers can apply directly in application code. These patterns help in gracefully handling exceptions, retries, and load spikes without overloading the application.

## Resilience4j

Resilience4j is a lightweight, easy-to-configure fault tolerance library designed for Java applications. It allows you to decorate your service calls with annotations or functional decorators, applying patterns such as:

- **Circuit Breaker**: Stops calling a failing service temporarily to allow it time to recover
- **Retry**: Automatically re-attempts failed operations based on rules

- **Rate Limiter**: Restricts the rate of requests to prevent overloading the service
- **Bulkhead**: Isolates failures in different threads or services
- **Time Limiter**: Aborts calls taking longer than a defined threshold

## Fallback Methods

A fallback provides an alternative response when the primary service call fails. This ensures users receive meaningful feedback instead of raw error messages. For instance, a product service might return cached product data if the inventory service is down.

## Timeout and Isolation

Timeouts ensure that service calls do not hang indefinitely and block resources. Isolation techniques, like limiting concurrent calls using bulkheads or separating execution into thread pools, prevent one slow service from degrading others while improving microservice resilience.

# Resilience at the Platform Level with Istio

Istio, a service mesh for Kubernetes, provides resilience features at the infrastructure level, abstracting fault-tolerance logic from application code. This allows you to enforce consistent resilience policies across microservices using configuration, rather than programming. Developers can focus on core business logic while platform teams ensure network reliability and security.

Istio proxies (Envoy) intercept traffic between services and enforce traffic policies such as retries, timeouts, load balancing, and circuit breaking.

- **Retries and Timeouts**: By specifying retry attempts and per-try timeouts, Istio ensures that transient errors are retried automatically without changing application code. These configurations improve success rates for operations prone to temporary failures.
- **Circuit Breakers**: Circuit breakers in Istio prevent repeated requests to failing services. They eject unhealthy service instances from the load balancer and prevent service overload. This improves overall system responsiveness by allowing healthy services to handle more traffic.
- **Load Balancing and Pooling**: Istio provides advanced traffic distribution mechanisms, such as round-robin, least requests, random selection, and connection pooling to optimize inter-service communication.
- **Fault Injection**: Fault injection simulates failures like delays or HTTP errors. It helps teams verify the system's fault-handling logic and observability tools before real incidents occur. It also enables chaos engineering practices within safe boundaries from the infrastructure layer, independent of application code. This is critical in large-scale deployments, where enforcing consistency and observability is difficult within code alone.

## Retries and Timeouts

Istio allows you to define request-level retries and timeouts in your `VirtualService` configuration as demonstrated in the figure below:

```yaml
spec:
  http:
  - route:
    - destination:
        host: reviews
    retries:
      attempts: 3
      perTryTimeout: 2s
```

**Figure 13.1**: *Retires and Timeouts*

# Circuit Breakers

Using Istio's **`DestinationRule`**, you can implement the illustrated circuit breaker patterns:

```yaml
spec:
  trafficPolicy:
    connectionPool:
      http:
        http1MaxPendingRequests: 1
        maxRequestsPerConnection: 1
    outlierDetection:
      consecutiveErrors: 5
      interval: 30s
      baseEjectionTime: 1m
      maxEjectionPercent: 100
```

**Figure 13.2**: *DestinationRule*

# Load Balancing and Pooling

Istio supports intelligent load balancing and connection pooling strategies to manage traffic between services effectively.

# Fault Injection

You can simulate delays and service errors to test your system's behavior under failure conditions, helping validate its resilience, just like in the following figure:

```yaml
fault:
  delay:
    percentage:
      value: 50
    fixedDelay: 5s
```

**Figure 13.3**: *Fault Injection*

# Combining Spring Boot and Istio for End-to-End Resilience

Spring Boot and Istio are complementary tools that together provide a layered approach to resilience. Application-level resilience ensures that business logic can recover from downstream failures, while mesh-level resilience facilitates robust network communication and global traffic policy enforcement.

For example, a Spring Boot service might retry a failed database call three times (in-process), while Istio can retry failed service-to-service HTTP calls automatically. Istio might also perform load balancing and enforce rate limits, while Spring Boot ensures each instance can handle failures locally using fallbacks or bulkhead isolation.

This separation of concerns ensures that platform teams manage communication-level reliability and security, while developers focus on resilience patterns tied directly to application logic. The combined observability from both layers also enhances traceability and root-cause analysis in complex distributed systems, as they are complementary. While Spring Boot handles in-process resilience (such as retries, fallbacks, and thread isolation), Istio manages cross-service communication (including circuit breakers, retries, and timeouts).

This layered approach allows developers to:

- Define business-specific resilience policies in the application layer
- Enforce global traffic control and reliability policies at the mesh layer
- Gain uniform observability through tools like Prometheus, Grafana, and Kiali

Building resilient microservices is not about avoiding failure, but about **embracing failure gracefully**. By leveraging Spring Boot's programmatic resilience patterns and Istio's service mesh capabilities, you can create robust, observable, and self-healing systems. As you scale your architecture, resilience evolves from a best practice into a survival requirement for modern cloud-native environments.

# Implementing Circuit Breaker Pattern with Resilience4j

A circuit breaker is one of the most fundamental patterns for building resilient microservices. It prevents a service from performing operations that are likely to fail, in turn allowing it to fail faster and recover gracefully. In this section, we explore how to implement the circuit breaker pattern in Java using Resilience4j, a lightweight and flexible fault tolerance library that integrates seamlessly with Spring Boot.

## Understanding Circuit Breaker

A circuit breaker acts like a safety switch in an electrical circuit. In a software system, especially in microservices architecture, it prevents an application from repeatedly trying to execute an operation that is likely to fail. For example, if a downstream service becomes unresponsive or starts throwing errors, the circuit breaker stops sending further requests to that service temporarily and prevents overwhelming the service, giving it time to recover.

The circuit breaker operates through three key states:

- **Closed**: During this state, the service is considered healthy. All requests go through and failures are monitored.

- **Open**: This is when the failure threshold has been exceeded. Requests are immediately blocked to prevent further failures.
- **Half-Open**: A limited number of test requests are allowed through to check if the service has recovered. If successful, the circuit breaker returns to the Closed state. A switch in an electrical circuit. When a service experiences repeated failures (for example: timeout, connection errors), the circuit breaker trips and prevents further calls to the failing service. Instead of making those calls, the circuit breaker immediately returns a fallback response, giving the failing service time to recover.

A circuit breaker has three states:

- **Closed**: Calls go through normally and failures are tracked.
- **Open**: Calls are blocked to prevent further failures.
- **Half-Open**: A few calls are allowed through to test if the service has recovered.

# Usage Of Resilience4j

Resilience4j is a lightweight, modular, and customizable library designed specifically for Java 8 and functional programming paradigms. It is a replacement for Netflix Hystrix, as it offers improved flexibility and better integration with modern Java frameworks like Spring Boot.

One of the primary advantages of Resilience4j is that it follows the 'choose what you need' approach. Instead of a monolithic fault-tolerance system, it offers separate modules for circuit breaking, retries, rate limiting, bulkheads, and timeouts. This makes it more efficient and easier to integrate with various types of applications.

Resilience4j can also integrate with popular monitoring tools like Micrometer, Prometheus, and Grafana and provide deep visibility into how resilience strategies are performing in production. For Java 8 and functional programming, it supports several resilience patterns, including circuit breakers, rate limiters, retries, and bulkheads. Unlike older libraries like Hystrix (now in maintenance mode), Resilience4j is modular and allows you to use only the patterns you need.

**Advantages:**

- Lightweight (no external dependencies)
- Functional and annotation-based API
- Native Spring Boot integration
- Metrics support (Micrometer, Prometheus)

## Adding Resilience4j to a Spring Boot Project

Add the following dependency to your **`pom.xml`**:

```
<dependency>
  <groupId>io.github.resilience4j</groupId>
  <artifactId>resilience4j-spring-boot3</artifactId>
</dependency>
```

# Defining Circuit Breaker Configuration

Before applying the circuit breaker in your code, it is important to define how it behaves under failure conditions. In Spring Boot, this is typically done through the **`application.yml`** file. The configuration allows you to fine-tune the behavior of each circuit breaker instance based on the specific requirements of the downstream service.

Key properties include:

- **slidingWindowSize**: Number of recent calls to consider when calculating the failure rate
- **minimumNumberOfCalls**: Minimum number of calls before the failure rate is calculated
- **failureRateThreshold**: The percentage of failed calls that triggers the breaker
- **waitDurationInOpenState**: Time to wait before transitioning from Open to Half-Open state
- **permittedNumberOfCallsInHalfOpenState**: Number of trial calls allowed in Half-Open state

Properly tuning these parameters is essential for avoiding both false positives and overly aggressive failure handling. It is demonstrated in **application.yml** as follows:

```
resilience4j:
  circuitbreaker:
    instances:
      weatherService:
        registerHealthIndicator: true
        slidingWindowSize: 10
        minimumNumberOfCalls: 5
        failureRateThreshold: 50
        waitDurationInOpenState: 10s
        permittedNumberOfCallsInHalfOpenState: 3
```

***Figure 13.4**: Circuit Breaker Configuration*

This configuration defines a circuit breaker for a service named **weatherService**:

- It trips if more than 50% of the last 10 calls failed.
- It stays open for 10 seconds before transitioning to half-open.

# Using the Circuit Breaker in Your Code

Once the circuit breaker configuration is in place, you can use it within your Spring Boot application in two primary ways: through annotations or programmatically. This section illustrates both methods, allowing developers to choose the one that best fits their project needs.

## Annotation-Based Example

Using annotations is the most straightforward approach. By applying the **@CircuitBreaker** annotation on a controller method, Spring Boot automatically handles the circuit breaker behavior behind the scenes. In this example, a call to **weatherService.callExternalApi()** is guarded by a circuit breaker named **weatherService**. If the external API fails beyond the configured threshold, the **weatherFallback** method is invoked instead of propagating the failure downstream.

The fallback method should have the same signature as the original method or accept a **Throwable** as the last parameter to handle exceptions more gracefully.

```java
@RestController
public class WeatherController {

  @Autowired
  private WeatherService weatherService;

  @GetMapping("/weather")
  @CircuitBreaker(name = "weatherService", fallbackMethod = "weatherFallback")
  public String getWeather() {
    return weatherService.callExternalApi();
  }

  public String weatherFallback(Throwable t) {
    return "Weather data is currently unavailable. Please try again later.";
  }
}
```

***Figure 13.5***: *Usage of Circuit Breaker*

# Programmatic Example

The programmatic approach gives you more control and is useful when you need to dynamically build or modify circuit breaker configurations at runtime. Here, we shall first retrieve or define a circuit breaker instance named **weatherService**. Then, we can wrap the original method call (**weatherService.callExternalApi()**) using **CircuitBreaker.decorateSupplier**.

The **Try** class from **Vavr** is used to handle success and fallback logic. If the original call fails, the fallback logic defined in **recover()** will execute and return a default response. This is helpful when the fallback logic is not static or when the resilience logic needs to be handled imperatively rather than declaratively.

```java
CircuitBreaker circuitBreaker = CircuitBreaker.ofDefaults("weatherService");
Supplier<String> supplier = CircuitBreaker.decorateSupplier(circuitBreaker, ()
-> weatherService.callExternalApi());
String result = Try.ofSupplier(supplier)
    .recover(throwable -> "Fallback response").get();
```

***Figure 13.6***: *Circuit Breaker Example*

# Observability and Monitoring

Understanding how and when your circuit breakers are triggered is essential for maintaining system health. Resilience4j integrates seamlessly with Micrometer, exposing the metrics and helping us visualize them via monitoring tools such as Prometheus and Grafana.

Typical metrics to monitor include:

- **resilience4j_circuitbreaker_calls_total**: Tracks the number of successful, failed, and not-permitted calls

- **resilience4j_circuitbreaker_state**: Indicates the current state of the circuit breaker (Closed, Open, or Half-Open)
- **resilience4j_circuitbreaker_failure_rate**: Shows the percentage of failed calls in the sliding window

By analyzing these metrics, teams can detect problematic dependencies, tune circuit breaker settings and quickly respond to production issues to expose circuit breaker metrics. These metrics can be scraped using Prometheus and visualized with Grafana.

Example metrics:

- **resilience4j_circuitbreaker_calls_total**
- **resilience4j_circuitbreaker_state**
- **resilience4j_circuitbreaker_failure_rate**

This helps you track how often the circuit is open, how many calls are being made, and when fallbacks are triggered.

Circuit breakers are a foundational resilience pattern that can protect your microservices from cascading failures. Resilience4j offers a powerful and modular way to implement this pattern in Spring Boot. By automatically rejecting requests when a service is failing and retrying only when safe, circuit breakers improve uptime, reduce load on dependencies, and enhance user experience during outages.

# Configuring Bulkhead, RateLimiter, and Retry Mechanisms

In resilient microservices architecture, handling load and failure gracefully is as important as ensuring uptime. Resilience4j not only supports circuit breakers, but also includes powerful patterns such as Bulkhead, RateLimiter, and Retry. These mechanisms help isolate failures, manage resource contention, and retry transient errors without overwhelming downstream systems. In this section, we will cover each of these patterns with detailed explanations and practical Spring Boot examples.

## Bulkhead Pattern

The **bulkhead** pattern is inspired by the structural design of ships, which use watertight compartments (bulkheads) to prevent the vessel from flooding. In a similar way, microservices use bulkheads to isolate different service components, so that a failure in one does not cascade to others.

In software, this is implemented by limiting the number of concurrent calls or threads allowed to execute a particular function. This prevents resource exhaustion and ensures that other parts of the application remain available even if one service or method is under stress.

For example, if a third-party service is known to be unreliable or slow, placing a bulkhead around the method that calls it ensures that it does not consume all the application threads, thereby preserving the health of the rest of the system. By ship compartments—each service operation is placed in its own '*compartment*' to prevent failures in one part of the system from affecting others. In Resilience4j, this is achieved by limiting concurrent threads or calls for a given method.

**When to Use:**

- To isolate failures from propagating across the system
- When calling external services with known contention or latency issues

```
resilience4j:
  bulkhead:
    instances:
      userService:
        maxConcurrentCalls: 5
        maxWaitDuration: 2s
```

***Figure 13.7**: Bulkhead Pattern*

This limits the number of concurrent calls to the **`userService`** method to **`5`**. Additional requests will wait up to **`2`** seconds or be rejected.

```
@Bulkhead(name = "userService", type = Bulkhead.Type.SEMAPHORE)
public String fetchUserData() {
    return restTemplate.getForObject("http://user-api/users", String.class);
}
```

***Figure 13.8**: Bulkhead Usage*

# RateLimiter

The **`RateLimiter`** pattern is designed to control the rate at which a method or resource can be accessed. This is particularly useful when calling external services that enforce strict usage quotas or when you want to prevent abuse from clients.

By restricting the number of allowed requests per time period, rate limiting helps maintain the stability of your services and ensures fair resource usage among users. It is especially useful for protecting sensitive endpoints such as login or payment APIs that are prone to brute force or denial-of-service attacks.

You can define how many requests are allowed per second (or other intervals), and how long a request should wait if the limit has been reached. If the request cannot be processed within the timeout window, it is rejected gracefully. This is useful to protect shared resources or external APIs from excessive calls.

**When to Use:**

- To prevent abuse of services
- To conform to third-party API usage quotas

```
resilience4j:
  ratelimiter:
    instances:
      loginService:
        limitForPeriod: 5
        limitRefreshPeriod: 1s
        timeoutDuration: 500ms
```

***Figure 13.9**: RateLimiter*

**Example:** This allows 5 requests per second to the **loginUser()** method. If the limit is exceeded, requests will either wait 500ms or be rejected.

```
@RateLimiter(name = "loginService")
public String loginUser() {
    return loginClient.authenticate();
}
```

***Figure 13.10***: *RateLimiter Example*

# Retry Mechanism

The **Retry** pattern is one of the most commonly used resilience strategies. It allows a system to automatically re-attempt failed operations that may have failed due to temporary glitches, such as brief network disconnects, DNS resolution delays, or short-lived backend service failures.

Retrying helps increase the success rate of operations without user intervention and reduces the impact of intermittent issues. However, it must be used with care to avoid retry storms that could amplify the failure.

Resilience4j allows you to configure the exceptions that should trigger a retry, the number of attempts for a retry, and the wait time between successive attempts. You can also combine retries with fallback methods so that users get a predictable and friendly response in the event of persistent failure.

**When to Use:**

- For idempotent operations prone to occasional failure
- For upstream services that frequently experience short-lived unavailability

**Configuration**

```
resilience4j:
  retry:
    instances:
      paymentService:
        maxAttempts: 3
        waitDuration: 1s
        retryExceptions:
          - java.io.IOException
          - java.util.concurrent.TimeoutException
```

***Figure 13.11***: *Configuration*

This configuration retries a failed call up to 3 times with 1-second intervals if the failure matches any of the listed exceptions.

```
@Retry(name = "paymentService", fallbackMethod = "paymentFallback")
public String processPayment() {
    return paymentGateway.charge();
}

public String paymentFallback(Throwable t) {
    return "Payment service is currently unavailable. Please try again
later.";
}
```

**Figure 13.12**: *Retry Configuration*

# Combining Patterns

These patterns can be layered together to build a comprehensive and robust fault-tolerant strategy tailored to your application's needs. In many real-world scenarios, a service call might require not just retry logic but also concurrency control and rate limiting to maintain performance and availability across distributed systems.

When combined, the patterns work collaboratively:

- **`Retry`** ensures transient faults (like intermittent network failures) are retried automatically.
- **`RateLimiter`** prevents excessive or abusive access, especially under load or attack.
- **`Bulkhead`** ensures that even if a dependency misbehaves or overloads, the impact is contained to just a portion of the system.

## Example Use Case

Consider an e-commerce application's **`placeOrder()`** method that calls multiple downstream services like payment, inventory, and shipping. Each of these services might face occasional downtime or delays.

```
@Retry(name = "orderService")
@RateLimiter(name = "orderService")
@Bulkhead(name = "orderService")
public String placeOrder() {
    return orderApi.submit();
}
```

**Figure 13.13**: *Example*

This method benefits from retry logic, concurrency limits, and rate limiting, while offering a comprehensive resilience strategy.

Using Bulkhead, RateLimiter, and Retry together equips your microservices to handle overload, transient failures, and external system instability. Resilience4j makes integrating these patterns into Spring Boot applications easy and configurable, giving you both fine-grained control and observability. By proactively managing failures, you can ensure smoother operation and a better user experience even under adverse conditions.

# Understanding and Implementing Fallback Methods

In a distributed microservices environment, failures are inevitable. Services might become unavailable, experience timeouts, or return errors due to overload or external issues. While resilience patterns like retries and circuit breakers help mitigate these failures, they do not always guarantee successful execution. This is where **fallback methods** come in as they provide an alternative execution path when the primary logic fails.

## Understanding Fallback Method

A fallback method is a predefined function or backup plan that gets executed when the primary business logic fails. This mechanism ensures that your application does not crash or propagate errors downstream when a dependency fails. Instead, it responds in a controlled and predictable way, often providing a default value, a cached response, or a helpful message to the user.

For instance, if your microservice fails to fetch product details from an external catalog service, a fallback method can provide a message indicating the temporary unavailability or return placeholder content until the service is restored. This approach helps maintain a consistent user experience and keeps other components functioning without disruption. It is executed when a protected method fails. Rather than propagating the exception to the user or crashing the application, the fallback method returns a safe response or default behavior, maintaining the application's stability and user experience.

Fallbacks can:

- Return default values (for example, cached results or hardcoded responses)
- Provide informative error messages
- Trigger alternative workflows
- Queue the failed request for later processing

## When to Use Fallbacks

Fallbacks are ideal in situations where availability and user experience matter more than strict accuracy or real-time data. They are most useful for non-critical operations or in cases where a partial response is acceptable.

Use fallbacks:

- When the application must remain responsive, such as returning cached data when a real-time service is unavailable
- To provide continuity of service in user-facing applications, even when backend dependencies are failing
- When system reliability is more important than eventual consistency, especially in read-heavy or data display scenarios

However, avoid fallbacks for operations that affect financial records, transactions, or critical system state. In such cases, retries and circuit breakers with proper alerts are more appropriate. They stay responsive even if upstream services fail.

- When partial data or a generic message is acceptable
- For non-critical components where graceful degradation is preferred over error propagation

Avoid using fallbacks for critical operations such as financial transactions unless it is safe to do so.

# Implementing Fallback with Resilience4j in Spring Boot

Resilience4j allows you to specify fallback methods using annotations or programmatic APIs. Fallback methods must match the signature of the original method or include an extra **Throwable** parameter to handle the exception.

**Example:**

```
@Retry(name = "inventoryService", fallbackMethod = "inventoryFallback")
public String checkInventory(String productId) {
    // Simulates a failing downstream API call
    return inventoryClient.getProductStock(productId);
}

public String inventoryFallback(String productId, Throwable t) {
    return "Inventory information is currently unavailable for product: " +
productId;
}
```

***Figure 13.14***: *Implementing Fallback Method*

In this example:

- The **checkInventory()** method is guarded by a retry mechanism.
- If all retries fail, the **inventoryFallback()** method is triggered.
- The fallback provides a meaningful message to the user without failing the system.

# Combining Fallbacks with Other Resilience Patterns

Fallbacks become even more powerful when used in conjunction with other Resilience4j patterns. This creates a layered defense system against various failure modes.

- With **Retry**, a fallback is invoked only after several attempts to recover from a transient failure. This allows some breathing room before declaring an operation as failed.
- With **CircuitBreaker**, the fallback is triggered immediately when the breaker is open, hence bypassing unnecessary calls to a known-failing dependency.
- With **Bulkhead** or **RateLimiter**, if the system is overwhelmed or call limits are exceeded, the fallback prevents further strain and makes way for graceful degradation.

# Other Fallback Mechanisms beyond Resilience4j

While Resilience4j is a widely adopted solution for implementing fallback strategies, the following alternative approaches can also be used, depending on your application's needs and technology stack:

- **Spring Retry**: Built into the Spring ecosystem, this library allows method-level retry and fallback annotations, offering an alternative to Resilience4j for basic use cases.

- **Manual Fallback Logic**: Developers can use traditional try-catch blocks to handle errors and return fallback responses directly, especially in smaller applications.
- **Netflix Hystrix**: Though it is presently deprecated, Hystrix provides a robust way to implement circuit breakers and fallbacks. It is still used in legacy systems.
- **Service Mesh Fallbacks (for example, Istio)**: At the infrastructure layer, tools like Istio can be configured to route traffic to backup services or mirror requests in the event of primary service failures.
- **API Gateway-Based Fallbacks**: API gateways can be configured to provide static or cached responses when a downstream service fails, especially useful in edge or proxy scenarios.
- **Frontend Fallbacks**: In modern web or mobile apps, fallbacks can be implemented on the client side, such as displaying cached data or placeholder UIs when APIs fail.

These strategies complement code-based fallbacks and provide a more holistic resilience approach across layers.

## Best Practices

Consider the following practices to use fallback methods effectively:

- **Ensure fallback logic is fast and efficient**: It should not perform any complex computation or external calls that could also fail.
- **Return meaningful responses**: Inform users about what is happening, such as "*Live data unavailable, showing last known value.*"
- **Avoid logic duplication**: Keep fallback code simple and distinct from your main service logic.
- **Monitor usage**: If fallbacks are triggered frequently, it is a sign that the dependent service needs attention.
- **Test regularly**: Validate that fallbacks work correctly under simulated failure conditions.

Following the mentioned practices ensures that your fallback methods enhance resilience without introducing hidden complexity or new failure points:

- Avoid putting business-critical logic in fallbacks.
- Keep fallback responses meaningful and consistent.
- Monitor fallback frequency to detect underlying issues.

Fallback methods are a vital part of the resilience strategy in a microservices system. They ensure continuity of service by providing alternate responses when the primary logic fails. When combined with other Resilience4j patterns like Retry and Circuit Breaker, fallbacks empower your application to remain stable, responsive, and user-friendly even during partial system outages.

# Monitoring and Logging

Resilience mechanisms like retries, fallbacks, circuit breakers, and rate limiters are critical, but their effectiveness depends heavily on observability. Without proper monitoring and logging, it is impossible to know when these patterns are triggered, how often they are used, or whether they are masking larger issues. In this section, we will explore how to monitor and log resilience behavior effectively, along with tools and best practices for production environments.

## Why Monitoring and Logging Matter

Monitoring and logging form the backbone of any production-grade, resilient system. While implementing fallback methods or circuit breakers helps applications remain responsive, observability tells us when, why, and how these mechanisms are being triggered.

Monitoring involves collecting metrics that show the health and performance of your system over time. On the other hand, logging records detailed, contextual information about specific events, such as failures or slow requests. Together, they enable teams to:

- Diagnose system bottlenecks and root causes of issues
- Proactively identify failing services
- Measure the effectiveness of resilience patterns
- Understand system behavior under failure conditions

These capabilities ensure that resilience is not a black box but an actively managed aspect of system health. Logging provides insight into system behavior, aiding debugging and root cause analysis. When implementing resilience patterns, observability helps answer key questions like:

- Are fallbacks happening too frequently?
- Which services are experiencing the most timeouts or failures?
- How often are circuit breakers opening?
- Are retries masking a persistent underlying issue?

These insights help you tune configurations, address bottlenecks, and improve system reliability.

# Metrics to Track for Resilience

Tracking the right metrics helps you validate whether your resilience mechanisms are effective and where improvements are needed. Without these insights, fallback and retry mechanisms might silently degrade performance or hide deeper issues.

Here are the most critical metrics to track along with what they entail:

- **Circuit Breaker Metrics:**
  - Total number of calls
  - Failed calls and their failure reasons
  - Number of times the circuit transitions to OPEN or HALF-OPEN
  - Time duration spent in each circuit breaker state
- **Retry Metrics:**
  - Count of retries per operation
  - Success rate after retries
  - Cumulative delay introduced by retries
- **Rate Limiter Metrics:**
  - Total calls allowed vs. rejected
  - Wait durations when throttling occurs
- **Fallback Metrics:**
  - How often fallback methods are triggered
  - Which service or endpoint triggered the fallback
  - Associated exception types or error responses

## Logging Patterns

Logging complements metrics by providing contextual information about individual requests and events. Structured logs written in a machine-readable format such as JSON facilitate advanced filtering and searching in logging platforms.

Resilience-related logs should include:

- The service name and endpoint that failed or was protected by resilience logic
- Timestamps to correlate events across systems
- Type of resilience pattern triggered (fallback, retry, circuit open, and so on.)
- Cause of failure (for example, **`TimeoutException`**, **`ServiceUnavailable`**)
- Execution duration to understand performance impact

Well-structured logs are crucial for debugging and incident response. They also aid in constructing user-friendly dashboards or audit trails for compliance with relevant metadata such as:

- Service name and endpoint
- Timestamp and latency
- Resilience pattern triggered (fallback, retry, etc.)
- Error cause or exception details
- Unique correlation ID (for tracing across services)

## Tools for Observability

To collect, store, and visualize the metrics and logs, modern observability stacks provide rich ecosystems. Choosing the right tool combination depends on your infrastructure and use case. Here is a breakdown of commonly used tools:

- **Spring Boot Actuator + Micrometer**
  - Exposes application health and resilience metrics through endpoints like **`/actuator/metrics`**
  - Works with various backends such as Prometheus, Datadog, New Relic
  - Integrates directly with Resilience4j and Spring Boot, requiring minimal setup
- **Prometheus + Grafana**
  - Prometheus scrapes metrics from Spring Boot applications
  - Grafana visualizes these metrics in time-series dashboards with alerts
  - Ideal for identifying trends like rising fallback counts or circuit breaker trips
- **ELK Stack (Elasticsearch, Logstash, Kibana)**
  - Centralized logging platform
  - Allows full-text search on logs with custom fields and filters
  - Kibana dashboards can reveal fallback patterns, error distributions, or latency spikes
- **Zipkin or Jaeger (Distributed Tracing)**
  - Essential for tracing requests across multiple microservices
  - Highlights where delays or failures occur in the service chain
  - Useful for visualizing retry attempts, slow dependencies, and fallback activation points

# Best Practices

- **Enable health indicators:** Use Spring Boot Actuator to expose the current state of your resilience components (for example, is the circuit breaker open?).
- **Alert on abnormal behavior:** Use Prometheus and Grafana alerts or ELK queries to detect when fallbacks or retries exceed healthy thresholds.
- **Tag logs with correlation IDs**: Attach unique identifiers to logs across microservices to trace a user's request from start to finish.
- **Aggregate fallback logs:** Analyze aggregated log data to detect which services consistently fall back, and why.
- **Visualize and baseline patterns:** Set up dashboards that track fallback counts, error rates, and retry trends over time. Compare against historical baselines to identify anomalies. Expose the state of circuit breakers and rate limiters.

Monitoring and logging are essential pillars of a resilient microservices system. With proper observability, you can track how the behavior of resilience patterns and optimize them for better user experience and system robustness. With tools like Micrometer, Prometheus, Grafana, and ELK, you can transform raw metrics and logs into actionable insights that improve uptime and confidence in your architecture.

# Conclusion

In this chapter, we explored key strategies for building resilient microservices systems that can maintain stability and continue operating even when parts of the system fail. We began by understanding resilience in microservices and recognizing the importance of designing for failure. Then, we implemented resilience patterns such as circuit breakers, bulkheads, rate limiters, retries, and fallback methods using Resilience4j, all of which help the system isolate and recover from faults effectively.

The chapter concluded with an in-depth discussion on monitoring and logging, reinforcing the idea that resilience is not just about implementing protective mechanisms, but also about observing and improving them over time. Observability empowers teams to measure resilience patterns in action and fine-tune configurations based on real-world data.

By combining these techniques, you now have a robust toolkit to build functional, highly available, and fault-tolerant microservices that form a strong foundation for scaling your systems in production environments.

In the next chapter, we will focus on effective data handling and testing strategies in microservices. You will learn how to manage databases using patterns like "*Database per Service*," handle transactions and consistency challenges, implement the Saga pattern, and perform robust testing using unit, integration, and end-to-end testing approaches tailored for microservices. With proper observability in place, you can not only track how resilience patterns are behaving, but also optimize them for better user experience and system robustness. By leveraging tools like Micrometer, Prometheus, Grafana, and ELK, you can transform raw metricss and logs into actionable insights that improve uptime and confidence in your architecture.

CHAPTER 14

# Effective Data Handling and Testing Strategies in Microservices

## Introduction

Handling data effectively and implementing robust testing procedures are crucial aspects of building reliable microservices. In this chapter, we will explore the best practices and techniques for managing data across distributed services and to ensure that your microservices are thoroughly tested for reliability and performance. We will begin with the database per service pattern and data management strategies, where you will learn about designing and managing data storage solutions tailored for the microservices architecture. The section will also cover the challenges and benefits of having a dedicated database for each service, along with the strategies for maintaining data integrity across multiple services.

Next, we will discuss managing transactions and data consistency in microservices, focusing on techniques which ensure that your data remains consistent even in the face of failures and distributed transactions. The section will lead us into eventual consistency and the saga pattern, which introduces patterns to manage long-running business processes and ensuring consistency across microservices that interact asynchronously. The chapter also covers JPA and Hibernate integration in microservices, guiding you on how to leverage Java Persistence API (JPA) and Hibernate effectively within a microservices architecture. You will also explore database migration and versioning techniques, which are essential for managing changes made to your database schema in a controlled and predictable manner.

On the testing front, we will explore a few strategies that will provide you with an overview of the specific testing approaches required for microservices environments. This will include Unit, Integration, and Contract Testing Approaches, which ensure that individual services function correctly, integrate seamlessly, and adhere to agreed contracts. Finally, the chapter will delve into End-to-End Testing Techniques to validate the entire application flow across all microservices and Mocking Techniques for External Services and Databases to simulate dependencies and ensure that your tests are both reliable and fast.

## Structure

This chapter will address the following topics:

- Database per Service Pattern and Data Management Strategies
- Managing Transactions and Data Consistency in Microservices
- Database Migration and Versioning Techniques
- Testing Strategies Tailored for Microservices

- End-to-End Testing Techniques
- Mocking Techniques for External Services and Databases

# Database per Service Pattern and Data Management Strategies

Autonomy is one of the foundational principles of microservices architecture. Each microservice along with its data layer, should be independently deployable and scalable. The Database per Service pattern reinforces this principle by giving each microservice the ownership of its own database. In this section, we will explore this pattern, its significance, and how to implement it effectively.

# Understanding Database per Service Pattern

The Database per Service pattern means that each microservice will manage its own private database. The said database is not shared with other services. This isolation helps enforce boundaries between services, reduces coupling, and allows for greater scalability, increases fault tolerance, and fosters team independence.

**Key Characteristics:**

- One database per service
- No direct access to another service's database
- Communication between services occurs via APIs or asynchronous messaging

## Benefits of Database per Service

- **Loose Coupling:** Services are truly independent. Changes in a service's schema do not affect others.
- **Autonomous Scaling:** Services and their databases can scale independently based on their load.
- **Technology Diversity:** Each service can choose the best database technology for its requirements, such as SQL, NoSQL, graph, and so on.
- **Faster Deployments:** Teams can evolve and deploy services without coordinating with others on shared schema changes.
- **Improved Fault Isolation:** Failures in a service's data store will not directly impact others.

# Challenges and Mitigations

While the Database per Service pattern has many advantages, it also introduces the following complexities:

- **Distributed Data Consistency across Services**
    - Since there is no shared database, achieving ACID properties across services becomes difficult.
    - Use eventual consistency and Saga patterns for distributed transactions.
- **Reporting and Analytics**
    - Aggregating data from multiple databases for reporting can be challenging.
    - Use data lakes or ETL pipelines to replicate data into a central warehouse.

- **Duplicated Data**
  - Some data might be replicated across services to fulfill business requirements.
  - Use versioning and service contracts to manage data duplication safely.

# Common Data Management Strategies in Microservices

As microservices evolve to handle distinct business capabilities, managing the data they produce and consume becomes increasingly complex. To support scalability, maintain loose coupling, and ensure consistency, developers apply a range of data management strategies tailored to complement the decentralized nature of microservices. The following patterns are widely used to handle data effectively across distributed systems:

- **Event-Driven Architecture (EDA):** Services emit domain events (such as `OrderCreated`, `PaymentProcessed`) that other services can subscribe to and act upon. This brings about eventual consistency and loosely-coupled updates.
- **Command Query Responsibility Segregation (CQRS):** Separates read and write models to optimize performance and scalability. Write operations change the state and emit events, while read models are updated asynchronously.
- **API Composition:** When a service has to fetch data from multiple services, it calls their APIs and aggregates results. This feature is useful for UI composition, but not ideal for high-performance needs.
- **Data Replication:** Services replicate relevant data (usually read-only) from other services via messaging or batch jobs.
- **Shared Kernel Pattern (as an exception):** In rare cases, a bounded context might share a schema if it is fully owned by the same team. However, it must be managed cautiously.

# Additional Data Management Patterns in Microservices

Beyond the foundational strategies, several advanced data management patterns are commonly adopted to ensure reliable, consistent, and scalable behavior across microservices. These are listed as follows:

- **Saga Pattern**: The Saga pattern manages distributed transactions by breaking them into a sequence of local transactions. Each transaction publishes an event or sends a command to trigger the next step. If something fails, compensating transactions are executed to rollback the previous steps. Sagas can be orchestrated (central controller) or choreographed (event-driven).
- **Outbox Pattern**: This pattern helps avoid dual-write problems by writing a message/event into an "*outbox*" table in the same transaction as the business change. A background process later reads from the outbox and publishes the event to a message broker, ensuring atomicity and consistency between the database and messaging layers.
- **Materialized View Pattern**: To optimize query performance and avoid cross-service joins, services maintain read-optimized projections of external data. These views are asynchronously updated via event streams or change data capture mechanisms, reducing latency for read operations.
- **Change Data Capture (CDC)**: CDC tools (for example, Debezium) monitor database transaction logs and convert changes into events. This enables services to react to real-time data updates from other systems without tight coupling or direct API calls.

These patterns address the operational and consistency challenges that arise from distributed data ownership and are critical when designing robust, production-ready microservices.

The Database per Service pattern promotes microservice autonomy and independence, enabling decentralized data governance, fault isolation, and scalable service ownership. Although it comes with trade-offs like complexity in achieving data consistency and centralized reporting, applying strategies such as EDA, CQRS, and data replication can address the underlined challenges. Ultimately, embracing this pattern is the key to realize the full benefits of microservices architecture.

# Managing Transactions and Data Consistency in Microservices

In monolithic systems, managing transactions is often straightforward because a single relational database can handle ACID transactions across all operations. However, in a microservices architecture where each service owns its own database, ensuring transactional consistency becomes more complex. This section delves into the strategies and patterns used to manage transactions and maintain data consistency across distributed systems.

## The Challenge of Distributed Transactions

In microservices, a single business process often spans multiple services and their respective databases. Coordinating a traditional ACID transaction across these boundaries is difficult due to:

- Network unreliability
- Independent service failures
- Latency constraints
- Lack of a shared transaction manager

Two-Phase Commit (2PC) is a classic protocol used in distributed databases to ensure all-or-nothing atomicity across multiple nodes. It works by first preparing all participating nodes to commit (the prepare phase), then issuing a final commit command (the commit phase). While 2PC provides strong consistency guarantees, it introduces tight coupling between services and can result in significant performance bottlenecks, especially in environments with high latency or unreliable networks. The protocol also suffers from blocking issues–if the coordinator crashes mid-way, the participants may remain in an uncertain state.

Instead of traditional 2-Phase Commits (2PCs), which introduce these drawbacks, microservices favor eventual consistency and asynchronous communication patterns. These approaches better align with the principles of decentralized ownership, scalability, and fault tolerance.

## Strategies for Managing Transactions

- **Eventual Consistency**: Eventual consistency is a consistency model that allows data to be temporarily inconsistent across services, with the guarantee that it will become consistent over time. This model is ideal for use in microservices, where synchronous operations can lead to tight coupling and latency issues.

  For example, in an e-commerce system, when an order is placed, the `Order Service` updates its local database and emits an `OrderCreated` event. The `Inventory Service` and `Billing Service` listen to this event and update their respective data stores asynchronously. If any service is temporarily unavailable, the event can be retried or replayed later, ensuring that consistency is eventually achieved without blocking the user.

  This model requires robust messaging infrastructure, retry mechanisms, and sometimes idempotency to handle message duplication. Eventual consistency allows each service to update its local state independently and notify other services via events. Over time, all systems become consistent, even if they temporarily diverge. This is a core principle of resilient distributed systems.

- **Saga Pattern**: The Saga pattern is a design approach to manage distributed transactions by breaking them down into a sequence of local transactions, each with its own compensating action. This approach avoids locking resources across services and improves scalability.

  **Orchestration Example:** In a hotel booking system, the `Booking Service` might orchestrate a saga by:

  - Reserving a room (Room Service)
  - Charging a payment (Payment Service)
  - Confirming the booking (Notification Service)

  If payment fails, the saga triggers a compensating action to cancel the room reservation.

  **Choreography Example:** Instead of a central orchestrator, services communicate via events:

  - `Booking Service` emits `RoomReserved`
  - `Payment Service` listens and processes payment
  - If successful, it emits `PaymentSuccessful`
  - `Notification Service` listens and sends a confirmation

  If a failure occurs, each service listens for compensating events like `PaymentFailed` to rollback previous operations. The Saga pattern manages distributed transactions using a series of local transactions coordinated through:

  - **Orchestration**: A central service (saga orchestrator) manages the sequence and execution of transactions
  - **Choreography**: Each service listens to events and reacts independently without a central coordinator

  Sagas also include compensating transactions to undo the effects of previous steps if something fails.

- **Transactional Outbox Pattern**: This pattern ensures that changes to a service's database and the generation of events are done atomically, thereby avoiding inconsistencies. The service writes an event to an "`outbox`" table in the same transaction as the business operation.

  **Example:** In the `Order Service`, when an order is placed, the order data and an `OrderCreated` event are saved to the database in one transaction. A background worker (or the Debezium CDC listener) reads the `outbox` table and publishes the event on Kafka.

  This pattern is essential when you want to guarantee that an event is published only if the transaction succeeds, and never if it fails. This pattern avoids the dual-write problem (updating a database and publishing a message simultaneously) by storing the message in an "`outbox`" table in the same database transaction. A separate process then reads the outbox and dispatches the message to a message broker.

- **Change Data Capture (CDC):** Change Data Capture allows services to respond to database changes without modifying application logic. CDC tools like Debezium monitor the database's transaction log and convert changes into events.

  **Example:** In a banking microservice, every time a `Transaction` record is inserted or updated, Debezium captures this change and emits it as a Kafka event. Other services (for example, audit service or analytics service) can subscribe to this stream and react accordingly.

CDC is a powerful technique to build loosely coupled, real-time integrations between services with minimal impact on performance. Tools like Debezium can listen to database transaction logs and capture changes in near real-time, which can then be published as events to other services. This decouples the producer from the consumers and helps replicate data consistently across services.

## Ensuring Data Integrity

To maintain consistency and reliability in distributed systems and asynchronous processing, especially in event-driven or message-based architectures, it is essential to implement strategies that safeguard data integrity.

- **Idempotent Operations**: Ensure that retrying a transaction does not lead to duplicate or inconsistent data
- **Message Ordering**: Use sequence numbers or timestamps to apply changes in the correct order
- **Deduplication**: Avoid processing the same event multiple times by checking for message IDs that have been handled already

## Testing for Transactional Consistency

In distributed systems, it is crucial to rigorously validate that transactional boundaries are respected and data integrity is maintained, even in the face of failures or asynchronous behavior. Robust testing strategies like the following, ensure that services behave predictably under stress and meet their data consistency guarantees:

- **Contract Testing**: Validate that services fulfill agreed data contracts, especially for events
- **Chaos Testing**: Inject failures to ensure that compensating transactions or retries work as intended
- **End-to-End Testing**: Simulate workflows involving multiple services to detect data loss or race conditions

Transactional consistency in microservices does not rely on traditional distributed transactions but rather on patterns and tools designed for autonomy and eventual synchronization. By embracing strategies like the Saga pattern, transactional outbox, and change data capture, teams can build systems that are both loosely coupled and consistent. These techniques allow microservices to scale independently while still ensuring data reliability and integrity across the entire system.

# Database Migration and Versioning Techniques

In a microservices architecture, every service typically owns its respective database. As services evolve, so do their data models. Managing database schema changes in a reliable, traceable, and automated way is essential to ensure smooth deployments, team collaboration, and rollback capabilities. This section focuses on how to manage schema changes using database migration and versioning tools.

# The Need for Database Migration Management

Microservices often follow CI/CD principles, where new features, bug fixes, and improvements are deployed rapidly; sometimes multiple times a day. If the schema is not kept in sync across different environments or team members' local databases, you may experience deployment failures, inconsistent behavior, or even data loss.

**Example:** Suppose you introduce a new column **`discount_code`** in the **`orders`** table to support promotions. If this migration is applied manually in dev but missed in staging, a deployment depending on that column could crash, leading to unnecessary debugging and downtime.

Using automated migrations helps ensure every environment evolves consistently with version-controlled changes, improving reliability and collaboration between developers and DevOps. where new features, bug fixes, and improvements are deployed rapidly. If the database schema changes are not properly versioned or applied consistently across environments, it may lead to:

- Application-database incompatibility
- Failed deployments
- Data corruption
- Rollback issues

To address these risks, teams adopt **database migration tools** that version schema changes, apply them in order, and track their execution.

# Popular Database Migration Tools

**Liquibase** is a powerful open-source tool designed for managing and tracking database schema changes across multiple environments. It uses a changelog file (in XML, YAML, JSON, or SQL) to define changesets, each of which represents an atomic change to the schema.

```
<changeSet id="1" author="dev">
  <createTable tableName="weather">
    <column name="id" type="BIGINT" autoIncrement="true">
      <constraints primaryKey="true"/>
    </column>
    <column name="city" type="VARCHAR(255)"/>
    <column name="temperature" type="VARCHAR(10)"/>
  </createTable>
</changeSet>
```

***Figure 14.1:** Liquibase ChangeSet*

Liquibase stores a history of applied changes in a special table (**`DATABASECHANGELOG`**) so it only runs changesets once, ensuring consistency. Liquibase is a widely used, flexible tool that supports both XML, YAML, JSON, and SQL formats to define database changes called **`changeSets`**.

The following points highlight some of the key features and advantages of using Liquibase for database schema management:

- Tracks executed changes via a dedicated table (**`DATABASECHANGELOG`**)
- Supports rollback and precondition checks
- Integrates with Spring Boot and CI/CD pipelines

**Flyway** is a simple, convention-over-configuration migration tool that uses SQL-based scripts or Java to manage database changes. Scripts are named using a strict versioning convention and applied in order.

```
V1__init_schema.sql
CREATE TABLE customers (
    id SERIAL PRIMARY KEY,
    name VARCHAR(100),
    created_at TIMESTAMP
);

V2__add_index.sql
CREATE INDEX idx_name ON customers(name);
```

***Figure 14.2***: *Flyway*

Flyway automatically tracks applied scripts and prevents accidental re-execution. It works well in projects where SQL is preferred over declarative formats like XML. Flyway uses SQL scripts or Java classes to manage migrations.

- Versioned migration files (for example, **`V1__init.sql`**, **`V2__add_table.sql`**)
- Applied in strict order
- Works well with Gradle/Maven builds and Spring Boot

Both tools support rollbacks, dry runs, and schema validation. Teams choose based on preference and project needs.

# Versioning Strategies

When using migration tools, a solid versioning strategy ensures that migrations are predictable, traceable, and reversible. Below are some common versioning strategies, each providing a way to organize, track, and manage database changes over time:

These approaches define *how* database changes are identified, applied, and maintained, helping avoid conflicts and ensuring consistent deployments across environments.

- **Semantic Versioning** helps developers correlate codebase updates and database changes. For example, a release **`1.3.2`** could include a **`V1.3.2__add_email_column.sql`** script.
- **One Migration Per Change** encourages granularity and reduces the blast radius of failures. Avoid grouping multiple unrelated changes in a single script.
- **Immutable Scripts** prevent unintended differences between environments. Once a migration is committed and deployed, it must never be modified–any correction must happen via a new migration file.
- **Rollback Scripts** are especially useful for critical production updates. For example, if you drop a column, prepare a rollback script to reintroduce it with default values. it is important to follow a clear versioning strategy:

# Integrating Migrations in CI/CD

To maintain schema consistency across environments like dev, staging, and prod, migration tools should be integrated into your continuous delivery process.

**Example using Spring Boot and Liquibase:** You can include migration execution in the build pipeline by enabling Liquibase in **`application.yml`** and running the app. Alternatively, use Maven plugins to trigger migrations as a build step:

```
<plugin>
  <groupId>org.liquibase</groupId>
  <artifactId>liquibase-maven-plugin</artifactId>
  <version>4.15.0</version>
  <configuration>
    <propertyFile>src/main/resources/liquibase.properties</propertyFile>
  </configuration>
</plugin>
```

**Figure 14.3:** *Example Using Spring Boot and Liquibase*

CI/CD platforms like GitHub Actions or GitLab CI can then apply migrations before service deployment, preventing drift between schema and application logic. Across environments (such as dev, test, staging, prod), the migration execution should be automated as follows:

1. Apply migrations during the build or deployment pipeline
2. Validate current schema state before applying new changes
3. Generate reports/logs for traceability

**Example**: In a Spring Boot project using Liquibase, migration scripts are automatically run on application startup or as a step in a deployment script.

# Best Practices

To ensure smooth and reliable schema evolution across multiple microservices, it is important to adhere to the following best practices that reduce risks, improve collaboration, and maintain consistency throughout the software lifecycle:

- **Keep migrations in version control**: Store migrations alongside code so that schema changes evolve with application features.
- **Test migrations with replica databases**: Simulate production-like databases in CI pipelines to validate that changes will apply cleanly.
- **Use preconditions**: In Liquibase, guard against unintended changes (for example, do not create a table if it already exists).
- **Maintain a detailed changelog**: Helps with audit compliance and rollback planning.
- **Coordinate schema dependencies**: For cross-service changes, communicate clearly and avoid tightly coupled updates.

**Example:** When adding a foreign key between services, ensure both services' databases are updated independently and do not rely on runtime assumptions about cross-database relationships. (Git) alongside service code

- Test migrations in CI with replica databases
- Use preconditions to guard against destructive changes
- Maintain a changelog history and rollback plan
- Coordinate cross-service schema dependencies carefully

Database versioning and migration techniques are crucial for maintaining data integrity and system reliability in a microservices architecture. Tools like Liquibase and Flyway provide automated, traceable, and repeatable processes for evolving your database schema. By integrating migration steps into your CI/CD workflow and following best practices, you ensure that your microservices can adapt and scale safely in a dynamic production environment.

# Testing Strategies Tailored for Microservices

Testing microservices introduces new challenges and opportunities compared to monolithic applications. Each microservice is a self-contained, independently deployable unit with its own logic, data store, and dependencies. To ensure quality, stability, and performance across services, teams must employ a layered testing approach that addresses both individual services and their interactions.

## The Importance of a Tailored Testing Approach for Microservices

Unlike monoliths, microservices communicate over networks, may fail independently, and rely on asynchronous behavior. Therefore, tests must account for:

- Network latency and unreliability
- Event-driven behavior and message brokers
- Distributed data consistency
- Version compatibility and contract adherence

A robust testing strategy minimizes the risk of breaking changes, ensures data integrity, and validates cross-service interactions.

# Types of Testing in Microservices

This section explains the five types of testing in microservices.

## Unit Testing

Unit testing is the foundation of your testing strategy. These tests focus on validating the correctness of isolated units—typically functions or methods—without external dependencies such as databases or services. They are fast, run frequently, and help catch logic errors early.

**Best Practices:**

- Use mocking libraries like Mockito or JMock to isolate dependencies.
- Keep tests deterministic (that is, they should generate the same result every time).
- Focus on logic boundaries and branch coverage.
- Write tests alongside the code to enable test-driven development (TDD).

**For example:** Suppose, we have to test the following discount calculation logic:

```
@Test
void shouldCalculateDiscountCorrectly() {
    double result = discountService.calculate(100.0);
    assertEquals(90.0, result);
}
```

**Figure 14.4:** *Testing a Discount Calculation Logic*

This test verifies a pure function and provides quick feedback during development. Unit tests validate isolated business logic within a service. They are fast, deterministic, and executed during local development and CI. Use tools like JUnit, Mockito, and AssertJ in Java to cover edge cases and logic branches.

## Integration Testing

Integration tests validate how different components of a single microservice work together. These may include REST controllers, service layers, database access, caches, message brokers, or external APIs.

**Best Practices:**

- Use in-memory or containerized databases (like H2, PostgreSQL with Testcontainers).
- Keep integration tests fast and stable.
- Clean up data between tests to avoid cross-test contamination.

**For example:** The following test verifies the persistence of an entity:

This Spring Boot test checks that an HTTP request results in a successful DB operation. Integration tests verify how components within a service interact, such as REST endpoints, databases, caches, and messaging. Spring Boot Test, Testcontainers, and embedded databases are common tools for integration testing.

```
@Test
void shouldPersistOrderToDatabase() throws Exception {
    mockMvc.perform(post("/orders")
        .content(orderJson)
        .contentType(MediaType.APPLICATION_JSON))
        .andExpect(status().isOk());
}
```

**Figure 14.5:** *Verifying Persistence of an Entity*

## Contract Testing

Contract testing ensures that services communicating via APIs adhere to a shared contract. This is especially important in microservices, where a client may expect certain response formats or request behaviors from a provider.

**Best Practices:**

- Define versioned API contracts using OpenAPI or Pact
- Run contract verification during CI
- Maintain backward compatibility as services evolve

**Tools:**

- **Pact** allows consumers to define expectations and generates testable contracts.
- **Spring Cloud Contract** provides auto-generated test stubs and contract validators.

**Example Workflow:**

1. Consumers define contract expectations.
2. Provider uses contract tests to ensure they satisfy those expectations.

3. CI pipeline fails if contract is broken. Contract testing ensures that services interacting via APIs conform to agreed expectations.

## End-to-End (E2E) Testing

End-to-End tests simulate real user flows across multiple services and external interfaces. These tests validate that an entire business scenario (for example, placing an order) functions as expected.

**Best Practices:**

1. Run E2E tests in a dedicated staging environment that mirrors production.
2. Use seed data and teardown scripts to manage test data.
3. Keep tests readable and focused on user behavior.

**Example:** Here is a full workflow from login to checkout:

1. Login via `AuthService`
2. Add items via `CartService`
3. Submit order via `OrderService`
4. Confirm inventory deduction via `InventoryService`

**Tools:**

- **Web**: Selenium, Cypress, Playwright
- **API**: Postman Collections, Rest-Assured, Karate E2E test simulate real user workflows across multiple services.

## Chaos and Resilience Testing

Resilience testing assesses how your system behaves under failure scenarios like timeouts, crashes, or latency. Chaos testing takes this a step further by intentionally injecting faults to assess system robustness.

**Why It Matters:**

- Validates fallback logic (such as, retries, timeouts, circuit breakers)
- Tests the observability and alerting setup
- Improves overall fault tolerance of distributed systems

**Tools:**

- **Chaos Monkey for Spring Boot**: Randomly disables endpoints or induces exceptions
- **Gremlin**: Enterprise-grade chaos engineering platform
- **Istio Fault Injection**: Simulate delays or aborts at the network layer

**Example:** Injecting a 5-second delay into `InventoryService` responses to test timeout resilience in `OrderService`. This testing simulates network failures, latency spikes, and service crashes to validate system resilience.

# Best Practices

To maximize the effectiveness of your testing strategy in a microservices architecture, it is essential to follow these best practices that ensure reliability, scalability, and maintainability across all testing layers:

- Automate all levels of testing and integrate into CI/CD pipelines

- Keep unit and integration tests fast and isolated
- Use dedicated environments for E2E testing
- Isolate flaky tests and add retry logic for transient failures
- Use mock servers or service virtualization for unavailable dependencies
- Monitor test coverage and address gaps proactively

Testing in microservices is multi dimensional and requires targeted strategies for logic, integration, contracts, and system behavior. By adopting layered testing approaches with modern tools and practices, teams can deliver scalable, resilient, and production-ready microservices with confidence.

# End-to-End Testing Techniques

End-to-end (E2E) testing in microservices verifies that the system as a whole is functioning as expected by simulating real-world workflows from the perspective of a user or client. It is crucial for validating complete business processes that span multiple services and ensures that the integration points and user-facing outcomes work as intended.

## The Critical Role of End-to-End Testing in Microservices

Unlike unit and integration tests that focus on individual components, E2E testing focuses on the system from a user's point of view. It validates whether services can collaborate to complete a full workflow, which is especially important in a domain like microservices, where services are deployed independently and may fail, or be updated in isolation. E2E testing also confirms that all systems, like API gateway, security, message queues, and data stores, are correctly wired and functioning cohesively.

For example, if **`AuthService`** undergoes an update that changes how tokens are issued, only E2E testing can reveal whether the change breaks access to **`OrderService`** or **`InventoryService`**. This holistic verification is vital before pushing changes to production. Since it focuses on isolated components or internal service interactions, E2E tests provide confidence that all services involved in a user journey communicate correctly and deliver the expected output. E2E testing is the last line of defense before a release goes live and helps:

- Detect misconfigurations in APIs, service registries, or gateways
- Validate inter-service communication (HTTP, message brokers, and so on.)
- Test service contracts, load balancers, and security rules

## Typical E2E Test Scenario

Consider the example of an e-commerce platform composed of multiple microservices. The user-facing journey, such as placing an order, may touch multiple services that must work in tandem.

For example:

1. **Login (`AuthService`):** Verifies token issuance and authentication flow
2. **View Products (`ProductService`):** Ensures product listing is fetched based on user role and availability
3. **Cart Operations (`CartService`):** Validates session persistence and cart operations

4. **Checkout (`OrderService`):** Checks for correct price calculations, inventory validation, and order recording
5. **Stock Update (`InventoryService`):** Confirms that inventory is decremented and synchronized across services

By scripting this entire scenario, E2E tests ensure that business goals and technical endpoints are achieved reliably via the following services:

- `AuthService`: User login and authentication
- `ProductService`: Product listing and availability
- `CartService`: Add or remove products from cart
- `OrderService`: Checkout and order placement
- `InventoryService`: Update stock post-purchase

# Tools and Frameworks for E2E Testing

Choosing the right tool depends on whether you're testing APIs, UIs, or workflows. These tools simulate real-user actions and validate service interactions and are mentioned as follows:

## API-Driven Testing

- **Postman:** Enables automated test collections using preconditions, assertions, and data files
- **Rest-Assured:** Perfect for writing fluent Java-based tests for RESTful APIs with JSON/XML payloads
- **Karate:** Combines BDD-style syntax with powerful assertions for easy test writing

## Browser-Based Testing

- **Selenium:** Legacy but powerful browser automation with language bindings
- **Cypress:** Modern, fast, and tightly integrated for front-end developers; supports API calls
- **Playwright:** Advanced capabilities like parallel browser sessions, network mocking, and cross-browser testing

## BDD and Workflow Testing

- **Cucumber:** Encourages collaboration between tech and non-tech stakeholders using Gherkin syntax to define behavior scenarios

# Best Practices for E2E Testing in Microservices

Following best practices helps reduce flaky test outcomes, improves feedback loops, and ensures repeatable success.

- **Use a Dedicated Staging Environment**: This environment should closely mimic production in terms of topology, versioning, environment variables, and secrets.
- **Isolate Test Data**: Tests should not depend on existing production data. Use dedicated test data with known states for reliable assertions.
- **Stub External Systems**: Mock third-party APIs using tools like WireMock, Mountebank, or sandbox environments to avoid rate limits or real charges.
- **Monitor System State**: Use logs and metrics to track service behavior under test. Integrate them with observability tools to trace request paths.

- **Keep Tests Idempotent**: Ensure that running the same test repeatedly does not change system state unexpectedly.
- **Use CI Pipelines**: Schedule E2E tests to run on merges, PRs, or nightly builds, and flag regressions early. It should mirror the production setup with similar service versions and configurations.
- **Isolate Test Data**: Use fixtures or setup scripts to prepare and tear down test records.
- **Stub External Systems**: If your system relies on third party APIs, use mock servers or sandbox environments.
- **Monitor System State**: Log response times, failures, and database states after test runs.
- **Keep Tests Idempotent**: E2E tests should be repeatable without side effects.
- **Use CI Pipelines**: Automate E2E test runs with build failures if critical flows break.

# Challenges of E2E Testing

Despite their importance, E2E tests can be time-consuming and sensitive to failures and present the following challenges:

- **Flaky Tests**: Network instability, shared test data, or timing issues may cause inconsistent results. Address these with retry logic, circuit breakers, and stable test harnesses.
- **Slowness**: E2E tests often spin up full environments, databases, and dependencies. Consider parallel execution or test sharding to speed up feedback.
- **Complex Setup**: Setting up reliable environments requires automation scripts, service discovery, mocking, and data seeding. Use tools like Docker Compose, Helm charts, or Kubernetes operators to orchestrate the full stack reliably.

Mitigation strategies include running lightweight smoke tests early, scheduling full regression suites during low-traffic hours, and improving observability to diagnose failures quickly. Network latency or service timeouts can cause intermittent failures.

- **Slowness**: E2E tests are slower than other types due to full-service orchestration.
- **Complex Setup**: Requires service discovery, database initialization, and external dependencies.

Mitigate these by:

- Running smoke tests before full suites
- Adding retry logic and timeout buffers
- Executing tests in parallel where possible

End-to-end testing plays a vital role in ensuring that the entire microservices ecosystem works together seamlessly to deliver value to end users. Although they are resource-intensive, their ability to simulate real production scenarios makes them indispensable. By combining robust tooling, good data hygiene, and automation, teams can be highly confident about their distributed systems.

# Mocking Techniques for External Services and Databases

In microservices-based systems, services often rely on third-party APIs, internal microservices, message queues, and databases. During development and testing, depending on real services or production-like databases can lead to instability, slow feedback cycles, and usher in environment constraints. Mocking and stubbing external systems ensures controlled, predictable behavior that enables isolated, fast testing.

## The Importance of Mocking in Testing

Mocking allows developers to:

- Test microservices in isolation without waiting for all dependencies to be ready
- Avoid calling expensive or rate-limited third-party APIs
- Simulate edge cases or failure scenarios that are difficult to reproduce in production
- Speed up test execution and reduce flakiness
- Develop in parallel by allowing teams to agree on service contracts and mock implementations

## Techniques for Mocking External Services

This section explains the four techniques for mocking external services.

### Stub Servers

Stub servers simulate external APIs by returning preconfigured responses to incoming requests.

**Tools:**

- **WireMock**: Allows creating dynamic HTTP stubs with JSON, delays, or conditional matching
- **Mountebank**: Supports HTTP, TCP, and more protocols
- **MockServer**: Ideal for setting expectations and validating HTTP interactions

**Example:** Stub `/currency-conversion` endpoint to return a fixed exchange rate.

```
{
  "from": "USD",
  "to": "INR",
  "rate": 82.54
}
```

### Service Virtualization

Simulates services you do not control or cannot fully replicate, including legacy systems, cloud services, and systems under development.

**Use Cases:**

- Tests when downstream services are unstable or unavailable
- Provides sandboxed environments for load testing

### OpenAPI/Swagger-Based Mocks

Auto-generate mock servers from an OpenAPI specification.

**Tools:**

- Swagger Codegen or Prism can create HTTP mock servers based on defined API specs.
- Stoplight Studio provides contract-first design and mocking features.

### Spring Boot Test Slices + MockBean

For internal integration testing, Spring Boot provides lightweight slices (for example, `@WebMvcTest`) and `@MockBean` to replace beans within the test context.

**Example:**

```
@MockBean
private PaymentClient paymentClient;
```

This replaces the real client with a mock object during the test lifecycle.

# Mocking Databases

When testing service logic that interacts with a database, you can:

## Use In-Memory Databases

Use `H2`, SQLite, or Derby to simulate relational databases.

**Pros:** Fast, lightweight, runs in memory.

**Cons:** May not reflect production-specific behaviors (for example, PostgreSQL-specific SQL).

## Use Testcontainers

Spin up actual DB containers (MySQL, PostgreSQL, MongoDB) for integration testing.

**Pros:** Matches production behavior.

**Cons:** Slower than in-memory tests but more reliable.

**Example:**

```
@Container
static PostgreSQLContainer<?> postgres = new PostgreSQLContainer<>("postgres:13");
```

## Repository Layer Mocks

Use Mockito to stub the repository's behavior for pure unit tests.

## Best Practices for Mocking

- Keep mocks up-to-date with actual API contracts.
- Use versioned mocks to match different deployment stages.
- Avoid over-mocking to the point that your tests do not resemble real scenarios.
- Incorporate mocking into your CI/CD pipeline.
- Test both success and failure responses.

Mocking external services and databases is a critical aspect of reliable and efficient microservices development and testing. By simulating dependencies, you reduce complexity, eliminate flakiness, and achieve faster feedback. Whether using stub servers, in-memory databases, or Testcontainers, these techniques empower teams to build resilient and testable systems.

# Conclusion

In this chapter, we explored the complete lifecycle of managing and testing data in microservices environments. We began with understanding the database-per-service pattern and various data management strategies, which form the foundational principles for scalable microservice design. We then delved into managing transactions and consistency and avoided the pitfalls of monolithic approaches like 2PC in favor of eventual consistency and sagas.

We also covered essential tooling and practices for database migration and version control with Liquibase and Flyway, followed by a comprehensive overview of testing strategies–from unit tests to robust end-to-end validations. We rounded up the chapter with mocking techniques for external services and databases, which empower teams to simulate environments, isolate tests, and build faster feedback loops with stability.

Together, these practices affirm the correctness, reliability, and testability of microservices from development through deployment. With a solid foundation in data strategies and testing, we shall now focus on cloud platforms. In the next chapter, we will explore Java deployment and service options across AWS, Azure, and Google Cloud Platform (GCP), providing guidance on choosing the right services for compute, storage, and orchestration. and Databases are a critical aspect of reliable and efficient microservices development and testing. By simulating dependencies, you can reduce complexity, eliminate flakiness, and achieve feedback quickly. Whether you are using stub servers, in-memory databases, or Testcontainers, these techniques will empower teams to build resilient and testable systems.

# Part 5
# Java Cloud Options
(Chapter 15)

# Chapter 15
# Cloud Options with Java

## Introduction

Cloud computing has become a cornerstone of modern software development, offering unparalleled scalability, flexibility, and cost efficiency. This chapter provides an in-depth exploration of the various cloud platforms available to Java developers, helping you make informed decisions about where and how to deploy your applications.

We will start with an **Introduction to Cloud Computing**, where you will learn the fundamental concepts of cloud technology, including its advantages and the different service models. Following this, we will also explore the **Options on AWS, GCP, Azure, Oracle Cloud, IBM Cloud,** and **Heroku**, with each section detailing the specific services, tools, and environments these platforms offer for Java development. Whether you are looking for robust infrastructure, advanced data services, or simplified deployment, you will find the complete guidance on selecting the best platform to meet your project's needs.

Finally, the chapter concludes with **Best Practices for Java Development** in the cloud, offering tips on optimizing your applications for performance, security, and scalability across different cloud environments. By the end of this chapter, you will have a comprehensive understanding of the cloud options available for Java and be equipped to deploy your applications effectively in the cloud.

## Structure

The following topics are addressed in this chapter:

- Introduction to Cloud Computing
- Options on AWS
- Options on GCP
- Options on Azure
- Comparing Java Support Across AWS, GCP, and Azure

## Introduction to Cloud Computing

Cloud computing has revolutionized the way individuals, organizations, and enterprises design, build, deploy, and manage applications and infrastructure. Rather than owning and maintaining physical servers and data centers, organizations can rent computing resources from cloud providers on-demand to gaining flexibility, scalability, and cost efficiency.

## Understanding the Fundamentals of Cloud Computing

Cloud computing refers to the delivery of computing services, including servers, storage, databases, networking, software, analytics, and intelligence, over the internet (also known as "*the cloud*"). It enables faster innovation, facilitates access to flexible resources, and results in economies of scale.

Consumers pay only for the cloud services they use, thus reducing operating costs, running infrastructure more efficiently, and scaling rapidly as business needs change.

## Characteristics of Cloud Computing

The characteristics of cloud computing distinguish it from traditional on-premises computing models and define its unique operational advantages that are mentioned as follows:

- **On-Demand Self-Service**: Provision computing resources as needed without human intervention
- **Broad Network Access**: Available over the network and accessible through standard mechanisms (for example: laptops, mobile phones)
- **Resource Pooling**: Providers serve multiple customers using a multi-tenant model
- **Rapid Elasticity**: Resources can be scaled up or down quickly according to demand
- **Measured Service**: Usage is monitored, controlled, and reported, offering transparency for both the provider and consumer

## Types of Cloud Computing Services

Different service models offer various levels of control, flexibility, and management, tailored to diverse business needs. These are mentioned as follows:

- **Infrastructure as a Service (IaaS)**: Provides virtualized computing resources over the internet. For example: AWS EC2, Azure VMs.
- **Platform as a Service (PaaS)**: Provides a platform allowing customers to develop, run, and manage applications. For example: Google App Engine, Azure App Services.
- **Software as a Service (SaaS)**: Delivers software applications over the internet on a subscription basis. For example: Salesforce, Gmail, Office 365.

# Cloud Deployment Models

Cloud deployment models define how cloud services are made available to users and organizations, shaping security, accessibility, and control strategies.

- **Public Cloud**: Services offered over the public internet and available to anyone who wants to purchase them. For example: AWS, Azure, Google Cloud Platform (GCP)
- **Private Cloud**: Cloud computing resources used exclusively by a single business or organization. These are either hosted on-premise or by a third party.
- **Hybrid Cloud**: Combines public and private clouds, allowing data and applications to move between them for greater flexibility and optimization
- **Multi-Cloud**: Using services from multiple cloud providers to avoid vendor lock-in and optimize specific capabilities

# Advantages of Cloud Computing

Cloud computing has significant business and technological benefits, helping organizations respond quickly to changing demands. Some of these are:

- **Cost Efficiency**: No upfront hardware costs; pay-as-you-go model
- **Scalability and Performance**: Easily scale resources up or down based on needs
- **Security**: Advanced security measures, compliance certifications, and access control

- **Disaster Recovery and Backup**: Simplified, cost-effective data recovery options
- **Speed and Agility**: Quickly deploy applications and services
- **Global Reach**: Cloud providers offer services across multiple geographic locations

# Challenges of Cloud Computing

Despite its advantages, cloud computing also introduces the following challenges that need careful consideration and strategic planning:

- **Downtime Risks**: Dependency on internet connectivity
- **Security and Privacy**: Protecting sensitive data remains a critical concern
- **Vendor Lock-In**: Migration between cloud providers can be complex
- **Compliance Requirements**: Must meet regulatory and legal standards (for example: GDPR, HIPAA).

Cloud computing is the backbone of modern digital transformation, as it offers unparalleled speed, scalability, and efficiency. It empowers organizations of all sizes to innovate faster and deliver services globally without the burden of managing physical infrastructure. As we move forward, understanding the different cloud models, service types, and their practical applications will be essential for developers, architects, and businesses that want to thrive in the digital era.

# Options on AWS

Amazon Web Services (AWS) provides one of the most mature, comprehensive ecosystems for deploying and managing Java applications in the cloud. Whether you are building monolithic applications, microservices, serverless functions, or containerized solutions—AWS offers highly scalable, reliable, and cost-effective options tailored for Java developers.

# Running Java Applications on AWS

Let us begin by understanding why AWS is a natural choice for deploying and scaling Java applications efficiently in the cloud.

AWS offers extensive support for Java applications, including:

- Managed OpenJDK distribution (AWS Corretto)
- Tight integration with build tools like Maven and Gradle
- Rich set of managed services for databases, compute, storage, and networking
- Comprehensive monitoring and security tools
- Deep ecosystem support for containerization and serverless architectures

# Key Java Services and Deployment Options

AWS offers a broad range of deployment options and services specifically tailored for Java developers, allowing flexible design patterns and architectures. These features and services are mentioned as follows:

**AWS Elastic Beanstalk**

- **Purpose:** Easiest way to deploy and scale Java web applications and services
- **Features:** Manages infrastructure (EC2, Auto Scaling, Load Balancing) automatically

- **Runtime Support:** Tomcat, Jetty, or custom Docker containers
- **Deployment Model:** Upload WAR/JAR file or Docker image

**Amazon EC2 (Elastic Compute Cloud)**

- **Purpose:** Full control over the environment
- **Features:** Configure custom JVM settings, install monitoring agents, tune memory/GC policies
- **Use Cases:** Stateful applications, legacy apps, or applications requiring OS-level customization

**AWS Lambda (Serverless Java)**

- **Purpose:** Event-driven, serverless computing
- **Features:** Write functions in Java 11 or Java 17 runtimes
- **Use Cases:** Lightweight microservices, scheduled jobs, API backends
- **Performance Tip:** Use GraalVM Native Images to reduce cold start times

**Amazon ECS and EKS (Containerized Java Applications)**

- **Purpose:** Deploy containerized Java microservices
- **ECS:** Fully managed Docker orchestration without needing Kubernetes expertise
- **EKS:** Managed Kubernetes control plane for running Spring Boot microservices in a Kubernetes-native environment
- **Tools:** AWS Copilot CLI, Amazon App Runner

**AWS RDS and Aurora**

- **Purpose:** Managed relational databases
- **Features:** Automated backups, high availability, read replicas
- **Use Cases:** Java applications using JPA/Hibernate for ORM
- **Aurora:** Optimized for high throughput and low latency, compatible with MySQL and PostgreSQL

**AWS CodePipeline and CodeBuild**

- **Purpose:** Fully managed CI/CD pipelines
- **Features:** Integrates with GitHub, AWS CodeCommit
- **Use Cases:** Automate build, test, deploy cycles for Java projects

**Amazon Corretto (OpenJDK)**

- **Purpose:** AWS-supported OpenJDK distribution
- **Features:** Regular security patches, long-term support, multiplatform availability
- **Use Cases:** Production-grade JVM for applications running on EC2, Lambda, or containers

# Example Architecture for a Java Microservice

Let us visualize how different AWS services can be combined to build a typical production-grade Java microservices architecture:

- **Frontend**: Hosted on Amazon S3 + CloudFront
- **API Gateway**: Handles routing, security, and throttling
- **Lambda (Java Functions)**: Stateless compute layer for API
- **Aurora Serverless**: Database backend

- **CloudWatch**: Monitoring logs and metrics
- **Secrets Manager**: Manage DB credentials and API secrets

AWS empowers Java developers to build highly scalable, secure, and resilient applications. Whether through traditional VMs, managed PaaS like Beanstalk, serverless functions in Lambda, or containerized deployments with ECS/EKS, AWS offers flexible solutions for every type of Java workload. Choosing the right mix of services based on application needs can help maximize performance and optimize cost-efficiency.

In the next section, we will explore how GCP provides equally powerful options for deploying and managing Java applications at scale.

# Options on GCP

Google Cloud Platform (GCP) offers a powerful and developer-friendly environment for building, deploying, and managing Java applications at scale. With a strong emphasis on Kubernetes, serverless, and managed services, GCP is particularly appealing to teams building cloud-native Java microservices.

# Why GCP for Java?

Let us begin by understanding why GCP is a strong platform choice for modern Java application development.

GCP provides robust support for Java developers, including:

- Native Java SDKs and APIs
- Fully managed Kubernetes with GKE
- Seamless integration with CI/CD pipelines
- Serverless options for lightweight Java functions
- Powerful data and machine learning services

# Key Java Services and Deployment Options

GCP offers a variety of tailored solutions to deploy Java workloads based on the application's architecture and scalability needs that are mentioned as follows:

**Google App Engine (PaaS)**

- **Purpose**: Fully managed platform for deploying Java web applications
- **Features**: Auto-scaling, zero server management, built-in security features
- **Deployment Model**: Deploy JAR or WAR files directly
- **Use Cases**: REST APIs, backend services, web applications

**Google Compute Engine (VMs)**

- **Purpose**: Full control over VMs for custom deployments
- **Features**: Custom machine types, persistent disks, GPUs
- **Use Cases**: Legacy Java apps, apps needing specific OS/JVM tuning

**Google Kubernetes Engine (GKE)**

- **Purpose**: Managed Kubernetes for containerized Java microservices

- **Features**: Auto-repair, auto-upgrade, integrated monitoring
- **Use Cases**: Highly scalable microservices, event-driven architectures, multi-cloud setups

**Cloud Run (Serverless Containers)**

- **Purpose**: Run Java containers serverlessly without worrying about infrastructure.
- **Features**: Autoscaling, pay-per-use, integrated with Cloud Build.
- **Use Cases**: Lightweight Java services, webhooks, APIs

**Cloud Functions (Java Runtime)**

- **Purpose**: Serverless event-driven compute
- **Features**: Native support for Java 11 and Java 17 runtimes
- **Use Cases**: Background processing, lightweight APIs, pub/sub event handling

**Cloud SQL and Spanner**

- **Purpose**: Managed relational databases for Java apps
- **Cloud SQL**: MySQL, PostgreSQL, SQL Server
- **Spanner**: Globally distributed SQL database with strong consistency
- **Use Cases**: High-availability backend storage for Java microservices

**Artifact Registry and Cloud Build**

- **Purpose**: Store Maven artifacts, container images; automate builds
- **Use Cases**: CI/CD pipelines for Java apps

# Best Practices for Java on GCP

Following these best practices helps maximize performance, security, and cost-efficiency for Java applications on GCP:

- **Use Cloud-native Services**: Prefer App Engine, GKE, Cloud Run over VMs for easier management.
- **Containerize Java Applications**: Use Jib or Cloud Buildpacks to containerize Java apps.
- **Enable IAM and Identity-Aware Proxy**: Secure applications and APIs.
- **Use Stackdriver (Cloud Operations)**: Monitor JVM metrics, logs, traces.
- **Implement Blue-Green Deployments**: Use App Engine versions or GKE rolling updates.
- **Integrate CI/CD**: Automate builds and deployments using Cloud Build and Cloud Deploy.
- **Optimize Memory Footprint**: Leverage Java 17's reduced memory overhead features for serverless.

# Example Architecture for a Java Microservice

Let us visualize how different GCP services can be combined to build a typical Java microservices architecture:

- **Frontend**: Hosted on Firebase Hosting or Cloud Storage + CDN
- **API Layer**: Cloud Run or App Engine Standard
- **Business Logic**: GKE with containerized Spring Boot apps
- **Database**: Cloud SQL or Cloud Spanner

- **Monitoring**: Cloud Operations (formerly Stackdriver)
- **Secrets Management**: Secret Manager
- **Authentication**: Cloud Identity and OAuth2 integration

GCP empowers Java developers to build cloud-native, scalable, and highly available applications with ease. With services like App Engine, GKE, Cloud Run, and Spanner, developers can choose the right level of abstraction and control for their application needs. Choosing GCP for Java workloads allows teams to embrace automation, resiliency, and innovation.

In the next section, we will explore how Microsoft Azure provides its own rich ecosystem of options for Java applications.

# Options on Azure

Microsoft Azure provides a robust, enterprise-grade cloud platform for developing, deploying, and scaling Java applications. Azure offers first-class support for Java workloads with a rich set of managed services, flexible deployment models, and deep integration with open-source tools.

## Empowering Java Developers with Azure

Let us begin by understanding why Azure is a strong choice for running Java applications at enterprise scale.

Azure offers comprehensive Java support, including:

- Managed OpenJDK and Azure-distributed Java binaries
- Native support for Maven, Gradle, and Jenkins integrations
- Spring Boot and Spring Cloud Azure integrations
- A wide range of managed services for compute, storage, messaging, and databases
- Enterprise-grade security, compliance, and global reach

## Key Java Services and Deployment Options

Azure provides the following solutions to deploy, manage, and scale Java applications, from traditional servers to full serverless computing.

**Azure App Service**

- **Purpose**: Fully managed platform for building, hosting, and scaling Java web apps and APIs
- **Features**: Auto-scaling, SSL termination, authentication integration, zero-downtime deployments
- **Deployment Model**: Deploy JARs, WARs, or container images
- **Use Cases**: Web apps, APIs, backend services

**Azure Virtual Machines (VMs)**

- **Purpose**: Full control over compute resources
- **Features**: Custom OS images, auto-scaling, integrated monitoring
- **Use Cases**: Legacy Java applications, custom JVM configurations, high-compute Java workloads

**Azure Kubernetes Service (AKS)**

- **Purpose**: Fully managed Kubernetes for containerized Java microservices
- **Features**: Built-in monitoring, auto-scaling, Dev Spaces, integrated CI/CD

- **Use Cases**: Complex microservice architectures, hybrid cloud scenarios

**Azure Spring Apps (formerly Azure Spring Cloud)**

- **Purpose**: Managed service for Spring Boot and Spring Cloud applications
- **Features**: Simplified deployment, service discovery, centralized configuration, circuit breaker patterns
- **Use Cases**: Microservices built using Spring Boot and Spring Cloud frameworks

**Azure Functions (Java Runtime)**

- **Purpose**: Event-driven, serverless compute service
- **Features**: Supports Java 8, Java 11, and Java 17 runtimes
- **Use Cases**: Lightweight APIs, background processing, scheduled tasks

**Azure SQL Database and Cosmos DB**

- **Purpose**: Managed database services
- **Azure SQL**: Relational database supporting Hibernate, JPA, and JDBC
- **Cosmos DB**: Globally distributed NoSQL database with multi-model support
- **Use Cases**: Persistent storage for Java web and microservices applications

**Azure DevOps and GitHub Actions**

- **Purpose**: CI/CD pipeline tools
- **Features**: Build, test, and deploy Java applications automatically
- **Use Cases**: Streamlined software delivery pipelines

# Best Practices for Java on Azure

The following best practices ensures optimal performance, security, and cost-efficiency for Java workloads on Azure:

- **Choose Managed Services**: Use App Service, AKS, and Azure Spring Apps for reduced operational overhead.
- **Secure Applications with Azure Active Directory (AAD)**: Implement OAuth2/OIDC flows for securing Java APIs.
- **Leverage Application Insights**: Monitor JVM health, requests, and performance metrics.
- **Use Azure Key Vault**: Secure secrets, database credentials, and certificates.
- **Enable Autoscaling and Load Balancing**: Configure Azure Load Balancer and scale sets.
- **Integrate CI/CD Pipelines**: Automate testing and deployments with Azure DevOps or GitHub Actions.
- **Containerize Java Applications**: Use Azure Container Registry and AKS for scalable microservice architectures.

# Example Architecture for a Java Microservice

Let us visualize how different Azure services can be combined to build a production-ready Java microservices solution:

- **Frontend**: Hosted on Azure Static Web Apps
- **API Gateway**: Azure API Management
- **Microservices**: Azure Spring Apps or AKS with Spring Boot containers

- **Database**: Azure SQL Database or Cosmos DB
- **Observability**: Azure Monitor and Application Insights
- **Authentication**: Azure Active Directory
- **Secrets Management**: Azure Key Vault

Azure provides a complete and integrated cloud solution for Java developers—from simple web apps to complex distributed systems. With services like Azure Spring Apps, AKS, Azure Functions, and robust database options, developers can build resilient, secure, and globally available Java applications. Choosing Azure allows enterprises to leverage Microsoft's cloud leadership, open-source commitment, and enterprise-grade reliability for their Java workloads.

In the next section, we will compare and summarize how AWS, GCP, and Azure stack up against each other for Java development.

# Comparing Java Support across AWS, GCP, and Azure

In this section, we comprehensively compare how AWS, GCP, and Azure support Java workloads, highlighting their similarities, differences, and best-fit scenarios for building cloud-native Java applications.

**Common Strengths across AWS, GCP, and Azure**

- **Managed Kubernetes Services**: (EKS, GKE, AKS)–All offer production-ready Kubernetes clusters for containerized Java microservices
- **Serverless Support**: All platforms provide serverless compute options for Java–AWS Lambda, GCP Cloud Functions, and Azure Functions
- **Relational and NoSQL Databases**: Fully-managed relational (RDS, Cloud SQL, Azure SQL) and NoSQL (DynamoDB, Firestore, CosmosDB) options are available
- **Native CI/CD Pipelines**: Integrated build and deployment services (AWS CodePipeline, GCP Cloud Build, Azure DevOps/GitHub Actions)
- **Security and Identity Management**: IAM services, role-based access control (RBAC), secret management (AWS Secrets Manager, GCP Secret Manager, Azure Key Vault)
- **Monitoring and Observability**: Full-stack monitoring via CloudWatch (AWS), Cloud Operations (GCP), and Azure Monitor

# Key Differences

While the major cloud providers offer similar core capabilities for Java development, each one has unique features, optimizations, and service integrations that may influence your choice depending on your application's needs. We have mentioned them in the following table:

| Feature/Capability | AWS | GCP | Azure |
|---|---|---|---|
| **PaaS for Java Apps** | AWS Elastic Beanstalk | Google App Engine | Azure App Service, Azure Spring Apps |
| **Serverless Java Performance** | Improving (Still cold starts) | Strong | Moderate |
| **Java Native Buildpacks** | AWS Lambda SnapStart | Built-in | Azure Functions Premium Plans |

| **Enterprise Java Support** | Partnered with Red Hat, Pivotal | Strong open-source focus | Deep Spring Boot and Spring Cloud Support |
|---|---|---|---|
| **Multi-Cloud and Hybrid** | EKS Anywhere, Outposts | Anthos | Azure Arc for hybrid Kubernetes |
| **Databases for Java Apps** | RDS, DynamoDB, Aurora | Cloud SQL, spanner,Firestore | Azure SQL, Cosmos DB |
| **Spring Boot Native Services** | AWS Spring Boot on Lambda | App Engine + Cloud Run | Azure Spring Apps |

***Table 15.1:*** *Comparison between Cloud Providers*

# Ideal Use Cases

- **AWS**: Best for enterprises already invested in AWS ecosystem; offers robust services for massive scaling and deep security integration
- **GCP**: Ideal for cloud-native, container-first development, AI/ML integration, and developers seeking fully managed serverless experiences
- **Azure**: Best suited for Spring Boot developers, enterprise Java applications (especially with Microsoft ecosystems), and hybrid cloud architectures

While all three platforms offer outstanding support for Java, the choice ultimately depends on your specific needs that are mentioned as follows:

- If you need vast service breadth, global reach, and resilience: **AWS**.
- If you prefer serverless-first, container-native development: **GCP**.
- If you are building enterprise-grade Java apps with strong Spring Boot dependencies: **Azure**.

Choosing the right cloud provider can enhance performance, reduce operational overhead, and accelerate your Java development journey.

# Conclusion

Congratulations on reaching the end of this comprehensive journey into cloud-based Java development! You now possess a solid understanding of how the three leading cloud providers like AWS, GCP, and Azure empower Java workloads, each offering a unique combination of tools, services, and architectural strengths. The path forward involves applying this knowledge in real-world scenarios to deepen your skills and refine your expertise. Begin by deploying Java microservices across each platform to get comfortable with their deployment pipelines and operational nuances. Containerize your applications and orchestrate them using Kubernetes engines like EKS, GKE, or AKS to build scalable and portable services. Set up CI/CD pipelines to automate your build, test, and release workflows using native DevOps tools offered by each cloud. Focus on optimizing cost and performance by leveraging observability features, auto-scaling, and resource tuning. As you progress, explore more advanced topics like multi-cloud strategies, service mesh integration with Istio, and serverless Java options through Cloud Functions or AWS Lambda. Remember, cloud computing is an ever-evolving space–by staying curious, hands-on, and up to date with best practices, you will be well-equipped to build secure, resilient, and modern Java applications across any cloud platform.

**Good luck with your Java cloud-native journey!**

# Index

## O



## P



## R

## T